# BOLD VENTURE

# BOLD
# VENTURE

## THE AMERICAN BOMBING OF
## JAPANESE-OCCUPIED HONG KONG, 1942–1945

STEVEN K. BAILEY

Potomac Books

AN IMPRINT OF THE UNIVERSITY OF NEBRASKA PRESS

∞

Library of Congress Cataloging-in-Publication Data
Names: Bailey, Steven K., author.
Title: Bold venture: the American bombing of Japanese-occupied
Hong Kong, 1942–1945 / Steven K. Bailey.
Other titles: American bombing of Japanese-occupied Hong Kong,
1942–1945
Description: Lincoln, NE: Potomac Books, an imprint of the
University of Nebraska Press, [2019] | Includes bibliographical
references and index.
Identifiers: LCCN 2018018094
ISBN 9781640121041 (cloth: alk. paper)
ISBN 9781640121621 (epub)
ISBN 9781640121638 (mobi)
ISBN 9781640121645 (pdf)
Subjects: LCSH: Sino-Japanese War, 1937–1945—Aerial operations,
American. | World War, 1939–1945—Campaigns—China—Hong
Kong. | Bombing, Aerial—China—Hong Kong. | United States.
Army Air Forces. China Air Task Force. | World War, 1939–1945—
Aerial operations, American. | Hong Kong (China)—History,
Military—20th century.
Classification: LCC DS777.533.A35 B34 2019 | DDC 940.53/73—dc23
LC record available at https://lccn.loc.gov/2018018094

Set in Minion Pro by Mikala R. Kolander.

# CONTENTS

# ILLUSTRATIONS

*Following page 170*

# ABBREVIATIONS

| | |
|---|---|
| ACG | Air Commando Group |
| AFC | American Ferry Command |
| AFCE | automated flight control equipment |
| AVG | American Volunteer Group |
| BAAG | British Army Aid Group |
| BG | bomb group |
| BS | bomb squadron |
| BTO | bomb through the overcast |
| CACW | Chinese American Composite Wing |
| CATF | China Air Task Force |
| CAVU | clear and visibility unlimited |
| CBI | China-Burma-India |
| CEF | China Expeditionary Fleet |
| CNAC | China National Aviation Corporation |
| CTSD | China Theater Search Detachment |
| FAW | fleet air wing |
| FG | fighter group |
| FS | fighter squadron |
| FSC | fighter squadron commando |
| GP | general purpose |
| GRS | Graves Registration Service |
| HMS | His Majesty's ship |
| HSBC | Hong Kong and Shanghai Banking Corporation |
| IJA | Imperial Japanese Army |
| IJN | Imperial Japanese Navy |
| IJNS | Imperial Japanese Navy ship |

| | |
|---|---|
| JAAF | Japanese Army Air Force |
| JNAF | Japanese Navy Air Force |
| KIA | killed in action |
| KIFA | killed in flying accident |
| KIPC | killed in plane crash |
| LAB | low-altitude bombing (radar system) |
| MACR | missing air crew report |
| MIA | missing in action |
| ONI | Office of Naval Intelligence |
| OSS | Office of Strategic Services |
| POW | prisoner of war |
| PRS | photographic reconnaissance squadron |
| PSP | pierced-steel planking |
| RAF | Royal Air Force |
| RCAF | Royal Canadian Air Force |
| TF | task force |
| TRS | tactical reconnaissance squadron |
| USAAF | United States Army Air Forces |
| USS | United States ship |
| VH | rescue squadron (U.S. Navy) |
| VHF | very high frequency |
| VPB | patrol bombing squadron (U.S. Navy) |

# BOLD VENTURE

# 1

## Eyes over Hong Kong

On September 22, 1942, Maj. Bruce K. Holloway took off from the dusty runway at Kweilin on a mission of special interest to Gen. Claire Chennault, commander of the China Air Task Force (CATF).[1] Rather than his usual P-40E, the twenty-nine-year-old Holloway flew a Republic P-43A Lancer with a supercharger that allowed for high-altitude recon work. He banked to the southeast and climbed steeply through overcast skies that masked the war-scarred Chinese landscape far below. Holloway hoped the soup would clear by the time he reached Japanese-occupied Canton and Hong Kong, where the general wanted him to scout out shipping, harbor installations, airfields, and other high-value targets for an upcoming CATF offensive in southern China.

Like all radial-engine fighters, the P-43 had a blunt nose that made it easy to spot on an airfield full of pointy-nosed inline-engine P-40s. The Lend-Lease program had supplied the Chinese air force with 108 P-43s, which had little in common with the P-40s flown by the CATF. Though the P-43 and the P-40 flew at roughly the same top speed and had about the same operational range, the Lancer climbed faster than the P-40 and with its turbo-supercharged engine could fly as high as thirty-six thousand feet. P-40s, in contrast, got sluggish above twenty thousand feet. However, the Lancer mounted only four .50-caliber heavy machine guns as compared to the six on a P-40E. The Lancer did not have as much armor for the pilot either, and most critically of all, it lacked self-sealing fuel tanks. Consequently, the P-43 remained far more vulnerable to enemy attack.

Even without bullet holes, the fuel tanks tended to leak, and the Lancer had acquired a reputation for fiery disaster. However, the P-43 turned out to be particularly well suited for recon missions in China because its speed and high-altitude performance made it difficult to intercept and invulnerable to flak. Since the CATF possessed very few recon aircraft of its own, General Chennault arranged to borrow more than a dozen Lend-Lease P-43s from the Chinese air force. CATF ground crewmen modified several of these P-43s by mounting a recon camera in the baggage compartment just behind and below the cockpit. The camera lens pointed downward through a hole cut in the bottom of the fuselage.[2]

From the cockpit of his loaner P-43, Holloway caught sight of the Canton airfields through broken clouds, which cleared out entirely as he approached Hong Kong at twenty-five thousand feet. Far below he could see a peaceful harbor clogged with small craft, though he made his recon run at an altitude that made it impossible to differentiate between civilian junks and military targets, such as cargo lighters, launches, and patrol boats. However, a large Japanese ship anchored between the Kowloon Peninsula and Hong Kong Island caught his eye, since he guessed it might weigh in at about twelve thousand tons. This made for a whale of a target. Holloway also spotted two large ships in dry dock on Hong Kong Island. He observed no activity at Kai Tak airfield and never encountered any enemy aircraft. He didn't see any flak puffs either. However temporarily, all signs of the war had vanished, and Holloway might as well have been flying over prewar Hong Kong.

Holloway touched down at Kweilin at 2:30 in the afternoon with a camera full of negatives that confirmed the presence of Japanese ships in Victoria Harbor, which was exactly what Chennault had been hoping for. Holloway also briefed Chennault on other potential targets. In his flight intelligence report, he wrote, "Cluster of five large oil reservoir tanks on north end of west side of Kowloon dock area very conspicuous target." Chennault concurred with this assessment, and on October 15 the general gave the order to launch the inaugural American raid on Hong Kong as soon as weather con-

2

ditions permitted. Holloway would fly the mission, but this time he would be strapped into a six-gun P-40 with a dozen seasoned combat pilots flying on his wing. This time Chennault would send a formation of B-25 bombers, too. And this time, Holloway knew, the Japanese fighter pilots would be waiting.[3]

# 2

## Chennault

I n the early summer of 1937, retired U.S. Army Air Corps captain Claire Lee Chennault arrived in China to reorganize and train the poorly equipped Chinese air force. The forty-seven-year-old fighter pilot and strong proponent of air power had been recruited by Song Meiling—a woman known to most Americans as Madame Chiang—on behalf of Chiang Kai-shek, her husband and the leader of Nationalist China. War broke out with Japan later that summer, and heavy casualties rapidly reduced the number of Chinese aircraft and aviators, leaving China with little defense against Japanese air attack. By October 1938 the pilots of the Japanese army and navy had achieved complete air superiority.[1] However, the Imperial Japanese Army (IJA) failed to defeat the Nationalist army on the ground despite conquering huge swaths of China. Faced with a stalemate, the Japanese high command tried to force Chiang's Nationalist government to sue for peace by bombing its wartime capital of Chungking. Japanese aircraft pounded Chungking and other Nationalist-controlled cities with impunity, an operation that killed a large number of civilians and caused heavy damage to targets that usually had little to do with the Chinese war effort.

Understanding that China desperately needed trained pilots flying modern fighter aircraft, Chiang tasked the newly promoted Colonel Chennault with organizing the 1st American Volunteer Group (AVG) in 1941.[2] The U.S. military showed little enthusiasm for supporting the AVG, as the unit would siphon off some of its best aviators at a time when hostilities with Japan and Germany looked increasingly likely. However, the AVG benefited from the discreet support of President Franklin D. Roosevelt, and the military grudgingly allowed its pilots and other support personnel to resign and join the AVG. The Nationalist government promised to pay AVG personnel an attractive salary supplemented with bonuses for every confirmed shoot-down of a Japanese aircraft. The Nationalist government also purchased one hundred P-40B Tomahawks for the AVG that had been manufactured at the Curtis-Wright plant in Buffalo, New York.

In the spring and summer of 1941, AVG personnel, supplies, and disassembled P-40Bs traveled by merchant ships to Rangoon, Burma. In the sweltering tropical heat, AVG mechanics went to work on assembling the P-40Bs, which had arrived in crates like giant model airplane kits. Once a sufficient number of Tomahawks had been assembled, AVG pilots began flight training under Chennault's supervision at a Royal Air Force (RAF) base just outside the town of Toungoo, some 170 miles north of Rangoon. On December 7, 1941, the Japanese navy attacked the American Pacific Fleet at Pearl Harbor, and the Japanese army invaded the British colonies of Hong Kong and Malaya. The AVG received orders from Chiang Kai-shek to defend the famed Burma Road, which served as China's supply conduit to the outside world after the fall of Shanghai and other coastal cities. Chennault immediately sent two of his squadrons across the Chinese border to Kunming. The third squadron remained in Burma to fight alongside the RAF, whose pilots flew Hawker Hurricanes and Brewster Buffaloes—nicknamed Flying Barrels on account of their stubby airframes.

In the weeks that followed, AVG pilots consistently chewed up Japanese bomber formations over Rangoon and Kunming. The two cities anchored each end of China's tenuous, one-thousand-mile supply line. In Rangoon the dockside cranes plucked Lend-Lease military supplies from the holds of merchant ships. The SS *Tulsa* alone brought in thirty-five M-3 armored scout cars, forty-eight 75 mm artillery pieces, five hundred Bren light machine guns, one hundred .50-caliber heavy machine guns, and at least eleven thousand Thompson submachine guns. The ship carried so much weaponry and ammunition, in fact, that it provoked an unseemly squabble between the British and the Chinese over who should get the equipment. Still more vessels arrived with cargoes of disassembled trucks, which factory workers assembled at the General Motors plant near the waterfront.[3] Longshoremen loaded the trucks and supplies onto railcars. Locomotives pulled the freight cars north through the Mandalay junction to the end of the line in Lashio, a city in northeastern Burma. Convoys of White, Mack, and Dodge trucks then hauled the ammunition, weaponry, gasoline, and spare parts to Kunming over the sinuous mountain switchbacks of the Burma Road.[4] Keeping the road open remained vital to China's war effort, as the Japanese army well knew. It planned to invade Burma, cut the road, and stop the flow of military supplies into China, which would then have to sue for peace.

The AVG pilots tasked with keeping the supply line open painted shark mouths on the pointy noses of their Tomahawks—a paint scheme borrowed from RAF P-40 squadrons in North Africa—and used combat tactics that Chennault had devised after years of observing Japanese fighters and bombers in action over China. He had even flown a captured Nakajima Ki-27 in mock dogfights against various Nationalist Chinese aircraft, such as the British-made Gloster Gladiator, the American-made Curtis-Wright P-36, and the Russian-made Polikarpov I-16.[5] Chennault knew the capabilities of Japanese aircraft and understood how Japanese pilots had been trained to fight, and unlike the American fighter squadrons that were being badly mauled elsewhere in the Pacific, his AVG consistently got the better of the Japanese. Rangoon-based journalists from the *Chicago Daily News*, *Time-Life*, the *New York Times*, and other prominent news outlets dubbed the unit the Flying Tigers. The name did not quite add up given that the unit flew P-40s with toothy shark mouths painted on their noses, but no matter—the American public seized upon this one story of Allied victory at a time when most of the front-page news involved Allied defeats.[6]

At the end of December 1941, the newspapers reported the surrender of Hong Kong. During the first weeks of February 1942, the newspapers recounted the fall of Malaya and the mass capitulation of British troops at Singapore. At the start of March, the newspapers covered the surrender of the Dutch East Indies. The papers also reported that the Japanese army had taken Rangoon and cut the flow of military supplies into China. The Burma Road still remained open, but the loss of the Rangoon docks ensured there would be no more supply convoys churning up the mud of its hairpin curves.

As the Japanese army advanced northward from Rangoon, its forward units overran the airfields used by the AVG. The sprawling RAF airbase at Mingaladon outside Rangoon went first. The AVG training base at Toungoo went next, followed by a reserve base at Magwe. Soon the AVG had been forced out of Burma altogether, and the first convoy of ground crewmen packed up a motley assortment of twelve jeeps, eighteen trucks, and one Buick sedan that had been liberated from an abandoned Rangoon showroom. The convoy carried fuel drums, aircraft and vehicle parts, tools, radio gear, small arms, ammunition, a three-month supply of canned goods, two Siamese cats, and many cases of Harvey's Bristol Cream sherry that had been found on the docks at Rangoon. Led by AVG chaplain Paul Frillman, who drove the Buick, the convoy traveled all the way to Kunming, where the sedan became the staff car of General Chennault.[7]

The AVG pilots, meanwhile, had been operating out of Loiwing, which lay just over the Chinese border to the northeast of Burma. At the end of April, however, Japanese columns took Lashio, and for the first time the boot prints of Japanese riflemen pocked the mud of the Burma Road. The hard-driving Japanese infantry marched up the serpentine highway and crossed the frontier into China, forcing the AVG to abandon the well-equipped aircraft repair facility at Loiwing as well. Along with an aircraft assembly plant, the AVG ground crews hurriedly attempted to destroy twenty-two irreplaceable P-40Bs that could not be repaired in time. Then they loaded up a second Kunming-bound convoy with as many spare parts and other supplies as the trucks and jeeps could carry. As Loiwing burned behind them, the ground crews joined the stream of refugees climbing the Burma Road into China. The AVG pilots, meanwhile, flew the remaining operational P-40s to Kunming. On May 3 Japanese troops entered Loiwing, where they found quantities of abandoned military supplies and half-destroyed American aircraft.[8]

Lead elements of the Japanese offensive drove up the Burma Road to the Salween Gorge, a formidable natural obstacle some three hundred miles to the west of Kunming. From a Chinese perspective, it appeared that the Japanese intended to take Kunming. Chennault concurred with this assessment and agreed with the decision to dynamite the only bridge over the Salween River.[9] In actuality the Japanese thrust consisted of a single motorized regiment tasked with mopping up retreating Nationalist Chinese troops that had participated in the Allied defense of Burma.[10] Supported by AVG pilots flying hazardous ground-attack missions, the Nationalist Chinese army stalled the advance of the much smaller Japanese regiment at the gorge. By the end of May, it had become clear to all sides that Kunming would remain in Chinese hands.

The western end of the Burma Road, however, had been lost to the Japanese. To compensate for the loss of this vital supply route, a small fleet of China National Aviation Corporation (CNAC) DC-3s and C-47s of the American Ferry Command (AFC) began shuttling supplies from Dinjan airfield in Assam, the easternmost point in British India, to Kunming. The only other supply conduit into China consisted of tortuous overland routes from Soviet Russia, which remained locked in a war of national survival with Germany. Stalin no longer had any war material to spare for Chiang Kai-shek's Nationalist government, so everything needed to keep China in the war would have to be flown in from India.

The CNAC—a venture jointly owned by Pan American World Airways and the Chinese government—had pioneered flights over the Himalayas in late 1941. Freight service began in March 1942 with Lend-Lease Douglas DC-3s, and daily passenger service started in June 1942. The U.S. government contracted the CNAC to fly military supplies, essential personnel, and mail to Kunming. As might be expected, given the contract from Washington and Pan American's stake in the company, many of the airline's pilots came from the United States.[11] However, the aircrews tended to be multinational in composition, since CNAC also employed Chinese pilots, flight engineers, and radio operators.[12]

India-based transport planes of the AFC began taking over supply operations from the CNAC in April 1942. Commanded by Lt. Col. Caleb V. Haynes, the AFC flight line in India could muster about twenty-five Douglas C-47s.[13] The total tonnage carried in the spring and summer of 1942 came nowhere close to the amounts needed for the AVG, however, much less the amounts needed for the army and air force of Nationalist China. Given the limited cargo capacity of the C-47, not to mention the limited number of C-47s, cargo had to be prioritized. The most vital items always flew first. From mid-April to mid-June of 1942, for example, the C-47 pilots of the AFC flew in two *tons* of cigarettes for the nicotine-addicted men of the AVG.[14] Aviation fuel, munitions, and spare aircraft parts also ranked high on the priority list.

Pilots referred to this hazardous five-hundred-mile journey from India to China as the "aluminum trail" in honor of the many crashed aircraft littering the flight path, which took pilots over the world's highest mountains in weather that regularly brewed up perverse amalgamations of every aviator's worst nightmares: iced-up wings, zero visibility, rivet-popping turbulence, a complete absence of navigational aids, and towering mountain faces that exceeded the ceiling for heavily loaded transports. Some pilots called the route the "rock pile" in honor of the many peaks they had to fly over or thread their way between.[15] Most pilots simply referred to this deadly flight path as "the Hump."

In addition to the risks presented by the weather and the mountainous terrain, the prospect of getting shot down was a real possibility facing the transport pilots. AFC and CNAC transports had to cross the Hump without fighter escort, and many of the C-47s that disappeared somewhere between Assam and Kunming fell to the tracer fire of Japanese Army Air Force (JAAF) fighter squadrons based at Lashio and Myitkyina in northern Burma. The KI-43 pilots tasked with intercepting American transports referred to their missions as *tsujigiri*, which translates somewhat roughly as "street murder" or "street ambush."[16] Transports caught by a *tsujigiri* fighter sweep had few options. Though solidly built, the slow-flying c-47s were extremely vulnerable and carried no defensive armament other than small arms. On one occasion Lieutenant Colonel Haynes and his crew chief fired .45-caliber Thompson submachine guns out the windows at an attacking fighter bent on some street murder. Fortunately, the pilot of the c-47 ended this unequal duel by diving down to treetop level, where the fighter broke off the attack for reasons that remained unclear but likely had nothing to do with the Tommy guns.[17]

A less imaginative or more cautious commander than Chennault might have settled into a defensive posture and used his dwindling number of p-40s to intercept Japanese air raids on Chungking and the vital airfield at Kunming, endpoint of the supply run across the Hump. Chennault rejected this strategy, however, which would have ceded the initiative to the Japanese and been reactive in nature, rather than proactive. Instead, the colonel decided to go on the offensive and launch a counter-air campaign that would strike Japanese airfields and wrest air superiority from the enemy. He conceptualized the AVG as an aerial guerilla army that would compensate for its small number of aircraft with superior combat tactics, a high degree of mobility, and the help of the civilian population.

Compared to Japanese air units based in China, Chennault had relatively few aircraft to work with. By the summer of 1942, the AVG flight line consisted of just fifty-one p-40s, including thirty-one of the AVG's original one hundred p-40Bs and twenty of the newer p-40Es that had been ferried in over the Hump as replacement aircraft. However, only about thirty of these aircraft remained in flyable condition. As the number of serviceable p-40s dropped below the number of available pilots, the AVG resorted to borrowing Republic p-43A Lancers—the forerunner of the p-47 Thunderbolt—from the Nationalist Chinese air force.[18] On the plus side, however, Chennault now had bombers under his command: seven well-traveled b-25c Mitchells transferred from the 10th Air Force in India.

Though short of aircraft, spare parts, ammunition, and just about everything else needed to keep a combat air group operational, Chennault did have an extensive network of gravel airstrips in southern China to operate from. The AVG began utilizing forward airbases five hundred miles to the east of Kunming, particularly the airstrips located among the limestone pinnacles of Kweilin and along the red-clay banks of the Siang River at Lingling and Hengyang. These larger airbases as well as the many smaller auxiliary airstrips allowed Chennault to extend the range of his aircraft, since squadrons could take off from Kunming deep inside China, stage at a forward field like Kweilin, and then fly onward to strike targets in the south of China or the north of French Indochina, such as Hankow, Canton, Hong Kong, and Hanoi. The gravel fields also allowed AVG fighters to scramble from one airstrip to shoot up an incoming Japanese bomber formation and then evacuate to another field hundreds of miles away so that when the pilots of the Japanese counterstrike arrived over the first field, they would find only an empty runway. The AVG ground crews and Chennault's headquarters staff shuttled from one field to the next on C-47 transport planes laden with spare parts, tools, machine-gun ammunition, communications gear, canned food, the general's black dachshund, Joe, and the Tommy guns that remained the favored sidearm of the AVG.

Chennault could also rely on a densely woven web of civilian aircraft spotters, who reported incoming Japanese aircraft. This allowed the AVG to vector fighters to the most advantageous intercept positions and to avoid being caught on the ground by Japanese bombers. Civilian laborers equipped with little more than shovels and bamboo baskets rapidly patched up runways pocked by bomb craters, often at considerable risk from delayed-action bombs and follow-up raids. After one particularly accurate Japanese air strike on Kweilin, work crews filled in forty-five bomb craters in less than two hours.[19] Civilians often risked their lives to assist downed American aviators as well. When AVG pilots bailed out or crash-landed in Japanese-occupied territory, the locals hid them, fed them, bandaged them, and guided them to friendly lines. When pilots came down alive in friendly territory, the locals often treated them like visiting celebrities, complete with fourteen-course meals, perfumed towels, and firecrackers.[20] If they came down dead, the Chinese extracted the body from the wreckage and organized elaborate funeral ceremonies that could stretch out for several days. The grateful inhabitants of one town west of Kunming even erected a memorial obelisk in honor of the American pilot who had died of his injuries after parachuting to earth in, of all places, the local cemetery.[21]

To increase the odds of a happy ending when it came to bail-outs and belly landings, AVG aircraft flew over friendly territory for as long as possible when approaching enemy targets. In the midsummer of 1942, when Chennault sent four B-25s to strike Canton for the first time, the twin-engine bombers flew above a salient held by Nationalist forces that pointed at the city like a spear. When the Mitchells and their P-40 escorts finally crossed Japanese lines, they had to cover only fifty more miles to Tien Ho airfield, which barely gave Japanese fighter pilots time to strap into their cockpits.[22] Surprise remained critical for the incoming AVG aircraft, since Tien Ho served as one of the largest Japanese airbases in southern China and could put a substantial number of interceptors into the air. As the bomber pilots approached the outskirts of Canton, they easily spotted Tien Ho, which looked like a giant crosshair when seen from the air. Hangers and revetments ringed a large grass circle, and two runways—one large and one small—intersected at right angles in the center of the circle. At least one aircraft was on the runway attempting to take off when the quartet of B-25s released their payloads and swung back toward friendly territory. All aircraft returned safely to Kweilin.[23]

The mission took place on July 4, 1942, and was the first American air raid in the Pearl River delta. The Americans serving in the AVG had signed a contract with the Chinese government that expired that day, so everyone knew that this would be the last mission flown by the AVG. At midnight on July 4, the unit officially disbanded and then immediately reconstituted itself as the China Air Task Force of the India-based 10th Air Force. The United States

Army Air Forces (USAAF) recalled Chennault to active duty, promoted him to brigadier general, and gave him command of the CATF. Brig. Gen. Clayton Lawrence Bissell, who commanded the 10th Air Force, served as Chennault's immediate superior. Bissell wanted all AVG personnel to return to active duty in the USAAF and continue their service in China. However, the terms Bissell offered for this return to service rankled pilots and ground crew alike. They felt he should induct them at higher ranks than he was offering. Some pilots wanted permanent commissions in the army as well, which Bissell refused to consider.[24] After a year in Asia and seven months of combat, though, most of the AVG men chose to head home for an all-too-brief respite from tracer fire and the flash of exploding wing tanks. They knew they would have to take their chances with the draft or proactively volunteer, which suited those men who had formerly served in the U.S. Navy and Marine Corps and preferred to return to those services. Other pilots opted to fly as civilian pilots with commercial airlines in the United States, a job that was considered essential to the war effort. Another seventeen pilots chose to fly DC-3s for the CNAC, which was a combat unit in all but name. However, a cadre of five AVG pilots cast its lot with Chennault, including David "Tex" Hill, a fighter ace newly promoted to major. A total of thirty-four ground crewmen also elected to remain with the CATF.[25]

The CATF continued to fly the AVG's patched-up P-40s, which escorted the equally battered B-25s when they struck Canton four more times in the summer of 1942. On July 6 the B-25s targeted the riverside docks in Canton. A gaggle of Ki-27 pilots attempted to intercept the formation of five Mitchells but wound up tangling with the four escorting P-40s instead. The American pilots claimed two Ki-27s in the dogfight that followed and successfully protected the B-25s. On July 18 a trio of Mitchells returned to Tien Ho and walked their bombs across the giant crosshair formed by its runways. The B-25s hit the runways and revetments twice more on August 6 and August 8. Japanese fighters intercepted in a blaze of tracer fire, but the P-40 pilots and B-25 gunners kept them at bay. No U.S. aircraft went down during the two missions, though according to the P-40 pilots at least two Japanese fighters trailed smoke plumes as they plummeted into the ground.[26]

News of the raids on Canton reached Hong Kong and filtered into the POW camps packed with thousands of British, Canadian, and Indian soldiers captured during the invasion of the colony at the start of the war. Much to the disappointment of the POWs, no American warplanes appeared over Hong Kong during the summer of 1942. General Chennault, however, had not forgotten about Hong Kong. As part of the ongoing counter-air campaign begun by the AVG and continued by the CATF, he wanted to lure Japanese fighter pilots into dogfights on terms that favored his P-40s. This would require hitting a target of high value, and the never-bombed port facilities at Hong Kong presented an obvious choice, particularly on days when intelligence operatives reported the presence of Japanese naval and merchant vessels. Chennault understood the strategic importance of sinking Japanese shipping in the South China Sea, but he gave priority to the suppression of Japanese air assets in China. He therefore saw attacks on ports and merchant vessels as a means to provoke a fight with JAAF fighter squadrons under conditions that would be advantageous to his own P-40 pilots. The destruction of Japanese shipping ranked as a secondary objective. Ultimately, Chennault viewed airstrikes on ports and ships as part of the CATF's counter-air campaign rather than an anti-shipping campaign in its own right.[27]

Chennault and his staff began planning for a series of air strikes on Hong Kong in the autumn of 1942. In the eyes of the U.S. military, Hong Kong remained a friendly city under enemy occupation, so the raids would be precision strikes designed to take out specific military targets, rather than Guernica-style terror bombings designed to level the urban areas of Hong Kong. Chennault envisioned a sequence of raids in rapid succession on Hong Kong, supplemented by diversionary attacks on Canton that would force the Japanese to split up their defending fighter squadrons.[28]

More than any other factor, the performance of the P-40 would determine the air combat tactics used during the Hong Kong raids. Since the P-40 fought best at fifteen thousand to eighteen thousand feet, the fighters would fly three thousand feet above the B-25s at eighteen thousand feet. Japanese pilots preferred to prowl at a higher altitude, where they could dramatically outfly the P-40, but they would have to sacrifice this performance advantage and dive through the gauntlet of escorting American fighters to get at the bombers. The resultant dogfight would take place at an altitude that best suited the P-40. Any Japanese fighter climbing to meet the bombers, meanwhile, would face the high-speed diving attacks that also favored the heavy P-40. If the Japanese pilots wanted to keep the bombers from hitting their targets—and Chennault felt certain that they would—they would have to engage in an aerial dual where the Americans had the tactical advantage.[29]

In preparation for the strikes on Hong Kong, Chennault and his staff acquainted themselves with the geography of the enclave, which consisted of three constituent parts that had been acquired by the colonial British at different times. Hong Kong Island had been ceded by the Chinese emperor in perpetuity to the British as a spoil of the Opium War in 1842. In a rerun of the first Opium War, in 1860 the British forced the Chinese emperor to cede the Kowloon Peninsula on the mainland, opposite Hong Kong Island. In between Hong Kong Island and Kowloon lay Victoria Harbor, the finest anchorage on the South China coast. In 1898 the British leased what became known as the New Territories. This gave Hong Kong a hinterland of mountains and isolated walled villages north of the Kowloon Peninsula. For good measure, the ninety-nine-year lease included more than 230 islands of various sizes. The smallest barely amounted to a few seaweed-slicked boulders exposed at low tide. The largest, Lantau Island, surpassed the size of Hong Kong Island by a considerable margin. The New Territories ended at the Shen Zhen River, which demarcated the border with China.

Renamed the Conquered Territory of Hong Kong by the Japanese, who saw no need to redraw its prewar borders, the enclave clung to the coast of the South China Sea along the vital shipping lane that ran between resource-rich Southeast Asia and resource-poor Japan. Hong Kong also sat at the mouth of the Pearl River estuary, a key waterway that led inland to Canton, the largest city in Kwangtung Province some ninety miles to the northwest of Hong Kong. Aside from its favorable geographic location, the former British colony boasted one of the finest harbors in Asia and an extensive collection of port facilities that the Japanese had captured largely intact. These installations included the Royal Navy base at Admiralty, the Hong Kong (HK) and Whampoa dockyard at Hung Hom, the Tai Koo shipyard at Quarry Bay, and the oil tanks at Lai Chi Kok. All this made Hong Kong a key supply hub for the Japanese military machine, and a steady stream of tankers and bulk carriers hauling oil, tin, rubber, bauxite, tungsten, and iron ore docked in Victoria Harbor during their long journey north from Southeast Asia to the home islands. Southbound transports, meanwhile, hauled the troops, weaponry, and munitions needed to seize and hold the territory of the expanding Japanese empire. In January alone over 120 transports transited through Hong Kong, including a nineteen-ship convoy that carried an infantry division earmarked for the conquest of the Dutch East Indies.[30]

Chennault wanted to destroy the maritime facilities lining the shores of Victoria Harbor, but he knew that Hong Kong presented a particularly difficult target due to its mountainous topography, variable weather conditions, distance from Kweilin, and layered defenses. Japanese fighter pilots from the 33rd Sentai guarded the skies over the Pearl River delta, where they staged from the airstrip on the island of San Chau south of Macau, the airbases of White Cloud and Tien Ho in Canton, and the airfield at Kai Tak in Hong Kong. Led by Maj. Tsutomu Mizutani, an experienced combat veteran, the pilots of the 33rd Sentai flew the nimble Nakajima Ki-43-1 Hayabusa (Peregrine Falcon), which had become the standard JAAF fighter in China.[31] Following a policy of code-naming Japanese bombers with female names and Japanese fighters with male names, American military intelligence referred to the Ki-43 as the "Oscar." However, a moniker as prosaic as "Oscar" failed to do the

KI-43 justice. The Japanese name did a far better job of capturing the character of the aircraft, which possessed the same sleek, predatory grace as the raptor for which it had been so aptly named. The lightweight construction of the Hayabusa as well as its large wing area and unique combat flaps made the fighter ideal for aerial close combat. In the hands of a skilled pilot—and the 33rd Sentai certainly had no shortage of such men—the Hayabusa could easily outmaneuver and outclimb the P-40.

The acrobatic qualities of the KI-43 came at the cost of armor and armament, however, since both items would have added weight to the airframe. As a result, the Hayabusa lacked steel plating for the pilot and self-sealing rubber sheathing for its fuel tanks. Even worse a high-pressure oxygen cylinder mounted behind the pilot's seat had a nasty tendency to explode when pierced by enemy fire, tearing open plane and pilot alike. The initial production model— the KI-43-IA—carried just two 7.7 mm light machine guns forward of the cockpit in the cowling of the radial engine. A synchronizing mechanism made it possible to fire the guns without hitting the twin-bladed propeller. The IB model mounted one 7.7 mm machine gun and one HO-103 12.7 mm heavy machine gun, while the fully up-gunned IC had two 12.7 mm machine guns with 250 rounds apiece. The HO-103 resembled the American M-2 Browning heavy machine gun, though the JAAF classified it as a cannon because it fired an explosive shell.[32] Of the 716 KI-43-Is built, all but 80 rolled off the production line as IC models, so Major Mizutani's 33rd Sentai almost certainly flew Hayabusas armed with twin HO-103s in October 1942. Even when equipped with these two powerful heavy machine guns, however, the KI-43-IC remained one of the most lightly armed fighters of the war. The P-40E, for example, carried six of the .50-caliber M-2 Brownings. Veteran JAAF pilots who had flown the under-gunned KI-27 against the Soviets during the Nomonhan Incident in 1939 had long advocated for a more heavily armed next-generation Japanese interceptor, but their entreaties had been ignored by the designers at Nakajima when they drafted the blueprints for the KI-43.[33]

Hong Kong's mountainous topography and propensity for unco-operative weather presented yet more dangers to incoming American aircraft. The 1,810-foot height of Victoria Peak on Hong Kong Island and the even higher ridges and mountains that hemmed in Kowloon complicated bomb runs for aircraft operating below 3,000 feet. Low-flying aircraft would have to weave between rock-studded ridgelines and peaks rising in near-vertical walls that could trap an unwary pilot and swat him from the sky like a bird slamming into a windowpane. The low clouds and heavy mist that often cloaked Hong Kong in a gauzy fog made for exceedingly hazardous low-altitude flying and often shut down air operations altogether.

Chennault and the CATF relied on weather reports supplied by Col. Lindsay Tasman Ride's British Army Aid Group (BAAG), which had agents gathering meteorological data for Hong Kong and Canton. A twice-wounded veteran of the First World War and a professor at the University of Hong Kong, Ride had commanded a medical detachment during the battle for Hong Kong. He surrendered with the rest of the garrison on Christmas Day of 1941, but escaped from his captors in January 1942. Acutely aware of the plight of the men and women left behind in the POW camps and the civilian internment camp at Stanley, and never once doubting the right of Britain to reclaim Hong Kong, Ride proposed to the British high command in New Delhi that he assemble a unit that would be known as the British Army Aid Group. The core of the unit would consist of British and Cantonese soldiers who had served in various military units in Hong Kong, surrendered when the city fell, and later escaped to unoccupied China. The innocuous-sounding unit name and its role as a provider of medical services and refugee relief would, Ride suggested, mask the covert nature of its mission, which would center on escape, evasion, and intelligence. With the grudging approval of Chiang Kai-shek, who mistrusted the British, the high command accepted Ride's proposal and the BAAG came into existence in July 1942.

Lt. Gen. Isogai Rensuke served as governor general of Hong Kong, but his garrison lacked the troops to maintain much of a presence outside the urban areas of Hong Kong. As a result BAAG agents could travel with a degree of safety in the New Territories. This allowed the BAAG to feed a steady stream of intelligence information to the CATF, including twice-daily weather reports. These proved to be of exceptional value, as the Americans had no other source of information for weather along the coast of the South China Sea.[34] BAAG intelligence summaries also provided extensive details on ship movements, troop concentrations, and antiaircraft defenses in Hong Kong. In addition to providing information on weather and weaponry, BAAG agents managed to steal the blueprints for the Kai Tak airport expansion before construction work on the project had even begun. This adroitly executed act of espionage so impressed General Chennault that he insisted the BAAG route its weekly intelligence summaries directly to his forward HQ in Kweilin in Kwangsi Province. Conveniently, the BAAG had moved its headquarters from Kukong to Kweilin in August 1942.[35]

The BAAG hoped to capitalize on this goodwill and get clearance for an airdrop of desperately needed medicines into the Sham Shui Po and Argyle Street POW camps in Kowloon. Due to poor nutrition triggered by a starvation-level diet, many prisoners suffered from beriberi and pellagra. BAAG officers hoped to use an American B-25 for the airdrop, since the RAF did not have a single plane in all of China. However, to assist the Americans who would fly the B-25, the BAAG managed to line up an RAF officer with the requisite night-flying experience and knowledge of Hong Kong's geography. In October 1942 BAAG officers ran the scheme past the British general staff in New Delhi as well as USAAF officers in China and suggested that the operation might enjoy a higher likelihood of success if the airdrop occurred simultaneously with a nocturnal raid on Hong Kong. The bombing would provide the necessary distraction for the airdrop, which would have to occur without the knowledge of the camp guards for it to succeed. New Delhi indicated its support for the BAAG proposal and procured seventy thousand ascorbic acid tablets in tins of one hundred pills. The tins would be packed in crates marked "chopsticks" and carried over the Hump by American transport planes. Meanwhile, the BAAG request worked its way up the American chain of command and reached the desk of General Bissell, commander of the 10th Air Force, who approved the delivery of the chopsticks to Kunming. Bissell then forwarded the request for the airdrop on to Lt. Gen. Joseph W. Stilwell, the commander of American forces in the China-Burma-India (CBI) Theater, for his final approval.[36]

Colonel Ride had long been concerned that the Americans' unfamiliarity with Hong Kong might cause them to inadvertently target the POW camps, which resembled Japanese barracks when seen from the air. He was particularly alarmed when an American officer pointed to a map of Kowloon during a meeting and declared that a particular installation in Kowloon seemed "mighty important and worth bombing." The officer happened to be pointing at the Sham Shui Po POW camp.[37]

To avert a friendly fire incident, Ride fostered intelligence sharing between the BAAG and CATF command centers at Kweilin, where a gravel airstrip slashed across a prairie-flat valley surrounded by angular limestone crags tufted with jungle. These geologic marvels rose nearly a thousand feet into the air, which prompted the Americans at Kweilin to describe them as giant stalagmites or upside-down ice-cream cones. Caverns had been carved into these pinnacles by a million years of dripping water, and in the larger caves the CATF had set up a radio room and an operations room, both bombproof and equipped with natural air-conditioning. When they stood in the mouth of the command cave, the CATF headquarters staff had a control-tower view of the entire field. The airbase had originally been built to handle American heavy bombers like the B-17, which necessitated a mile-long runway built of gravel and clay as well as spacious revetments that could easily hold the smaller B-25s. American pilots deployed to Kweilin stayed in a hostel about five miles from the field. Built of camphor wood, the hostel featured American-style furniture and food, hot-water showers, and a bar with a pool table.[38]

As the only bomber unit in the CATF, the 11th Bomb Squadron

would lead the raid on Hong Kong, though it would be bolstered by the India-based B-25s of the 22nd Bomb Squadron, which would fly over the Hump to Kunming for temporary deployment. Both squadrons belonged to the 341st Bomb Group, though only the 11th had been permanently assigned to the CATF. Collectively the two squadrons would allow Chennault to launch the largest bomber raid ever mounted by American forces in China. Escorted by P-40 pilots from the 75th and 76th Fighter Squadrons, the B-25s would stage their attack from Kweilin, though to preserve mission secrecy all aircraft would remain at Kunming until the pilots received word from Chennault to launch the raid. At that point the strike force would fly east to Kweilin, where the warplanes would be refueled and the aircrews briefed by Chennault and his staff. During this briefing the pilots would be told for the first time that they would be going to Hong Kong. After just a few hours on the ground, the P-40s and B-25s would then rumble aloft for the final run to the target zone.

On September 22 Major Holloway flew his reconnaissance mission over Hong Kong in a P-43A Lancer borrowed from the Chinese air force. Based on Holloway's recon flight as well as intelligence reports from the BAAG, Chennault gave the Hong Kong operation the green light. In the days that followed, however, BAAG agents reported poor weather conditions over Hong Kong, forcing Chennault to delay the raid. For Col. Robert L. Scott, the thirty-four-year-old commander of the 23rd Fighter Group, the wait at the airbase in Kunming was agonizing. He slept fitfully, dreamed of his friends plummeting in flames during unwinnable dogfights with massive formations of Japanese fighters, and woke each morning at 3:00 a.m. in the hope that the weather had cleared and the raid was a go. Simultaneously, he wrestled with the deep-rooted fear that all airmen experienced before a dangerous flight into enemy territory. He dreaded the mission, but he would not have missed the first strike on Hong Kong for anything.[39]

On October 24 the weather turned clear and cool at Kunming. Favorable weather reports for Hong Kong finally arrived from the BAAG as well, and Chennault gave the order to launch the raid the next morning. He then sent a coded message to Song Meiling, wife of Chiang Kai-shek, that read, "Please notify Generalissimo Chiang Kai Shek that Japanese ships and docks at Hongkong will be attacked on October 25th. The same will be in celebration of his birthday, and I sincerely wish a long life and good health."[40]

# 3

## Fried Eggs or Scrambled?

Chennault had limited resources for making good on his birthday promise to Chiang Kai-shek. With the arrival of several Mitchells from the 22nd Bomb Squadron, the size of the strike force had grown to a dozen B-25s under the command of Maj. William E. Bayse. The 75th and 76th Fighter Squadrons scraped up eleven P-40s for the escort, plus one P-43A for recon work.[1] Maj. David L. Hill, a former U.S. Navy dive-bomber pilot and one of the highest-scoring aces in the AVG, commanded the 75th. Lanky, light-haired, and blue-eyed, the twenty-seven-year-old major had been born in Japanese-occupied Korea to missionary parents. His father had later served as chaplain to the Texas Rangers, and the young David Hill had grown up in the Lone Star State. Somewhat inevitably, the major went by the nickname "Tex."[2]

Caleb Haynes—the former AFC commander who had poked his Tommy gun out the window of a C-47 and opened fire on a pursuing enemy fighter—also planned to join the raid. He had been promoted to brigadier general and now had overall command of the American B-25s based in China. Japanese intelligence officers remained well aware of his new posting and promotion, just as they knew he had previously commanded the C-47 transports carrying avgas, ammunition, and other supplies over the Hump. In an attempt to discredit General Haynes and sap the morale of the men under his command, Japanese propaganda broadcasts had begun referring to him as "the old broken-down transport pilot." In response Haynes printed thousands of rice-paper leaflets, which his B-25s dropped with their bomb loads on the Japanese. The multilingual leaflets read in both English and Japanese: "These bombs come with the compliments of the old broken-down transport pilot Haynes."[3] In preparation for the Hong Kong raid, Haynes had ordered a fresh batch of leaflets from the local printer. When his B-25 reached the target zone, a crewman would toss out the leaflets, which would fall like a flurry of rice-paper propaganda onto the streets of Kowloon.

In Kunming the officers and enlisted men assigned to fly the raid received a briefing from Lt. Col. Harold "Butch" Morgan, the chief bombardier of the 11th Bomb Squadron. As he listened to Morgan speak in the crowded, smoke-filled operations room, Staff Sgt. James Nelson Young knew that something big must be in the works. After all he had flown nearly three-dozen combat missions, but he had never been asked to attend a formal briefing. Such affairs remained the preserve of the officers—the pilots, navigators, and bombardiers—and almost always excluded enlisted men like Staff Sergeant Young.[4]

A radio operator and belly gunner, Young had been assigned to the B-25 piloted by 1st Lt. Howard C. Allers. He had never flown with Allers or any of the other crewmen aboard his B-25, but this did not strike Young as particularly unusual. Enlisted airmen grew used to being rotated from aircraft to aircraft like spare parts. Young came from a hardscrabble background in Klamath Falls, Oregon, and had enlisted in the army on December 31, 1940, almost a year before Pearl Harbor. Like all American pilots and aircrew, he had volunteered for flight school, survived a rigorous selection process, and undergone extensive training. He had arrived in the CBI in May 1942, flown his share of missions, and managed to stay alive. After flying thirty-four combat missions aboard B-25s from both the 11th and the 22nd Bomb Squadron, Young had become rather philosophical about his chances of surviving the war. He knew he could be killed at any time but preferred not to dwell on it. He found it preferable to focus on the mundane tasks of preparing for air combat: cleaning and oiling the belly guns, checking the radios, stowing and mending gear, and preparing the next meal. Should it be fried eggs, he thought, or scrambled?

Lieutenant Colonel Morgan stood before the pilots and airmen during the briefing and ordered them to be on the flight line by 3:30 the next morning in preparation for a 4:00 a.m. departure. The B-25s would leave Kunming with empty bomb bays and fly to a forward airbase, Morgan told them. Citing the need for military secrecy, however, he did not reveal the name of the staging field or the final target of the mission.

At the conclusion of the briefing, Young returned to the airfield, where Chinese sentries stood vigilantly at each aircraft revetment. Still more soldiers stood watch in the machine-gun emplacements ringing all four sides of the field. Young could hear his boots crunching softly on the gravel taxiway, which like everything else on the field had been built largely by hand. He found the B-25 assigned to First Lieutenant Allers and supervised the loading of oxygen canisters and multiple boxes of .30- and .50-caliber machine-gun ammunition in belts that included plenty of tracer rounds. Packed with white phosphorous, tracer rounds burned brightly when fired, which meant that Young would be able to track the flight of the bullets he fired and correct his aim as needed. He had learned during the briefing that five five-hundred-pound bombs and ten small incendiary bombs would be taken aboard when the squadron landed to refuel at the forward airfield on the way to its target. When a Studebaker fuel truck rolled up, Young also monitored the fueling of the wing tanks with five hundred gallons of avgas. A faulty generator on one of the engines required his attention as well, but with some coaxing, he got the component to function normally with the help of Sgt. Paul "Rusty" Webb, the top-turret gunner and flight engineer. They both worked alongside the ground crew until well after dark. In the revetments scattered around the airfield, the other B-25 crews performed similar preflight routines. Nobody wanted the shame of having to abort the mission due to mechanical failure, and nobody wanted an engine to start coughing over enemy territory either.

Not many hours later the fighter pilots and bomber crews assembled in the predawn darkness, the air crisp and the stars bright overhead. Kunming's elevation of 6,200 feet made for cold mornings.

After an early breakfast, Young climbed into the fuselage of the B-25 commanded by First Lieutenant Allers. Aside from Young, Webb, and Allers, the crew included the copilot, 2nd Lt. Nicholas Marich, and the bombardier, 2nd Lt. Joseph W. Cunningham. The navigator, 2nd Lt. Murray L. Lewis, had just arrived in-theater and would be flying his very first combat mission.[5] Allers and Marich started both engines and taxied out toward the airstrip as dawn began to break. Young strapped himself in, expecting that they would begin barreling down the gravel runway at any moment, but the aircraft came to a halt instead, and he felt the vibration from the twin propellers fade as the engines quit. Word came back from Allers and Marich that they had throttled down and cut the engines on a signal from the lead plane. An airman soon drove down the line of motionless aircraft, passing the word for all crews to double-check their engines. One of the squadron's B-25s had apparently been sabotaged, and nearly thirty gallons of engine oil had drained from a loosened connection before the leak had been discovered. Young and his crewmates climbed out of their aircraft, thoroughly inspected the engines and other vital systems, and found no sign of tampering. All the other crews reported in with similar findings. After an hour's delay, the squadron cranked up its engines once again, taxied onto the runway, and roared aloft at 5:00 a.m.

Young still had no idea where they were going, but he felt pretty sure they would need the protection of Colonel Scott's P-40s no matter where they went. As an enlisted man, Young expected to be kept in the dark when it came to mission details. Some of the scuttlebutt circulating among the squadron claimed they would be hitting the home islands of Japan in a reprise of the famed Doolittle raid. However, after several hours of flying Young saw the weird, stalagmite-like topography of Kweilin come into view far below. This allowed him to get his bearings, since he knew that Kweilin lay five hundred miles to the east of Kunming. Young figured that a refueling stop among the stalagmites pretty much ruled out a strike on Japan, which would have required a more northerly trajectory, but it did position them for raids on targets throughout central and southern China.

FRIED EGGS OR SCRAMBLED?

The bombers began landing at one-minute intervals, and soon Allers and Marich had eased their big twin-engine airplane onto the gravel runway, taking care to avoid the soft spots where bomb craters had been filled in by Chinese work crews. Young's watch said 8:00 a.m. when Allers cut the engines and shut down the aircraft. Scott's fighter pilots had already touched down at their usual landing speeds of about one hundred miles per hour, fortunately without any blowouts of their badly worn tires. Along with just about every other part needed to keep the P-40s in the air, landing-gear tires remained in short supply.

Allers, Marich, Lewis, and Cunningham climbed up a slope to the operations cave at the base of one of the limestone pinnacles for an officers-only briefing. Young figured the four lieutenants were about to find out where they would be dropping their load of five-hundred-pound bombs. He and Webb would simply have to wait until they returned, but the two enlisted men had plenty to keep them busy in the meantime. As the hot metal of the plane ticked in the heat, they locked ten seventeen-kilogram incendiary bombs into the racks in the fuselage, helped the ground crew hoist five M-43s into the bomb bay, and supervised the pumping of aviation fuel into the wing tanks. The air smelled of avgas and the omnipresent red dust of the unpaved airfield, which coated the sweaty Chinese and American mechanics as they performed last-minute checks of the engines and other equipment. As he tinkered with the still-recalcitrant generator, Young wondered when—or if—they would get to eat before returning to the air, as he had not had a bite since his 3:00 a.m. breakfast.

Meanwhile, the officers assembled in the operations cave for a briefing from General Chennault. At this time Chennault finally revealed the mission target, which had been a secret that only Scott, Bayse, Haynes, Morgan, and a few other senior officers had been privy to. The B-25s would target the Japanese ships reported to be in Victoria Harbor, the general said. The oil tanks, wharves, and godowns on the Kowloon Peninsula would serve as secondary targets if it turned out the ships had left port.[6] To preserve the element of surprise, the strike force would take off from Kweilin as quickly as possible. Follow-up raids that night and the next day would continue to hit shipping in Victoria Harbor as well as the electric power plant and dry docks on Hong Kong Island. A few B-25s would fly diversionary raids on Canton as well. The bombers would keep pounding away at Hong Kong until the stockpile of fuel and bombs at Kweilin ran out, Chennault told the roomful of aviators, while the P-40 pilots would lure any defending Japanese interceptors into a dogfight on terms that favored the Americans. Time on the ground in between missions would have to be minimized due to the threat of Japanese counterstrikes on the Kweilin airfield.

When Allers and the other lieutenants returned from the briefing, Young was standing on the right wing monitoring a fuel hose as it pumped gasoline from a tanker truck into the wing tank. The officers stood under the wing, which offered the only available shade, and talked quietly about the briefing. "Hong Kong," Young heard Allers say, which solved the mystery of their target. Young knew that Hong Kong would be heavily defended, both by flak and by fighters based at fields at Hong Kong, Canton, and San Chau. His greatest concern centered on escape and evasion, however. If he had to jump over enemy territory, he wanted to be well prepared.

Young always flew with plenty of survival gear. He carried a .45 pistol in a shoulder holster, a scarf his mother had given him for Christmas, and a small jungle kit attached to his parachute pack that contained a survival knife, quinine pills, some Nationalist Chinese currency, a pair of one-pound chocolate bars, a head net, fishing line and hooks, extra shells for the .45, and a small silk Nationalist Chinese flag embroidered with Chinese characters identifying him as an American flyer who should be given aid and assistance. American airmen referred to the little flags as "blood chits," and some sewed them to the backs of their leather flight jackets. Like virtually all U.S. aviators in China, including General Chennault, Young did not speak Chinese, so he would have to rely on his blood chit to explain to friendly locals who he was and what he needed.

In addition to preparing his survival gear before each mission,

Young had also gotten into the habit of studying maps of the target area so that if he had to bail out, he would have some sense of where to go once he hit the ground. He had heard the rumors about how the Japanese treated downed American aviators, and he had no desire to become a prisoner of war. Since he had not been given advance notice that Hong Kong would be the target, however, he had never consulted any maps of the former British colony. He had a general sense of Hong Kong's location on the South China coast, but that was about it. If he had to hit the silk during the raid, it would all be guesswork and good luck once his boots plopped into the rice paddy mud.

As Young pondered his odds of avoiding capture should he have to pull the ripcord over Hong Kong, Colonel Scott prepared to climb into the cockpit of his P-40E. His fighter force had already been significantly reduced. One P-40 had refused to start, and the pilot of another had damaged his plane when he taxied into one of the many craters and potholes pitting the airstrip. Scott had already lost two of his twelve aircraft before they had even left Kweilin.[7] Scott's plane checked out, however, and he clambered onto the left wing laden down with helmet, goggles, oxygen mask, earphones, parachute, life vest, .45 pistol, Thompson submachine gun, movie camera, and assorted other gear. He flung one leg over the fuselage and into the cramped cockpit, then swung in the other leg and wiggled down into his armored seat. Then he somehow found space to stow the camera and the submachine gun. Scott planned to use the camera to film the raid, but he hoped that he would never have to use the Tommy gun, which he carried in case he belly-landed in Japanese territory. Come out of the cockpit shooting, he always said, since like most American airmen he feared capture more than death.[8]

Scott strapped in, adjusted his seat and rudder pedals, and clicked on the radio. Then he toggled the starter switch, primed the engine, turned on the ignition, pressed the starter with his foot, and watched the eleven-foot propeller lurch to life in a snort of exhaust smoke. The triple blades quickly spun to a blur beyond the windscreen as he moved the mixture control from idle cutoff. Scott knew from experience that the Allison engine required very little warm-up time, and that extended idling risked fouling the plugs, so he taxied straight out to the runway. He began bumping down the airstrip at 11:45 a.m., less than three hours after he had touched down at Kweilin. His plane trailed a plume of red dust, which swirled and writhed down the length of the gravel strip like the tail of a vengeful dragon. Compensating for propeller torque with some right rudder, Scott saw the revolutions per minute hit three thousand. His tail wheel left the dirt, which leveled out the nose and gave him an unobstructed view forward. Then the Shark hit one hundred miles per hour, and Scott left the runway behind. He immediately retracted the landing gear and adjusted the cowl flaps as he climbed for altitude and positioned himself on the wing of Major Holloway. Major Hill took off in a P-40E that could be easily identified by the number 151 painted on the fuselage between the cockpit and the tail. Six more fighter pilots—Maj. John R. Alison, Capt. John F. Hampshire, 1st Lt. Robert F. Mayer, 1st Lt. William E. Miller, 1st Lt. Mortimer D. Marks, and 2nd Lt. Morton Sher—left the ground in quick succession.[9]

Young finished fueling up the tanks as the fighters roared aloft. From his vantage point atop the wing, he had been keeping an eye on a flatbed truck as it worked its way down the line of parked bombers with sandwiches for the crews. To his dismay the truck turned around before reaching his plane as word came to get the bombers off the ground as quickly as possible. Young climbed down from the wing, still hungry, and clambered into the broiling innards of the Mitchell with the rest of the crew. As he did so, he heard First Lieutenant Allers grousing about getting switched to the rearmost position by a captain who wanted to move his aircraft closer to the tip of the formation. The captain's B-25 had a tail gun, Allers pointed out, while their own ship did not. The guns manned by Webb and Young could dish out devastating streams of cigar-sized .50-caliber slugs, but these weapons were housed in turrets with restricted arcs of fire. Webb and Young would not always have clear shots at any pursuing fighters. With no tail gun, Young reflected, they made for a less than logical choice for flying as tail-end Charlie, but logic wasn't the issue. The issue was rank, and Allers just didn't have enough of it.

As the pilot in command of the aircraft, Allers settled into the left seat up in the cockpit, while Marich took the copilot's seat beside him on the right. Cunningham wormed into the greenhouse at the front of the aircraft. Both engines stuttered to life, blasting a hot breeze down the tube of the fuselage where Young, Webb, and Lewis strapped themselves in for takeoff. Young could smell engine exhaust and the night soil spread on the paddy fields as they taxied out to the airstrip. They waited as the other eleven ships of the squadron lifted off, and then Allers spun the plane on its tricycle landing gear at the end of the runway, throttled up the engines, and released the brakes. The aircraft began jolting down the airstrip, half obscured by the clouds of dust raised by the propellers. Allers had a mile-long runway to work with, which left plenty of room for him to reach the minimum takeoff speed of about eighty or ninety miles per hour. Young felt the tail dip when the nose gear left the ground, and then the plane rattled aloft as the ochre dirt of Kweilin fell away behind them.

The B-25s climbed steadily through widely scattered cloud, and First Lieutenant Allers ordered Young and the rest of his crew to don their oxygen masks when they passed ten thousand feet. The unheated and uninsulated fuselage provided little protection from the frigid, high-altitude air. Chilled, ravenous, and deafened by the drone of the twin engines, Young felt quite alone. He figured that all the bomber pilots must have felt the same way since they closed up into an unusually tight pattern. Each flight—A, B, and C—arranged itself in a diamond formation. Each diamond comprised one point in a larger triangle formation. As ordered Allers positioned his B-25 as the trailing point of the Flight C diamond. Cruising at seventeen thousand feet, the squadron headed southeast on the final leg of the 350-mile run to Hong Kong.

# 4

## Tai-tai! Planes Are Coming!

The men of the 11th Bomb Squadron flew B-25Cs, an early variant of an aircraft that had proven to be rugged, dependable, easy to maintain, and highly versatile. Like the P-40 the B-25 could withstand tremendous amounts of punishment and remain in the air. A Mitchell could fly with one engine shot out, or one of its pilots incapacitated, or one of its twin tail fins blown to pieces, or even all three things at once. CATF B-25s also carried substantial defensive armament, which further enhanced their ability to survive combat missions. The standard North American B-25C rolled out the factory door with twin .50-caliber machine guns in a belly turret, two more .50 calibers in a top turret, and one forward-firing .30 caliber in the nose. Though this sounded formidable in blueprint theory, in actuality B-25 crews dismissed the .30-caliber nose gun as hopelessly inadequate and found the gun turrets to be highly unreliable and prone to failure during combat. Moreover, CATF crews had quickly realized that the omission of any tail guns left the Mitchells vulnerable to attacks from behind, since the belly and top turrets lacked clear fields of fire to the rear. To address these problems, CATF mechanics and armorers had modified the defensive armament of the unit's B-25s during the summer of 1942 under the supervision of the squadron armament officer, 1st Lt. Elmer L. Tarbox. Tarbox had the mechanics place twin .50-caliber machine guns in the nose, giving the aircraft much heavier forward firepower. The ground crews also removed the troublesome bottom turret and replaced it with twin .30-caliber guns in a mount designed by Tarbox, and they improvised a tail-gun position by mounting another .30-caliber machine gun in the rear of the plane. All these field modifications presaged changes that would be made to later production models of the B-25.[1]

In addition to serving as the squadron armament officer, Tarbox also flew as a bomber pilot. He sat in the cramped cockpit of number 63 during the Hong Kong raid, and in all likelihood his B-25 bristled with specially designed machine-gun positions. However, Tarbox and the squadron armorers had not had time to modify the plane flown by First Lieutenant Allers, which still carried the standard defensive armament for a B-25C. From his armored bucket seat in the ribbed Plexiglas nose compartment, Cunningham could fire his .30-caliber machine gun by inserting the weapon into ball-and-socket gun ports to his front, left, and right. The original idea had been that the gun could be moved as needed to target enemy fighters, but in practice it took far too long to switch the heavy Browning from one socket to another. Like most bombardiers Cunningham left his .30 pointing straight ahead and ignored the left and right sockets. Webb operated the twin .50 calibers in the powered top turret, which served as the most formidable gun position on the aircraft when it operated correctly, which it frequently did not. The hydraulics failed, the sights fogged up, and the nine yards of ammunition belts jammed when the aircraft pulled heavy g's in a dive or climb. As for Young, he had the worst deal of all, since he had to kneel and peer down through a periscope while working the belly turret controls with both hands. What he saw through the series of mirrors mounted in the periscope—assuming they hadn't fogged up—represented reality backward, so he had to move his hands in counterintuitive fashion and hope he managed to hit something.[2]

The B-25C commanded by First Lieutenant Allers also lacked the incendiary bomb racks that had been mounted on many of the aircraft in the 11th Bomb Squadron. Installed in the field by CATF ground crews, the racks eliminated the need to drop small incendiary and fragmentation bombs by hand. This slow and rather fraught method of hand-dropping the diminutive frags and incendiaries had been standard practice when the 11th first arrived in China.[3] Staff

Sergeant Young had been assigned the delicate job of arming and releasing the seventeen-kilogram incendiaries the old-fashioned way. The bombs worked somewhat like a hand grenade. Young would pull a bomb from a wall rack inside the fuselage and yank a cotter pin from the bomb's fuse shaft, which had a small propeller attached to it. He would then jettison the bomb through the gun port in the floor. Once the bomb was tossed overboard, its propeller would spin for a few seconds and detach from the shaft, at which point the fuse became fully armed and ready to detonate upon impact. The cotter pin served as the safety device that kept the propeller from spinning and the bomb safely inert while it rested in its rack. To help get the bombs out of the aircraft as quickly as possible once they reached the target zone, Second Lieutenant Lewis had been tasked with feeding the seventeen-kilogram bombs to Young, who thought the bombs looked like tubes of bologna sausage.

The B-25Cs flown by the CATF carried six-man crews. The pilot and the copilot flew side by side in the cockpit, where they were deafened by the roar of the 1,700-horsepower Wright-Cyclone GR-2600 radial engines mounted on each wing. The twelve-foot propellers powered by these engines could theoretically hurl the plane through the skies at over three hundred miles per hour, though most of the aircraft winging toward Hong Kong had racked up so many hours on their engines that they could no longer reach such optimum speeds. The navigator worked in a small compartment or "pit" just behind and slightly below the cockpit. The bombardier sat up front in the greenhouse with its Plexiglas nose bubble, bombsight, and .30-caliber nose gun. To reach his position, the bombardier had to crawl through a narrow, low-ceilinged tunnel that ran beneath the flight deck from the navigator's pit. The bomb bay rested behind the cockpit and between the wings, and to reach the rear compartments of the plane the crewmen had to step down from the cockpit into the navigator's pit and then squeeze past the bombs on a narrow catwalk that stretched the length of the bomb bay. In the main fuselage compartment behind the bomb bay, the flight engineer manned the twin .50-caliber guns mounted in the top turret, which jutted up from the fuselage not far from the twin rudders of the tail. A fifth crewman had responsibility for the radio and, in the case of Staff Sergeant Young, the belly guns. An armored door separated the rear crew compartment from a smaller tail compartment, which contained a toilet, tools, parachutes, and other crew gear. In the modified B-25s, the compartment also housed a jury-rigged tail-gun position. Crucially, the rear compartment also had a floor hatch with an emergency release. If the gunners had to bail out, they would tumble themselves out through this hatch and into the slipstream. The pilots, navigator, and bombardier would use a hatch in the floor of the navigator's pit.

When Young looked up through the top turret, he was reassured to see the P-40s shadowing the bombers a few thousand feet overhead. He rather optimistically guessed that their escort numbered twenty to twenty-five fighters, which seemed like a sufficient number to keep enemy bandits at bay and prevent any scenario that had him opening hatches in the floor. Young could just make out the teardrop-shaped auxiliary fuel tanks hanging from the center bomb rack of each Shark. To extend their range and time over target, all nine of the escorting P-40s carried these disposable belly tanks. When they had leveled out from their climb, Scott and his fellow pilots had adjusted their fuel selectors to begin drawing fuel from their belly tanks, which could be jettisoned as soon as they ran dry. Belly tanks slowed the performance of a P-40, so pilots always used the fuel in the disposable tanks first so that they could be dropped before engaging the enemy.[4] Pilots frequently had to punch their tanks off, which lead to a chronic shortage of drop tanks. To overcome this supply shortfall, the CATF relied on homemade fifty-gallon bamboo belly tanks.[5]

Unfortunately, the belly tank slung beneath Major Alison's P-40E refused to feed. He tried rolls, dives, turns, banks, and just about every other acrobatic maneuver his plane could handle in an attempt to restore fuel flow, but the tank stubbornly refused to function. Without the extra fuel in the drop tank, Alison knew he would never make it back from Hong Kong. He banked back toward Kweilin. An engine malfunction forced an equally disappointed Major Holloway back to Kweilin as well. The remaining seven p-40 pilots maintained position above the b-25s, which had better mechanical luck. None of the twelve Mitchells had to abort.[6]

Lieutenant Colonel Morgan flew in the nose compartment of the lead b-25. Morgan was not a small man, which made the already cramped compartment feel even smaller. He shared this space with a pair of .50-caliber machine guns, belts of ammunition, his parachute, oxygen tanks, interphone, and toggle switches for the bomb-bay doors and bomb shackles. Most importantly of all, he shared the crowded compartment with the squadron's only Norden bombsight.[7] Morgan would use the top-secret device to aim the bombs that would be dropped by the entire squadron. When the Norden automatically released the five-hundred-pounders cached in the bomb bay of Morgan's b-25, the other eleven ships in the formation would immediately drop their bombs as well.

Fifty minutes out from Kweilin, Colonel Scott adjusted his oxygen mask for the hundredth time, but it was no use—the rubber continued to chafe his sunburned neck. As planned, the strike force bypassed Canton and its concentration of enemy airfields by keeping a good thirty miles to the west, though Scott could still make out the twisting veins of the Pearl River estuary. Flying beneath a clear blue sky, he watched the undulating green terrain pass far below and, in the distance, saw the sun glaring off the surface of the ocean. Hilltops protruded from islands shrouded in fog, reminding him of Catalina Island on the Southern California coast. The formation soon reached the South China Sea and banked to the left over Macau, some forty miles southwest of Hong Kong.

Staff Sergeant Young took up his position over the belly guns, while Staff Sergeant Webb positioned himself on the firing steps of his top turret. The steps protruded from a shaft running from the floor up into the turret, and when Webb stood on the steps, he could get his head and shoulders into the turret between the twin .50-caliber guns. When the turret rotated, the shaft did as well, moving Webb in synchronized turns with the guns. While Webb could actually see his targets, Young had to peer through a mirrored gun sight that worked somewhat like an upside-down periscope on a submarine. He knelt on a foam pad, braced his torso against a chest plate, and reached forward to grab the gun controls. Then Young nodded his head down and nestled his cheek against a cushioned eyecup, which rested atop a shaft that drilled down through the fuselage and emerged between the guns dangling beneath the aircraft like a pair of gigantic stingers. A series of mirrors allowed Young to see out through the optical gun sight mounted on the bottom of the shaft. With his cheekbone pressed against the eyecup, he could scan the skies beneath and behind the bomber like a submarine captain scanning the waves for enemy ships.

Young could see San Chau and Macau falling away behind the American aircraft as they continued on a northeasterly bearing across the wide mouth of the Pearl River delta. Soon the mountainous bulk of Lantau Island appeared off the left wing. The planes flew along the West Lamma Channel, passed to the west of Stonecutters Island, and then continued over the crenelated terrain of the New Territories. When they reached their prearranged turning point seven miles north of Kowloon, General Haynes led the formation in a sharp bank to the south and commenced his bomb run at approximately 1:30 p.m. In the Plexiglas nose bubble, Lieutenant Colonel Morgan quickly ascertained that the Japanese ships reported to be in Victoria Harbor had left port, so he prepared to bomb the mission's secondary target: the wharves, godowns, and oil tanks along the western coastline of Kowloon.[8]

A few thousand feet above the bombers, Colonel Scott and his fellow P-40 pilots split into two separate flights. Hampshire, Sher, and Hill stayed with Scott, while Marks, Mayer, and Miller formed a second group. The two flights wove back and forth above the bombers, alert for enemy fighters, in a maneuver known as "S-ing." Scott's gloved hands sweated profusely in anticipation of combat, and when he tore off a glove and wiped his palm and fingers on his pants, they left a rust-red smear of airfield dust. His throat felt as dry as the Kweilin runway, and he found it difficult to swallow.

Scott did, however, have complete confidence in his aircraft despite its growing reputation as an obsolete, outmoded, and outclassed cement truck of a fighter plane. The Curtis-Wright P-40 had certainly performed poorly in the early days of the Pacific war, when all too many of them had spiraled down in flames over Hawaii, the Philippines, the Dutch East Indies, northern Australia, and other battle zones, but these aerial debacles were the result of inexperienced and ill-prepared American pilots who had failed to capitalize on the P-40's strengths while simultaneously failing to exploit the weaknesses of Japanese fighter aircraft.

To be fair the American pilots at Pearl Harbor, Manila, Java, and Darwin had almost always been outnumbered, though the same could be said of the pilots of the AVG and the CATF. Chennault's battle-honed aviators could hold their own against larger Japanese formations, but then again they knew their P-40s intimately. "Sharks," they called them, or "Forties." They had flown them on dozens of missions and logged hundreds of hours in the cockpit. They knew that the P-40's top speed of about 350 miles per hour in level flight would outpace Japanese fighters, and that the Shark could go even faster in a dive. However, even with its liquid-cooled 1,150-horsepower Allison V-12 engine running flat out, the heavier Shark had no chance of outclimbing the more lightly constructed Japanese fighters, which performed far better at higher altitudes anyhow. The Allison had only a single-stage supercharger, which meant that at higher altitudes the supercharger could not compress the oxygen-lean air flowing into the engine sufficiently to keep it running at full power. A combat-loaded P-40 flying above twenty-two thousand feet reacted with the sluggish imprecision of a rice-wine drunk, and no CATF pilot wanted to fight at such rarified altitudes.[9]

CATF pilots also knew from experience that the nimbler Japanese fighters could easily outmaneuver P-40s in a close-in dogfight, so they avoided such encounters at all costs. Instead, CATF pilots had learned to enter combat with an altitude advantage that allowed them to swoop down, close with the enemy in a blaze of tracer fire, and then break away at dive speeds that could hit 450 miles per hour. In a serious emergency, the performance envelope could be pushed even further. One P-40B pilot with an enemy fighter on his tail recorded a power dive of 515 miles per hour, which exceeded the speed that should have torn off the wings by a solid 75 miles per hour.[10] The lighter weight and less robust construction of Japanese fighters ensured they could rarely hang on to a P-40 in a dive.

Climbs remained an entirely different matter, however. The P-40 could gain only about two thousand feet of altitude per minute, which an enemy fighter like the Ki-43 Hayabusa could easily surpass by a substantial margin. Due to the P-40's slow rate of climb, CATF pilots could scramble aloft and ascend to an advantageous interception altitude only when they had sufficient advance warning of incoming enemy air raids. For this reason the CATF relied on a web of Chinese aircraft spotters to report incoming enemy aircraft, as this gave the unit time to position its slow-climbing P-40s in the best possible ambush positions before the Japanese aircraft arrived over the target. This practice provided the CATF pilots with a crucial advantage that P-40 pilots fighting elsewhere in the Pacific often lacked. Vectored into position with the assistance of an extensive aircraft spotter network that often worked with radar-like efficiency, CATF pilots could then execute the kind of hit-and-run diving attacks that played to the strengths of the heavily armed P-40.

Shark pilots had also learned to take advantage of their six .50-caliber heavy machine guns, which outgunned the weapons package mounted on their most common adversary, the Ki-43. The heavier armament of the P-40s allowed the American pilots to score hits on Japanese fighters before they could close to a range where their agility made them lethal. The M-2 Browning substantially outranged the 7.7 mm machine guns carried by many Japanese aircraft, and while the M-2 was roughly equivalent to the Japanese HO-103 heavy machine gun, no Japanese fighter carried six at a time. The Ki-43-IC, for example, carried just two. Due to their lower muzzle velocity, even the deadly 20 mm cannons carried by some Japanese aircraft were outranged by the American .50-caliber guns. The cigar-sized 12.7 mm rounds packed enormous power, and the hammering recoil of the six guns mounted on a P-40 packed so much energy that if a pilot fired the .50 calibers in just one wing, his aircraft would slew off course.[11] When a stream of six 12.7 mm slugs hit a Japanese fighter, the result was much like a shotgun blast hitting a beer can—the aircraft simply disintegrated in a gush of smoke, flame, blood, and shredded aircraft parts. Even winging a Japanese fighter often proved sufficient to end its flying career. While the lightweight airframes of Japanese interceptors allowed for impressive maneuverability and rates of climb, that same fragile construction often meant that even if the pilot of a shot-up fighter managed to make it back to the ground, his plane would more than likely never fly again.

The P-40, meanwhile, could take multiple hits and keep on flying. The plane's self-sealing gas tanks minimized fuel leakage and the risk of conflagration when perforated by machine-gun slugs or flak shrapnel. Many fighters with liquid-cooled engines had their heavy radiators mounted in the wings or belly to better distribute the weight toward the aircraft's center of gravity. However, spreading the coolant system throughout the aircraft made it more vulnerable to enemy fire—and it only took a single well-placed rifle bullet to disable the coolant system, which would soon cause the entire engine to seize up. However, the distinctive pointy nose of the P-40 housed not just its liquid-cooled engine but also its radiator and oil cooler. As a result the compactly packaged coolant system presented a smaller target that was much harder to hit. Armor sheathing for the engine provided further protection.[12]

In addition to the nose armor, a steel plate mounted behind the cockpit shielded the pilot. More than one P-40 pilot with a Zero on his tail had the rivets of this plate blasted into his back when 20 mm cannon shells exploded against the steel armor, but such wounds could be survived, and the bloodied pilots landed their ships safely.[13] One AVG P-40B wobbled back to base with sixty-six bullet holes, including five in the pilot, who escaped a fatal wound courtesy of his armor plating.[14] Some P-40 pilots even managed to safely land their mangled ships after head-on collisions with enemy fighters, which almost always failed to survive the impact.[15] P-40s sometimes collided with other obstacles as well—one Shark pilot flying just above the deck in heavy rain ran into some telephone lines strung across a river and returned to base with 1,200 feet of phone cable trailing behind his aircraft. Another pilot hit a high-tension line during a strafing run, lassoed himself with 200 feet of wire, and still managed to fly home to make a normal landing.[16] The rugged construction of the P-40 meant that ground crews could repair badly mangled planes and send them back into the air along with the bandaged-up pilots.

As Colonel Scott continually scanned the skies for Japanese fighters and Lieutenant Colonel Morgan readied his Norden, the air-raid sirens started to wail in Hong Kong. When the American author and old China hand Emily "Mickey" Hahn first heard the urgent blaring of the sirens, however, she dismissed them as a drill.

"Tai-tai!" her amah, Ah Yuk, told her. "Planes are coming!"[17]

"Nope," Hahn said. "It's false, Ah Yuk, it's a practice alarm."

"Practice?" said Ah Yuk, heading for the safety of the basement with Hahn's young daughter. "This is real. Come on, Tai-tai!"[18]

After avoiding imprisonment in the Stanley internment camp with the other Allied civilians—on the grounds of her marriage to a Chinese husband, albeit one not currently residing in Hong Kong—the thirty-seven-year-old Hahn had taken up residence in Tregunter Mansions, a block of flats on May Road near the stop for the Peak Tram. Like so many structures on Hong Kong Island, the brick building clung to the side of a steep slope far above the city center, which meant that from the north-facing basement door Hahn and Ah Yuk could look out over the trees toward Kowloon. To their disappointment they failed to spot any American planes, though they saw flak bursts high overhead and heard the distant boom of explosions rumbling across the harbor from Kowloon.

In the greenhouse of the lead B-25, Morgan dialed the speed, heading, and altitude of his aircraft into the mechanical computer of his Norden bombsight. He also factored in the crosswind. Steadying himself with one arm, he hunched over the device and peered into the eyepiece, which featured crosshairs made from two strands of human hair. With his other arm, he continued to adjust the dials of the bombsight, which had begun flying the plane through the automated flight control equipment (AFCE). In the cockpit General Haynes and his copilot had relinquished control of the aircraft to the autopilot. Morgan felt the plane shudder as the bomb-bay doors opened. Flak bursts began to pepper the air just ahead of the bombers, and the black and white balls of smoke twisted into fanciful shapes as they whipped past.

Through the eyepiece of the Norden, Morgan watched the jagged peaks of the New Territories flow past far below until they gave way to the urban street grid of Kowloon. Whitfield Barracks slid into the crosshairs and remained pinned like a photo thumbtacked to a bulletin board. Milliseconds later the bombsight automatically released the bombs from an altitude of 17,200 feet. The planes following behind Morgan's B-25 immediately dropped their five-hundred-pound bombs as well, which began to fall in long strings, their noses slowly tilting downward until they were falling fuse-first toward the streets of Kowloon.

Sitting in the rear of the B-25 flown by First Lieutenant Allers, Staff Sergeant Young felt the sudden rush of air as the bomb-bay doors opened, turning the interior of the fuselage into a wind tunnel. Young counted off the five-hundred-pounders as they tumbled free in quick succession, but his count stopped at four—for some reason the last of the five five-hundred-pounders remained in the bomb bay. Before Young could report the hung-up bomb to the pilot, Second Lieutenant Lewis handed him the first incendiary, and he pulled the cotter pin and tossed the seventeen-kilogram bomb overboard. In short order the two crewmen had dropped all ten of the sausage-shape weapons.

Nearly 60 five-hundred-pound bombs spattered across the street grid of Kowloon, where they detonated like strings of giant firecrackers, and 120 of the seventeen-kilogram incendiary bombs, each pregnant with fire, rained onto the rooftops of the city. In a rapid sequence of explosions, the bomb train from the northernmost flight of B-25s blasted its way down Jordan Road and adjacent side streets, particularly Woosung and Nanking Streets. With a brilliant flash, shophouses crumpled and spilled out onto the pavement. Still more flashes left burning vehicles and deep craters in the middle of Jordan Road. Morgan's flight struck Whitfield Barracks and the Austin Road area, where bombs cracked open military buildings like eggshells and torched a gasoline depot. One stick of bombs from the rearmost plane tore up the Gun Club Hill barracks. The southernmost flight scattered twenty five-hundred-pounders between Haiphong and Salisbury Roads, with residential buildings and shops at the intersection of Hankow and Haiphong Roads taking the brunt of the destruction. Along Salisbury Road the bombs inflicted varying degrees of damage to the Peninsula Hotel, the Star Ferry pier, the Kowloon railway station, and the switching yard tracks. A pair of unexploded bombs landed on the grounds of the Marine Police Headquarters as well, where they rested half buried in the dirt. One outlying string detonated along Cameron and Carnarvon Roads, where several buildings sustained catastrophic direct hits. A trio of smoke columns began to spire over Kowloon as leaflets emblazoned with the phrase, "These bombs come with the compliments of the old broken-down transport pilot Haynes" slowly fluttered downward in a flurry of rice-paper propaganda.[19]

From the cockpit of his P-40, Colonel Scott glimpsed the flash of the exploding bombs, but he focused his attention on the telltale plumes of dust moving down the runway at Kai Tak. He knew those gritty trails marked the trajectory of Japanese fighters scrambling aloft in pursuit of the American B-25s. Scott nervously toggled his gun switch off and on as he watched the twin-engine aircraft ascend at a rate he knew no P-40 could ever match. At this point he spotted a second group of single-engine fighters—likely Ki-43s from Major Mizutani's 33rd Sentai—climbing toward the bombers. Using the generic term for all Japanese fighters, Scott thumbed the mike button on the throttle and announced, "Bandits ahead—Zeros! At eleven o'clock."

Despite Japanese attempts to block the frequency, Scott heard Major Hill reply, "Yes, I see 'em."

Scott jettisoned his belly tank, checked once again that he had activated the red gun switch on his instrument panel, rolled his plane onto its back for maximum dive speed, and hurtled toward the lead Ki-43. He took a long shot from a thousand yards out when he saw that the enemy fighters would reach the bombers before he could get any closer but registered no hits. Before Scott could close with the first enemy fighter, Hill slid in front of him in number 151, followed the Ki-43 as it turned tightly into the bombers, and opened fire with his .50 calibers. Scott and Captain Hampshire observed the plane trailing flame before smashing into the waters just west of Hong Kong Island.

As the B-25s closed their bomb bays, the flak intensified and the pilots observed muzzle flashes winking on the northern shore of Hong Kong Island. General Haynes led the B-25s in a diving right-hand turn over Victoria Harbor and Stonecutters Island, then banked in the opposite direction to confuse the attacking enemy fighters. Staff Sergeant Young kept a tight grip on his gun handles as he continually scanned the skies for incoming enemy fighters. Out the right window, he saw the blurred streak of a Japanese fighter diving past just a few hundred feet to the right of his B-25, and when he snapped his neck to look downward through his gun sight, he spotted the same fighter leveling out and crossing under the bomber at a distance that fell well within the range of his .50-caliber guns. Acting on instinct Young pointed his twin belly guns straight down and depressed the thumb trigger. The barrels spat out a volley of what looked like brilliant orange tennis balls, and he watched the fighter flip over onto one wing and corkscrew downward in a scrawl of smoke. His guns fell silent when he released the trigger, but he could still hear Staff Sergeant Webb firing his guns above him in the top turret and Second Lieutenant Cunningham popping away with the .30 caliber in the nose.

Young never saw the enemy fighter that perforated the right engine, but he felt his B-25 shudder and lose airspeed as the Wright-Cyclone caught fire. He spotted another fighter zooming in on their tail, and though he doubted his belly guns could elevate high enough to get any hits, he opened fire anyhow. His tracers streaked behind in a volley of incandescent orange lines that faded into the distance without striking the trailing fighter. A tail gun, Young thought, thumb mashed against the trigger, would have done the job.

In the cockpit First Lieutenant Allers and Second Lieutenant Marich radioed the P-40s for help as they activated the fire-suppression system, which triggered carbon-dioxide charges mounted under the engine cowling. This action extinguished the flames streaming out from the right engine, but the big GR-2600 continued to trail smoke and oil. In dismay Allers watched the oil pressure fall to zero. Soon the engine began cutting out. As his air-speed decreased, Allers saw the other B-25s pull ahead and vanish from sight after crossing over Hong Kong Island. His plane had become a straggler, the term used for wounded bombers that fell behind the main formation, and Allers knew that stragglers usu-ally got picked off. In desperation he pushed the yoke forward and put the ship into a quick dive over the harbor, then hauled up and rolled the airplane upward in a series of evasive maneuvers, but the nimble enemy fighters easily kept pace with the crippled Mitchell.

Captain Hampshire heard the distress call from First Lieutenant Allers, while Second Lieutenant Sher saw one of the Mitchells drop-ping out of the bomber stream with a smoking engine. Both avia-tors attempted to ward off the attacking Japanese fighter pilots, who saw the damaged B-25 as easy prey. In the dogfight that followed, Hampshire chewed bits of flap and other debris from the wing of one enemy fighter but lost contact with Sher. His engine failing, Sher gave up the fight. He dove free of the melee with three enemy fighters in pursuit and headed northward in the hopes of making it back to Kweilin before his engine gave out.

Staff Sergeant Young felt the aircraft bank sharply as First Lieu-tenant Allers and Second Lieutenant Marich attempted to get them back over land on a northwest heading. Out the window he saw an enemy fighter pilot pull up alongside their bomber, in no apparent hurry to finish them off. Young swung his fifties around but could not get the fighter into his gun sights. In the top turret, Staff Sergeant Webb had no better luck. A second fighter came up behind the bomber and shot out the left engine. Allers and Marich feathered the dead left engine, a procedure that turned the knife's edge of the frozen propeller blades into the wind to reduce drag. With the right engine sputtering and both nacelles trailing smoke, the stricken B-25 soon fell below ten thousand feet. Young tossed aside his oxygen mask and tore off his fleece flight jacket as the plane descended into the warmer air. His eyes and nose burned from the cordite fumes from his guns, which he continued to fire at incoming enemy fighters.

An enemy fighter raked the rear portion of the stricken B-25 with a well-aimed burst. A machine-gun bullet punched downward through Webb's top turret, peppering one of his hands with shards of Plexiglas, and slammed into an ammunition canister for the belly guns. The box exploded in a blast of powder smoke and sent brass shrapnel whizzing throughout the narrow fuselage and into the bicep of Young's left arm. He frantically attempted to clear the resultant jams in both of his .50 calibers but only managed to saw his finger open on the jagged edges of the ruined ammo box. He quickly ascertained that the explosion had fused the belted rounds to the action of his guns, rendering them inoperable. The electrical power to Webb's revolving top turret had been severed by enemy fire as well, which meant he could not swing or elevate his twin .50s. Both airmen made split-second assessments on the status of their aircraft—four of the five guns aboard had been knocked out, their one remaining engine had begun to fail, and they could feel the B-25 dropping from the sky at a terrifying rate of speed. Young and Webb instantly reached the same conclusion, yanked open the armored door at the back of the plane, and staggered into the rearmost compartment. As Webb began pulling on his chute, Young yanked on the emergency release that would open the floor hatch. The mechanism, however, refused to budge.

Colonel Scott, meanwhile, had lost sight of the badly scattered P-40s as well as the bomber formation, which had banked to the northwest and headed for Kweilin at fifteen thousand feet. However, he could see six of the twin-engine fighters that had scrambled from Kai Tak climbing for altitude below him. Firing at extreme range, he sent tracers into the right engine of the lead fighter, which he identified as a "Nick," the American codename for a two-seat Kawasaki Ki-45 Toryu. The enemy pilot immediately snapped into a dive. Scott knew that he had him then, since P-40s dove faster than anything the Japanese could put in the air. Since the Japanese pilot should have continued to climb at full throttle, Scott began to wonder if his long-range gunnery had inflicted some crippling damage after all. As the twin-engine fighter rapidly lost altitude, the pilot made no effort to evade the pursuing P-40 and the 7.7 mm machine gun of the rear-seat gunner remained silent. Soon Scott came within easy firing range. All six of his .50-caliber guns hammered in unison, and the sudden deceleration caused by the recoil of the weapons snapped Scott's head forward as if some invisible hand had smacked him on the back of the skull. Three lines of tracers streaked out from each of his wings and converged on the Ki-45. Smoke began streaming back in an angry black smear, and Scott could see the Toryu lurching with the impact of the .50-caliber slugs. First the right engine began to flame, then the left. Just short of a fog bank, the Toryu hit the swells west of Hong Kong Island and disintegrated in a spray of wreckage. Scott then attempted to close with the remaining Ki-45s, but his P-40 lacked the climb rate necessary to catch them. He tried another burst of long-range gunnery, could not ascertain if his rounds had struck home, and called off the chase.

The acrobatics of the dogfight had taken Colonel Scott to the southern side of Hong Kong Island, where he approached the Stanley Peninsula at an altitude of just one thousand feet. In level flight the wings blocked the view of the ground directly beneath his plane, so he rolled his P-40 from side to side as he overflew the rocky peninsula. With his left wingtip pointed straight down, he caught a glimpse of what he took to be Allied soldiers in a prison compound. Their enthusiastic waves told Scott that they had seen the American markings on his plane. In actuality Scott had just overflown the Stanley Civilian Internment Camp, where the sight of the first

Allied aircraft to appear over Hong Kong since the start of the war provoked spontaneous cheers from the compound's 2,500 British, American, and Dutch prisoners. As the drone of Scott's P-40 faded, the morale of the civilian inmates popped like a champagne cork as they dared to dream of liberation by Christmas.[20]

"If that's a P-40 in front of me, waggle your wings," Scott heard through his earphones as he continued out to sea, and he immediately began rocking his ship from side to side to avoid being mistaken for a Ki-43. He felt pretty certain that Major Hill had him lined up in his gun sight. As the pursuing plane drew closer and finally pulled up alongside, Scott saw the number 151 on the fuselage. With Hill on his wing, Scott set the prop controls to maximum cruising position to conserve fuel and prevent the engine from overheating. Hill did the same in his own cockpit, and together they streaked to the northwest for Kweilin.[21]

# 5

## Paddy Mud

In the tail compartment of the B-25 flown by First Lieutenant Allers, Staff Sergeant Young continued to stomp on the frozen floor hatch, knowing that if it popped open and he lost his balance, he would tumble out of the plane without a parachute. Suddenly the hatch released and fell away behind the aircraft, leaving a hole in the floor just big enough to drop a man through. Young could see that they had lost a great deal of altitude and would soon descend below the point where they could safely bail out. Staff Sergeant Webb, who had already fastened his own parachute, helped Young strap on his own pack. Second Lieutenant Lewis had never followed them into the rear compartment, and no word had come back from the cockpit, but the sergeants knew they could not stop to worry about the officers. They feared the plane might explode at any moment and figured they had just a few seconds to bail out before they slammed into the rice paddies. Young stood closest to the floor hatch, so without hesitation he crouched by the opening in the floor, his knees pressed against his chin, facing the tail. Then he pitched himself forward like a single falling domino and tumbled out of the bottom of the aircraft into the open air. Webb followed just seconds later.

Young's chute slapped open immediately. As he swung in his harness, he caught a glimpse of a Japanese fighter zooming past just above his canopy. The pilot fired a burst of tracer fire, perhaps in an attempt to kill Young as he floated toward the ground or perhaps in an attempt to deliver the coup de grâce to the bomber he had just bailed out of. Young's boots punched into the dirt seconds later, for he had jumped at just five hundred feet, and his collapsing canopy swished softly down behind him.

Unaware that his gunners had bailed out, First Lieutenant Allers continued to wrestle with the yoke of the plummeting B-25. He could see that the left engine had stopped burning, and Marich reported that the fire in the right engine had been extinguished as well. This reduced the threat of a midair explosion, much to the relief of both lieutenants, but with the engines shot out, they knew that they would have to bail out immediately while they still had the altitude needed to safely deploy their parachutes. Allers gave the order to jump. Standard procedure called for the copilot and the navigator to leave the ship first. However, Second Lieutenant Lewis, the navigator, could not get his parachute strapped on. Rather than leave Lewis to his fate, all four officers chose to ride the ship down. Allers kept the wheels up, aimed for a rice paddy, and belly-flopped the plane into the mud. The propellers folded like taffy and the windows blew out in a spray of Plexiglas, but the airframe held together as the B-25 slid to a halt on its fuselage.

The four officers vaulted from the top hatch, fearing that the plane might explode. Marich, Cunningham, and Lewis sprinted for cover from an approaching trio of enemy fighters, but Allers drew his sidearm and ran around to the front of the downed bomber instead. As per his orders, he intended to destroy their bombsight with a few well-placed shots from his pistol. The bombsight might not have been a Norden, but it was still considered a top-secret device. Standing outside the shattered greenhouse and taking careful aim, Allers managed to put seven rounds into the device before the incoming Japanese fighters opened fire. Rounds tore up the downed bomber and a machine-gun bullet rammed into the top of Allers's right foot. The slug traveled on a downward diagonal trajectory and blasted out just behind his big toe, turning the bones to powder and pulling shreds of boot, sock, and lace into the wound. Marich, Cunningham, and Lewis pulled Allers beneath the cover of the vegetation bordering the paddy field before the fighters could circle around for another gun run. When the fighters did not return, Cunningham retrieved the medical kit from the wreck, and they bandaged Allers's foot as best they could. Then the four of them began moving away from the crash site in a direction that they hoped would lead to friendly territory. Allers could not walk, so he had to drape his arms over the shoulders of two of his comrades and hobble along on his left foot.

Young had landed on a raised dirt path some distance from the crashed B-25. An irrigation ditch ran along one side of the path, and a rice paddy bordered the other side. An ominous buzzing sound alerted Young to an approaching fighter, probably the same one that had taken a shot at him while he was swinging like a pendulum beneath his silk canopy. Young punched the release on his parachute harness, tossed aside the straps, and rolled into the muck of the ditch. Seconds later a string of bullets chewed up the path as the fighter zoomed overhead at treetop height. Young untangled himself from his chute, splashed down the length of the ditch, and threw himself up against a wooden sluice gate that the local farmers used to irrigate the rice paddy. The gate offered just enough concealment to hide Young from the fighter, which made one more pass without firing and then left the scene. Young figured the pilot had probably rattled off all his ammo or depleted his fuel tanks.

Numb and disoriented, Young staggered down the ditch in search of his parachute. At first he could not find it, but then his head began to clear and he realized that he had stumbled past the sluice gate in the opposite direction from where he had landed. He retraced his steps and found the crumpled parachute, which rested atop the paddy dike like a signal flag. After the deafening clamor of air combat, the countryside seemed strangely quiet. Thinking that it might be useful for shelter or to trade for food, Young began cutting a large swath of parachute silk. He planned to stow the cloth in his jungle kit, hide the rest of the chute, and then strike out for territory held by the Nationalist Chinese. He had no idea where he had landed, however, and no map of southern China.

A few simple homes built of mud and bamboo stood nearby, and Young caught a glimpse of two men watching him from inside one of these small structures. When the engine noise of the Japanese fighters overhead had completely died out, the men began walking toward Young, who unsnapped the fastener on his shoulder holster as a precautionary measure. Seeing this hostile move, the men retreated until Young lost sight of them. He went back to stuffing parachute cloth into his jungle kit, then noticed a young Chinese man approaching him without any apparent fear. Young showed him his blood chit, though the man already seemed to understand who the American was and what he needed. Using sign language he indicated to Young that Japanese patrols regularly swept the area and that he would need to disguise himself to avoid detection. Young should take off his uniform, he pantomimed, and wear his own clothes instead. Soon Young found himself outfitted in the simple peasant garb of southern China—a loose, grayish-black cotton shirt and pants—while the young Chinese man stood stripped down to nothing more than his loincloth and hat. In gratitude Young gave him 1,200 "mex," the term used by American fliers for Nationalist Chinese currency. Young kept his fleece-lined flight boots, shoulder holster, and the scarf his mother had given him for Christmas.

A second man joined Young and his benefactor in the loincloth, and after a short conversation in Cantonese, the two of them led the American aviator down the canal path. Young padded along awkwardly in his oversized fleece boots, only dimly aware that he had a dripping red gash in one finger, shrapnel in his left arm, and a broken collarbone. After five minutes of walking, the two Chinese men suddenly looked back down the path and then gestured urgently for Young to conceal himself beneath a pile of straw heaped on the trail. They helped cover him up and signaled that he should remain absolutely still and quiet. Though Young had no idea why this concealment had become necessary, he felt it best to comply, so he lay under the baking-hot pile of straw. The footfalls of the two Chinese men quickly faded away. After what he guessed to be a quarter of an hour, Young heard a group of men making their way down the canal path. He assumed it was a Japanese patrol. The men stopped by the mound of straw and soon hands began pulling apart the pile.

Young looked up, heart thudding like one of his belly guns, and found himself staring into the downcast face of Staff Sergeant Webb.

"Well, I'll be damned," Young said and rose to his feet, giddy with relief. He held out his hand with a grin.

"I guess you know we'll get out of this," Webb replied, as if trying to convince himself.

The half-dozen Chinese men who had arrived with Webb led the two Americans down the canal path to a crossing point, where they carried the downed aviators piggyback across the mucky channel. Webb had lost his sidearm when he bailed out, a not uncommon occurrence for parachuting U.S. airmen. The whistling slipstream of free fall and the neck-snapping violence of the chute popping open often tore loose critical survival gear. Young still had his .45 securely fastened in its shoulder holster, however, and as the eight men walked across an open field, the leader of the Chinese indicated that he wanted Young's pistol. Though he wasn't entirely sure that he was making the right move, Young decided that maintaining a spirit of goodwill among their rescuers remained far more important than retaining the rather false sense of security offered by the .45. He handed the weapon over, hoping that it would kill its share of Japanese before the war was over. The leader stowed the pistol away without comment but appeared satisfied with the deal.

A belt of tall reeds bordered the far side of the field. Beyond the reeds Young could see the waters of what he assumed to be a saltwater bay. The leader of the Chinese men indicated that Young and Webb should enter the dense stand of reeds and hide. Seeing little alternative the two Americans parted the reeds, stepped into the muck, and pushed their way through the stalks and mud until they could not see the field or the bay. The band of Chinese men, meanwhile, had departed without explanation. Young and Webb realized they had been left entirely alone and without direction, so they made their way deep into the reeds. The concealment calmed their nerves somewhat, and Webb had time to tell Young the story of his bailout. Webb had followed Young out the floor hatch of their plummeting bomber, popped his chute, and splashed down in the waist-deep soup of a rice paddy. As he flailed about in the brownish water, tangled up in his shrouds, lines, and harness, he had lost his jungle kit, sidearm, and most importantly, his cigarettes. To top it off, he had amoebic dysentery. Young gave him half his money and half his chocolate, but could do little for Webb's more immediate need for antibiotics and nicotine.

The sun began to set, and the temperature dropped. An increasingly morose Webb sat on a little hump of ground nursing his tortured bowels. Young's morale began to crumble as the shadows grew, the cold began to chill his bones, and the dire nature of their predicament sank in. Soon, however, the two Americans heard voices in the field beyond the reeds. Young crept carefully to the edge of the reeds and saw several Chinese men working their way along the edge of the reeds as if looking for the downed aviators. Young decided to take a chance and gamble that the men would guide them to friendly territory and not sell them for a bounty to the Japanese military. When Young stepped out of the reeds, the closest Chinese man splashed through the muck and handed him an unsigned note that read: "If you are English, come to me and I will help you."

Young convinced Webb that they should trust the good intentions of the unknown person who had penned the offer of assistance. The mud-spattered man who had given Young the note led the two aviators back across the field to the canal path where Young had originally floated to earth, been strafed, and then hid under a haystack. A young Cantonese man dressed in white—a sure sign he did not make his living in the rice paddies—greeted them in accented and grammatically eccentric English. Despite the man's attempt to be courteous, Young thought that he actually looked rather startled to see the two airmen, who had appeared from the marsh like apparitions. Overcoming his surprise the man explained that he had watched their bomber spewing flame as it dropped like a meteor from the sky, and though he had not witnessed the crash, he doubted that anyone could have survived it. The man in white explained that he had worked for the British in Singapore and had made his way back to Kwangtung after the supposedly impregnable fortress-city had fallen to the Japanese in February. He promised he would guide the Americans to a unit of friendly guerrillas about five miles away and indicated that if they walked all night, they could ghost past the Japanese positions and reach the guerillas before sunrise. Despite the limitations of his English, he also made it clear that he would be risking his life. If the Japanese caught him, the best he could hope for would be a swift execution.

Young and Webb followed the man from Singapore down the canal path as dusk gave way to night. After a short distance, the man stopped at the door of a one-room home with a thatch roof. He ushered the two Americans into the dimly lit interior, where an older man welcomed them in Cantonese, smiled, and gestured for them to take a seat on the floor. A young woman fussed over the large clay stove that dominated the room, feeding rice stalks into the firebox and stirring a massive pot. Soon she presented her guests with chopsticks and bowls of rice and shrimp. Webb and Young had not eaten since three that morning and had gone eighteen hours without food, but they found they had little appetite and could barely eat. Both appreciated the warmth of the fire, but the fear of the Japanese made sitting in the little home unbearable. After twenty minutes had passed and the heat of the massive clay stove had begun to sink into their bones, Young and Webb both agreed that they needed to keep moving. Young offered some Nationalist currency in gratitude for the hospitality they had enjoyed, but the man who owned the home refused to accept the money and presented them instead with a ration of rice wine in a canteen fashioned from a quart bottle and a length of string.

With the man from Singapore in the lead, Young and Webb began walking single file in the darkness. They skirted a walled village, which rested down a gentle slope about a quarter mile away, its walls glowing dimly in the moonlight. Another man soon materialized out of the darkness to converse in hushed tones with the man from Singapore, who then translated their conversation into English. Though Young found it difficult to understand the man's accent, he gathered that the local gendarmes in the village had apprehended two American officers from Young's bomber, and that for the right payment, both men could be released. However, one of the officers had been wounded in the leg and could not walk. Webb argued that they should secure the release of the two officers, though Young remained unconvinced that entering the village was a good idea, since they had no proof the officers were actually within its walls. Still, Webb convinced him that they should try it, particularly since their guide appeared intent on taking them into the village anyhow.

The three men crept down the hill to the protective brick wall that encircled the village. Though rural communities in China barred their gates at night, the gates to this particular village remained wide open. The three men stepped cautiously through the portal, and soldiers immediately jumped out in front of them with rifles and bayonets at the ready. Young glanced over his shoulder and saw that another soldier now stood just outside the gate holding an automatic weapon. Young could not tell what kind, but the make and model hardly mattered. He knew that if they tried to run, it would cut all three of them down. Young, Webb, and their guide stood three abreast and completely still, hemmed in by a thicket of bayonets so long it almost seemed the soldiers had lashed swords to the ends of their rifle barrels. "Are they Japanese?" Young whispered, and their guide gave a single nod in reply.

Staff Sgt. James Nelson Young had just become a prisoner of war.

# 6

## Night Raid on North Point

Colonel Scott and Major Hill reached Kweilin at about the same time that Sergeants Young and Webb went to ground in the reeds somewhere in southern China. As Scott performed a victory roll over the field, his P-40 emitted a telltale whistling sound that told General Chennault and the other Americans on the ground that the ship had seen combat. They all knew that P-40s took off with their gun barrels taped over to protect against dust and moisture, just as they knew that the tape stayed there until a pilot fired his guns, whereupon the tape disintegrated in a blast of superheated cordite. They also knew that open gun barrels, unlike those covered in tape, whistled loudly in the slipstream.[1] When the Americans on the field at Kweilin heard the mechanical shriek from Scott's P-40, they immediately understood what it signified.

Hill landed first, and Scott touched down shortly thereafter. They were the last two pilots to return from the mission. Scott quickly determined that Second Lieutenant Sher had failed to return and that the B-25 piloted by First Lieutenant Allers had gone missing as well. The exact circumstances of how the two aircraft had disappeared remained unknown, but since the planes would have long since run out of fuel, everyone agreed that Sher and Allers had gone down. Nobody was ready to consign the seven missing men to the ranks of the killed in action, however. The lore of the AVG and the CATF abounded with tales of airmen who had gone down during a mission, been given up for dead, and then turned up weeks later very much alive after a long trek back through enemy lines with the help of friendly locals and Communist guerrillas.

At dispersal points scattered around the edge of the sprawling airfield, the ground crews began the process of repairing, refueling, and rearming the B-25s for the follow-up raids scheduled for that night. Dust-coated trucks picked up the exhausted bomber crews and conveyed them over badly rutted roads to the hostel, where the men ate a hasty meal, smoked, and caught a quick nap if they were lucky. After sunset they returned to the field for another preflight briefing by Lieutenant Colonel Morgan, who informed them that they would fly two raids that night against Hong Kong and Canton. They could expect CAVU—clear and visibility unlimited—conditions over the target zones and a full moon that would provide enough illumination to see the target. Morgan did not need to say that the bombers would proceed without a fighter escort, since everyone knew the Sharks lacked the capability to fight at night. However, Morgan cautioned that the enemy would likely have their own night-fighters over the target. None of the B-25s had exhaust dampeners, which meant that their exhaust flames would be visible in the darkness, particularly to enemy pilots flying at an altitude beneath the bombers. All crews were advised to be vigilant against attack, particularly from six o'clock low.

Six B-25s under Major Bayse, commanding officer of the 11th Bomb Squadron, took off at 9:30 p.m. and flew toward Hong Kong on the first night mission ever flown by the CATF over the Pearl River delta. Each ship carried six American-made M-43 five-hundred-pound bombs and ten Chinese-made seventeen-kilogram fragmentation bombs. Because all supplies had to be flown over the Hump, the CATF preferred whenever possible to drop bombs that had been previously cached in-country by the Chinese. Sometimes they dropped American-made weapons, but most of the time they used Chinese models or drew from the stockpile of Russian-manufactured bombs that China had purchased from the Soviets on extremely favorable terms. The CATF had also dropped Chinese and French ordnance, and at one point the unit had stocked machine-gun ammunition manufactured in eleven different countries, including Japan.[2]

At 11:00 p.m. Major Bayse arrived over Hong Kong at thirteen thousand feet and commenced his bomb run against the North Point power station. The power plant supplied electricity for Hong Kong Island and was clearly running at peak capacity that night, since Bayse found the entire city lit up like a peacetime metropolis. Between the moon, the brightly electrified city, and the reflective waters shimmering just offshore from the target, Bayse's bombardier had little difficulty pinning the power plant in his bombsight. In the cockpit Bayse felt the aircraft buck as three thousand pounds of high explosive left the bomb bay. A string of detonations soon lit up the streets below, and the entire city went dark, causing Bayse to conclude that they had thoroughly demolished the power station. Antiaircraft tracers started slashing through the darkness like a Chinese New Year fireworks display, and a single searchlight began sweeping its beam over the city. The searchlight failed to locate the bombers, however, leaving the Japanese gun crews with no other option than to take literal shots in the dark.[3]

Back in his command cave, Chennault received new orders from Brigadier General Bissell in India. The orders read, "Hit Lashio at daylight with all B-25s available."[4]

Earlier that month Chennault had presciently warned Bissell to expect Japanese air attacks on the Hump airbases in Assam, India.[5] Just when Chennault had opened his air offensive against Hong Kong, more than a hundred Japanese aircraft had raided the 10th Air Force bases at Dinjan and Chabua. Five P-40s, two P-43s, and five C-47 transports had been shot down or shot up on the ground. Another four transports and thirteen fighters received varying amounts of damage.[6] The 10th Air Force had been badly mauled and Hump flights badly disrupted. Bissell wanted to launch an immediate retaliatory strike against Lashio, the field in Burma that he believed the Japanese raiders had staged from.

Based on reconnaissance flights flown by CATF aircraft, Chennault believed that the Lashio airfield could not have supported a major Japanese strike on the Hump bases in India, and that the raiders had likely come from Chiang Mai in Thailand or Toungoo in Burma—the very field where the AVG had trained in 1941. An enraged Chennault realized that he would have to scrub further raids on Hong Kong, redeploy the B-25s to Kunming, and bomb an empty airfield in Burma instead. Despite his anger Chennault understood that he had no choice but to follow Bissell's orders. Though under the command of Chennault, the CATF remained a subordinate unit of the 10th Air Force and thus under the overall command of Bissell in India. Seniority mattered, too. Bissell and Chennault held the same rank, but Bissell remained the senior officer because he had been promoted to brigadier general one day before Chennault. After weighing his options, Chennault decided to continue with the Canton mission as planned, since the bombers would be back before sunup. After sunrise all B-25s at Kweilin would depart for Kunming.

Bayse's flight returned from Hong Kong at 1:00 a.m., and just two hours later a trio of B-25s commanded by Lieutenant Colonel Morgan headed for Canton to bomb the aviation fuel stockpiles at Tien Ho airfield. Each aircraft carried a dozen Chinese-made fifty-kilogram incendiary bombs and ten seventeen-kilogram fragmentation bombs, which the bomber crews called "haircutters." With Morgan flying as first pilot in the lead plane, the flight of B-25s arrived over Canton to find the entire area blacked out and Tien Ho smothered in ground fog. Morgan diverted to their secondary target, which they could locate by the shape of the river branches at Canton. Unhindered by antiaircraft fire or searchlights, the bombardiers dumped their mix of incendiary and fragmentation bombs on the riverfront godowns stuffed full of rice sacks, rifle ammunition, oil drums, and all the other supplies that the Japanese army needed to keep fighting in China. All three Mitchell crews reported that their bombs ignited substantial conflagrations punctuated by secondary explosions so bright that it seemed like someone had taken a flashbulb photo inside the cockpit. As feared enemy night-fighter pilots caught sight of the bombers' glowing engine exhausts. Morgan led the flight in a three-hundred-mile-per-hour dive down to the deck and ran full throttle toward Kweilin. The night-fighters hound-dogged the three bombers for over a hundred miles but never managed to pull within effective firing range. Out of frustration the JAAF pilots banged out a few long-range bursts in the hopes of scoring a lucky hit. Then they broke off the chase. All three B-25s returned safely to Kweilin by 5:15 a.m.[7]

Major Holloway climbed into the cockpit of the lone P-43A at Kweilin not long after Lieutenant Colonel Morgan's B-25s had returned from Canton. At 7:00 a.m. he taxied out to the runway and lifted off into the sunrise on yet another solo reconnaissance mission to Hong Kong. When Holloway or any other American pilot flew a recon mission in a P-40E, they always flew with at least one wingman. P-40Es could be bounced from above by Japanese fighters. However, when Holloway piloted the faster and higher-flying P-43A, he always flew alone. The turbocharged P-43A could operate at a height and speed that the P-40Es simply could not match. Since the high-altitude performance of the P-43A made it very difficult to intercept, Holloway saw no need for an escort anyway.

Holloway had an uneventful flight to Canton. As White Cloud airfield came into view far below, he could see at least thirteen enemy aircraft on the tarmac, but the skies remained empty. He put his olive drab P-43A into a steep dive that took him down to as low as ten thousand feet and made as much noise over the field as he could for about ten minutes, but his acrobatics failed to provoke any activity on the runway below. Even the flak gunners seemed to be taking the day off. He filmed the airfield, then overflew Tien Ho and the various satellite runways, which all appeared to be just as somnolent as White Cloud. Holloway continued on to Hong Kong, where he counted eleven ships in Victoria Harbor that he estimated to be larger than three thousand tons. However, he saw no smoke plumes and no sign of any damage from the B-25 raids. He could even make out the unscathed smokestacks of the North Point power station. Holloway took more movies, then banked his Lancer around to the northwest, and cruised back to Kweilin at a comfortable three hundred miles per hour. He returned to base by 10:30 a.m. and made his report to General Chennault, who had no doubt hoped for news of more visible damage to Hong Kong.[8]

While Holloway ran his recon mission over the Pearl River delta, the B-25 crews began firing up their radial engines. Nobody had got much sleep, but the fuel tanks had been filled, the oxygen bottles swapped out, the guns cleaned, and the ammunition cans replenished. In quick succession all the B-25s on the field took off for Kunming, where they would be loaded up with an assortment of Russian and Chinese ordnance and sent onward to pummel the Japanese field at Lashio. General Chennault dispatched Colonel Scott to Kunming as well, where he would be better positioned to coordinate the actions of the 23rd Fighter Group.

Chennault, however, stayed behind with the P-40 pilots and the stockpile of five-hundred-pound bombs that had been meant for Hong Kong. He had not forgotten Holloway's report on the eleven ships in Victoria Harbor and had no intention of leaving Kweilin without first taking another crack at Hong Kong. The P-40Es at Kweilin had centerline bomb racks that could hold a five-hundred-pounder, and if the pilots could refuel midway between Kweilin and Hong Kong, Chennault figured they could haul a bomb that size to Victoria Harbor and put those eleven ships underwater. Deep in the limestone command cave, Chennault and his pilots began planning for another raid. This time they would dive bomb.[9]

# 7

## Somewhere in Southern China

Somewhere in southern China, Staff Sgt. James Young, Staff Sgt. Rusty Webb, and a nameless Chinese guide stood motionless in the moonlight. They dared not move as Japanese soldiers hemmed them in with their bayonets. A Japanese officer took the rice-wine canteen from Webb, sniffed the contents, and then smashed the bottle against a heap of mortar and brick. His soldiers separated the Chinese guide from the Americans and led him away, perhaps to receive a cash bounty or perhaps to receive a bullet to the back of the head. Young had no way of knowing which it would be. In truth he did not feel all that confident about his own prospects and imagined torture sessions and firing squads.

Bayonets held at the ready, Japanese soldiers herded Young and Webb into the shell of a house that had been thoroughly scrambled by artillery fire or a bombing raid. Much to Young's surprise, First Lieutenant Allers and Second Lieutenant Lewis waited inside. Allers limped over, and they shook hands all around. Despite the thick cocoon of bandages encasing his foot, Allers appeared in good spirits. Though uninjured Lewis seemed more beaten down. As the ranking officer, Allers felt responsible for keeping up morale, so he offered some encouraging words and said that things were not over yet.

The guards made it clear that the four of them would have to keep moving. Since Allers could not walk, Young and Lewis draped his arms over their shoulders and walked three abreast back out the village gates and into the surrounding rice paddies. Webb's dysentery had worsened, and it took all his energy just to keep himself on his feet, so the job of carrying Allers fell to Lewis and Young, despite his broken collarbone. When the four of them came to a hill, however, Young and Lewis had to switch off carrying the 160-pound lieutenant on their backs for what Young estimated to be a quarter mile. The Japanese soldiers pushed them along until they crested the hill, where an army truck sat waiting.

The truck carried Young and his comrades to a nearby village, which had been heavily bombed or shelled. Japanese soldiers pushed the downed aviators into a grimy upstairs room furnished with a sleeping pallet and some straw. One of the guards brought a sheet of canvas, which the four Americans used as a communal blanket to ward off the cold. A single guard kept watch over the men, but throughout the night soldiers would climb up the stairs, light up the room with a flashlight or lantern, and check out the prisoners like zoo-goers watching a cage full of exotic animals.

Exhausted, Young slept until well past dawn. He woke to bright sunlight and joined his fellow prisoners on the room's small balcony. The guard had one of the local Chinese bring bowls of shrimp and rice much like the meal that Young and Webb had been offered the previous evening. Like most American servicemen, the four bomber crewmen had never acquired a taste for rice and found it difficult to stomach. Allers was in considerable pain, as he had received no medical treatment for his mangled foot. He told Young about how he had been shot and said that after their crash landing he, Lewis, Marich, and Cunningham had made their way to the same dirt-poor village where Young and Webb had been captured. However, they had arrived before the Japanese soldiers. A Chinese doctor had swaddled Allers's foot in bandages after giving the wound a super-ficial cleaning but had not been able to do anything more. The four airmen had then departed the village and started climbing up into the surrounding hills, but they soon saw the flashlights of a pursu-ing Japanese patrol. Marich and Cunningham took the lead, and Allers assumed that they had managed to elude the Japanese. He and Lewis had been overtaken by the Japanese and brought back to the village. Shortly thereafter Young and Webb had walked through the village gates and been taken captive as well.

In the warmth of the sun, all four of the Americans found themselves nodding off. Even the guard fell asleep. The shock of their sudden change in fortune had left Young feeling strangely numb. Rather than think about what their captors might do to them, he dozed instead, cloaked in a surreal sense of confusion and denial. In a break between catnaps, Young saw the NCO who commanded the Japanese soldiers walking in the street below, so he woke the sleeping guard. Young figured that if the NCO had discovered his soldier drowsing on duty, they would have immediately been assigned a new and likely far less benign guard.

Young and his comrades stayed on the balcony with the sleepy guard until late afternoon, when the NCO and his men escorted them to an open-topped truck. The truck slammed its way down a series of pitted and rutted roads, an experience that Allers endured in stoic agony, his foot cushioned on Young's lap. Not long after sunset, the truck swung through the gates of a walled compound. The guards lined the prisoners up against the side of a small building as two civilians approached with cameras. Young soon understood that guards and prisoners alike would have to pose for a carefully arranged propaganda photo. As the guards held their Arisaka rifles at hip position, ready to thrust their long bayonets into the guts of their prisoners, the Americans raised their hands in the universal signal of surrender. A series of flash photos captured the tableau, and then the guards shoved the prisoners into the building, which turned out to be an unlit prison cell complete with barred windows and three disheveled Chinese captives.

Young huddled on the dirt floor next to Allers and pulled a straw mat over the two of them for warmth. Lewis and Webb did the same. Allers feared that gangrene had begun to eat at his untreated foot wound, and he whispered to Young that he did not expect to survive their imprisonment. He asked Young to contact his wife, should Young survive the war, and tell her what had happened to her husband. Young assented, though he doubted he would be able to follow through on the lieutenant's request.

One of the Japanese guards brought a bucket of rice and a tin of salmon, and he patiently supervised the parceling out of the food into four equal portions. The three Chinese received no food, however, and apparently knew better than to ask for any. Not much later the guards loaded the Americans back into the truck, which moved the airmen to yet another badly damaged village. In what appeared to be the front room of an abandoned shophouse, the four aviators settled in for the night. A guard stepped in from the alley outside and handed them four small bags of lard-heavy pastries. Young had regained his appetite, but Allers had completely lost his. Though he could not really say what he was eating, Young devoured his bag of greasy pastries. Despite the rats and the cold, the men slept.

In the morning the Japanese soldiers marched the four Americans through the narrow lanes of the village to a nearby railroad line. The airmen climbed aboard a truck fitted to run on the rails like a miniature train, which then conveyed them across a patched-up bridge that could no longer bear the weight of a regular locomotive. On the opposite side of the bridge, the guards loaded them aboard a passenger coach on a regular train, only to have an officer angrily boot the Americans out and consign them to an empty boxcar. The locomotive lurched forward, the steel couplings between the railcars slammed tight, and the train began to slowly creak down the tracks.

Young fantasized about jumping out the open door of the boxcar as the train clanked slowly through the hinterland of Kwangtung. He reckoned he could shove past the three drowsy guards, hurl himself into a passing rice paddy, and be safely under cover before the guards could take a shot at him with their rifles and submachine gun. After that his plans reached a dead end. He had no map, no compass, no food, no water, no money, and no weapon. He did not speak Cantonese, and he had only his floppy, fleece-lined flight boots on his feet. He had a broken collarbone and a torn-up finger, too. Most of all, however, he did not want to leave his comrades behind. He chose to stay in the boxcar.

The train soon reached Canton, and not much later Young and his comrades found themselves within the walls of a military prison. Guards escorted them to a large room and ordered them to sit at a table. A Japanese civilian interpreter with a high forehead and deep voice asked in English what they wanted to eat. "Eggs," the four of them responded, and to their surprise, each man received two small eggs for lunch.

Guards then carried Allers to the camp hospital, while Young, Webb, and Lewis were placed in separate cells with cement walls, a bunk with no blankets, a table, and a chair. Before Young could settle in, the guards returned and took him to an interrogation room, where a uniformed officer sat behind a desk with the deep-voiced civilian interpreter. The guards positioned themselves by the door. Young did not need to be told that he stood before the Kempeitai—the Japanese military police—and that the unit had a reputation for savagery and ruthlessness.

Using the interpreter as his mouthpiece, the officer told Young to state his military rank.

"Staff sergeant," Young told the officer.

The officer then asked if Young thought the Allies would win the war.

Young carefully stated in a flat tone of voice that he expected an Allied victory.

Instead of debating how the war would turn out, the officer asked what type of bomber Young had been flying in.

"A B-25 Mitchell," Young said, figuring the Japanese had found the wreck and already knew the answer to the question.

The officer then wanted to know the name of the airbase that Young's squadron had used to launch its raid on Hong Kong.

Young considered lying or refusing to answer, since the names of airbases qualified as sensitive intelligence information. However, since the Japanese had bombed Kweilin on numerous occasions, he saw no harm in divulging this notional military secret.

"Kweilin," he finally said.

The officer then asked whether Lieutenant Colonel Morgan had been on the mission.

In as neutral and unprovocative a tone as possible, Young said that he could not answer the question. He had decided that the

Kempeitai meant to execute him regardless, so he might as well keep his silence.

The officer repeated the question, and the interpreter assured Young that he would not be killed.

Unconvinced, Young replied that he did not have to answer the question.

With a nod from the interpreter, the guards tied Young's wrists together with insulated wire, yanked his hands up into the small of his back, and ran the wire around his neck. Then they rammed him down on a bench, his hands beneath his back and his head hanging over the end. Nobody spoke a word during this process. One of the guards then approached with a chipped brown teakettle. Young attempted to hold his breath, but the guards slapped open his mouth and thrust the spout of the teakettle between his teeth, forcing him to gulp down the water to keep it out of his lungs. Soon he could drink no more, and he began to drown. He lost consciousness, came to when the guards removed the teakettle spout from his mouth, and puked up the water. The guards then jammed the spout back in his mouth and poured water down his throat. Soon he blacked out.

Young regained consciousness and vomited up the water. He heard the officer asking about Lieutenant Colonel Morgan again, but before he could decide whether to answer, the guards thrust the refilled teakettle between his teeth and filled his guts back up with water. Once again Young blacked out.

When he regained consciousness, the officer repeated the question about whether Lieutenant Colonel Morgan had taken part in the mission.

Young agreed that yes, Lieutenant Colonel Morgan had been on the mission.

Many more questions followed, and Young answered those that seemed militarily unimportant and tried to dissemble on those that did. After an hour the guards returned him to his prison cell. Young could hear the agonized cries of Chinese prisoners echoing through the concrete building and the shouts of their Kempeitai interrogators. He saw bare-chested Chinese inmates hauling the corpses of dead prisoners past his cell, and the living and the dead alike often had gashes and welts running in angry red stripes across their backs. All the prisoners appeared to be civilian Chinese.[1]

In one of the random moments of decency that punctuated his prison experience, the guard assigned to watch over Young's cell provided him with tooth powder and had him rinse out his mouth, apparently as a medicinal remedy for the dirty water he had been forced to drink and vomit back up in such copious quantities. The guard then sat outside his cell, bored, until a second guard arrived with a wooden tablet that he mounted on the door frame. The first guard then became more interested in Young, and through hand gestures he indicated that the tablet stated the American's name, rank, and specialty as a radioman.

Young spent the night in his cell. He could not feel his left thumb, which the wiring binding his hands had paralyzed, and he could tell that he had injured his throat as well. Screams from the interrogation rooms ricocheted down the hallway outside his cell. Panic clawed at his every thought with sharp jolts of terror. At midnight October 27 melted into October 28. The sun eventually rose and spilled shafts of light through the barred windows of the prison.

# 8

## Dud Bombs and Dead Fish

The deafening roar of v-12 Allison aircraft engines broke the predawn silence at Kweilin on the morning of October 28. Led by Major Holloway, the pilots of eleven p-40Es throttled up, bounced down the gravel strip, and lifted into the blue-black sky. Six more p-40E pilots led by Captain Hampshire followed, though they all needed a bit more runway to get their machines aloft due to the weight of the five-hundred-pound demolition bombs slung beneath their bellies. In total seventeen p-40 pilots from the 75th Fighter Squadron as well as the just-arrived 16th Fighter Squadron assembled over the limestone crags of Kweilin and headed east into the rising sun.

During the preflight huddle in the command cave, General Chennault had briefed the p-40 pilots on the targets they would go after in Victoria Harbor. Holloway had observed eleven ships of at least three thousand tons during his recon flight in the p-43, the general said, and intelligence sources had since reported the arrival of additional merchant vessels and an aircraft carrier. The ships had docked along the Kowloon waterfront but would soon continue south on their run to the Solomon Islands. Chennault wanted to add Japanese freighters and flattops to the CATF trophy shelf, and he believed that some well-placed five-hundred-pound bombs would do the trick. Since the b-25s had been recalled to bomb Japanese airfields in Burma, his p-40 pilots would have to dive-bomb the ships in Victoria Harbor instead.

The six p-40s assigned to the bombing flight carried maximum payloads consisting of a five-hundred-pound bomb, 1,800 rounds of .50-caliber ammunition, and fully topped-up internal gas tanks. The pilot added just a bit more weight—malaria, lousy food, and stress had kept the American aviators as lean as racehorse jockeys. Still, the load exceeded 2,500 pounds and pushed the threshold of what the aircraft could carry.[1] As a result, the twelve-cylinder Allison engines would guzzle fuel at a prodigious rate during the inbound flight to Hong Kong. To complicate matters further, the six P-40s in the bombing flight could not carry drop tanks, bamboo or otherwise. This last fact necessitated staging at Namyung, a primitive forward airfield to the north of Hong Kong that was held—albeit just barely—by Nationalist Chinese troops. Even after refueling at Namyung, however, the high rate of fuel consumption and lack of belly tanks would still mean less time over the target and less gas for dueling with enemy fighters. All the pilots ran the risk of running out of fuel on the return leg, but for the pilots in the bombing flight the risk remained particularly acute. If they failed to locate the unfamiliar field at Namyung, which they were told during the briefing resembled a giant Chevrolet symbol from the air, they would run out of fuel and have to slide into the nearest rice paddy.

Assuming the refueling at Namyung went as planned during the inbound flight, the P-40s could still be intercepted by enemy fighters during the final seventy-five-minute run into Hong Kong. Holloway and the other ten P-40 pilots assigned to the cover flight had the job of keeping enemy fighters away from the six pilots hauling the bombs. If enemy fighters broke through Holloway's screen of escorting P-40s and attacked the six bomb-laden P-40s, however, the pilots in the bombing flight would have to scrub the mission and jettison their loads, given how dramatically the weight and drag of a five-hundred-pounder reduced the performance of a P-40. No Shark pilot wanted to dogfight while strapped to a quarter-ton bomb.

Even if Hampshire and the other pilots in the bombing flight made it to Hong Kong with their five-hundred-pounders, they would still face a number of challenges, with flak ranking chief among them. However, they would also have to contend with the inconvenient fact that the P-40 had never been designed for dive-bombing.

A navy dive-bomber like the SBD Dauntless came equipped with dive brakes, which slowed its near-vertical descent to controllable speeds. The Dauntless also had a mechanism that swung its bomb away from the underbelly of the plummeting aircraft when released so that the bomb would not strike the propeller. The P-40E did not have dive flaps and a bomb swing, however. The P-40E only had a simple centerline rack that kept the bomb tucked in tight against the underside of the aircraft. Experienced P-40 pilots knew that if they pitched too far forward during their dive the bomb might hit the eleven-foot propeller when released, particularly if the massive torque produced by the V-12 Allison sent the aircraft into a skid. Or the pilot might successfully drop his bomb but then be unable to pull the nose-heavy fighter out of its dive. P-40s had a scary tendency to "mush" at the bottom of a power dive, which was a colorful way of saying that the heavy plane could build up so much velocity that the pilot could no longer haul the aircraft out of its dive. No matter what magic he performed with the flaps and stick, the Forty would still keep on dropping until it belly-flopped onto the ground at four hundred miles per hour.[2]

All seventeen P-40s refueled at Namyung without incident, and soon the entire strike force had climbed back up to sixteen thousand feet on a heading for Hong Kong. The attack plan called for the two flights to approach Victoria Harbor from different directions, with the cover flight arriving just before the bombing flight. As planned the eleven P-40s providing top cover came in from the northeast and arrived over Hong Kong at about 11:00 a.m. Holloway banked his P-40 on its side so that he could look down to observe the target area, but a layer of undercast hanging at six thousand feet obscured the harbor. After checking their sixes for Japanese interceptors above the clouds, Holloway and the rest of the flight corkscrewed down and punched through the undercast.[3] As they dropped through the clouds into clear visibility, they flew into heavy antiaircraft fire between four thousand and six thousand feet. Most of the flak came from gun positions at various points in Kowloon, though the gun crews aboard a destroyer anchored near the HK and Whampoa dockyard enthusiastically pumped out an impressive volume of fire as well.

A minute after the arrival of the cover flight, Hampshire and the five other pilots in the bombing flight streaked in from the east at sixteen thousand feet with the sun at their backs. Once over the harbor, they spiraled downward through the clouds, the flak, and Holloway's circling P-40s. With no sign of the promised aircraft carrier, the six pilots made snap decisions to bomb a tanker and several large freighters instead, including one with a canvas deck covering that they later surmised could have been mistaken for a flattop by an intelligence operative unfamiliar with naval vessels. All six of the pilots kept their plummeting aircraft under control, successfully released their five-hundred-pounders, and managed to pull up without mushing or colliding with their own bombs. As the cover flight circled in a protective umbrella overhead, its pilots observed one solid bomb hit on a sizable freighter. Damaging near misses raised fifty-foot geysers of salt water directly beside two more ships.

The top-cover pilots also saw a Japanese radial-engine fighter pounce on the P-40 flown by Capt. Philip B. O'Connell just as he recovered from his dive. Tracer fire raked his P-40, set the left wing afire, and quite likely killed O'Connell in the cockpit, since his aircraft plunged straight down into Victoria Harbor. Led by Hampshire the remaining P-40s in the bombing flight flew low and fast to the northeast over Junk Bay and Sai Kung.

Meanwhile, several pilots in the cover flight tried to nail the fighter that had knocked O'Connell out of the sky. Two or three additional Japanese fighters suddenly joined the fray, which complicated matters, since nobody knew exactly where they had come from. Holloway later speculated that the fighters had lifted off from the airstrip at San Chau. However, some of the other pilots believed that the interceptors had scrambled from Kai Tak, given the sudden appearance of these planes and the fact that they had observed at least two more aircraft rolling out onto the runway in an attempt to take off and join the dogfight. First Lt. Jack R. Best bored in on one of these planes, fully intent on blowing it to pieces and killing whoever might be in the cockpit. He became so focused on shooting up his target, in fact, that he almost lost track of his altitude and rammed the airstrip with his plane instead. Aviators called this potentially fatal tunnel vision "target fixation," and more than one fighter pilot had flown his ship into the dirt when he kept on firing at a ground target when he should have been focused on pulling up. Best squeezed off a quick thirty-round burst that raised dust across the runway in front of his target, then yanked back on the stick just in time to avoid burying the nose of his Shark in the airstrip.

While Best strafed Kai Tak, 1st Lt. Robert H. Mooney shot up a building on Hong Kong Island that he thought looked important. His six .50-caliber wing guns fired slugs that easily punched through the building's brick walls, though he had no idea whether they hit anything worthwhile inside. Meanwhile, squadron-mate 1st Lt. Dallas A. Clinger—who actually hailed from Wyoming rather than Texas despite his first name—burned through six hundred rounds while strafing one of the freighters and an antiaircraft gun position on the Kowloon waterfront.

The outnumbered Japanese fighter pilots decided not to press their luck and opted to disengage after making their initial run against the bombing flight. In their post-mission debriefing, the American pilots disagreed on exactly what their adversaries had been flying. Some said twin-engine Ki-45s; others said single-engine Ki-27s. As for the "Zero" that had shot down O'Connell, some pilots averred that it had been a navy A6M, but others reckoned that maybe it had been a Ki-43 or perhaps even some other esoteric model that they had never encountered before, such as a German Messerschmitt. Many of the pilots swore they had run into ME-109s and ME-110s, and remained so confident of these sightings that Hampshire included them in the official flight intelligence reports filed after the mission. His willingness to do so likely stemmed from his familiarity with the War Department's *Basic Field Manual 30-38: Identification of Japanese Aircraft*, which had been issued in March 1942. The very first Japanese aircraft profiled in this secret document was the ME-

109, which American intelligence erroneously believed the Germans had exported to Japan in substantial numbers.[4]

Ever conscious of his fuel gauge, Holloway led the top flight to the rendezvous point over a lake to the northeast of Hong Kong, where it formed up with Hampshire's bomber flight. As the two flights continued on a northeast heading, Hampshire and three other P-40 pilots had to crash land in friendly territory when their tanks ran dry before they could reach Namyung. The sturdy airframes of the P-40s held together for all four pilots, who walked away from their wheels-up landings and eventually rejoined their squadrons at Kweilin. In the end the 23rd Fighter Group could account for every pilot on the mission except for O'Connell, the first American to be killed in action over Hong Kong during the Second World War.[5]

THE AMERICAN AIR raids on Hong Kong generated rumors about massive Japanese casualties, particularly the visually spectacular night attack on the North Point power station. One wild rumor circulating among the POWs in the Sham Shui Po camp claimed that 1,800 Japanese soldiers had been killed or wounded when bombs delivered during the first raid had demolished Whitfield Barracks in Kowloon. Other rumors claimed that several hundred Cantonese locals had perished in the raids as well, which depending on the rumor were said to have been carried out by American or British or Chinese warplanes.[6]

The *Hongkong News*, which had a Japanese editor and had consequently been the only English-language newspaper permitted to continue publishing after the takeover of the colony, attempted to counteract such rumors by downplaying the impact of the raids in a story published the day after Lieutenant Colonel Morgan and his Norden bombsight scattered high explosives across Kowloon. Titled "Little Damage Done by Enemy Raids on H.K.," the story opened with a lead indicative of the newspaper's editorial position: "The raids by enemy planes on Hongkong caused only slight damage to property but great suffering to the Chinese. It can be seen, therefore, that these nuisance raids are without any regard for the lives and property of the Chinese mass, but merely for the benefit of Britain and America, who, up to now, have been preaching about their humanitarian methods of conducting warfare."[7] A follow-up story a day later rather indignantly pointed out that the North Point power station and the shipyards that relied on electricity from that plant were all operating normally, which contradicted official communiqués from Chungking and proved that both the Nationalist Chinese and the American accounts of the raids could be dismissed as little more than wishful propaganda.[8]

To cast further doubt on American claims, the Japanese triumphantly placed the tail assembly of a shot-down American bomber in Statue Square in Victoria, the urban center of Hong Kong Island. The tail had likely come from the B-25 crashed by First Lieutenant Allers, since no other American bombers had been brought down in the Pearl River delta. In an indictment of Allied ammunition manufacturers, the Japanese also displayed four small bombs— most probably seventeen-kilogram incendiaries of the sort dropped by Staff Sgt. James Young—that had failed to explode during the American raids.[9]

As the Japanese had so vituperatively asserted, American estimates of the bomb damage proved to be overoptimistic. BAAG agents sent in poststrike assessments indicating that while the first raid had managed to hit some barracks and set oil and ammunition stocks ablaze in Kowloon, the three raids had done little damage to the port facilities that enabled Hong Kong to serve as a key way station for Japanese vessels making the long journey between Southeast Asia and the home islands. Furthermore, no ships had been damaged, much less sunk. Some Japanese military personnel had been killed at Whitfield Barracks and other locations, and a much larger number of Japanese and Cantonese civilians had died when bombs struck residential tenement buildings. "As a result of all the reports received," the BAAG concluded, "the bombing of Hong Kong cannot be regarded from the military point of view as a great success."[10]

Moreover, and no doubt much to the disappointment of the old broken-down transport pilot, BAAG reports never mentioned the blizzard of leaflets dropped by General Haynes. The *Hongkong News* made no reference to them either. Certainly the POWs at Sham Shui Po never saw any of the leaflets, which was much to their loss— toilet paper had become a rare luxury in the camp. In the end the leaflets may have simply fallen into the harbor and been flushed out to sea with the tide.[11]

The BAAG also confirmed that the B-25s had failed to damage the North Point power station. One of its operatives reported that the bomb train had stretched in a straight line from the edge of the power plant all the way to Blue Pool Road at the end of Happy Valley, tearing up the tram tracks, blasting a series of tenement buildings, and causing a hundred civilian casualties of both genders and all ages. Errant manufacturing in the American Midwest had apparently saved more than a few lives, however, since a BAAG agent reported that at least two and perhaps as many as four five-hundred-pound bombs had failed to explode. The words on the side of one sturdy bomb casing could still be read by the BAAG operative: "Cleveland Chemical Works, Ohio, 500 lbs. 1938."[12]

The same BAAG operative also assessed the third raid by the dive-bombing P-40s as completely ineffective. Captain Hampshire and his pilots believed they had landed at least one solid hit on a freighter and splashed two more bombs so close alongside two more ships that they had likely suffered hull breaches and shrapnel damage topside. However, the BAAG report made no mention of sunk or damaged ships. The operative confessed that he was not even sure what the intended targets of the dive-bombers had been, since the bombs had all detonated in the harbor, leaving the waters strewn with a sheen of dead fish. "I heard that the boat people want more of these raids!" the operative reported, proving that the BAAG had managed to keep its sense of humor despite the dire situation in Hong Kong.[13]

Emily Hahn never lost electric power at her flat and saw no signs of damage whatsoever in the days that followed the bombing. "Viewed as more than a token raid," she later wrote, "it was disappointing."[14]

If the raids failed to do much damage, however, they did raise the spirits of Graham Heywood, a meteorologist from the Royal Observatory in Kowloon who had been imprisoned in the Sham Shui Po camp despite his civilian status. With considerable jubilation Heywood and his fellow POWs had tracked the American B-25s as they came over the Kowloon hills, watched the freefalling sticks of bombs, and witnessed the eruptions of flame and smoke in the streets nearby. When the Japanese guns positioned close to the camp perimeter began firing, however, the POWs scrambled for cover. Heywood knew that a junk-metal rain of what he called "rubbish" would soon start falling from the sky. Spent tracer rounds arced into the camp, and shrapnel pelted down from the flak bursts overhead. Since Heywood and the POWs had never been allowed to construct any form of air-raid shelter, they had to improvise as best they could. Heywood fashioned a one-man shelter from his camp cot, crawled beneath, and listened to the rubbish knock holes in the roof. As he feared, shrapnel and stray rounds bloodied several unlucky POWs, but none of the wounds proved to be life threatening.

Lieutenant Colonel Morgan and the other bombardiers had been briefed on the location of the Sham Shui Po camp thanks to the efforts of Colonel Ride and the BAAG, so no American bombs had impacted within the camp fence. However, no tins of ascorbic acid tablets had fallen into the camp either, as the BAAG initiative to air-drop "chopsticks" to the prisoners had fizzled, perhaps due to the long supply line from India, or different American priorities, or the inherent inertia of military bureaucracies, or doubts that such a scheme could ever actually work. Since Heywood and the POWs had no inkling of the plan, however, its failure had no impact on their soaring morale. Despite the danger posed by the raids, many of the prisoners found them exhilarating. Like the civilian internees in the Stanley camp, they took the sight of the American aircraft as sure proof that Hong Kong had not been forgotten.[15]

The same BAAG operative who had reported on the dead fish noted that the raids had initially caused considerable panic among the civilian population of Hong Kong, but that this panic had subsided once it became apparent that the Americans had been aiming—

however inaccurately—at military targets. Civilian morale improved with the knowledge that the Americans had not forgotten the people of Hong Kong and that the USAAF would not do to the city what Japanese bombers had done to Chungking. However, Emily Hahn observed that while the appearance of American warplanes had initially boosted the spirits of the civilian population, the exaggerated Allied claims about the effectiveness of the raids had quickly brought those spirits back down. Allied broadcasts claimed that the raids had destroyed the North Point power station and left military targets in Kowloon in flames, but Hahn only had to flip on a light switch or gaze across the harbor for proof of the bogus nature of these claims. If the Allies had lied about the results of the Hong Kong raid, everyone concluded, then Allied reports about victories elsewhere could no longer be trusted. "We heard the Japanese laugh at the Allies for their lies," she later wrote, "and we knew the laughter was justified, and we were ashamed. Until then we had thought that only Axis people lied and boasted." In the end the post-raid boost to civilian morale proved to be as ephemeral as Hong Kong's beloved Bauhinia blossoms.[16]

While General Chennault had hoped to inflict crippling damage on the port facilities at Hong Kong, he had also intended to deal a psychological blow to the Japanese. He wanted them to know that the Americans could, and would, strike Hong Kong whenever they pleased. However, the raids had little impact on Japanese morale, at least in part because they had not come as a surprise. Understanding that a raid was imminent, the JAAF had deployed fighter aircraft to Canton and Kai Tak for the express purpose of countering American air attacks in the Pearl River delta. The BAAG later reported that one Japanese officer had informed a Chinese friend to expect an American raid on Sunday, October 25. In the hours just before the raid, the Health Department in Hong Kong had called its employees in to work, which suggested that the impending attack was widely known not just to the Japanese but to the local Cantonese as well. Even the city's small Indian community had known of the impending air strikes. Three Indian civilians who later fled Hong Kong reported when interviewed by American intelligence officers that everyone in their temple had been aware of the incoming American raids. Despite the expectation of an American air attack, however, the BAAG reported that the Japanese administration had failed to issue any advance warnings to the civilian population and that no air-raid precautions had been taken ahead of time.[17]

The pilots and gunners who had flown the first raid on October 25 believed they had completely routed the defending screen of Japanese interceptors. Colonel Scott claimed that his seven P-40s had shot down ten enemy fighters for certain, including the two that he had personally dispatched, and racked up another eight kills that could not be confirmed. By the reckoning of the 11th Bomb Squadron, their gunners had flamed seven fighters and probably nailed an additional eight. Based on pilot and aircrew debriefings as well as Chinese intelligence sources, Chennault and his staff concluded that about twenty Japanese fighters had been shot down on October 25.[18]

However, fighter pilots and gunners on both sides frequently overestimated their victories, and the actual Japanese losses were likely quite lower and perhaps no higher than those suffered by the Americans.[19] Major Mizutani's 33rd Sentai did not report any of its pilots killed in action over the Pearl River delta during the last week of October. Possibly the unit had lost some of its aircraft, however, since unlike American air groups, Japanese *sentai* typically reported pilot casualties but did not tabulate their own aircraft losses. BAAG intelligence did report that one shot-up Japanese fighter had crashed and burned at Kai Tak during the final raid on October 28, but its operatives could provide no documentation of any other downed Japanese aircraft over Hong Kong. Even allowing for the possibility that one or more twin-engine Ki-45s had been shot down by Colonel Scott, Japanese losses had been unquestionably light.[20]

Regardless of the casualties they had sustained, however, the Ki-43 pilots of the 33rd Sentai could claim a successful intercept of the American attackers. Major Mizutani and his pilots believed they had brought down two B-25s on October 25 and a P-40 on October 28, and this tally proved to be pretty close to the mark.[21] In actu-

DUD BOMBS AND DEAD FISH

ality on October 25 the *sentai* had downed the B-25 flown by First Lieutenant Allers and had nearly bagged the P-40 flown by Second Lieutenant Sher, who had been forced to land in a field far short of Kweilin due to a sputtering engine. Sher attempted a risky wheels-down landing in an open field, caught his gear in a deep hole, nosed over, and pretzeled the propeller.[22] During the raid on October 28, the 33rd Sentai had shot down the P-40 flown by Captain O'Connell. In the resultant dogfight, the other P-40s guzzled so much fuel that four pilots had to crash land when they ran out of gas during the run home. While the 33rd Sentai and fuel exhaustion had taken their toll of CATF aircraft, the same could not be said of the Japanese flak gunners. Despite the heavy volume of antiaircraft fire, no B-25 pilots and only two P-40 pilots returned to Kweilin with flak damage, and in both cases ground crews easily repaired the shrapnel and bullet holes.[23]

In total one American P-40 pilot (O'Connell) had been killed, and four B-25 crewmen (Young, Webb, Allers, and Lewis) had been captured. Two more downed airmen (Marich and Cunningham) had managed to evade capture and make their way to friendly territory. On October 29 the BAAG reported that both airmen had passed through friendly lines and that a BAAG agent would escort them back to their squadron in Kweilin. As for Second Lieutenant Sher and the four P-40 pilots who had drained their tanks dry, all five had managed to crash land in friendly territory without serious injury, so they soon rejoined their squadrons. The force-landed P-40s could be repaired and returned to service, but in the short term six P-40s and one B-25 had been lost or rendered nonoperational, which likely amounted to a casualty rate higher than the loss rate for the Japanese fighters defending Hong Kong.

Accounts of the first air strikes on Hong Kong claimed that the raids marked the first loss of a CATF bomber to enemy action, as if to emphasize how unusual it was to lose a B-25.[24] The qualifying adjective "enemy" was important, however, because a fighter aircraft had in fact shot down a CATF B-25 several months before the inaugural Hong Kong raids. The unfortunate catch was that the fighter had been an AVG P-40 flown by an American pilot who clearly needed to brush up on his aircraft identification skills. Fortunately, all five bomber crewmen survived this friendly fire fiasco courtesy of their parachutes. Moreover, in June four other B-25s had been destroyed when they crashed into mountains or ran out of fuel during the initial deployment of the 11th Bomb Squadron to Kunming. In total five CATF bombers had been lost before the Hong Kong raids, and a sixth had been rendered nonoperational for mechanical reasons and cannibalized for spare parts.[25]

General Chennault launched another round of raids from the bomb-cratered Kweilin airfield at the end of November. In a continuation of his counter-air campaign, he targeted Japanese airbases in the Pearl River delta and sought to lure Japanese pilots into dogfights on terms that favored his P-40 pilots. By this point the CATF had gathered nearly two-dozen P-40s at Kweilin from the 16th, 75th, and 76th Fighter Squadrons in addition to the B-25s from the 11th Bomb Squadron. Ground crews had also been flown into Kweilin aboard C-47s along with their tools and spare parts. Aviation fuel, bombs, and machine-gun ammunition had been cached around the dusty field. To keep up morale, the transport pilots flew in 150 pounds of turkey and some hams for Thanksgiving dinner.[26]

On November 23, 24, and 27 the well-fed and well-armed P-40 pilots and B-25 crews bombed and strafed the Japanese airstrip on San Chau as well as the larger Canton airbases at Tien Ho and White Cloud. While inbound CATF aircraft feinted toward Hong Kong on at least one of the missions that hit Canton, and American reconnaissance flights overflew the city on several occasions, no CATF aircraft targeted Hong Kong in November. Chennault had certainly hoped to hit Hong Kong, but two factors had caused him to drop the city from the target list: a shortage of seventy-five-gallon drop tanks at Kweilin and strong headwinds. The former factor limited the gas a P-40 could carry on a mission to Hong Kong, while the latter factor would increase the rate of fuel consumption. Given that a Kweilin-to-Hong Kong combat flight pushed a P-40 to the outer limits of its operational range under the best conditions, a vigorous headwind and lack of belly tanks would likely lead to more planes running out of gas on the return flight to Kweilin. Rather than take this risk, Chennault opted to instead hit the airfields at Canton and San Chau.[27]

In addition to Japanese airfields, CATF pilots also hit maritime targets on the Pearl River. On November 24 they bombed a large freighter and shot up the IJNS *Suma*, a gunboat of the 2nd China Expeditionary Fleet (CEF) that had originally been named the HMS *Moth*. In dry dock during the invasion of Hong Kong, the *Moth* had been scuttled in the harbor along with numerous other vessels to keep them from falling into Japanese hands after the colony surrendered. The Imperial Japanese Navy (IJN) raised and repaired the *Moth*, renamed it the *Suma*, and assigned the vessel to the 2nd CEF, which had responsibility for the waters around Hong Kong and in the Pearl River delta. According to intelligence gathered by the BAAG, about ten sailors on the bridge and in the wardroom sustained injuries during the American attack, and the executive officer had been killed. On November 27 CATF aircraft caught the Japanese freighter *Ryokusei Maru* at the Canton docks, where it had been unloading cargo, and left it a disabled wreck.[28]

Dive-bombing in a P-40 proved once again to be a particularly hazardous undertaking. A Shark piloted by 1st Lt. Patrick H. Daniels of the 76th Fighter Squadron went down while dive-bombing an aircraft assembly factory in Canton on November 24. The P-40s rigged for dive-bombing carried three thirty-five-pound fragmentation bombs under each wing, and the frags shackled to the Shark flown by Daniels had apparently exploded on release, tearing off a wing. The P-40 came down near Tien Ho, and the violence of the impact rammed the engine and other wreckage six feet into the dirt.[29] The squadron mates of First Lieutenant Daniels speculated that his plane had gone into a skid, which could happen easily enough when diving a heavy P-40, particularly when the pilot had to take one hand off the stick to pull the bomb-release handle. As a result of the skid, the bombs may have struck the propeller or collided with each other. An alternative scenario credited the antiaircraft gunners at Tien Ho with a lucky hit on a bomb or fuel tank. No other American aircraft went down during the November raids, though one P-43 pilot and at least one P-40 pilot executed forced landings.[30]

Based on pilot debriefings as well as Chinese intelligence sources, General Chennault and his staff believed that the raids had damaged or destroyed more than forty Japanese aircraft of various kinds on the ground at Canton, and that nearly the same number had been shot down while tangling with the P-40s in the air. Colonel Scott thought as many as twenty-nine Japanese fighters had been blown out of the sky.[31] As with the earlier Hong Kong raids in October, however, the Americans likely overestimated the number of enemy aircraft damaged and destroyed during the November raids. Japanese records indicate that the raids cost the JAAF just three pilots—two from the 25th Sentai who got caught on the ground by American bombs and another from the 33rd Sentai killed in the air in his Ki-43-I.[32] Whatever the level of Japanese losses, however, American casualties had been unquestionably light with just one pilot killed and one aircraft shot down. Satisfied with the results of the raids on Canton and facing the onset of winter with its poor flying conditions, Chennault withdrew his squadrons to Kunming from their exposed position at Kweilin at the end of November.

AT THE START of December, the guards rousted Staff Sgt. James Young from his cell for a cold-water shave with a straight razor. He had acquired a thick beard during his imprisonment in Canton, and the guards had been ordered to make him presentable for his journey to a POW camp in Japan. Young anticipated his transfer with considerable elation, since leaving Canton would mean the end of his nightly interrogation sessions. Moreover, he reckoned conditions in Japan would have to be better than those in China. He figured they certainly could not be worse, and his guards seemed to genuinely believe that POW camps in Japan offered a safe and relatively comfortable place to ride out the war.

The next morning Young traveled to one of the Canton airfields with Staff Sergeant Webb, Second Lieutenant Lewis, and an entourage of escorting soldiers. Young hoped that their arrival on the tarmac would not coincide with another American air raid, as he had no desire to be shredded by a fragmentation bomb. On two different occasions he had glimpsed American aircraft flying over the prison, including B-25s that he felt certain had come from his own unit. When Young, Webb, and Lewis arrived at the wind-blown airfield, however, they saw no sign of an impending air raid. To their surprise they found First Lieutenant Allers waiting on the flight line with his own posse of guards. None of them had seen Allers since the night they had been captured. He looked pale and had lost weight, but he still possessed both of his feet and appeared to be on the mend. The lieutenant told them that he had spent the month of November in the hospital, where doctors had treated the gunshot wound to his foot. Life in the hospital had not been luxurious, and Allers had his doubts about the quality of his medical care, but he had not been abused.

Young soon ascertained, in fact, that Allers, Webb, and Lewis had never been called to the interrogation room for a chat with the teakettle. Young, however, had endured an entire month of nightly interrogations, which had run the gamut in severity as well as in technique. He had spent one evening drinking sugary tea with a pleasant young female interlocutor who asked cagey questions designed to ferret out his dissembles and deceptions. On most evenings, however, uniformed officers whom he presumed to be Kempeitai asked him a series of questions that began with his early childhood and ended with his final mission over Hong Kong, then doubled back in an attempt to catch him in a lie. Each time he had to answer a question, Young found himself mentally scrambling to remember how he had answered it the last time he was asked the same question. No matter how he responded, he almost always received a beating. Sometimes his questioners found his answers entirely inadequate and resorted to the teakettle or some similar engine of torture. Young figured his supposed expertise in secret codes and communications gear had been what attracted the attention of the

Kempeitai, particularly since his interrogators had on several occasions presented him with American-made cryptology and communications gear and asked him to show them how to use it. Young, of course, had no idea how most of the equipment worked and realized his captors probably already knew how to operate it. Still, they took his inability to make sense of the machines as a refusal to cooperate, which led to sustained thrashings with fists, boots, bamboo canes, and sheathed swords.

Odd moments of kindness had punctuated the rhythm of his nightly beatings. His fleece flying boots had been confiscated not long after his capture, leaving him barefoot. However, his captives found his shoes in the wreckage of the bomber—Young had swapped them out for his boots while airborne—and returned them to him just as the nights began to grow brutally cold in Canton. In general his prison diet consisted of gruel, and not all that much of it, but for Thanksgiving, the sergeant of the guard arranged an improvised feast in honor of the American holiday. As they sat together at a table, Young, Webb, and Lewis each received a small morsel of chicken, a banana, an egg, a bit of cheese, rice, soy sauce, a piece of toast, and a splash of sake. When Indian POWs from the British garrison in Hong Kong arrived in the prison as part of a work detail, one of the soldiers discreetly handed Young a small bar of soap. When Young tried to pay him with the Chinese currency he had managed to keep hidden in the purple scarf from his mother that he wore around his waist like a money belt, the Indian soldier refused and said, "You are my brother." Young never saw him again.

At the Canton airfield, the four men clambered into the fuselage of a twin-engine bomber that they recognized as a Mitsubishi Ki-21. They sat on the floor of the unheated and empty bomb bay as the aircraft lifted off and began climbing through the turbulent weather. For company the American prisoners had just a single guard who had apparently never flown before. Wooden sword sheath clacking against the ribs of the fuselage, he spent the flight peering gleefully out the windows at passing clouds. Though the plane cruised at the frigid altitude of ten thousand feet, Young and his comrades had to make do with their thin prison garb and a single canvas tarp that failed to adequately cover all four of them. Allers had to endure the throbbing ache of his shot-up foot, while Webb had acquired a malady of the urinary tract. Every thirty minutes or so, he had to relieve himself, but the Ki-21 had not been equipped with a relief tube, so Webb urinated in the only receptacle available—a shoe belonging to First Lieutenant Allers. With one foot in bandages, Allers only needed one of his shoes, so he had carried the other one aboard with him. His spare shoe still had a machine-gun bullet hole in the tongue and sole, so each time Webb relieved himself into the shoe, the urine simply dribbled out through the hole in the bottom of the shoe. A minute later it had frozen solid.

Young and Lewis—a navigator by training—determined by dead reckoning that they had landed at Taihoku airfield, Formosa. Out of respect for fellow airmen, perhaps, the JAAF aviators at the airbase gave the disheveled American prisoners the same meal of pickled vegetable and fish that they had been eating themselves. Once the Ki-21 had been refueled, the guard ordered them back into the bomb bay. They made another frigid overwater flight at ten thousand feet and then began to descend. Though the guard had ordered the men to cover their heads with the canvas tarp so that they would not be able to look out the windows, the improvised shroud failed to block Young's view. He furtively watched miles and miles of parallel canals pass by far below as the plane dropped its landing gear during the final approach to what he presumed would be an airbase at Shanghai.

As the four men deplaned onto a cold, windswept airfield, Young saw a 1936 Ford sedan and a phalanx of guards with drawn pistols and out-thrust rifles tipped with long bayonets. After handcuffing the Americans, the guards shoved them into the car, which motored into the flat, gray, treeless outskirts of Shanghai. When the Ford turned down a brick lane, Young saw a compound standing alone in an expanse of open ground that reminded him of a slaughterhouse. An eight-foot-tall brick wall topped with triple strands of electrified wire enclosed the compound. Sentries pulled the gates open, and then the driver put the sedan in first gear and motored over the threshold. Guards peered in at Young, Webb, Allers, and Lewis as the car slowly moved forward. With a sound like the bang of a judge's gavel as he sentenced a condemned man, the gates of Kiangwan POW camp slammed shut behind them.

# 9

## It Was a Honey

On a warm, clear-skied summer afternoon in Hong Kong, the American writer Emily Hahn heard the drone of aircraft far above her apartment, followed shortly thereafter by the rumble of exploding bombs. The date was July 29, 1943, and over eight months had elapsed since the last round of American raids on Hong Kong. During those eight months, Hahn had continued to avoid internment in the Stanley camp, though life in occupied Hong Kong had grown increasingly difficult as essential goods became harder to procure and utility services failed or became too expensive to pay for. Despite these hardships Hahn had chosen to remain in Hong Kong rather than be repatriated with several hundred American nationals in the Stanley camp, who left in June 1942 as part of a civilian prisoner swap brokered by the Red Cross. Hahn had opted to stay behind so that she could be near Maj. Charles Boxer, the father of her daughter Carola. Boxer had been wounded during the Japanese invasion and taken to the British Military Hospital on Bowen Road, where he convalesced under armed guard within walking distance of Hahn's apartment.

The first raids in October 1942 had failed to impress Hahn, but this time around she could tell that her fellow Americans meant business. They had brought big four-engine bombers, for one thing, and they had clearly brought more bombs as well. The concussions shook Hahn's apartment on May Road, which sat perched on a hillside not all that far from where the bombs slammed across the navy dockyard and up into the steeply pitched streets of Victoria. Smoke and dust mushroomed above the roofs of the city as flak crackled in the faded denim sky. As raids went, Hahn later wrote, "it was a honey."[1]

Though Hahn could not have known this at the time, the blast of all those exploding American five-hundred-pounders signaled the inaugural attack on Hong Kong by the B-24s of the 308th Heavy Bomb Group. Moreover, the raid marked the first strike against Hong Kong by the newly activated 14th Air Force, the successor unit to General Chennault's CATF. When first created in July 1942, the CATF had been an expeditionary wing of the India-based 10th Air Force. However, on March 10, 1943, the CATF had become an independent command designated as the 14th Air Force. Chennault had finally been granted permission to fight his air war as he saw fit.

While commanding the CATF, General Chennault had felt increasingly restricted by an unwieldy chain of command that often prioritized operations in Burma over those in China. A particularly galling example of this problem had occurred during the first raids on Hong Kong in October 1942, when General Bissell had suddenly recalled Chennault's B-25s from Kweilin to bomb the Japanese airbase at Lashio in Burma. The activation of the 14th Air Force gave Chennault the command authority to wage an air campaign on his terms and with an exclusive focus on China. He no longer had to answer to Bissell, though Bissell did retain control over the resupply operation over the Hump, which gave him considerable leverage over the 14th Air Force. Chennault also gained more independence from General Stilwell, the commander of all American personnel in the CBI Theater, including both Bissell and Chennault.

The genesis of the 14th Air Force particularly pleased Chiang Kai-shek, who had pressured Washington to create an independent China-based U.S. air force commanded by Chennault. Resistance in China, Chiang had warned, could not continue without a substantial increase in American air support and military resupply via the Hump. Both Chiang and Chennault believed that the 14th Air Force would give Chennault the tactical freedom and combat aircraft necessary to go on the offensive against the Japanese in eastern China, including in areas north of the Yangtze that had previously been beyond the range of U.S. aircraft. Chennault even envisioned 14th Air Force bombers venturing out over the South China Sea to hunt Japanese freighters, tankers, and other maritime big game.

When it came to pilots and planes, however, the initial activation of the 14th Air Force represented little more than a change in nomenclature. The four fighter squadrons and one medium bomber squadron of the CATF became the core units of the 14th Air Force, which continued to be known as the Flying Tigers and retained the striped feline on its unit patch. On a good day in March 1943, the flight line of the nascent 14th Air Force still numbered less than a hundred aircraft, and not all of them could fly due to shortages of aviation gasoline and spare parts. The fighters included eighty-six P-40BS and P-40ES, all of them worn out and patched up. A few of the P-40BS even dated all the way back to July 1941, when they had arrived with the first AVG contingent in Burma. Seven P-43AS on loan from the Chinese air force supplemented the P-40s, primarily as reconnaissance aircraft, since no pilots wanted to take them into combat. For bombers the 14th Air Force had only a dozen early model B-25s, which had seen just as much action as the P-40s.[2]

However, thirty-five B-24D Liberators of the 308th Bomb Group had been assigned to the 14th Air Force, which gave Chennault his first heavy bombers. Unfortunately, they would take several months to arrive; moreover the 308th would be the only reinforcement that the 14th Air Force could expect to receive for the time being. No additional units could be spared from other theaters. The rate of Hump resupply flights for the 14th Air Force did not increase either, since the necessary transport aircraft simply did not exist. Chennault had gained tactical freedom, but at the strategic level his operational orders for the 14th Air Force remained unchanged—it would continue to guard the eastern end of the supply line over the Hump and support Allied operations in northern Burma. These two mandates would continue to take priority over the support of Nationalist troops or offensive air operations in eastern China. Washington had believed that these strategic, tactical, and logistical factors were sufficient reason to postpose the activation of the

14th Air Force indefinitely, given the lack of transport and combat aircraft as well as the strategic prioritization of Burma over China. Despite these limitations Roosevelt had ultimately chosen to support the creation of the 14th Air Force as a way to encourage continued Chinese resistance. The upgrade to full-fledged air force status thus represented a substantial political victory for Chiang Kai-shek, who gained an independent American air force in China. He also obtained commitments from Roosevelt for an increase to ten thousand tons a month in Hump cargo and the provision of five hundred combat aircraft for American and Chinese pilots. The activation of the 14th Air Force also enhanced the power and status of Chennault, who received a one-star promotion from brigadier general to major general.[3]

At the point when the CATF became the 14th Air Force, Chennault had recalled all four of his fighter squadrons as well as his one medium bomber squadron to Kunming from Kweilin and other forward airfields due to the shortage of gasoline and the decrepit state of his aircraft, many of which needed complete overhauls. These factors as well as poor weather conditions limited the scope of air operations by the 14th Air Force in March and April 1943. Japanese air raids on the American fields further limited the scope for offensive operations, since the P-40 pilots had to focus on defensive interceptions of incoming Japanese bomber formations. Despite these limitations the 14th Air Force managed to mount a series of small strikes on phosphate mines in French Indochina and on Fort Bayard, the principal city in the Japanese-occupied French colonial enclave of Kwangchowan on the South China coast. The 14th Air Force also hit assorted targets in Burma.[4]

The 308th Bomb Group began deploying to Kunming from Chabua airfield in India in late March. However, the treacherous flight conditions over the Hump cost the group four B-24s and nearly every man on board the crashed airplanes, including a squadron commander. A ground collision with a transport plane wrecked a fifth B-24. Despite these misfortunes by May the 308th had ferried across the Hump virtually everything it needed to commence offensive operations in China, including one hundred thousand gallons of aviation gasoline, two hundred thousand pounds of bombs, thousands of .50-caliber machine-gun rounds, miscellaneous supplies and spare parts, the ground personnel, the flight crews, and, of course, the B-24s.[5]

In May and June, the 14th Air Force focused on supporting the Nationalist troops defending against a two-pronged Japanese offensive. In early May IJA forces in the Hankow area drove south toward Changsha with the goal of taking the city along with the forward airfields of the 14th Air Force at Hengyang, Lingling, and Kweilin. Another IJA column advanced up the Yangtze River toward the wartime capital of Chungking. Though the IJA units at the tip of the spear managed to thrust so far up the Yangtze River gorges that they caused panic in Chungking, the Japanese offensive finally ground to a halt in early June. After seizing the spring rice harvest in the areas they had overrun, IJA units withdrew back toward Hankow in good order despite the continual air attacks by units of the 14th Air Force. Understrength and poorly equipped Nationalist army units had taken heavy losses, but the immediate threat to Chungking and the American airbases had ended.[6]

With the Japanese offensive over and his eastern airbases secure, Chennault judged the time to be right for a shift to a strategic campaign against Japanese maritime supply lines. In July 1943 the 14th Air Force launched a sustained series of attacks against Japanese-held coastal cities in China and Indochina. This campaign also targeted Japanese shipping moving along the north-south supply line in the South China Sea. Chennault understood this campaign would invite Japanese counter-air offensives against his airfields. He also knew that if the 14th Air Force succeeded in sinking enough ships, the Japanese might even launch another ground offensive against Kweilin and his other forward airfields. General Stilwell, in fact, had long argued that aggressive attacks by American squadrons operating out of Chinese airbases would force the IJA to take these fields. However, Chennault and many other American officers believed that the IJA and the Nationalist Chinese had reached a stalemate, with both armies unable to mount significant offensives. They concluded that the likelihood of a successful IJA drive on the American airfields therefore remained unlikely, and that even if the Japanese did go after the airbases, the offensive would siphon military resources they needed elsewhere in the Pacific theater. All things considered Chennault judged the antishipping campaign to be worth the risk, as slashing the enemy supply lines in the South China Sea would have a significant impact on the Japanese war machine. The newly arrived 308th Bomb Group would take a lead role in these strikes with its B-24 heavy bombers.[7]

The Consolidated Aircraft Corporation in San Diego had designed and built the prototype YB-24 in 1939 and completed a small production run of early model Liberators, which the USAAF initially designated as the LB-30. However, in addition to Consolidated, the aviation manufacturers Douglas and North American as well as the automotive manufacturer Ford Motor Company took on the job of mass-producing the aircraft for the U.S. military during the war years. Assembly-line workers at the sprawling Ford plant at Willow Run outside Detroit built over 8,000 of the 18,482 Liberators produced during the war. In all likelihood many of the Liberators assigned to the 308th had been welded and riveted together at Willow Run. Some of the 360,000 rivets holding each plane together might even have been punched by Rose Monroe, an assembly line worker at Willow Run who became famous as Rosie the Riveter in a propaganda poster campaign designed to ease the wartime labor shortage by encouraging women to enter the workforce.[8]

The Liberator—referred to by some aircrews as "the flying boxcar"—had an ungainly appearance when viewed from the side due to its capacious, slab-sided fuselage. When viewed from above, however, the B-24 had a graceful silhouette created by its slender, fifty-five-foot wings. At 110 feet no other aircraft flying in the United States had a longer wingspan when the B-24 first came into service. Like some kind of mechanical juxtaposition, the Liberator's fragile-looking wings mounted four powerful Pratt and Whitney R-1830 radial engines that could collectively generate 4,800 horsepower—the equivalent of the power generated by fifty-six Ford v-8 sedans.[9] On the ground the bomber stood on tricycle landing gear supplemented with a retractable bumper that hung down from the rear fuselage to prevent the twin-rudder tail from striking the ground during rough landings. In the air the Liberator proved to be impressively fast for its size, thanks to its engines and unique wing design. A newly built Liberator in mint condition had a cruising speed of 175 miles per hour and could hit a top speed just over 300 miles per hour, though the battered and often overloaded ships of the 308th could not always achieve this level of performance. The B-24 could also fly as high as twenty-eight thousand feet, which meant it could top all but the very highest peaks when flying over the Hump.

General Chennault believed the Liberator to be better suited for China operations than the famous Boeing B-17 Flying Fortress because it had a longer range. Eighteen rubber fuel tanks in the wings held more than 2,700 gallons of one-hundred-octane aviation fuel, and this load could be supplemented by auxiliary tanks mounted in the bomb bay when the mission demanded extended flight time. Under ideal conditions the B-24 could fly 2,850-mile round-trip missions with the standard fuel load in the eighteen tanks. This meant it could hit targets in eastern China from the airfields in and around Kunming. Moreover, from forward bases like Kweilin in southeastern China, the B-24 would be able to venture far out into the South China Sea in search of maritime targets.

Regardless of the target and mission, the Liberator packed plenty of destructive power. The B-24 could haul up to eight thousand pounds of bombs in variable mixes of one-hundred-pound incendiary, fragmentation, and general purpose (GP) bombs; five-hundred-pound GP bombs; one-thousand-pound GP bombs; and two-thousand-pound blockbusters. Bomb loads had to be balanced against fuel loads and cross-referenced with the range of the mission, which meant that in China B-24s often carried fewer bombs, with a dozen five-hundred-pounders a typical load. Rather than drop open as they did on the B-17 or B-25, the bomb-bay doors on the Liberator retracted up into the sides of the fuselage like garage doors. With topped-up fuel tanks and a fully loaded bomb bay, the takeoff weight of a b-24 could approach an impressive sixty thousand pounds.

Like most American warplanes of the time, the Liberator had been designed to absorb combat damage and keep on flying so that it could complete its mission and bring its crew home. Since a sharp knife could punch through the lightweight aluminum skin of the fuselage, the pilot and copilot sat in armored seats. If flak shrapnel or machine-gun bullets punctured the fuel tanks, their self-sealing rubber design minimized leaks and the risk of explosion. The plane could fly with one pilot dead, with multiple engines shot out, or with one of the twin tail rudders disabled. It could even fly with all three of these eventualities in play. However, the Liberator could only take so much punishment, and it had a notorious tendency to catch fire. In the event the plane did go down, the Liberator had multiple escape hatches for bailing out and two life rafts in roof compartments just aft of the cockpit that could be released and automatically inflated during a water landing.

When it came to crew survivability over targets defended by enemy fighters, however, no feature mattered more than the Liberator's defensive battery of .50-caliber heavy machine guns. In the early-model b-24ds flown by the 308th when it first arrived in China, everyone on board except the pilot and the copilot had his own personal machine gun. Even the navigator and the bombardier did double duty as air gunners. Their compartment in the front of the plane bristled with two or even three guns that poked through sockets in the front and sides of the Plexiglas nose cone. The flight engineer also served as a gunner. He stood behind the pilot and the copilot with his head and shoulders stuffed inside a powered twin-gun turret mounted atop the forward fuselage. Aft of the bomb bay, the left and right waist gunners each fired a manually aimed .50-caliber machine gun out the fuselage windows. Often one of the waist gunners also had responsibility for the aircraft's radio set, which sat just behind and below the pilots in the flight engineer's compartment. At the very back of the aircraft, a lone gunner worked the tail turret with its two rear-firing guns.

A combat-loaded B-24 carried thousands of belted 12.7 mm rounds for its .50-caliber guns, though the ammunition type varied depending on availability, mission, and personal preference of the armorers and individual gunners. However, an all-purpose ammunition belt of .50-caliber shells often consisted of one solid armor-piercing round, one incendiary round, one explosive round, and one tracer round for every four cartridges on the belt. Such a mix could be used effectively against aircraft as well as ships and ground targets.[10]

The "D" model B-24s initially assigned to the 308th lacked Sperry ball turrets as well as powered nose turrets. However, as replacement aircraft arrived in China to make up for combat losses and operational accidents, the unit soon gained later-model B-24s with the retractable belly turrets and powered nose turrets. This additional armament increased the crew to ten men and ten .50-caliber machine guns, all but two of them in twin-gun powered turrets. Collectively, the various gun positions ensured that late-model B-24s could fire on enemy fighters approaching from almost any angle.

Chennault's antishipping campaign gathered momentum in June and July 1943, with both the B-24s and the B-25s hitting maritime targets at Canton, at Haiphong in French Indochina, and out at sea. However, the first strikes on Hong Kong did not occur until July 27, when a half-dozen Mitchells from the 11th Bomb Squadron escorted by P-40s from the 74th Fighter Squadron bombed a five-hundred-foot freighter near Stonecutters Island from seventeen thousand feet. The bombardiers failed to score a single hit, though they did kill many more fish. Another six B-25s struck Hong Kong again the next morning, but due to heavy cloud cover their high-altitude bomb runs on the Tai Koo dockyard proved so inaccurate that they did little damage. Still more fish died as the bomb trains chugged across the harbor. However, Japanese fighter pilots refused to engage, and the flak remained desultory at best. No American aircraft went down during either raid, though one P-40 had to force land while returning from the target.[11]

On the morning of July 29, the 308th Heavy Bomb Group launched the honey of a raid so memorably described by Emily Hahn. In total nineteen B-24s from all four squadrons of the 308th lifted off from Kunming and flew toward Hong Kong with three thousand pounds of bombs cradled in the bomb bay of each aircraft. One ship aborted with engine trouble and returned to Kunming, but the remaining eighteen Liberators still constituted the most powerful strike force to ever head for Hong Kong.

Many of the pilots who had played leadership roles during the early raids on Hong Kong and Canton in 1942 had been rotated home to the States, including Colonel Scott and Major Hill. However, Bruce Holloway still remained in-theater and had been promoted to colonel. As the new commander of the 23rd Fighter Group, he led the Kweilin-based fighter escort, which consisted of a dozen P-40s and a trio of newly arrived Lockheed P-38 Lightnings. The twin-engine P-38s belonged to the 449th Fighter Squadron, which had been the second unit after the 308th to reinforce the 14th Air Force. The first five P-38Gs had arrived with their pilots in Kunming in July, not long before the premiere B-24 mission to Hong Kong.[12] The 449th pilots loved their P-38s, which had proven to be fast, rugged, heavily armed, and highly maneuverable. Best of all the Lightning could lose an engine and keep on flying. In addition to the P-38s, replacement P-40Ks and P-40Ms had been dribbling in to Kunming to make up for combat losses and worn out P-40Bs and P-40Es.

The 14th Air Force had been slowly gathering strength, but it remained severely constrained by the tenuous supply line over the Hump. In the absence of a land route from India, virtually everything the squadrons needed had to come over the Himalayas by air—aviation fuel, spare parts, bombs, machine-gun ammunition, medical supplies, tools, mail, rations, small arms, and communication gear. Given the logistical limitations faced by the 14th Air Force, General Chennault had concluded that single-engine fighters and twin-engine medium bombers would best constitute the bulk of his combat power. He appreciated the capabilities of the new P-38s, but he could not afford to deploy more than a single squadron of the twin-engine fighters, which required twice the number of spare engine parts compared to a P-40 and burned more fuel as well. Chennault had needed heavy bombers and was glad to have received the 308th Bomb Group, but fueling and maintaining the unit's four-engine aircraft remained an ongoing challenge. Continually short of aviation fuel and ordnance, the 308th often had to send its own B-24s back over the Hump to fetch more bombs and gas, which slowed the tempo of its combat operations.

At noon the Kweilin-based fighter escort rendezvoused with the incoming B-24s. The P-38 pilots flew top cover at twenty-five thousand feet, while Holloway and the rest of the P-40 pilots held steady at twenty-three thousand feet. Flying through hazy skies at twenty-one thousand feet, the B-24s reached Hong Kong in the early afternoon and split into three formations of six planes apiece. Each formation had been assigned one of the three major dockyards in Hong Kong—the HK and Whampoa dockyard, the Tai Koo dockyard, and the Royal Navy dockyard. Collectively the trio of dockyards provided the Japanese with the finest ship-repair facilities in all of occupied China. The destruction of these dockyards as well as Hong Kong's capacious oil storage facilities remained a key objective of the ongoing antishipping campaign launched by the 14th Air Force.

The Hong Kong and Whampoa Dock Company commenced operations in 1868 and by 1941 had developed into one of the largest shipyards in East Asia. Known locally as the "Kowloon docks," the complex sprawled along the coast of Hung Hom in eastern Kowloon and featured three dry docks where large ships could be constructed or comprehensively overhauled. In addition the dockyard operated three slipways where smaller vessels could be pulled from the water on marine railways for hull-scraping, painting, and other routine maintenance. The self-sufficient dockyard had everything it needed for ship construction and repair as well as housing for its European staff and Chinese dockworkers. For decades the dockyard had been a dominant feature of the Kowloon side of the harbor, though its visibility dramatically increased with the installation of a one-hundred-ton hammerhead crane in 1937.[13]

The Taikoo Dockyard and Engineering Company belonged to the firm of Butterfield and Swire, which had roots that stretched back to the founding of the British colony. Swire had significant shipping interests, so it made natural business sense to open a dockyard in Victoria Harbor. Construction of the dockyard at Tai Koo—the name meant "Great and Ancient," the Chinese name for Butterfield and Swire—began at the turn of the century at Quarry Point, an undeveloped area on the northeast shore of Hong Kong Island that lay close to Lei Yue Mun, the eastern entrance to the harbor. Since Quarry Point lacked flat terrain suitable for a building site, an army of laborers overseen by the world's best architects and engineers leveled a rock-studded hillside along the coast and used the rubble to extend the shoreline. In this manner Swire created 52.5 acres for its shipyard and a companion enterprise, the Tai Koo Sugar Refining Company. The dockyard ranked as one of the most technologically advanced shipyards in Asia when it opened in 1910, with a dry dock that could handle the largest ship then afloat—the 685-foot *Oceanic*. Cranes ran on rails alongside the dry dock and slipways, including a ten-ton crane, a twenty-five-ton crane, and a one-hundred-ton crane that rivaled the hammerhead across the harbor at the HK and Whampoa dockyard.[14]

The third major dockyard in Hong Kong belonged to the Royal Navy and enjoyed a prime location just to the east of the city center on Hong Kong Island. The navy laid the foundation stone in 1902 at about the same time that construction began at Tai Koo. When completed the navy dockyard included a nine-acre tidal basin where ships could dock for repairs, re-coaling, and reprovisioning. A pair of ten-ton cranes and the obligatory one-hundred-ton crane rolled on tracks that ran the length of the basin quays. The dockyard's 550-foot dry dock—called a "graving dock" in navy parlance—could accommodate ships as large as the aircraft carrier HMS *Hermes*. The dockyard had its own godowns, barracks, fire station, and parade ground. It even fielded its own security force, the Royal Naval Yard Police, who fought as militia during the Japanese invasion in 1941.[15]

The British military attempted to destroy all three dockyards before the colony surrendered to the Japanese, but this attempt to execute a scorched-earth denial of assets to the enemy had been half-hearted and last minute. The IJN quickly repaired the navy dockyard and designated it the Number 2 Repair Facility.[16] By mid-1942 the Japanese had restored operations at the HK and Whampoa dockyard and the Tai Koo dockyard as well. The three facilities repaired merchant ships scuttled in the harbor by the British and completed the various half-constructed vessels that had been in the dry docks at the time of the invasion. One of the first ships to leave the Number 2 Repair Facility had been the scuttled HMS *Moth*, which had been raised from the harbor floor and reincarnated as the gunboat IJNS *Suma* of the 2nd CEF. When the B-24s appeared overhead on July 29, the navy dockyard had just hauled the *Suma* back into the dry dock for refitting and repairs.[17]

Far above the three dockyards, the eighteen B-24s opened their bomb-bay doors and released twenty-five tons of bombs—a quantity that massively exceeded the bomb weights dropped during earlier raids by the twin-engine B-25s. In total 104 demolition bombs whistled down toward the dry docks, wharves, warehouses, and one-hundred-ton cranes. According to the bomb-damage assessment conducted by the 308th after the mission, fourteen five-hundred-pound bombs detonated within the perimeter of the Tai Koo dockyard, including two direct hits on the dry dock. The same number of bombs slammed into the navy yard as well, including one that hit the dry dock and another that struck a freighter in the tidal basin. A mere five bombs fell on the HK and Whampoa dockyard, with four more straddling a merchant vessel attempting to leave the docks and the rest going into the harbor.

The Japanese garrison had positioned its flak guns to defend the three dockyards, and the gun crews immediately went into action as the Liberators appeared high overhead. However, the shells burst harmlessly below the bombers cruising nearly four miles above the harbor. The only two Japanese fighter pilots on the scene enjoyed greater success when they attempted to intercept the B-24s despite being outnumbered by the American fighters by a margin of seven to one. In the ensuing dogfight, the Japanese fighters—most likely Ki-

43s from the 33rd Sentai—attacked from a height above the bomber formation and managed to riddle a P-38, which later had to force land in friendly territory, and a P-40, which Holloway reported as missing in action. As for the two intrepid Hayabusa pilots, the Americans claimed them as "probables," an optimistic term used for a shoot-down that could not be visually confirmed.

While no B-24s sustained any damage over Hong Kong, one plane from the 373rd Bomb Squadron crashed on the return leg when it ran all eighteen of its tanks dry. Unlike many of the Liberators flown by the 308th, this particular aircraft had a ball turret. Apparently the increased weight and drag of the belly turret caused the crew to miscalculate how far they could fly with the fuel aboard. Capt. William Chenowith ordered the rest of the crew to bail out and then nursed his last few gallons of gasoline in an attempt to make the airbase at Kunming. Chenowith and the two copilots—one American and one Chinese—nearly made the field. However, fifteen miles from the airstrip at Kunming, the engines quit. Chenowith attempted a dead-stick belly landing in a rice paddy, but the resulting crash wrecked the plane and killed all three pilots. Official records compiled by the 308th claimed that this crash marked the unit's first loss during a combat mission in China, and while this remained true, the assertion obscured the inconvenient fact that the 308th had already lost at least six aircraft and a good many pilots and crewmen to crashes, collisions, and Japanese air raids.[18]

Emily Hahn gave the first B-24 raid much higher marks than the October 1942 raids, which she reckoned had hit little of value. "The bombers had improved in their aim so much," she later wrote, "that you couldn't think of those first raids in the same class." Hahn noted with satisfaction that the bombers had specifically targeted the dreaded Kempeitai, which she described as the Japanese version of the Gestapo. "They are envied and enviable," she wrote, "because, officially, they take orders from nobody but the Emperor, and everyone knows that actually they don't even take orders from him. They do just what they like."[19] Hahn believed that the bombers had hit the Kempeitai headquarters situated in the Court of Final

Appeal building near the Royal Navy dockyard. The only thing the bombers had missed, she reported, was the Central Police Station.

However, Hahn's post-strike analysis proved to be as inaccurate as the American bombing, which had only managed to place a third of the bombs within the perimeter of the targeted dockyards, with the rest going into the harbor or nearby city streets. The five-hundred-pounders that had landed around the Kempeitai headquarters should have been landing in the nearby Royal Navy dockyard, not on the heads of the Kempeitai. In any case the bombs missed the court building where the sword-wielding gendarmes had set up shop. The bombs that Hahn believed had missed the Central Police Station had also been meant for the dockyard, and they had fallen even wider of the mark and demolished civilian buildings far from their intended target. Hahn reported that three hundred Chinese had been killed by errant bombs exploding around the police station, and while this number may have overstated the casualties, civilians had certainly died during the raid.[20]

The 308th believed that it had pulverized at least one ship in dry dock, but postwar analysis of Japanese ship losses concluded that no vessels of any size had been sunk on July 29 in Hong Kong. Bombs had fallen around the IJNS *Suma* as it lay cradled in the Number 2 Repair Facility dry dock, but the gunboat sustained no damage and even contributed to the antiaircraft fire arching up into the sky. The postwar analyses concluded that only the partially completed minesweeper *W-101* had been hit during the raid, and that the damage to the ship had been minor. In the end the raid had not exactly been a honey, but it had been visually spectacular and it had certainly shaken the city—and it presaged, as the Japanese well knew, more-frequent and more-devastating raids on the shipyards that, aside from the harbor itself, remained the most valuable strategic assets in Hong Kong.[21]

Like everyone else in Hong Kong, Hahn could tell that the tempo of the American air campaign had begun to increase. After the initial spate of raids in October 1942, she had waited for eight long months for the Americans to return to Hong Kong. However, after the raid by the B-24s in July, she waited for less than thirty days for American bombers to reappear over Hong Kong. On August 25 the 14th Air Force targeted the dockyards twice in a single day. In the morning eight Kweilin-based B-25s from the 11th Bomb Squadron flew over Kowloon at 16,500 feet and sprinkled nearly fifty five-hundred-pound bombs across the HK and Whampoa dockyard. Colonel Holloway served as flight leader for the seven escorting P-40s from the 74th Fighter Squadron. From the cockpit of his olive-drab P-40—easily identifiable by the white number "1" on the fuselage—he saw numerous fires burning in the dockyard and a vessel ablaze in one of the dry docks. He also noted at least three more merchant ships in the harbor. In the afternoon seven B-25s returned to Hong Kong to try to sink those ships. However, the vessels had apparently put to sea, most likely to avoid catching a salvo of American quarter-ton bombs. The Mitchells attacked the Tai Koo dockyard instead but failed to score a single hit on the sprawling waterfront complex when their entire bomb train of forty-two five-hundred-pound demolition bombs splashed into the harbor. All the P-40 pilots in the air that day returned to Kweilin with full ammunition trays, since they had not encountered a single Japanese fighter, and none of the bombers suffered flak damage, as the antiaircraft fire over Hong Kong had been no more accurate than on previous raids.[22]

Early the next afternoon a strike force of fifteen B-24s from the 308th Bomb Group returned for another crack at the HK and Whampoa dockyard. A mixed bag of ten P-38s from the 449th Fighter Squadron and seven P-40s from the 74th Fighter Squadron shepherded the heavies eastward with Col. Clinton D. "Casey" Vincent in command. This time eight JAAF fighters intercepted, including some that had scrambled from Kai Tak, where they had apparently been deployed in response to the raid on the previous day. The Japanese pilots had clearly been briefed on best practices for attacking American heavy bombers and made frontal gun runs on the B-24s from the ten o'clock and two o'clock positions with the goal of hitting the cockpit and engines.

JAAF pilots defending Hankow had successfully employed the

same tactics just a few days earlier when the 308th had attempted to bomb the city on August 21 and August 24. Due to poor coordination and plain bad luck, the B-24s had been caught without their fighter escort on both days. As a result the Hankow-based pilots of the 25th and 33rd Sentai had been able to shred the American bomber formation. Maj. Toshio A. Sakagawa, the thirty-three-year-old commanding officer of the 25th Sentai, had personally downed the lead B-24 of Maj. Walter B. Beat, the commander of the bomber formation. A highly experienced combat pilot, Sakagawa had fought the Russians during the border war at Nomonhan, the British and the Americans over Malaya and Burma, and the Americans and the Chinese over China. In total the KI-43-II pilots of the 25th and 33rd Sentai had destroyed an unprecedented seven B-24s, which amounted to 20 percent of the entire bomb group and drove home the lesson that even heavy bombers bristling with .50-caliber gun turrets could not fly missions into airspace patrolled by enemy interceptors unless they brought along their own bodyguard of friendly fighters.[23]

The mission over Hong Kong on August 26 further reinforced this lesson since, due to the protective screen of P-38s and P-40s, the Japanese pilots failed to score a single hit on the bombers. The Liberators, meanwhile, placed about half of their fifty-six bombs within the boundaries of the HK and Whampoa dockyard and also inflicted collateral damage on the nearby China Light and Power electric plant. Moreover, the American fighter pilots and B-24 gunners claimed to have shot down at least five of the attacking enemy fighters, which appeared to be flown by less experienced and less aggressive pilots than the ones defending Hankow. Though the Japanese losses had likely been overstated, the American pilots had nonetheless come out ahead. No American aircraft went down, though one P-38 trailed a line of smoke from an engine nacelle as it wobbled unsteadily back to a safe landing at Kweilin. Three P-40s force landed on the return leg as well, though two flew back to Kweilin later in the week and all three pilots escaped without injury.[24]

On a hot afternoon four days later, a quartet of P-40s from the 74th Fighter Squadron—two with bombs and two flying top cover—

pounced on three small freighters and an escort vessel as they left Hong Kong. The two P-40s in the bomb flight carried five-hundred-pounders on centerline bomb shackles with seventy-five-gallon bamboo drop tanks hanging just behind on specially built racks. Rather than attempt a risky dive-bombing attack, the two pilots opted for an entirely new tactic that they had never tried. Each pilot approached a freighter at mast height and released his bomb just short of the target in the hopes that it would strike the water and then skip—or perhaps more accurately, bounce—into the hull of the ship. The unpracticed pilots failed to score direct hits, but they landed their bombs close enough for the blast to buckle hull plates and send shrapnel tearing through the superstructure. All four fighters then gave the convoy a two-thousand-round hosing down with their wing guns. When the pilots left the scene for the return run back to the refueling point at Namyung, smoke obscured all four ships, one of the freighters had acquired an ominous list, and the entire convoy had swung around on a heading that would take it back to Hong Kong. Upon landing all four P-40 pilots agreed that their experiment with skip-bombing had proven the validity of the tactic.

Less than twenty-four hours later, another four pilots from the 74th took off for Hong Kong to try to polish off the convoy. One of the top-cover pilots aborted, but his three comrades approached Hong Kong from the south, winged over the northeast edge of Hong Kong Island, and flew east to west down the length of Victoria Harbor. They spotted the *Shirogane Maru* near Stonecutters Island, which the bombing flight skip bombed. In the strafing that followed, all three pilots fired 1,500 rounds into the damaged freighter and sank a fifty-foot launch. The two raids marked the first use of skip-bombing by American fighters in the China theater, and the results suggested it should become the primary bombing technique for going after enemy ships.[25]

Earlier in the year, Emily Hahn had predicted that September would make for "good bombing weather."[26] Her prediction proved rather prescient when the 11th Bomb Squadron went after the Lai Chi Kok oil depot on September 2. Hong Kong boasted a constellation of oil-storage facilities, which in prewar days had been owned and operated by Western firms like Standard Oil, Texaco, Sacony, Asiatic Petroleum, and Vacuum Oil. Captured largely intact and used by the Japanese to fuel their military machine, the oil-tank farms had long been considered high-value targets by the 14th Air Force.

Ten B-25s unloaded fourteen tons of bombs during the noonday raid on Lai Chi Kok, and the resultant detonation of at least seven large oil tanks spawned a mushroom cloud that rose higher than the Kowloon hills. Errant five-hundred-pounders plunged into the cove that separated the conflagrant oil depot from the Sham Shui Po POW camp. This caused considerable consternation among the prisoners, who had still not been allowed to construct air-raid shelters. Instead, the guards ordered them into their barracks, which offered scant protection. Many of the guards then proceeded to gamely fire their rifles at the American aircraft, which contributed to the general pandemonium in the camp. Further chaos ensued when two late-arriving P-40s skip bombed a tanker anchored off Stonecutters Island and then shot up the fireboats attempting to douse the flames at Lai Chi Kok.[27]

Heavy black smoke continued to boil up into the sky long after the American aircraft had returned safely to Kweilin, much to the satisfaction of meteorologist Graham Heywood and the other prisoners at Sham Shui Po. They enjoyed the view of the blaze while taking their meager evening ration of rice on the barracks parade ground. If the raid had raised the spirits of Heywood and his fellow inmates, it had certainly squashed the morale of the guards, who only had to look across the cove to the inferno at Lai Chi Kok to understand how the war was going. The tanks burned for an entire week, and the resultant smoke plume rose to an altitude of thirteen thousand feet and stretched for a hundred miles along the coast.[28] Civilian trucks and buses began to disappear from the roads as their tanks ran dry due to a shortage of gasoline and diesel. Rickshaws, horse-drawn carriages, and hand-pulled carts soon replaced these sidelined motor vehicles. The Japanese military reserved what fuel remained in Hong Kong for its own trucks and other machinery, but the IJA, the IJN, and the Kempeitai nonetheless faced the prospect of running out of gas.[29]

Rumors of repeated American raids on Canton likely contributed to the general decline in morale of the Japanese garrison in Hong Kong. Over the summer months, American bombers had hit the airfields and port facilities at Canton on five different occasions. On September 9, just as the petroleum bonfire at Lai Chi Kok finally burned itself out, the B-25s of the 11th Bomb Squadron executed a sixth strike, this time on White Cloud airfield. A substantial force of JAAF fighters from the 3rd Hikoshidan—usually translated as "air division" and roughly equivalent to an air force–sized unit in the USAAF—intercepted the B-25s. The 3rd Hikoshidan had just relocated its headquarters to Canton along with a number of its air units, though its commanding officer, Lt. Gen. Moritaka Nakasono, had not yet arrived. From the airfields at Canton, Nakasono and the headquarters staff of the 3rd Hikoshidan—the highest operational unit of the JAAF in China—planned to coordinate a major offensive against American airbases at Kweilin, Kunming, and other locations. Major Sakagawa's 25th Sentai had deployed from Hankow to Canton along with the 85th Sentai in preparation for this offensive, and the Ki-43s and Ki-44s of these units tangled with the escorting P-40s of the 74th Fighter Squadron. Unlike at Hankow, where they had decimated American heavy-bomber formations on two different occasions, Sakagawa and his Hayabusa pilots managed to damage only a single B-25, which straggled back to Kweilin on one engine. At least one JAAF pilot—Capt. Yoshiaki Nakahara of the 85th Sentai—died in the confused dogfighting over Canton.[30]

Later that day four P-38 pilots from the 449th Fighter Squadron arrived over Canton at seven thousand feet. Unlike the P-40 the P-38 lent itself to dive-bombing runs because its contra-rotating twin propellers minimized torque, making the plane relatively easy to control in a dive. Furthermore, its powerful dual engines meant that it could outdive enemy fighters on the way down and then outclimb them on the way back up after bomb release. Though tailed by 25th Sentai pilots who had been patrolling over Canton at thirteen thousand feet, each Lightning pilot nosed into a dive, dropped a pair of five-hundred-pound bombs on the docks and godowns lining the Pearl River, and powered clear of the pursuing Ki-43s.

As the four P-38 pilots began their return run back to Kweilin, 2nd Lt. Billie M. Beardsley spotted a Japanese twin-engine transport plane. Unknown to Beardsley the Mitsubishi Ki-57 had lifted off that morning from Kagi, Formosa, and flown across the South China Sea to Canton. The passengers aboard the transport included Lieutenant General Nakasono, commander of the 3rd Hikoshidan.[31] Key members of Nakasono's staff accompanied the general, including officers in charge of operations and intelligence. The flight crew of the inbound transport either failed to hear or failed to heed the warning from JAAF air control to avoid the Canton airfields due to enemy air activity. As a result Nakasono's transport arrived over Canton at the same time as the American P-38s. After confirming he did not have a B-25 in his gunsight, Beardsley opened fire. The general and his staff officers may well have been killed when the lethal mix of .50-caliber machine-gun bullets and 20 mm cannon shells ripped into their unarmed and unarmored transport. In any case the Ki-57 caught fire, crashed into the Pearl River, and disintegrated. All aboard perished. However unintentionally, Beardsley had single-handedly gutted the command structure of the 3rd Hikoshidan. Major Sakagawa and his 25th Sentai could have matched this midair assassination only by catching General Chennault's C-47 in the landing pattern at Kunming. However, the opportunity for revenge did not present itself. JAAF attacks on American airfields, which had been ongoing all summer, began to taper off, though poor flying weather had as much to do with this as the death of Lieutenant General Nakasono.[32]

The 449th returned to Canton the next day to hit the docks and godowns again, which they accomplished without loss despite interception by the 85th Sentai, and then two days later they headed for Hong Kong, on September 12. As six P-38s flew top cover, four P-38s laden with five-hundred-pounders went after targets of opportunity that included the dam of a water reservoir on Hong Kong Island, the police station at Stanley, several merchant ships, and the 2nd CEF gunboat *Saga*. The bombs lobbed against the face of the dam failed to explode, but the other three pilots believed they had scored hits or damaging near misses on three different vessels. In actuality only the *Saga* had been damaged by strafing. A P-38 flown by 2nd Lt. Ivan A. Rockwell had an engine shot out by antiaircraft fire, however. The lieutenant feathered the propeller of the dead engine and managed to make it almost all the way back to Kweilin before the second engine failed. Though he attempted to bail out, Rockwell went down with the plane and became the first pilot from the 449th to be killed in a raid on Hong Kong.[33]

Emily Hahn, meanwhile, learned in early September that the Red Cross had brokered a second prisoner swap between the government of Japan and the governments of the United States and Canada. As a result she would soon be repatriated along with the few American civilians still left in Hong Kong, most of the remaining Canadian passport holders, and a few stray citizens from South American countries. Under the terms of the deal, Japanese diplomats and other civilians detained in the United States would be swapped for American civilians held in Hong Kong and other locations in Asia. One ocean liner from Asia would carry the American and Canadian internees to Goa, a neutral Portuguese colonial enclave on the west coast of India, where it would meet a second liner carrying Japanese civilians from New York. Under the watchful eyes of Red Cross officials, the Japanese and the American and Canadian passengers would switch ships, at which point they would be free to return home to their respective countries. Hahn had little reason to stay in the increasingly unsafe and hungry Hong Kong, since Major Boxer expected that he would soon be sent to Japan for slave labor like so many of the other POWs in the city. The Japanese occupation authorities wanted Hahn gone, too. She knew it was time to take her daughter and go.

On September 22, 1943, the *Teia Maru* dropped anchor in Stanley Bay, where it rode with the tide in full view of the British civilians who would be left behind in the Stanley camp. The ship already carried hundreds of American civilians from internment camps in Tokyo and Shanghai, and they pressed against the rails, taking in the view of the Stanley camp and comparing it to the compounds that they had only just been released from.

The next morning many of the British internees walked up to the old military cemetery, which had been incorporated within the camp boundaries along with the campus of St. Stephen's College. They sat on the stone wall or leaned against the hand-carved gravestones scattered beneath the casuarina trees. From their hillside vantage point, the internees had an unobstructed view over St. Stephen's Beach and out into Stanley Bay. They watched as launches shuttled the Americans and Canadians out to the *Teia Maru*, which took some time in the choppy waters and intermittent rain. Hahn and her daughter Carola boarded the *Teia Maru* together with two dozen Americans and about seventy-five Canadians. As for the British and Dutch internees, they faced the prospect of spending the entire war in the Stanley camp. There had been no word of any prisoner exchanges between the British and Japanese governments.

Hahn felt the vibration of the ship's engines beneath her feet as smoke began to billow from the stacks of the *Teia Maru*. At 9:30 that evening the ship departed for Manila, where it would take aboard the last of the 1,500 internees—fully half of them missionaries—who would be repatriated. Three giant white crosses painted on the hull of the ship identified the *Teia Maru* as a noncombatant vessel to any American submarines that might be hunting in the South China Sea, as did the fact that it sailed with all its lights on.

A crowd of British internees watched in silence as the brightly lit liner eased out of Stanley Bay. The drizzle and the gravestones matched the somber mood. As the wind ruffled the casuarinas, the ship slowly faded into the haze until they could see it no more.[34]

# 10

## Colbert's Walk Out

At noon on the first day of December 1943, David "Tex" Hill taxied his fighter plane out onto the familiar airstrip at Kweilin. Out of the corner of his eye, he could see his wingman, Flight Officer Wilson, taxiing along beside him. The extra-wide gravel runway and strangely shaped mountains that surrounded the dusty airbase had not changed much while he had been back in the States, but just about everything else at Kweilin had. For one thing Hill had been promoted to lieutenant colonel. In addition he had taken command of the 23rd Fighter Group, which meant that he now had responsibility for three squadrons, a couple dozen fighter aircraft, and several hundred pilots, ground crewmen, and assorted other American and Chinese personnel. Moreover, Hill had left his P-40 days far behind and now sat in the cockpit of a sleek P-51A Mustang. The 23rd had received fifteen Mustangs, all worn-out hand-me-downs from the 311th Fighter-Bomber Group in India, but their arrival in October 1943 nonetheless symbolized the growing strength of the American war machine and its ability to crank out increasingly sophisticated aircraft.[1] Like everyone else in the 23rd Fighter Group, Hill expected a long war, but he had no doubts about which side would win.

In December 1942 Hill had received orders to return to the United States, where he commanded the Proving Ground Group at Eglin Field in the Florida Panhandle. Under top-secret conditions the test pilots at Eglin put new aircraft designs through their paces over the palmetto swamps of the sprawling military base. Hill himself took the opportunity to fly the new P-51A, an aircraft he thought ideal for service in China. He also got to work with some of his old AVG comrades as well as with Charles Lindbergh, who had come to Eglin to evaluate the performance of various American fighter aircraft.[2] In October 1943 Hill returned to the CBI and took command of the 23rd Fighter Group in November. Like Colonel Scott and Colonel Holloway, who had both continued to fly combat missions when they had been in command of the 23rd Fighter Group, Hill chose to lead from the front. In this regard he had much in common with his adversaries, since the commanders of JAAF fighter *sentai* in China also led their units into combat.

With Wilson on his wing, Hill powered down the runway and felt the sudden acceleration press him back into his armored seatback. The two aircraft lifted off in unison, and the landing gear on both fighters retracted into the wings. Hill and Wilson formed up at four thousand feet with eight other pilots from the 76th Fighter Squadron, all flying olive-drab P-51As emblazoned with the signature shark mouth of the 23rd Fighter Group. Hill could also see a formation of eight P-40s from the 74th, which would provide additional fighter strength for the mission. On the field far below, dust plumes on the runway told Hill that the B-25s had begun to waddle aloft, their bellies stuffed with six five-hundred-pound GP bombs. Six of the B-25s came from the 11th Bomb Squadron, a veteran unit of the 14th Air Force, while six more came from the relatively new 2nd Bomb Squadron of the 1st Bomb Group, Chinese American Composite Wing (CACW). A unit of the Chinese air force equipped with American aircraft, the CACW remained under Chennault's operational control. Chinese and American pilots from the 3rd Fighter Group provided additional escort in seventeen P-40Ns, the workhorse of the CACW fighter squadrons. The CACW P-40Ns brought the total fighter strength for the mission up to thirty-five aircraft.[3]

American aircraft had been attacking targets in and around Hong Kong with increasing frequency during the autumn of 1943. After Emily Hahn and the last American internees had boarded the *Teia Maru* and left Hong Kong in late September, there had been a relative lull in air strikes on the city in October. However, the war raged unabated out in the South China Sea, with U.S. Navy submarines and aircraft of the 14th Air Force sinking a number of Japanese vessels offshore from Hong Kong. In November B-25s sank the auxiliary minesweeper *Genchi Maru* in the Pearl River delta and badly damaged a single-stack freighter in Kowloon Bay. In total at least nine merchant vessels succumbed to American air strikes and mines in or close to Hong Kong in November alone.[4]

To complement the attacks against ships at sea, B-24s from the 308th Bomb Group targeted port facilities in Hong Kong. Three sizable air strikes on November 3, 15, and 16 hit the Kowloon waterfront but inflicted little damage due to poor weather conditions and inaccurate bombing. However, on the night of November 15, five B-24s spread twenty antiship mines in the waterways of the Pearl River delta as well as in the channels used by vessels steaming in and out of Victoria Harbor.

The November missions to Hong Kong cost the 308th three B-24s, though only one of the big four-engine bombers went down as a direct result of enemy action. Many of the crewmen aboard the stricken aircraft bailed out over enemy-held territory, but in the end all but four eventually found their way back to Kweilin. Several P-40 pilots had to belly in during these raids as well, and at least one Japanese aviator from the 85th Sentai—1st Lt. Yoshiji Shiki—died in combat with the Americans.[5]

Lieutenant Colonel Hill fervently hoped that more JAAF pilots would die over Hong Kong as he led his Mustangs up to ten thousand feet. Two P-51 pilots reported mechanical issues—a faulty tachometer and an engine that kept cutting out—and aborted soon after takeoff from Kweilin, reducing Hill's flight to eight aircraft. Hill lost two more aircraft to the northeast of Hong Kong when one pilot ran out of gas in his wing tank and then went into a dive in a frantic attempt to restart his stalled engine after switching tanks. More than six thousand feet of altitude later, he got the engine started, but by then he and his wingman had lost Hill's formation. Both pilots returned to Kweilin, leaving Hill with just six of the original ten Mustangs assigned to the mission.

The half-dozen remaining pilots continued as a single flight sub-divided into three pairs of aircraft. Lieutenant Colonel Hill led the formation with his wingman, Flight Officer Wilson. Next came Capt. James M. "Willie" Williams, commander of the 76th Fighter Squadron, and his usual wingman, 1st Lt. Robert "Bob" T. Colbert. The third element consisted of 1st Lt. Harry G. Zavakos with 1st Lt. Dale Bell on his wing.

With Hill and Wilson still in the point position, the Mustangs began to climb to twenty-one thousand feet as the strike force reached a predetermined point northeast of Hong Kong and swung to the south for the final run into Hong Kong. The P-40s began to ascend as well but leveled out several thousand feet below the P-51s. The B-25s, in turn, cruised a few thousand feet below the Sharks. The P-40s and the bombers held their formation through the turn and climb, but Hill discovered that his own flight had become danger-ously spread out, with Zavakos and Bell trailing behind Hill, Wil-son, Williams, and Colbert.

The American aircraft overflew the corrugated terrain of the New Territories, where ground haze pooled in the fissures between boulder-studded peaks. After passing over the final ridgeline that separated Hong Kong's hinterland from Kowloon, ten of the B-25s executed conventional medium-altitude bomb runs on the HK and Whampoa dockyard and the wharves and godowns lining the Kow-loon Peninsula. Two more B-25s made a simultaneous low-level attack on the Tai Koo dockyard. The CAVU weather conditions allowed Hill to observe the impact of the bombs, which appeared to be on target as far as he could tell. Fortunately, he could not say the same for the enemy antiaircraft fire, which proved to be completely inaccurate. White and black flak puffs with tentacle-like streamers of smoke peppered the sky below or behind the bombers. Still more shells burst at the same height as Hill's Mustang but nowhere near close enough to cause any harm. Unscathed, the empty bombers and their P-40 fighter escort banked sharply to the northeast for the return run back to Kweilin.

Between Hong Kong and Canton, a pair of KI-44s backed by three

Ki-43s made a single frontal pass on the B-25s, though they scored no hits, and then climbed back above the bomber formation. The P-40 pilots guessed that the Japanese aviators hoped to pounce on any stragglers, but the B-25 pilots stayed bunched up tight so their gunners could pour out interlocking streams of defensive machine-gun fire. The P-40s, however, had been scattered by the Japanese attack and headed for Kweilin alone or in pairs.

Hill and his Mustang pilots missed the skirmish between the P-40s and the mixed bag of Ki-43s and Ki-44s. With no targets in sight, Hill banked his aircraft to the north for the run back to Kweilin. At this point the formation of six P-51s began to fragment into three separate pairs of aircraft. Hill and Wilson continued to lead the formation. Williams and Colbert followed some distance behind, with Bell and Zavakos trailing even further back in the tail-end Charlie position. All six pilots had lost contact with the P-40s and the bomber formation.

Instead, Hill and the rest of his flight ran into the crack fighter pilots of the 85th Sentai, who swooped down on the isolated pairs of Mustangs, which they correctly ascertained to be in a vulnerable position. That the pilots of the 85th Sentai had perfectly positioned themselves to ambush Hill's flight could hardly be chalked up to mere good luck. For one thing Japanese radar units stationed in Canton might have provided them with advance warning or vectored them into position. In addition by late 1943 a Japanese radar unit may have been in operation atop Tai Mo Shan, the tallest peak in Hong Kong. From the 3,140-foot mountain, the Japanese radar—most likely a Tachi-3 or Tachi-6 system—would have been able to spot incoming American aircraft out to 155 miles under ideal conditions, leaving plenty of time to scramble the detachment of Ki-44s that had been deployed to Kai Tak for the air defense of Hong Kong.[6]

In any case the 85th Sentai had some of the best fighter pilots in the 3rd Hikoshidan. They relied on combat experience and gut instinct, not radar, when it came to bouncing enemy aircraft. In 1942 the 85th Sentai had transitioned from the obsolete Ki-27 to the cutting-edge Ki-44-II Shōki in Manchuria. Only pilots with over one thousand hours in the air received clearance to qualify in the Shōki, which considerably upped the quality of the trainees; moreover, these trainees were granted sufficient time to transition from the horizontal dogfighting tactics of the agile Ki-27 to the dive-and-climb maneuvers that best suited the Shōki. In July 1943 the well-prepared unit deployed to central and southern China, where its pilots began to acquire a reputation as the best Shōki pilots in the JAAF.[7]

Codenamed the "Tojo" by American military intelligence, the Nakajima Ki-44 Shōki took its name from a mythological Taoist deity famed for the ability to protect homes and temples against devils, demons, and other evil denizens of the underworld. The Shōki differed substantially from the Ki-43 Hayabusa, which had long been the mainstay of JAAF fighter units based in China. Though the Hayabusa could outmaneuver the Shōki, the faster Ki-44 could hit 375 miles per hour in level flight and dive at an even higher speed. One brave test pilot even pushed his Shōki into a 528-mile-per-hour power dive. The Shōki also packed twice the punch of a Hayabusa, as it carried four HO-103 heavy machine guns with 250 rounds apiece. In many respects the Ki-44 actually had more in common with its principle adversaries in China, the P-40 and the P-51. Japanese Shōki pilots discovered, for example, that they could fight like American P-40 pilots by snapping into a high-speed dive and hitting U.S. and Chinese pilots from above with a deadly burst from four 12.7 mm machine guns very similar to the ones mounted in the wings of American aircraft. The impressive dive speed of the Ki-44 then allowed the Shōki pilots to make good their escape in a maneuver that had long been the favorite tactic of P-40 pilots.

Major Sakagawa had a long history with the Ki-44. In December 1943 he flew a Ki-43 Hayabusa and commanded the 25th Sentai, but he had once led the 47th Chutai, a special unit tasked with testing the preproduction version of the Ki-44 in combat. Equipped with nine early-model Ki-44s, the 47th Chutai fought against Commonwealth forces over Malaya, Singapore, and Burma in the early months of 1942. The 47th Chutai also tangled with the AVG on a few occasions. Sakagawa and his pilots found much to like in the

Ki-44, including its dive speed, rate of climb, and the fact it packed heavier armament than other JAAF fighter aircraft, but they also noted some critical deficiencies. For one thing landing the Ki-44 proved to be particularly dicey because the aircraft required a high landing speed but offered poor visibility from the cockpit. Moreover, those pilots in the 47th who had formerly flown the nimble Ki-27 and Ki-43 grumbled at the more limited acrobatic abilities of the Shōki. The performance of the Ha-41 air-cooled radial engine proved to be inadequate as well. In response to the latter concern, Nakajima built just forty Ki-44-Is before swapping out the Ha-41 engine for the more powerful Ha-109. The up-engined version of the fighter became known as the Ki-44-II and first entered service with China-based units in 1943.[8]

Ki-44 pilots of the 85th Sentai first ambushed the middle pair of Mustangs flown by Captain Williams and First Lieutenant Colbert. The two Mustang pilots checked their sixes and spotted five enemy fighters trailing behind them out of gun range. However, a second flight of Shōki pilots apparently came in from above and behind Williams and Colbert, who never saw them coming. Captain Williams got hit first, and while his aircraft might have survived a gun run by a more lightly armed Hayabusa, the four-gun Ki-44s immediately scored a fatal wound. Williams could hear and feel his engine roughen up, and a quick check of the instrument panel told him that he was rapidly losing oil pressure. Moments later the engine quit altogether.

"This is Willie," he reported over the radio. "I've been shot down and am not over the lines."[9]

Rather than bail out over enemy terrain, Williams opted to glide as far to the west as possible in an attempt to reach friendly territory. The Ki-44s had caught him at about seventeen thousand feet, so he had some altitude to trade for time and distance. Fortunately, the Shōki pilots did not attempt to finish off the crippled Mustang, perhaps because they had been distracted by the arrival of Zavakos and Bell. Williams finally attempted to bail out north of Macau when he had just one thousand feet of altitude left. At a speed of

120 miles per hour, he pulled the emergency canopy release and tried to go out the right side of the aircraft. However, he could not get free of the cockpit because the plane rolled as soon as his hands and feet left the controls. Williams pulled himself back down into the cockpit and leveled the Mustang out, at which point the aircraft went into a stall. He pushed over into a dive to shake the aircraft out of its stall, but by this point he had just a few hundred feet of altitude left and knew that he would have to belly in. Williams had the presence of mind to strap himself back in before sliding the plane wheels-up across a rice paddy.

Like Captain Williams, First Lieutenant Colbert never spotted the Ki-44 that drilled his Mustang and shattered its coolant system, the Achilles heel of any liquid-cooled fighter plane. The heavy 12.7 mm shells also wrecked the elevators, radio, and instruments. Aviation gasoline spurted into the cockpit and shrapnel peppered Colbert's legs, shoulder, and face. Instinctively, Colbert pushed his plane into a dive. He pulled out of the dive at about five thousand feet, discovered that he had escaped his attacker, and put his plane on a northeast heading over the Pearl River delta. As his engine sputtered and aviation gasoline continued to spill into the cockpit, Colbert knew that he would have to bail out. However, he felt pretty sure that parachuting into the Pearl River would end badly, so he opted to stay with the plane despite the risk of explosion. He pulled the emergency release handle as soon as he cleared the delta and had solid land below, but only the top and left panels of the canopy blew out. Between the wind and his wounds, he found it difficult to get out of the cockpit, but he managed to drape his uninjured left leg over the side. Then he leaned out of the cockpit and let the slipstream suck him out of the aircraft at 200 miles per hour. His parachute snapped open seconds later and tossed him around like a rag doll. As he descended, he saw his P-51 hit the ground and disintegrate in a fiery explosion.

From his position at the trailing end of the strung-out formation of Mustangs, First Lieutenant Zavakos had observed a Ki-44 on Colbert's tail as he nosed into a shallow dive, trailing coolant like an aerial blood trail. Zavakos had then lost sight of Colbert as he turned to defend his wingman—First Lieutenant Bell—from another attacking Ki-44. In the dogfight that followed, Zavakos got separated from his wingman, managed to get in two bursts of tracer fire at one of the Ki-44s, and then attempted to evade the more numerous Shōki pilots by nosing over into a high-speed dive. Much to his consternation, a determined Shōki pilot hung on to him throughout the 400-mile-per-hour plunge and then chased him like a hound dog on the scent as he flew at treetop height at speeds of up to 325 miles per hour. Zavakos noted with alarm that the pursuing aircraft bore the black paint scheme of what he and his fellow American pilots had taken to calling the "Black Dragon Squadron." In reality, however, the dark-colored aircraft belonged to the inconsistently painted 85th Sentai, which flew planes painted gray, olive, or olive and brown, or, for reasons that remained obscure, olive and brown over-sprayed with a thin coat of black.[10] Zavakos eventually shook off his sable-colored pursuer but flew so far off course in the process that he wound up landing at Lingling, which actually lay further north than Kweilin. Bell and Wilson, meanwhile, successfully returned to Kweilin.

As for Colonel Hill, he observed a trio of green-colored Ki-44s ascend to a point several thousand feet above him at twenty-four thousand feet. The first Shōki made a diving attack, shot up Hill's Mustang, and broke away. Then the second Shōki made a similar attack, and this time Hill reported that he raked its fuselage and sent pieces of the aircraft spinning into the slipstream. The third Ki-44 declined to engage with Hill, who guessed that the Shōki pilots had either drained their fuel tanks or run out of 12.7 mm shells. He headed back toward Kweilin after first attempting to find the rest of his formation. He soon ascertained that he had lost visual and radio contact with his fellow Mustang pilots, who had been completely scattered by the Japanese attack, and that his aircraft had been hit multiple times.

For the 85th Sentai, the dogfight had been an unqualified victory, a fact Hill all too readily understood when he landed at Kweilin and discovered that his flight had lost two pilots and failed to down any ᴋɪ-44s. "They riddled me," Hill later said of the Shōki pilots. "I think the only thing that saved me was that the guy probably ran out of ammunition. I made myself very scarce behind that armor plate."[11]

Hill told General Chennault that he wasn't sure that the ᴘ-40s and ᴘ-51s flown by the 23rd Fighter Group could match the ᴋɪ-44 in air-to-air combat. The general responded with his usual pragmatism. If Hill and his Mustang pilots couldn't take down the ᴋɪ-44s in the air, Chennault told him, then the 14th Air Force would bomb and strafe them on the ground instead.[12]

Though the aviators of the 85th Sentai had bested their American counterparts, the pilots of the ᴘ-40s and ᴘ-51s had still managed to accomplish their primary mission of keeping the ᴋɪ-44s away from the ʙ-25s. The outnumbered aircraft of the 85th Sentai had been unable to seriously disrupt the raid and had failed to damage any of the bombers. At the Tai Koo dockyard, the ʙ-25s pounded the 2,645-ton *Teiren Maru*—formerly the *Gouverneur General A. Varenne* of Vichy French registry—and made a general mess of things. While neither the Tai Koo dockyard nor the ʜᴋ and Whampoa dockyard suffered critical blows, the Japanese had to write off the *Teiren Maru* as damaged beyond repair.[13] As for the Americans, they had to accept the loss of two ᴘ-51s and a pair of combat pilots.

Tʜᴇ 14ᴛʜ Aɪʀ Force had to accept the continual loss of planes and pilots, who flew when tired, traumatized, or terrified, and often all three. This led to dangerous lapses in judgment, as did the fact that pilots often flew when they were wired on adrenaline or completely drained of it. Pilots also flew with too little combat experience, which could also prove fatal, or too little knowledge of a particular aircraft type. Pilots who knew their ᴘ-40s intimately strapped themselves into unfamiliar cockpits, swapping their Sharks for the ᴘ-38, ᴘ-43, or ᴘ-51. They quite literally learned how to pilot a Lightning, a Lancer, or a Mustang on the fly or died in the attempt. Some pilots were stricken with paralyzing fear, others were entirely fearless, and both emotional positions could be fatal. Some pilots were too focused, some not focused enough. All of this led to mayhem in the clouds and mishaps on the tarmac. Pilots executed flawless landings, except that they forgot to lower their landing gear and bellied into the runway. Other pilots collided with jeeps and trucks on the taxiway or aircraft on the strip. They crushed and chopped up Chinese civilians patching the potholed gravel runways. In the air they switched the fuel selector to their belly tank, even though they actually had a five-hundred-pound demolition bomb hanging from the centerline rack, and then had to frantically switch over to their internal tanks and restart the engine when it ran out of gas. Meanwhile, in the flak-spattered chaos of combat, jittery bomber crewmen in the greenhouse or the caboose popped the hatch and bailed out, certain that their aircraft was about to explode in midair or spiral down in flames, and then found themselves swinging in their shrouds as their B-24 or B-25 powered serenely back to base. Fighter pilots sometimes forgot to toggle their gun switches before a dogfight and missed fish-in-a-barrel shots. They succumbed to target fixation during strafing runs and kept firing until they rammed the target with their own aircraft. They bombed the wrong targets. They forgot to release their bombs. They landed on the wrong runways. They overshot runways. They undershot runways. Occasionally, they shot each other down. They got lost. They collided in midair with friend and foe alike. They flew into mountains. They stalled at altitude and ground-looped on the tarmac, bending propellers and shredding wing tips. They buzzed the field to show off like prewar barnstormers, then pin-wheeled across the paddy dirt in a whirl of disintegrating aircraft parts. They got shot to pieces by Shōkis and shredded by flak. They went straight down and disintegrated in an orange orchid of fire. They had augered in, said their fellow pilots. They had mushed. They had bought the farm, or more specifically, they had invested in some prime Chinese real estate.

More than a few pilots, however, came back from the dead. They bailed out or bellied in far behind enemy lines, bloody and sometimes quite literally on fire. They went MIA and were often presumed KIA. They disappeared for days, weeks, and months, sheltered and fed by Chinese peasants who often could barely feed themselves.

Barefoot Communist guerrillas guarded and guided them, bolt-action Mausers at the ready. Sometimes Nationalist army commando units or BAAG agents lent a hand as well, and eventually the missing pilot found his way back to Kweilin, where he reappeared like the white rabbit in a magician's trick. The intelligence debriefing reports written up by the squadron s-2 officers rarely used terms like "escape and evasion" when describing the return of a missing pilot. Rather, the reports simply said with understated precision that the pilot had "walked out."

First Lieutenant Colbert fully intended to join the ranks of shot-down American flyers who had returned from their missions on foot, but the way home did not seem readily apparent to him. Colbert had completed his parachute descent without further mishap and landed on a small knob somewhere to the northeast of Hong Kong, but he had no way to more precisely determine his geographical location. His immediate position clearly rated as the most immediate concern, since the Chinese working in the fields below him signaled that he should withdraw further back into the hills. Fearing that Japanese patrols might be in the area, Colbert took his jungle kit and limped back into the crenelated landscape, where he hid himself in a screen of brush. As Colbert sat in the brambles, bloody and reeking of aviation gasoline, he knew that he was in no condition for a cross-country trek.[14]

A short time later, two of the Chinese who had been working in the fields began walking toward Colbert's hiding spot. By their expressions he judged that they had good intentions. Colbert had little choice but to parlay with the men anyhow, as his injured knee meant he could not outrun them. He had no way to resist them either, since he had chosen to fly that day without a pistol. When the pair reached his position, Colbert showed them the blood chit sewn on the back of his leather flight jacket. Both men smiled in response, and one of them spoke a few words of English and identified himself by the common Cantonese surname of Leung, but he could not understand anything Colbert said.[15] Like nearly all American aviators in China, Colbert spoke no Chinese, so he fell back on his *Pointee Talkie* instead.

Many American pilots believed that their *Pointee Talkie* ranked as the single most important item in their survival kit. The U.S. military issued these multilingual phrasebooks to American pilots and ground crew in China, though BAAG personnel used them, too. The Chinese section of the booklet contained sentences phrased in both English and Chinese, though it also included sections for other languages that downed American aviators might encounter in the CBI, including French, Vietnamese, Thai, and Lao. English sentences with Chinese translations allowed an airman who did not actually speak the language to ask questions in Chinese, while Chinese sentences with English translations allowed Chinese speakers who could not understand English to respond to the questions presented by the pilot. Most chapters focused on routine matters that Americans working at airbases would need to explain to Chinese ground crew. For example the section of the book devoted to handling air cargo contained sentences like, "This is fragile cargo, so handle with care." Or, to prevent munitions or avgas from going up in flames, another sentence admonished in both English and Chinese, "No smoking or fire near this cargo; it is dangerous."[16]

In all likelihood, however, Colbert would have thumbed open the booklet's blue fabric cover and proceeded straight to the chapter titled "In Enemy Occupied Territory." He would have then pointed to this sentence: "I am an American airman helping China in its war of resistance and have been forced down here." Having established his identity and the reason for his unannounced arrival, Colbert would likely have next pointed to this sentence: "If the enemy or puppet troops come please help conceal me."[17]

Colbert's benefactors indicated that it would be safe to come out of hiding, and they helped him hobble down the hill to where he had left his parachute shroud. The medical kit attached to the harness had been thoroughly looted by the farmers who had been laboring in the fields, but Leung and his companion convinced them to return the purloined bandages, iodine, and other items to Colbert. The two men then led him to another hill, where they rested in a clearing near the town of Tingtsum. A gaggle of curious men, women, and children soon appeared, eager to see the spectacle of a downed American pilot, and they provided Colbert with hot water to drink and to clean his wounds. After bandaging his injuries as best he could, Colbert amused himself by painting iodine on the sores and abrasions of his civilian admirers, who clearly lacked even the most basic of health care. He found the medical kit to be useless for anything more severe than cuts and bruises, so he did not mind sharing its contents. He judged the medical supplies in his jungle kit to be somewhat more useful, though he knew that if he had been severely wounded they would have been completely inadequate.

Using the *Pointee Talkie*, Leung and the other civilians explained that Colbert would have to abandon his flight gear and anything else that could identify him as an American aviator. This struck Colbert as good advice, so he changed into simple country clothes and held on to only a ring, his silk survival map of China, and the *Pointee Talkie*. He also kept his wad of Nationalist Chinese currency, though he gave nearly half of the bills to Leung to cover food and generate goodwill. The deal also turned out to include the services of a local barber, who shaved Colbert's head in short order. With his bare scalp and farmer's garb, Colbert thought he could blend in with the locals when observed from a distance. He had far less faith in his ability to pass for Chinese at closer range, however.

By this point darkness had begun to fall, and Leung and a small group of men escorted Colbert to another clearing north of the first one. The group rested there until about nine in the evening and then continued on to a small dwelling tucked away back in the hills. Leung explained that they would spend the night there and then stood guard with a partner as Colbert slept under a thick Chinese quilt on a straw bed. At two in the morning, however, Leung woke Colbert and indicated that they would have to move to a more secure hiding place. Moving furtively though the chilly night air, the two men brought Colbert to the mouth of a cave concealed in the bank of a stream. The three men wormed into the cramped confines of the cave, which smelled of earth and sweat. Colbert estimated the cave to be just seven feet deep, four feet wide, and three feet high. In this earthen cocoon the men dozed fitfully, lulled by the gurgle of the stream bubbling past the mouth of their hideout.

At daybreak a half-dozen civilians from Tingtsum arrived with rice, sausages, and fish. Colbert, however, struggled to eat the unfamiliar food. Fortunately, the meal also included oranges and bananas, which he found more palatable. Leung and the new arrivals explained through the *Pointee Talkie* that the Japanese knew Colbert had parachuted into the area and that patrols had begun searching for him. Leung and the other residents of the town wanted to move Colbert out of the area in a civilian bus, but he refused because he knew that bus traffic would have to cross the heavily patrolled Kowloon-Canton Railway line. Colbert asked them to get in touch with Nationalist army units or local guerrilla bands instead, but Leung indicated that both Nationalist and Communist troops remained too far away to reach on foot. Leung and the other civilians believed that an extended trek in search of friendly military units would be far too risky. The Japanese fighter aircraft that passed overhead midmorning and again in the afternoon hardly boosted their confidence. As he watched the fighters pass by high overhead, Colbert no doubt wondered if the six-plane formations included the pilot who had shot him down.

In the end Colbert, Leung, and the second guard spent another night cocooned in the damp confines of the cave. As he lay in the dirt, Colbert perhaps took heed of the advice provided in his *Pointee Talkie*: "Don't be too impatient. This is the slow moving East." Though this advice stemmed from simplistic American assumptions about Chinese culture, it nonetheless offered Colbert an important reminder: Successful walk outs never happened quickly.

In the morning after another extended conversation with Colbert, Leung and several of the other Chinese men agreed to escort the American pilot to friendly forces. Shortly thereafter it began to rain, and the group agreed that foot travel would not be feasible in such inclement weather. Rather than return to the sodden cave, however, Leung and Colbert decided to risk taking shelter in the dwelling where they had spent part of the first night. Colbert took refuge inside while Leung and another man stood guard outside.

At nine that morning, Leung and the other guard entered the house and told Colbert that two strangers wanted to speak with him, but that they should not be trusted. Shortly thereafter two wet but very well-armed men arrived and ducked through the doorway. One of the two men spoke English, much to Colbert's relief. He identified himself by his nom de guerre—Mr. Chung—and explained that he belonged to the Chungking Special Operations Unit. As the rain drummed on the thatch roof, Chung explained that his commando unit operated behind Japanese lines and assisted with the exfiltration of downed American aviators. Chung and the other members of his detachment had been searching for Colbert as soon as they received word that an American pilot had parachuted into the area. Communist guerrilla units had also been looking for Colbert, though their search had been an entirely separate operation with no connection to Mr. Chung's outfit.

Colbert spoke with Chung for more than ninety minutes and decided that the man could be trusted. He confirmed that travel by bus remained out of the question due to the risk of discovery by the Japanese. Moreover, Chung explained that Leung and the other civilians from Tingtsum did not seem to know that the bus route had been rendered impassible by retreating Nationalist troops, who had trenched the road to deny its use to advancing units of the IJA several years earlier. Chung felt that Colbert had been kept in the area too long, but he also cautioned against hasty action. Chung assured Colbert that he would consult with his commanding officer and devise an escape plan. After promising to return as soon as possible, Chung stepped out into the rain with his comrade and disappeared into the surrounding hills.

Leung sent a young boy into Tingtsum to procure more fruit and other victuals for Colbert, but he soon returned and reported that the IJA had entered the town. Colbert, Leung, and the other guard immediately retreated to the cave, where they remained for the rest of the day and throughout the night. Japanese troops discovered the dwelling where Colbert had met with Chung and searched a number of caves as well, but the American and his two Chinese companions remained undetected. Since there appeared to be no safe alternative, Colbert spent the next day in the cave as well as the following night. Though Colbert felt they should attempt to contact friendly forces, Leung indicated once again that the distant location of Nationalist army units would make walking to their position too risky, particularly when enemy forces had begun searching for Colbert.

In the morning Chung arrived with a seven-man team from the special operations unit. He explained that Communist guerrillas had been searching for Colbert in Tingtsum, not the Japanese, though IJA detachments had been sweeping the vicinity for the American pilot as well. For this reason Chung wanted to move Colbert to a more secure location about fifteen miles to the east. He ordered some of his men to reconnoiter the way forward, and when they passed back the all-clear signal at midmorning, Chung and Colbert set out after them with several of the special operators acting as bodyguards. The remainder of Chung's men walked point or trailed behind as a rearguard. Though a civilian Leung also continued on with the soldiers, as Chung valued his knowledge of the local terrain.

The column soon reached the crash site for Colbert's P-51, which had come down not far from the cave. Though his wounds caused him considerable pain, Colbert found that he could still make reasonable time over the uneven terrain. He figured he was in far better shape than his Mustang, which had blown itself to pieces when it nosedived into the soil of southern China. Colbert assessed the sooty jumble of scrap metal and quickly ascertained that nothing of intelligence value to the Japanese could have survived the crash and resultant fire. Chung told him that the local civilians had already stripped the wreckage of anything that might be usefully repurposed, but that he had warned them to keep the salvaged metal well hidden from the Japanese. Anyone caught with a piece of an American aircraft would face severe retribution.

The group left the blackened bones of the shattered Mustang behind and continued east. When they had covered about seven miles, Colbert heard the crackle of small arms fire in the distance. Chung immediately halted the column to assess the situation. He listened to the popping of distant rifle and revolver fire and concluded that the Communist units in the area had engaged one of the Japanese patrols searching for Colbert. Since getting tangled up in a firefight would jeopardize his mission of rescuing Colbert, Chung led his column on a detour over some hilly terrain that took them away from the shooting.

At about six in the evening, Chung halted the column so that he could speak with Leung. He told the civilian that he could not reveal the escape route they were going to take, and that Leung would have to leave the column for this reason. Chung and Colbert both thanked Leung for his service and gave him cash to cover his expenses. Chung then detailed one of his men to escort Leung to the nearest village, where he could spend the night before returning to Tingtsum in the morning.

Chung, Colbert, and his bodyguards trekked eastward as the sunset pressed against their backs like an impatient comrade urging them to pick up the pace of their flight. After moving carefully through the darkness for two hours, they reached a cluster of homes and outbuildings where shadowy figures with rifles murmured friendly greetings in Cantonese. Chung whispered that these men also belonged to his special operations unit and introduced Colbert to their commanding officer, Mr. Chin. Colbert never did manage to ascertain the real identity of Mr. Chung, but Mr. Chin proved more willing to drop his wartime disguise. Colbert came to know him as Captain Wong.

As for the village, it turned out to go by the rather grandiose name of Taiping, which meant "Great Peace." The village hardly merited the adjective "great," as it consisted of just a handful of houses, all but one of which stood vacant, and "peace" certainly remained a rather elusive item in occupied southern China. A family displaced from Shanghai lived in the only occupied dwelling, though unlike just about everyone else Colbert had encountered since floating to earth under his parachute, they did not appear to be destitute rice farmers just a few meals ahead of starvation. Some members of the family even spoke English, which allowed Colbert to dispense with his *Pointee Talkie*, and they treated Colbert as an honored guest in their well-kept home. He enjoyed hot meals, a real bed and quilt, and the first chance to bathe since he had climbed into his cockpit at Kweilin.

As Colbert enjoyed the Shanghainese family's hospitality the next morning, Captain Wong explained that Taiping would serve as the jumping off point for crossing the Kowloon-Canton Railway. At periodic intervals both men could hear trains rumbling down this strategically important rail line, which lay just four miles to the east of the village. Captain Wong told him the Japanese had been stockpiling railway ties, perhaps to extend the railway or perhaps in anticipation of having to make repairs after American airstrikes or sabotage by Communist guerilla units. From intelligence briefings Colbert knew that the Kowloon-Canton Railway provided the only rail link between Hong Kong and Canton, and for this reason was likely to be heavily guarded by the IJA. He also knew that he would have to cross these tracks to get to friendly territory. Captain Wong agreed that crossing the railway would be the riskiest moment of their attempt to pass through the Japanese lines into terrain held by the Nationalist army. Fortunately, however, the men he had sent forward to reconnoiter their escape route had reported no sign of the IJA cavalry detachments that they had previously spotted patrolling the tracks. Captain Wong judged that they could safely make their crossing of the rail line that evening.

To take full advantage of the darkness, Captain Wong, Colbert, and a half-dozen soldiers left Taiping at one in the morning. Scouts patrolled in advance of the main group, and a rearguard kept watch for pursuers. In anticipation of a firefight with IJA patrols, the soldiers bore an impressive assortment of Mauser automatic pistols, revolvers, rifles, grenades, bayonets, and even a few light machine guns. Nobody in the heavily armed party offered Colbert a sidearm, which suited him fine, but Wong advised him to carry one the next time he flew over Japanese territory.

After a winding five-mile hike, the party reached the Kowloon-Canton Railway. Colbert could see the steel rails glinting faintly in the darkness, but the silence of the night air told him no train would be passing by anytime soon. As far as he could tell in the early morning blackness, the railroad was in good condition and in need of some attention by the 14th Air Force. Colbert gathered from Captain Wong that while his men had not detected any sign of the enemy during their march to the railway, they knew that an IJA strongpoint watched over the tracks nearby. For this reason their crossing of the railway would need to be swift and silent. When told to do so, Colbert moved out into the open and onto the gravel rail bed. He heard his shoes crunching softly on the crushed stone as he stepped over the polished steel tracks. Just a few seconds later, he dropped back into cover on the other side.

Captain Wong and his men immediately led Colbert away from the railroad tracks, which vanished into the darkness behind him after just a few steps. A two-mile trek to the east brought them to a river, but the column had veered off course in the night and the captain could not locate the ford that he had planned to use. The sky had begun to lighten in the east, and Wong feared his men would be caught with their backs to the river as the sun rose. He knew that a shootout with the IJA would not end well for his small force, which could be easily overwhelmed. In such a scenario, Colbert might well be captured.

The captain sent two of his men in search of a local civilian who could guide them to the river ford, regardless of whether that person actually wanted to do so. His men soon found an early-rising farmer with a pair of chopsticks held in his callused hands. The man had just sat down to his breakfast, and despite the offer of a cash payment for his services, he appeared resolute in his desire to finish his meal. Acutely aware of the need to get across the river before full daylight, Captain Wong's men leveled their gun barrels at the farmer. Understanding that he had no choice in the matter, he laid down his chopsticks. In the end the hungry farmer not only showed the group where to cross the waist-deep river. He also had the honor of piggybacking Captain Wong across the one-hundred-foot-wide torrent, as the officer wanted his Nationalist army uniform to stay dry. Once across the river, Wong paid the sodden farmer, warned him to keep his mouth shut, and sent him back home to his breakfast. One of the special operators then picked up Colbert, whom the farmer had not been allowed to see and had never been told about, and carried the pilot across the chill waters like a human backpack.

The column formed up on the far side of the river and continued marching until about two in the afternoon, when the unit reached another small village and rendezvoused with the commanding officer of the special operations unit, Maj. Wong Chi-Pan.[18] The major and his men had lunch waiting, as nobody in Captain Wong's column had eaten since leaving for the crossing of the Kowloon-Canton Railway. At the conclusion of their meal, Major Wong hired a sedan chair for Colbert, who found it increasingly difficult to walk due to his shrapnel-peppered knee. Major Wong and Captain Wong then led their combined unit on to a second village for the night.

In the morning Colbert set out in a sedan chair escorted by Major Wong, Captain Wong, and a substantial number of men from the special operations unit. The column trekked over hilly terrain to Chanlung, which had a functioning telephone exchange, a hotel, and other trappings of prewar normalcy. In the evening Major Wong telephoned the headquarters of the Waichow-Tamshui garrison to report the successful extraction of an American lieutenant from occupied territory. The garrison commander in turn passed the word to the BAAG Advance Headquarters in Waichow. Colbert spent the night in a local hotel, and though the threat of interception by the IJA had receded, Major Wong and Captain Wong nonetheless took turns guarding him in his room. Meanwhile, the rest of the special operations unit fanned out around the building to provide additional security. When a representative from the BAAG—codenamed Agent No. 21—arrived at the hotel unannounced, the sentries concluded that they should kill him. Fortunately, however, the quick-witted agent rapidly established his bona fides and avoided having his throat cut. Maj. Wong allowed Agent 21 to speak with Colbert and offer him the services of the BAAG.

Early the next morning, Colbert traveled by sedan chair to Waichow in the company of Agent 21. Major Wong and his men continued to provide a substantial escort. The column reached Waichow in the afternoon, where a BAAG doctor immediately went to work on Colbert's wounds. He removed as much shrapnel as he could with the surgical facilities on hand but left the shrapnel lodged in Colbert's knee and beneath his eye. For nearly a week, Colbert remained under the care of the BAAG, which paid all expenses associated with his treatment and recuperation. A steady stream of Waichow city officials and Nationalist officers presented Colbert with a variety of gifts, including bouquets of just-picked flowers, cotton towels, canned milk, tins of cocoa, sausage links, smoked duck, and an array of fresh fruit.

At the BAAG Advance Headquarters in Waichow, Colbert posed for a celebratory photograph to commemorate his rescue, surrounded by British BAAG officers, Cantonese BAAG agents in civilian dress, and Nationalist officers holding drawn Mauser pistols. In preparation for the photo, Colbert had shaved, bathed, and shed his Chinese peasant garb. The BAAG officers in Waichow had provided him with a new uniform, albeit a Royal Army one, complete with British battle-dress jacket. Colbert's hair had begun to grow back, and his injuries had started to heal, though he knew his gaunt exhaustion would be obvious to anyone viewing the photograph.[19]

The BAAG had hoped to fly Colbert from Waichow to Kweilin, but given the small size of the Waichow airstrip and its proximity to Japanese lines, this plan had to be abandoned in favor of an extended journey by riverboat, sedan chair, truck, and train. Colbert left for Hengyang on December 15 with a wad of BAAG cash in the pocket of his British uniform, exactly two weeks after he had been shot down, and arrived in the city just before sunrise on December 23. An American doctor assigned to the 14th Air Force met him in Hengyang, tweezered out the remaining bits of shrapnel from his right knee, and pronounced him in good health.

On Christmas Eve Colbert climbed into the familiar olive-drab fuselage of a USAAF transport aircraft and flew to Kweilin. He discovered upon arrival that his comrades in the 74th and 76th Fighter Squadrons had just flown the second of two escort missions over Canton in concert with P-40 pilots from the CACW. First Lieutenant Zavakos had failed to return from the second mission, though everyone in the 76th hoped he would walk out just like Colbert had, and two Chinese pilots from the CACW had been killed in action by the Ki-43-II Hayabusa pilots of the 11th and 25th Sentai and the Ki-44 Shōki pilots of the 85th Sentai. One B-24 had been lost, and a second Liberator had been so badly shot up that some of its crew had chosen to abandon ship and take their chances parachuting into what they hoped to be friendly territory. In the end, however, the pilot and flight engineer managed to return the badly perforated ship to Kweilin, where they executed a successful landing on three engines.[20]

Colbert also learned for the first time that the Shōki pilots who had shot him down had also bagged Captain Williams. Like Colbert Williams had been rescued by friendlies, in this case a unit of Mauser-toting Communist guerrillas. The 76th Fighter Squadron suspended operations for Christmas Day and threw a party to celebrate the return of Captain Williams—who was, after all, still the squadron's commanding officer—and his wingman, First Lieutenant Colbert.

The day after Christmas, the 76th Fighter Squadron deployed from Kweilin to the forward airfield at Suichuan, which lay in Jiangxi Province directly to the north of Hong Kong. Williams and Colbert, however, had flown their last combat missions. They knew that they would soon be ordered back over the Hump to train replacement pilots in India, since 14th Air Force policy stipulated that pilots who escaped from behind enemy lines could not return to combat duty. If a pilot ever had the bad luck to be shot down a second time, the theory went, he could be captured and coerced into revealing the names of those who had helped him the first time he had hit the silk. The policy worked to prevent this scenario and protected the Chinese who assisted downed American fliers from Japanese retribution.[21]

Before leaving for India, Colbert underwent an extended debriefing by the s-2 officers of the 76th Fighter Squadron and the 23rd Fighter Group. As per standard procedure, the two officers wrote up a lengthy intelligence report on the lieutenant's escape and evasion. "This is the narrative of 1st Lt. Robert T. Colbert," the typewritten report began, "who recently 'walked out' after bailing out of his ship between Hongkong and Canton on the December 1st raid on the Kowloon Docks."[22]

# 11

## *Sweepy-Time Gal*

By April 1944 the civilian internees at Stanley had long since come to understand that deliveries of food rations and other basic necessities would be sporadic at best. When the camp had shifted from the control of the Japanese Foreign Affairs Department—a civilian bureau—to direct military administration in January 1944, the prisoners had hoped that this transfer might result in a more stable and balanced food supply. In the end not much changed except the name of the camp, which underwent a small but significant revision. Rather than the Stanley *Civilian* Internment Camp, the internees now officially occupied the Stanley *Military* Internment Camp.[1] Food supplies remained as erratic as ever under the new regime, and the ever-hungry prisoners continued to rely on their own ingenuity when it came to procuring their next meal, however meager it might be.

In this abundance of scarcity, the prisoners knew they could rely on just one thing: the regular arrival of the *Hongkong News*. The camp administration believed that the prisoners should be fed a steady diet of Japanese propaganda, even if they had little interest in providing the internees with much of anything else to eat. Though a mouthpiece of the occupation authorities, the *Hongkong News* still provided the prisoners with useful information on local conditions as well as a chance to read between the lines and gather some sense of how the war was actually unfolding. The prisoners understood that much of the content in the newspaper could be dismissed out of hand. Some simply refused to read the paper, in fact, though those who did figured that they could discover moments of truth in the mix of falsehood and fantasy. In a camp where everything remained in short supply, readers and nonreaders alike appreciated the many uses that the *Hongkong News* could be repurposed for, particularly in the lavatory.[2]

Still, it is hard to know how the Stanley internees would have reacted to the photograph of a demolished American bomber in the April 20 issue of the *Hongkong News*. They would perhaps have viewed the picture as yet another propaganda ploy designed to conceal how badly the air war had been going for the Japanese. The photo, which appeared in the local Chinese-language newspapers as well, showed a derrick hoisting the wreckage of a large aircraft onto the quayside in the city center. The caption read, "Photo above shows the remains of the enemy Consolidated B-24 bomber which was shot down over Hongkong on Tuesday." The scene in the photograph almost looked like something from the Willow Run plant in Detroit, as the plane appeared to be half-assembled rather than half-demolished. The aircraft lacked its nose and cockpit, though the top gun turret could be clearly seen atop the forward fuselage. The wings remained intact, but the rear fuselage, the tail, and most of the propellers had gone missing.[3]

Regardless of whether the prisoners viewed the photograph as authentic, rumors would have soon filtered into the camp about the hulk of an American bomber on display on the waterfront opposite the Hong Kong and Shanghai Bank. The bodies of two dead American airmen had also been laid out like trophies as well, said some of the rumors, until the stench of decomposition finally forced the Japanese to organize a work gang to bury the corpses in some nameless location.

On April 21, after paging through the *Hongkong News*, one internee pulled out his journal and wrote, "Jap paper ridiculous in most of its reports." He made no mention of the wrecked B-24, however, though he did note that a ration of peanut butter had been issued to the internees that day. For the famished and food-obsessed prisoners, a dollop of peanut butter mattered more than a salvaged bomber that might or might not be an American aircraft shot down over Hong Kong.[4]

At the headquarters of the 68th Composite Wing in Kweilin, however, the identity of that salvaged bomber mattered a great deal and did not prove particularly difficult for American intelligence officers to ascertain. They debriefed aircrews, listened to Japanese media broadcasts, and read incoming BAAG reports, which suggested that two crewmen had survived the crash of the bomber and been taken prisoner. The BAAG reports also described the *Hongkong News* photograph of the wrecked aircraft.[5] The long, slender wings of the plane in the picture unmistakably identified it as a B-24. Only one Liberator from the 14th Air Force had recently gone missing in or near Hong Kong: a B-24D that had failed to return from a mission over the South China Sea on April 20. The USAAF had designated the B-24 as aircraft number 42-40622, but everyone in the 373rd Bomb Squadron knew the ship by the nickname emblazoned on the slab-sided fuselage just below the cockpit: *Sweepy-Time Gal.*

IN LATE 1943 General Chennault had reorganized the 14th Air Force into four combat wings. Responsibility for air operations in western China went to the Kunming-based 69th Composite Wing, which consisted of the 51st Fighter Group and the 341st Medium Bomb Group. Colonel Vincent took command of the Kweilin-based 68th Composite Wing—so named for its mixed-mission blend of fighter, tactical reconnaissance, and medium bomber squadrons—and assumed control of air operations in eastern China. Colonel Hill's 23rd Fighter Group composed the heart of the wing, though the 11th and 491st Bomb Squadrons from the 341st Bomb Group often came under Vincent's tactical command when they operated out of Kweilin, Liuchow, and other southeastern airbases. The third combat wing consisted of the expanding CACW, while the 312th Fighter Wing represented the fourth wing of the 14th Air Force.[6]

As the sole heavy bomber outfit in China, the 308th Bomb Group remained an autonomous unit unaffiliated with any of the combat wings and answerable directly to 14th Air Force headquarters in Kunming. The 308th had been flying sea sweeps since July 1943, when General Chennault had directed his medium and heavy bomber squadrons to interdict merchant vessels in the South China Sea. As Chennault's orders made clear, only the attainment of air superiority within the 14th Air Force's sphere of operations topped the antishipping campaign in importance. Air strikes against ports along the coast of southern China and French Indochina constituted a key component of the antishipping campaign, with raids on Hong Kong ranking as the highest priority. Captain Williams and First Lieutenant Colbert had been shot down during this type of mission, which could be costly in terms of lost aircrews and aircraft. Sea sweeps, however, proved to be equally dangerous undertakings.

From Kweilin and other forward airfields in southeastern China, the B-25s had sufficient range to venture out into the Gulf of Tonkin and the Formosa Strait. The B-24s had even greater endurance and could patrol south to Vung Tau—known to American aircrews by its French colonial name of Cap St. Jacques—or almost to Okinawa in the north. During the latter months of 1943 and the early months of 1944, the B-24s and B-25s went out virtually every day that had decent flying weather. They typically hunted in pairs—two B-24s or two B-25s—and flew parallel courses within sight of one another at altitudes under five hundred feet. Many of these missions proved to be uneventful, with aircraft returning to Kweilin with full bomb bays and empty gas tanks.

When a pair of B-25s did encounter Japanese ships, however, a short, vicious engagement invariably followed. The outcome remained uncertain, and things could just as easily end badly for the bomber crews as they could for the sailors aboard the enemy vessels. During the run into the target, the B-25s descended to mast height or lower, with the first B-25 flying in the point position just ahead and to one side of the second B-25. As the flight approached the enemy ship at a right angle, the crew of the lead B-25 used their forward-firing machine guns to suppress enemy antiaircraft fire, which allowed the pilot and the bombardier of the trailing plane to focus on skip-bombing their five-hundred-pounders into the hull of the target. If the trailing plane failed to sufficiently damage the vessel or simply missed it altogether, the two bombers would then swap positions and make a second pass. B-24 pilots followed a somewhat different procedure, as they flew slightly higher, approached the target ship at an angle, and dispensed with skip-bombing tactics in favor of sailing their bomb load directly into the hull or the superstructure. However, pilots flying both aircraft types had to release their bombs close in to the bull's eye—so close, in fact, that even small-arms fire from otherwise unarmed merchant ships presented a significant risk. However, the automatic antiaircraft weapons mounted on armed freighters and their *kaibōken*—escort vessels—remained particularly deadly, as they worked the most effectively against aircraft making exactly the kind of low-level attack favored by the American bomber pilots. The crew of a B-24 or B-25 bearing down on a well-armed vessel often had the element of surprise on the first run, but the risk increased exponentially when making a second run on a fully alerted ship equipped with machine guns and 25 mm automatic cannons.

A typical engagement involved a pair of B-24s that had departed Kweilin for a sea sweep on January 20, 1944. Capt. Richard D. Furbush and First Lieutenant Byron piloted aircraft number 320—aircraft were often referred to by the last three digits of their serial number—while First Lieutenant Ritter and 2nd Lt. Samuel Auslander flew number 430. At midmorning the pilots spotted two unescorted merchant ships to the southeast of Hong Kong—the 2,165-ton *Menado Maru* and the smaller 1,000-ton *Kuzan Maru*. The bombers immediately commenced low-level attack runs. Understanding that they faced a life or death struggle, the crews of the two ships frantically banged away at the oncoming Liberators with rifles and 7.7 mm machine guns. As Captain Furbush and First Lieutenant Byron opened the bomb-bay doors on number 320, a series of well-aimed slugs slammed into the nose and the cockpit. Bullets struck Furbush in his right hand and left arm, leaving him unable to control the aircraft, while razor-edged bullet fragments sliced up Byron's legs. Other bullets penetrated the bombardier's compartment, causing the entire bomb load to salvo prematurely, and the sudden jettisoning of the payload further destabilized the airplane. For a terrible second or two, the B-24 lurched out of control, the pilot incapacitated and its wings perilously close to catching a wave, but then Byron took control and stabilized the aircraft despite the wounds to his legs. The gunners on number 320 strafed the decks as they passed over the ships at not much above mast height, and then Byron withdrew from the battle space. Number 320 would not be fighting anymore that day.

Ritter and Auslander in number 430 made four runs on the ships, however, and scored bomb hits on both. The gunners aboard number 430 sprayed enough .50-caliber fire to suppress the sharpshooting riflemen and machine-gun teams aboard each vessel, though the Liberator still absorbed multiple hits. After the final run, Ritter and Auslander circled the ships for fifteen minutes at a distance and altitude that kept them safely out of gun range. When Ritter finally wheeled number 430 back to the west, the smoking wreck of the *Kuzan Maru* had nearly foundered, with water washing over its decks. The *Menado Maru*, meanwhile, listed drunkenly to one side while belching steam and smoke from breaches in the hull plating. All surviving crewmembers had taken to the lifeboats by this point, despite the risk of getting strafed in the water. The Liberators left the life-jacket clad men unmolested, however, perhaps because number 320 had been so seriously shot up and needed to get its wounded pilot and copilot back to Kweilin. Though the airmen in the perforated nose compartment of the bomber had escaped injury, the well-aimed defensive fire from the ships had knocked out the front turret and disabled the interphone system that the crew used to communicate. Despite the considerable damage to number 320, Lieutenant Byron brought the ship back for a safe landing at Kweilin.[7]

With the bomber crews so heavily engaged in sea sweeps—the 308th sank three more merchant ships near Hong Kong just two weeks after destroying the *Menado Maru* and the *Kuzan Maru*—the 14th Air Force mounted just four raids on the city in the first four months of 1944. The first mission took place on January 11, when two B-24s dropped more antiship mines in the harbor channels; the second air strike occurred on January 23, when Lieutenant Colonel Hill returned to Hong Kong for the first time since he had tangled with the 85th Sentai and lost Captain Williams and First Lieutenant Colbert. Rather than the Mustang-equipped 76th Fighter Squadron, this time around Hill led eleven pilots from the 74th Fighter Squadron. The 74th had still not received any P-51s, so Hill strapped himself into the familiar cockpit of a P-40 instead. An additional sixteen P-40s from the 3rd Fighter Group of the CACW joined the raid, bringing the total number of escorting aircraft to twenty-eight.

Six of the B-25s came from the 11th Bomb Squadron, with two more from the CACW rounding out the formation. The failure of the bomber crews to maintain strict radio silence irked Lieutenant Colonel Hill and the other fighter pilots, however. "Gunners, get ready to put on oxygen masks," they heard one of the bomber pilots order when forty miles out from the target. "Your engine is smoking," radioed a different B-25 pilot to another plane in the formation.

Though less than perfect when it came to staying off the radio, the B-25 pilots maintained a tight formation as they made a conventional bombing run on Kai Tak airfield from 15,500 feet. Lieutenant Colonel Hill observed multiple bomb blasts among the warehouses and other buildings along the eastern edge of the runway, the intended target. He saw no evidence of Japanese aircraft at Kai Tak, but he did spot a pair of merchant ships and a large naval vessel in the harbor. Five Ki-43-IIs that likely came from either the 11th or the 85th Sentai bounced the B-25s as they left the target area, but the engagement proved inconclusive, with the 74th claiming one Hayabusa as damaged and the CACW pilots claiming one as shot down. Two P-40s crash-landed in friendly territory as a result of battle damage and dry tanks, so the dogfight represented, arguably, a draw. Still, the B-25s had been able to complete their runs unimpeded by enemy interceptors, and even though their bomb trains had missed the runway, the larger win could still be claimed by the Americans.[8]

Three weeks later the 14th Air Force launched a follow-up attack against Kai Tak on February 11. The Kweilin-based strike force consisted of B-25s drawn from the 11th Bomb Squadron—the unit excoriated for its poor radio hygiene during the previous raid on Hong Kong—and the 2nd Bomb Squadron of the CACW. Fourteen Chinese and American P-40 pilots from the 3rd Fighter Group of the CACW provided the escort, with further backup from six P-40 pilots of the 74th Fighter Squadron. Japanese Ki-43-IIs and Ki-44-IIs intercepted in force—again most probably from either the 11th or the 85th Sentai—and in the resultant aerial melee four P-40s went down. The JAAF pilots nailed two P-40s from the 74th, but both pilots successfully walked out after hitting the silk west of Hong Kong. The CACW lost two planes as well, though only one pilot survived. Due to battle damage, 1st Lt. Ying Qiu Yang crash-landed his P-40N in friendly territory but later died of his injuries. Meanwhile, 1st Lt. Donald W. Kerr bailed out over Kai Tak and fluttered to earth on the south side of the Kowloon ridgeline. Despite the risks involved, local civilians concealed him from pursuing Japanese troops in a cave that proved to be far more capacious than the narrow, low-roofed slit in the earth that had sheltered First Lieutenant Colbert. Communist guerrillas later shepherded Kerr to freedom. The American and Chinese fighter pilots claimed nine Ki-43s, though the JAAF likely lost fewer aircraft and may, in fact, have lost none at all. Japanese military documents do not record any pilots as killed in action over Hong Kong that day. However, the *Hongkong News* accurately reported the loss of four American aircraft, though the story erroneously claimed one of them as a B-25.[9]

At four aircraft and one pilot, the price had been high, but the P-40 squadrons had nonetheless successfully protected the B-25s, which completed their medium-altitude bomb runs unimpeded by enemy attack and without suffering any losses. The bombs worked over the buildings along the perimeter of the airfield, though whether these structures contained anything of military value could not be determined. In fact whether the raid accomplished anything at all remained open to question. Like most Japanese airstrips in occupied China, Kai Tak had proven to be just as resilient as the Chinese fields used by American aircraft, since the Japanese could draw on civilian labor—whether paid or prodded at the point of a bayonet—to quickly repair cratered runways. Ample warning times facilitated by ground spotters and IJA radar units, meanwhile, made it difficult to catch JAAF aircraft on the ground at Hong Kong. JAAF fighters had sufficient time to take off and, in many cases, climb to altitudes where they could pounce on incoming American aircraft. If any operational bombers, reconnaissance aircraft, or transports happened to be on the field, they could be safely taken aloft and out of harm's way before the American bombers arrived. Aviation fuel, spare parts, munitions, maintenance equipment, starter trucks, and fuel tankers could all be dispersed away from the field as well. Even the IJA antiaircraft guns squatted in the surrounding hills rather than the open expanse of the airfield. In the end walking a stick of five-hundred-pound bombs across the face of Kai Tak airdrome may have done little more than rearrange the gravel and sod.

Hong Kong endured just one additional pounding between January and April. On March 10 eleven B-24s laden with one-thousand-pound bombs and parachute flares mounted a night strike on the HK and Whampoa dockyard. The raid apparently came as no surprise to the Japanese garrison, perhaps due to the radar unit perched atop Tai Mo Shan, and the city went black at 9:30 p.m., just thirty minutes before the arrival of the Liberators. As explained to the bomber crews during the S-2 briefing before the mission, the lead B-24s would illuminate the target with the flares, and the remaining ships would then drop their load of half-ton demolition bombs. In the end, however, the flares failed to light up the target area, perhaps due to improper release procedures or perhaps due to incorrect fuse settings, and the bombardiers could barely discern the outline of the dockyard. Some of the bombardiers did not even bother to release their bombs and advised the flight deck to carry their payload back to Kweilin. All eleven Liberators returned to base by midnight. Whether any solid hits had been registered on the docks could not be ascertained, the aircrews told the S-2 staff during the poststrike debriefing, though they felt certain that they had managed to wake up just about everybody in Hong Kong.[10]

FOR THE 308TH Bomb Group, war paint remained as integral to combat missions as aviation fuel, oxygen bottles, cigarettes, and links of .50-caliber tracer rounds. In the best tradition of the Flying Tigers, squadron artists painted giant shark mouths on the olive-drab noses of the unit's B-24s. Other aircraft featured finely detailed portraits of improbably buxom women, most of them naked and all in suggestive poses, as if serving as advertisements for some kind of high-altitude flying bordello. Virtually every aircraft sported a nickname painted on the side of the fuselage just below and forward of the cockpit—*The Goon, Tennessee Belle, Jungle Pussy, Georgia Peach, Sherazade, Esky, Doodlebug,* and *Miss Beryl.* The crew of *Sweepy-Time Gal* had named their aircraft after their primary mission type—the sea sweep—and then, apparently content with their clever play on words, never got around to painting a toothy shark grin or stark-naked pin-up girl on the side of their plane.

First Lt. Glenn A. McConnell served as the aircraft commander for *Sweepy-Time Gal,* a radar-equipped B-24D. In April 1943, after completing his basic flight training, McConnell had been commissioned as a second lieutenant at Douglas Army Airfield, a blaze of tarmac scraped across the arid face of southern Arizona not far from the hazily defined Mexican border. He had hoped to fly the Martin B-26 Marauder, a hot little number of a twin-engine bomber with stubby wings and a reputation for killing its pilots. Instead, McConnell's orders assigned him to flight training in the pencil-winged quad-engine B-24. Five months after his commissioning, he crossed over the Hump and arrived in China as an untested copilot assigned to the 373rd Bomb Squadron, 308th Bomb Group.

McConnell flew bombing raids over land targets and sea-sweep missions that carried him far out into the South China Sea. He also made twenty-three runs over the Hump, hauling fuel and bombs from India to Kunming on resupply missions nearly as perilous as his combat flights. By March 1944 McConnell had logged 250 combat hours, which gave him enough experience to make the shift over to the captain's seat as a first lieutenant.[11] He often flew with 2nd Lt. Samuel Auslander, a seasoned copilot who had also racked up his share of missions. Auslander had been one of the pilots who sank the *Menado Maru* and the *Kuzan Maru* off Hong Kong, in fact, though on that mission he had been flying in a different aircraft with a different pilot. McConnell and Auslander achieved a measure of fame in the 308th when they shot down a "Mavis"—the Allied codename for a Kawanishi H6K5 four-engine flying boat. Very few pilots in any theater of the war could claim to have engaged in a dogfight between four-engine aircraft, and even fewer could claim to have survived the battle.

McConnell and Auslander had the advantage in this aerial dual, since the yokes in the cockpit of *Sweepy-Time Gal* had been rigged with fighter-plane-style gun buttons that triggered a pair of forward-firing .50-caliber machine guns. Auslander pressed the gun button as the two aircraft approached each other on head-on trajectories, and as *Sweepy-Time Gal* vibrated with the hammering recoil of the twin machine guns, McConnell saw the .50-caliber slugs rip into the twin-rudder tail of the flying boat. The noise, vibration, and smell of cordite increased as the gunners in the top turret and right waist position started banging away at the Kawanishi, which droned past just above and to the right of *Sweepy-Time Gal*. Incandescent streaks of tracer fire crisscrossed between the two aircraft as the IJN air-men manning the gun positions aboard the dark blue flying boat let loose with their own weapons. Both the American and the Japanese gunners had been trained to take a bead on fighter planes rather than four-engine aircraft, so they had no trouble scoring plenty of hits on such large, slow-moving targets. The flying boat began to trail a streamer of smoke and flame. Meanwhile, *Sweepy-Time Gal* took multiple hits. A 7.7 mm bullet from one of the gunners aboard the IJN aircraft punched through the left windshield, whizzed past McConnell's throat, and disintegrated against the armor plate behind his seat. The resultant spray of bullet fragments peppered McConnell and the flight engineer. The big Kawanishi, meanwhile, pan-caked into the swells and disintegrated.

Having eliminated the threat from the Kawanishi, McConnell turned his attention to getting his crew home. A quick damage assessment determined that *Sweepy-Time Gal* had been badly per-forated, with the navigational and electrical systems knocked out, a severed hydraulic line spurting fluid into the bomb bay, and a serious oil leak in engine number three. McConnell knew that the useless weight of the five-hundred-pounders would slow the plane's return to Kweilin, narrow the margin for error by burning up more fuel, and present a serious hazard upon landing. Since the electrical and hydraulic systems had been wrecked, he ordered two crewmen to squeeze their way down the narrow catwalk that ran through the center of the bomb bay and manually crank open the inoperative doors. McConnell then jettisoned the entire bomb load into the sea and swung the Liberator around to a westerly bearing as the crewmen cranked the doors shut. *Sweepy-Time Gal* held together for the return flight to Kweilin, though during the approach to the field two crewmembers had to unjam the front landing gear and lower the big rubber tire by hand. To further complicate things, the brakes for all three wheels of the tricycle landing gear had been disabled by the loss of hydraulic pressure, but McConnell and Auslander nonetheless managed to land the battered B-24 and bring it to a halt at the far end of the mile-long gravel runway.

At Kweilin the ground crew started patching up *Sweepy-Time Gal*. The medical staff, meanwhile, performed equally efficient work on McConnell and the flight engineer, whose wounds did not prove serious enough to warrant their removal from flight status. When *Sweepy-Time Gal* had been sufficiently repaired, McConnell and the rest of the crew flew from Kweilin to Kunming without incident. However, the mechanics at Kunming discovered something that their counterparts at Kweilin had overlooked. An unexploded 20 mm cannon shell—a parting shot from the tail gunner on the Kawanishi—had punctured the nacelle of engine number three and come to rest atop the supercharger. Even without exploding the shell had possessed sufficient kinetic energy to damage the engine, but if the shell had actually gone off the blast might well have proved fatal to *Sweepy-Time Gal*.[12]

ON THE MORNING of April 18, a month after the shoot-down of the Kawanishi, First Lieutenant McConnell taxied *Sweepy-Time Gal* out to the end of the runway at Kweilin. Auslander sat beside him in the right seat. The offending 20 mm shell had been extracted from engine number three, and all four of the big Pratt and Whitneys roared in response as McConnell moved the throttles forward. *Sweepy-Time Gal* began bumping down the gravel runway and finally wallowed into the air with full wing tanks and a belly-load of high explosives. The crew totaled a dozen men altogether—the two pilots, the navigator, the bombardier, the flight engineer, the radio operator, four gunners, and a pair of radar technicians. The straightforward mission plan called for McConnell to cruise out into the South China Sea and hunt for maritime targets of opportunity. A second B-24 with the same mission brief would fly a parallel search to broaden the expanse of ocean covered by the sea sweep, though the two aircraft would fly tracks beyond visual range of each other, as per standard procedure.[13]

With the assistance of the navigator, McConnell piloted *Sweepy-Time Gal* on a southeasterly course over the mainland. He bypassed Canton and then brought the aircraft down to two hundred feet as they crossed over the island of San Chau to the south of Macau and headed out over the open waters of the South China Sea. The marginal weather would have scrubbed a visual sea sweep, which relied on keen eyesight, binoculars, and a stock of good luck. However, *Sweepy-Time Gal* had been fitted with radar equipment that could locate targets in all weather conditions, from CAVU to zero visibility. The crews of the radar-equipped Liberators referred to their aircraft as "sniffers" because they could detect enemy vessels hiding in a fog bank or the protective darkness of a moonless night. A "straight" B-24, meanwhile, lacked the search radar necessary for a low-visibility or nocturnal sea sweep.

About an hour after McConnell had passed over San Chau, he heard one of the radar technicians announce over the interphone system that he had acquired a target. The radar had painted contacts twenty miles ahead, and as the Liberator raced closer, McConnell and Auslander could soon discern the silhouettes of two vessels—an escort that McConnell believed to be a destroyer and a smaller merchant ship. McConnell made an initial run on the destroyer, trading incandescent streaks of tracer fire the entire way in, and released half of his five-hundred-pound bombs. The resultant explosions raised impressive geysers of salt spray, but the gunners in the rear of the plane reported that the bombs had failed to register any hits.

Frustrated, McConnell brought the Liberator around for a second run—a risky move, as the gun crews on both ships had now been fully alerted—and pickled everything left in his bomb bay. Auslander, meanwhile, slid back the side windscreen, poked the barrel of his .45 pistol out the window, and squeezed off a couple shots as they passed over the freighter. Perhaps a few of his slugs plinked against the steel hide of the ship along with the much more lethal .50-caliber rounds fired by the gunners, who hosed down the decks and the superstructure of the little steamer. The ship survived the bomb run, however, and the gunners reported that the five-hundred-pounders had just killed more fish.

With the bomb bay empty, McConnell banked to the west on a heading back to San Chau, some one hundred miles south of Hong Kong. Due to a malfunction in the navigational gear, however, the plane strayed off course by a good twenty or thirty degrees and wound up approaching the mainland at Hong Kong. By the time McConnell and Auslander realized what had happened, they had already passed Tathong Point on Tung Lung Chau, one of the islands that crouched like a bodyguard at the mouth of Victoria Harbor, shielding it from the swells of the South China Sea. Still flying at very low altitude, McConnell and Auslander began to thread *Sweepy-Time Gal* through the eastern passage to the harbor, with Kowloon on the right and Hong Kong Island on the left.

The locals referred to the narrow eastern channel into Victoria Harbor as Lei Yue Mun—a place name that could be loosely translated as Carp Channel, though the American and British militaries never bothered and simply referred to the passage in English as Lyemun Channel. If a flight crew winged through this opening between the opposing coastlines of Kowloon and Hong Kong Island, they would likely glimpse small fishing communities clinging to the boulder-strewn shores. They would perhaps even make out the sampans that had been pulled ashore like barnacles stranded above the high-tide line. If the clouds had not descended to swaddle the coastal ridges in mist, the copilot could glance out the right-hand side of his aircraft and spot Devil's Peak rearing up over the waters, its apex capped with a crown of ramparts. On the left-hand side of the cockpit, meanwhile, the pilot might catch a quick glimpse of the shrapnel-pocked carapace of Lei Yue Mun Fort squatting on a rocky headland. Both positions had been constructed by local laborers under the supervision of the colonial British, who had well understood the need to fortify the eastern entrance to the harbor. Various Chinese dynasties had obeyed the same imperative for millennia, and the remnants of one ancient fort could still be found on Tung Lung Chau.

The Japanese also saw the necessity of guarding the eastern approach to the harbor, which consisted of northern and southern channels bisected by the bulk of Tung Lung Chau, where the Japanese had built a coastal artillery position on Tathong Point.[14] Some of the ground fire spitting toward *Sweepy-Time Gal* may have originated from this position, which watched over the wider southern channel. However, the B-24 faced a much more serious threat as it roared down the strait with the 720-foot-high bulk of Devil's Peak looming overhead: a trio of Japanese Ki-44-II Shōki trailing the bomber like seagulls chasing after a fishing boat. These fighters probably belonged to the 85th Sentai, the same unit that had shredded Lieutenant Colonel Hill's flight of Mustangs in December. Unintimidated by the American gunners frantically attempting to get a bead on them, the Ki-44 pilots proceeded to pound the Liberator with their 12.7 mm heavy machine guns.

The number three and four engines on the right wing sustained multiple hits and began to trail orange ribbons of flame. McConnell and Auslander attempted to feather the propellers, but the blades failed to respond, and as the pilots struggled to keep the plane airborne at an altitude under two hundred feet, pieces of the right wing began to peel off in the slipstream. The unfeathered propellers produced a catastrophic amount of drag, and the burning wing began to dip down toward the waves while the intact and fully powered left wing continued to produce lift and swung upward. A quick glance at the instruments told McConnell they had slowed to just ninety-five miles per hour, while an even quicker glance out the windscreen told him that they had flown nearly to the shoreline of Hong Kong Island. Moments later a line of spray jetted behind the tip of the right wing as it carved through the surface of the sea. The wing tip caught a swell and then the front of the plane swung into the water, which hit its glassed-in nose like a giant hammer. The force of the crash snapped off the tail, tore off the engines and propellers, and destroyed everything forward of the top gun turret.

The impact hurled McConnell free of the disintegrating cockpit in a spray of Plexiglas, wiring, rivets, oxygen bottles, aviation fuel, and crumpled sheets of aluminum. He sank to the bottom along with everything else, but he had been torn loose from his armored seat, so his Mae West quickly brought him back to the surface. McConnell gasped for air as his head popped above the water, and as he spun around in the waves, he thought he caught sight of several other survivors, including Auslander. He spun around again, but they had vanished. He saw no sign of the life rafts carried by *Sweepy-Time Gal* either. Over the sound of the water sloshing against his ears, he heard the distinctive buzz of low-flying fighter aircraft and spotted the three ki-44s swinging around to strafe the hulk of *Sweepy-Time Gal*, which had come to rest in shallow water. The Shōki pilots also gunned for McConnell, who shucked his Mae West and dove under the frigid salt water each time the fighters passed over. Though he could see the white trails of machine-gun bullets streaking for the seabed, he managed to avoid getting shot.

By this stage of the war, both American and Japanese combat pilots routinely strafed the survivors of sunken ships or crashed aircraft. The JAAF had learned from fighting the Soviet air force during the Nomonhan border war that killing enemy pilots had a far greater impact than merely destroying enemy aircraft. Consequently, JAAF pilots in China did not hesitate to machine-gun enemy aviators hanging from their chutes. American pilots rarely returned the favor, and while this sometimes involved moral and ethical objections to shooting unarmed men, it had more to do with the fact that relatively few Japanese pilots ever bailed out. American aviators viewed the survivors of Japanese merchant and naval vessels as legitimate targets and frequently shot lifejacket-clad men to pieces as they bobbed in the oil-slicked halo left by their sunken ship.[15]

Despite their reputation for complete ruthlessness, Japanese pilots could be quite chivalrous, particularly the pilots of the JNAF. In one instance the famous ace Saburo Sakai encountered a DC-3 while flying a lone patrol east of Surabaya, Java, on February 28, 1942. As he pulled his A6M up alongside to inspect the unarmed airliner, he saw a blonde-haired woman and a small child peering back at him through one of the windows. In the end Sakai opted not to shoot the aircraft down. In an entirely separate incident in the Marshall Islands, JNAF fighter pilot Ensign Isamu Miyazaki spared a badly damaged Grumman F6F Hellcat flown by Ensign Fletcher Jones of VF-10 on January 30, 1944. Miyazaki flew parallel to Fletcher as he struggled to keep his Hellcat airborne just one hundred feet above the ocean. When Miyazaki had determined beyond a doubt that the American pilot could no longer fight, he simply let him go. Fletcher thus escaped a coup de grâce from his adversary, but his reprieve proved to be short lived. He drowned in the warm Pacific waters when he had to ditch his mortally wounded Hellcat.[16]

As for McConnell he had no intention of drowning. Once the circling Ki-44s had emptied their ammunition trays into the carcass of *Sweepy-Time Gal*, he started swimming for shore. He had not made much progress before the crew of a navy launch took up where the Ki-44 pilots had left off and started shooting at him with rifles. The bullets cracked past his head to splash into the waves in front of him, though McConnell had no way of knowing whether this represented poor marksmanship or a volley of warning shots. The launch overtook him in any case, and the crew hauled him out of the channel like some kind of prize fish. McConnell thus became the first trophy salvaged from the crash of *Sweepy-Time Gal*, though hardly the last. The launch crew also pulled Staff Sgt. Tony Spadafora, one of the gunners, from the fuel- and oil-slicked water. The crew immediately blindfolded both Americans and tied their hands behind their backs. McConnell and Spadafora came ashore at Causeway Bay, where their captors took them to the St. John Ambulance Brigade compound on Tung Lo Wan Road, which had been repurposed as a military holding facility by the IJN.

*Sweepy-Time Gal* turned out to be the real prize, however, since the battered but intact wreck could be presented to the civilian population as proof that the JAAF could shoot down the huge American bombers that seemed to cruise over the city with impunity. A massive four-engine Liberator had never been placed on public display in Hong Kong, though pieces of other American aircraft had been deposited in Statue Square for public inspection. The tail of the twin-engine B-25 that First Lieutenant Allers had crash-landed near Canton had been brought to Statue Square after the first raids on Hong Kong in October 1942. As recently as February 1944, just two months before the loss of *Sweepy-Time Gal*, a mangled P-40 had been displayed outside a Japanese store in Hong Kong as a war trophy.[17] The plane had most likely been flown by First Lieutenant Kerr of the CACW, who had been shot down over Kai Tak on February 11 and evaded capture. Still, no American heavy bombers had ever come down in Hong Kong, leaving the Japanese garrison unable to prove that it could handle the giant American planes. The Japanese had repeatedly claimed to destroy large numbers of American bombers, as reported in the *Hongkong News*, but they had lacked any evidence to present to the civilian population. At long last *Sweepy-Time Gal* offered hard proof of the Japanese ability to take down the American Liberators.

Aware that they had just reaped a propaganda windfall, the Japanese wasted no time in hoisting the pieces of the wreck onto a lighter. The rear fuselage and tail had broken loose and had to be raised from the water separately from the wings and midsection of the fuselage. A tug towed the lighter to Victoria City, where a derrick swung the wreckage ashore. The Japanese puzzle-pieced the aircraft back together and left it resting flat on its belly like a dead bird in a poorly executed taxidermy project. This hardly mattered, however, since anyone viewing the wreck could clearly see the star-and-bars insignia of the USAAF on the dented fuselage, which made for first-rate propaganda photos. As an added bonus, the name *Sweepy-Time Gal* could still be made out on a salvaged piece of the disintegrated nose and cockpit.

At the St. John Ambulance Brigade headquarters, an IJN officer who spoke English showed McConnell the April 20 edition of the *Hongkong News* with its photograph of the wreckage of *Sweepy-Time Gal*. Given the mangled state of his aircraft, McConnell marveled at his own lack of injuries. Spadafora had been less fortunate, as he had fractured his right knee, but he could still count himself lucky. As far as McConnell and Spadafora knew, the other ten men in their crew had died in the crash or subsequent strafing of the wreck.

In fact a BAAG intelligence summary shared with the intelligence staff of the 68th Composite Wing in Kweilin reported that the bodies of two airmen from the crew of *Sweepy-Time Gal* had been brought ashore at Blake Pier, not far from where the wreck had been displayed along the harbor front. "They were thrown about as if to torture the men even when they were dead," stated the summary. "The bodies were on display for two days until they started to decompose."[18]

Though the aircraft remained on display for much longer than the bodies of the dead airmen, the wreckage eventually disappeared. A work crew armed with acetylene torches likely carved up the carcass for scrap metal. For more than two years, the Japanese administration had been systematically stripping Hong Kong of anything made of metal, including its colonial statuary. In the end a wharfside crane likely spooned chunks of *Sweepy-Time Gal* into the hold of a bulk carrier bound for the home islands with a load of scrap iron, steel, aluminum, and bronze for the blast furnaces.

McConnell likely made it to Japan first, however. Upon arrival at the St. John Ambulance Brigade headquarters, he had been subjected to several days of interrogation by IJN personnel. His initial refusal to divulge more than his name, rank, and serial number provoked a series of beatings with a ship's hawser, which the prison guards used to whip the back of his legs between his knees and buttocks. McConnell's interrogators asked various questions about 14th Air Force units in China, USAAF aircraft, and the training of American pilots. He soon lost interest in military secrecy and became focused entirely on saying whatever he thought might end the whippings with a rope heavy enough to tether a Kawanishi flying boat to a mooring buoy in the harbor. After several days of agonizing interrogation sessions, the IJN officer in charge of the holding facility apparently concluded that he could gain nothing more of use from the badly lashed American aviator. The beatings stopped, and the guards dumped McConnell in his cell, barefoot and handcuffed but otherwise left alone. To help him get through the chilly nights, the guards even gave him a leather flight jacket bearing the name of Tech. Sgt. Robert Berman, the radio operator aboard *Sweepy-Time Gal*. McConnell donned the coat without hesitation, though he assumed the coat had been stripped from Berman's dead body.

After McConnell had spent two weeks in the St. John Ambulance Brigade compound, the IJN locked him in a cage on a destroyer, which put to sea shortly thereafter. McConnell understood that if an American aircraft or submarine sank the destroyer, its IJN crew would not be unlocking his cage before the ship went under, but fortunately the vessel survived the increasingly perilous three-day sprint to Formosa. A bomber then flew McConnell to Japan, where he wound up in Ōfuna prison camp outside Yokohama. Spadafora eventually found himself there as well. The secret IJN-run compound held American and British POWs whom naval intelligence considered of high value, such as submarine crewmen, bomber pilots, radar and radio technicians, and fighter aces like U.S. Marine Corps major Gregory "Pappy" Boyington of the famed Black Sheep Squadron. McConnell had no opportunity to meet his fellow inmates, however, because as soon as he arrived at Ōfuna the guards locked him in solitary confinement, still barefoot and still clad in the leather jacket of his dead crewmate.

# 12

## Gulls, Pigeons, and Jays

Though B-24Ds like *Sweepy-Time Gal* had been loaded with some of the world's most cutting-edge radar gear when they rolled off the assembly line, the next generation of radar-equipped B-24Js soon went into production. This latest model of radar-equipped Liberator could do more than just detect maritime targets in total darkness or zero visibility. Using the automated low-altitude bombing (LAB) system, which meshed an onboard radar with a specialized bombsight, the B-24J LAB could lob five-hundred-pounders at ships without the pilots ever seeing the target.

In April 1944 twenty specially trained crews in an equal number of brand-new B-24Js configured for low-altitude bombing deployed over the Hump and entered service with the 308th Bomb Group. Ground crews painted the undersides of the new aircraft black to foil enemy searchlights and emblazoned some of the aircraft with the shark mouths that had become the signature of the 14th Air Force. In addition to the new radar system, the B-24J LABs carried extra fuel tanks in the bomb bays, which under ideal cruise-control conditions allowed aircraft to fly fifteen-hour missions. Since the aircraft would be operating at low altitude, the ball turrets had been stripped out. However, each of the J-model Liberators featured a power gun turret in the nose, which substantially increased the aircraft's forward firepower.

Equipped with their new radar system, the pilots and crewmen of the 308th dispensed with daylight sea sweeps and started working the night shift instead. Detachments of B-24 LABs—sometimes referred to as SB-24s—deployed to Kweilin and Liuchow. From these forward airbases in southeastern China, the B-24 LABs flew out into the South China Sea in search of targets.

At the usual search altitude of 2,500 to 5,000 feet, the SCR-717 search radar in the waist of a B-24 LAB could pick up targets as far as fifty miles away, though radar operators found that the unit worked most reliably out to thirty miles. When the radar operator detected a radar signature, the pilots circled the potential target at a range of ten to fifteen miles so that the operator could confirm the size and number of ships.

Once the specific target had been selected—LAB crews preferred lone ships or convoy stragglers—the pilots gradually decreased altitude to four hundred feet as they approached the target under the direction of the radar operator. All B-24 LABs carried an absolute altimeter, which allowed the pilots to descend to low altitude without plowing into the waves in the darkness. As an added safety feature, one of the gunners deployed the trailing wire radio antennae from a reel in the fuselage of the plane. The gunner kept one hand on the radio cable as it fluttered in the slipstream. If the metal weight— referred to by aircrew as a "fish"—at the end of the cable struck the water, the gunner would feel the impact through the line and could immediately use the interphone to call for an emergency ascent.

Maintaining an airspeed of about 170 miles per hour, the B-24 pilots approached the target ship at a forty-five-degree angle, which could be difficult to achieve against vessels taking evasive action or firing their antiaircraft weaponry. At this point the pilots handed over control of the aircraft to the bombardier in the nose compartment, who relied on a complex assemblage of symbiotic electronic equipment to make blind runs on ships in complete darkness. The search radar manned by the radar operator sent images to the AN/ APQ-5 system in the nose, which linked the Norden bombsight to an auxiliary radarscope. As the plane approached the ship, the bombardier kept his crosshairs centered on the target blip displayed in the radarscope, and the AFCE responded by adjusting the bearing of the aircraft. At the optimum moment, the AN/APQ-5 released the bombs automatically.

Though the AN/APQ-5 system chose when to release the bombs, the bombardier had to preset the number, spacing, and fusing of the bombs. Typically the bombardier opted to release three five-hundred-pound bombs per run with the intervelometer set so that they would impact fifty to seventy feet apart. He would usually fuse the bombs for a two- to five-second delay to ensure that they would penetrate the hull or the deck before exploding. Though the bomb load varied depending on the range of the mission and other factors, B-24 LABs typically carried ten to twelve five-hundred-pound GP bombs, which allowed for three or four runs on a target. The first run often took ships by surprise, which meant that if a B-24 LAB sank its target on the first go, the aircraft and its crew could escape without drawing any return fire. However, the risk of taking hits from antiaircraft fire dramatically increased if the ship remained afloat and the big, relatively slow-moving B-24 had to make additional bomb runs.

Between May 24 and October 31, 1944, the B-24 LABs from the 308th Bomb Group attacked 222 ships during 243 sea-sweep sorties. Exactly how many of those 222 ships actually sank remained difficult to determine, however, and not just because night missions often precluded visual confirmation of sinkings. The effectiveness of the radar units depended on the skill of the radar operator, the distance involved, weather conditions, coastal geography, and other variables. Shorelines, islands, and thunderstorms all confused the search radar and could fool even the best radar operator. Consequently, B-24 LAB crews sometimes mistook the radar echo of a rocky shoal or a small island for an enemy ship. Even the sails of Chinese junks could sometimes produce radar signatures that suggested a much larger vessel. B-24 LAB crews believed that they could tell whether a bomb had hit a ship or the water by the bomb flash and blast concussion. However, B-24 LABs sometimes bombed faux targets like reefs and islets, though the 308th eventually assembled charts of the patrol areas based on radarscope returns that reduced this problem. In addition the search radar could not reliably determine target size, meaning that a crew might claim to have sunk a merchant ship when it had actually sunk an unlucky Chinese junk. Even the fact that a ship had vanished from the radarscope after a bomb run could not necessarily be taken as proof that the ship had gone under, since any number of factors could take the ship off the radar screen. The finicky radar units sometimes malfunctioned, for example, and ships could blend into the radar signature of a coastline or two vessels could coalesce into one radar echo. The problem of B-24 LAB crews making duplicate claims further complicated matters. Though the LAB crews claimed to have sunk 67 of the 222 ships that they attacked between May 24 and October 31, postwar assessment could only confirm that 10 ships had been sent to the bottom.

Due to careful army-navy coordination, no American submarines numbered among the ships attacked by B-24 LAB crews. The army aviators flying the B-24 LABs worked in special zones designed to prevent friendly fire incidents. The naval officers operating the submarines had been briefed on the zones and knew to avoid them. Standing orders forbade the B-24 LAB crews from attacking ships outside their designated zones unless they hit a harbor. Free-fire zones for the B-24 LABs included a semicircle with a one-hundred-mile radius with Shanghai at its center. A second zone in the South China Sea included the Formosa Straight, the South China Sea approaches to Swatow, Hong Kong, and Hainan, and the Gulf of Tonkin. Everything outside those zones belonged to the submarines, which generally operated on the surface at night.

Hong Kong figured prominently in one of the most common search patterns flown from the airfield at Liuchow. On this search route, the B-24 LABs ventured from Liuchow out over the waters in the Hong Kong area, proceeded to the port of Takao on the southwestern coast of Formosa, and then returned down the south China seaboard to Hong Kong, which would be bombed as a secondary target if no ships had been found out at sea. Whenever possible pilots avoided returning to base with a full bomb bay, and Hong Kong became one of the preferred disposal points for excess ordnance.[1]

Known as "snoopers" to their crews, the B-24J LABs did more to wreck everyone's sleep in Hong Kong than any other kind of American aircraft. Nocturnal sea sweeps often failed to find any Japanese ships, which meant flight crews had to drop their bomb loads on Hong Kong in the middle of the night. B-24J LABS returning from fruitless sea sweeps flew one-plane raids on the Tai Koo dockyard on August 3 and the Kowloon dockyard on August 10, though due to a malfunctioning radar unit and a fumble on the part of the bombardier, the aircraft on the latter raid never released its bombs and returned to Liuchow with a full bomb bay. More one-plane raids followed on the Royal Navy dockyard on August 14, the HK and Whampoa dockyard on August 25, the oil tanks at Lai Chi Kok on September 7, and Tsim Sha Tsui on September 29 and 30.[2]

Japanese searchlight units at Hong Kong occasionally pinned one of these lone raiders in a beam of brilliant light so that the flak gunners could get a bead on the intruding aircraft. Though B-24 pilots could usually shake off the searchlight beam before taking any anti-aircraft fire, they had to execute the maneuver while temporarily blinded, as two rookie pilots discovered. Late in the afternoon of August 25, a "snooper" from the 375th Bomb Squadron piloted by 2nd Lt. Milton Wind and copiloted by 2nd Lt. Elmer E. Haynes took off from Liuchow to fly a sea sweep over the Tonkin Gulf. For both pilots as well as the rest of the crew, the flight marked their inaugural combat mission. Haynes had wondered how he would react to his first exposure to combat and discovered that flying the plane demanded all his attention and left little room for nerves. The sea sweep proved to be uneventful in any case. After failing to locate any ships in the vicinity of Hainan, the two pilots opted to hit their secondary target, the HK and Whampoa dockyard. With Second Lieutenant Wind at the controls, they overflew the harbor at seven thousand feet and commenced their bomb run.

Haynes felt a surge of exhilaration when the bombardier released all twelve of their five-hundred-pound bombs, nine of which impacted on the eastern fringe of the dockyard. However, this momentary elation turned to sudden terror when two searchlight beams filled the cockpit with a light that seemed brighter than the sun. Both pilots immediately lost their vision. Seconds later they heard flak bursts cracking behind them. Caught by surprise, Second Lieutenant Wind acted on instinct. He had to quite literally fly by feel, since he could not see anything except dazzling white light, but faced with no other option, Wind rolled over and dove for the deck as Haynes pulled down his sunglasses and sank low in his armored seat. Plummeting through the darkness, unable to see the instrument panel, they managed to shake the searchlight and pull out of the dive. Over the interphone the crew reported no damage or injuries, though they had all been knocked around like beads in a rattle. Roaring along at 1,500 feet over the Pearl River delta, Haynes suddenly realized that a cold sweat had glazed his entire body and soaked through his flight gear. Though the flak had never really frightened him, Haynes had no trouble admitting that the searchlight beams and the long swan dive in the darkness most certainly had. His trembling became so uncontrollably spastic that he began to doubt whether he could still pilot the aircraft. Strapped in beside him in the captain's seat, Second Lieutenant Wind looked no better, but between them they wrestled the aircraft back to Liuchow and completed their inaugural combat mission.[3]

To complement the nocturnal activities of the radar-equipped B-24 LABS, the B-25s of the 341st Bomb Group continued to fly visual sea sweeps during daylight hours in late spring and early summer of 1944. The 341st belonged to the Kunming-based 69th Composite Wing, but the wing routinely seconded detachments to the Kweilin-based 68th Composite Wing under the leadership of Colonel Vincent. Due to their shorter range, the B-25s had to operate closer to shore, but they found no shortage of maritime targets along the coast. On May 12 the B-25s caught the IJNS *Saga* of the 2nd CEF near Lantau. Built in 1912 the 208-foot *Saga* hardly represented the cream of the IJNS, but its crew could still put up a fight with a trio of 3.1-inch antiaircraft guns and a battery of machine guns. The ship had survived an attack by P-38s in 1943 with minor damage, and its luck continued to hold out as it steamed beneath the brooding mountains of Lantau. Though thoroughly strafed, the little river gunboat once again escaped serious harm.[4]

IN MID-APRIL 1944 the IJA launched Ichigō sakusen—Operation Number One—an ambitious, multiphased ground offensive involving twenty divisions, eight hundred tanks and armored cars, 1,550 artillery pieces, 15,550 trucks, and one hundred thousand cavalry, draft, and pack horses.[5] From a strategic standpoint, the offensive had three basic objectives. First, the IJA would capture Kweilin and the other American airbases in southeastern China so that the USAAF would be unable to use these airfields as bases for flying sea sweeps or, more crucially, as launch points for future strategic bombing raids on Japan. Second, the offensive would drive south through Hubei, Hunan, and Kwangsi Provinces to open up an overland supply route between Southeast Asia and northern China. Third, in the process of accomplishing the first two objectives, the IJA would rout the Nationalist Chinese army and knock Chiang Kai-shek—whose best troops had been sent to Burma at Allied insistence and whose warnings about the impending offensive had been discounted by Allied intelligence—out of the war once and for all.[6]

Like so many of the previous campaigns fought on Chinese soil, the route of the national rail network determined the lines of advance for Ichigō. A single rail line ran like a spine down the length of the country from north to south, passing through territory controlled by both Chinese and Japanese forces. Like ribs connecting to the spine, spur railways ran inland from the port cities of Shanghai and Canton to connect with the main north-south railroad line. The IJA planned to focus its assault on three Chinese-held sections of the national railway grid: the portion that ran from Hankow north to Peking, the portion that ran from Liuchow north to Hankow, and the portion that ran from Canton north to Hengyang. Control of these railway lines would allow the Japanese to move raw materials and other critically needed supplies overland from Southeast Asia rather than by sea, where Japanese shipping had been decimated by American aircraft and submarines. Japanese-held China, Manchuria, and Korea would gain an internal supply line running north from Hanoi and Saigon. Moreover, raw materials moving along this supply line could be transshipped across the relatively secure Sea of Japan to the home islands.

GULLS, PIGEONS, AND JAYS

In mid-April the IJA launched the initial phase of the offensive, which sought to capture the last Chinese-controlled portions of the Hankow-Peking railway. IJA troops surged north from occupied Hankow, which sat astride the railway, while additional units moved south from Kaifeng in the north. The two converging columns punched through the Nationalist army lines and gained complete control of the Hankow-Peking railway line in early May. The IJA executed the next phase of the offensive when troops surged south out of Hankow and captured Changsha, the first Chinese-held city on the rail line below Hankow, on June 18.

In response to the threat posed by the offensive, General Chennault directed the 68th Composite Wing under the newly promoted Brigadier General Vincent to support the Chinese defense of Hengyang, the next major city south of Changsha. Though the Nationalist army resisted with inspired tenacity, the IJA nonetheless captured the Hengyang airbase at the end of June and the city itself on August 8. Both the 68th Composite Wing and the 308th Bomb Group continued to harry the advancing IJA, but the offensive had broken the Nationalist army and could not be stopped. Both Chennault and Vincent understood that more American airbases would be lost in the months to come.[7]

With the 68th Composite Wing committed to slowing the Ichigō offensive, the 11th and 491st Bomb Squadrons had to ratchet back their antishipping work. Daylight sea sweeps by B-25s had been almost entirely curtailed by the end of June. The few overwater missions flown by B-25 crews for the rest of 1944 remained sporadic sideshows to what had become the primary mission of the 11th and 491st Bomb Squadrons: close air support for the Nationalist Chinese army, air interdiction of IJA supply lines, and destruction of JAAF air assets.[8]

Operating out of Liuchow, the 11th and 491st Bomb Squadrons flew daylight strikes designed to slow the advance of Japanese troops during Ichigō, while at night the squadrons focused on suppressing JAAF air units, which had been doubled in strength to more than 240 aircraft tasked with supporting the ground offensive.[9] The two squadrons regularly hit Tien Ho, White Cloud, and Kai Tak airfields, with occasional targeting of dockyards, wharves, river traffic, and other targets. Since the B-25s lacked the numbers and payloads to knock out the airfields, the missions sought to hound and harass the JAAF instead. Between July 4 and October 6, the 11th and 491st Bomb Squadrons hit the airfields on twenty-five different nights. A typical mission called for anywhere from two to twelve Gulls, Pigeons, and Jays—as the 491st referred to the different models of their B-25s—from either or both squadrons to execute staggered takeoffs so that each B-25 arrived over White Cloud or Tien Ho airfield just as the previous aircraft peeled off to head home. To maximize surprise they avoided flying over Japanese-held towns where the garrison could phone a warning to Canton. With six to twelve aircraft, the Canton airfields could be harried from dusk to dawn. A variant of the mission plan called for a single aircraft to loiter over the target and release its payload incrementally as it made multiple runs spread out over an hour or more.

To keep the Japanese guessing, the Mitchells always approached the target zone from different directions and bombed from a wide variety of altitudes ranging from 1,000 to 9,500 feet, though one flight crew executing evasive maneuvers bottomed out at 50 feet and then shattered a searchlight with its .50 calibers. Pilots flew at airspeeds of 180 to 270 miles per hour and carried a wide variety of munitions. They dropped 100-pound AN-M30 GP demos as well as 100-kilogram GP demolition bombs—likely of Russian manufacture—and AN-M1 clusters of six 20-pound fragmentation bombs with the noses fused for instant detonation. They dropped 100-pound incendiary bombs in train with the intervelometer set for either 100, 200, or even 300 feet and started fires visible to the tail gunners when the pilots had put sixty miles behind them. They released 250-pound AN-M57s. They pickled 500-pound AN-M43s, some with delayed fusing set to detonate anywhere from one to twelve hours after the raid. They hauled 500-pound incendiary clusters. They scattered packages of JM-3 and JA-5 propaganda leaflets. They dumped parachute fragmentation bombs. On rare occasions they toggled AN-M44 1,000-pounders packed with a mix of Amatol and TNT. They hurled invectives when pink gouts of flak went off like flashbulbs in front of the windshield. When searchlights flooded the cockpit with eye-dazzling illumination, they dispatched prayers to the Almighty.

Japanese reactions to these harassment raids varied, and on some nights the B-25 crews could spot the airfields from miles away because the runway lights were on. On other evenings the entire delta hid in complete darkness. Sometimes the searchlight beams scissored smoothly across the sky and pinned bombers where the beams crossed. Sometimes the searchlights seemed uncoordinated and jerky, as if manually operated, and flailed about without ever spotting a B-25. Sometimes the searchlight crews never turned on their beams at all, but strings of red tracers rose up toward the B-25s, and white, yellow, pink, red, and orange bursts of flak flashed in the skies. In their mission reports filed after such nights, the crews simply referred to the fire as "intense." On one mission over Kai Tak, a bomber crew observed the firing of a projectile with a reddish streamer that appeared to be a rocket, which arced above the aircraft without exploding. On still other nights Japanese night-fighters prowled in search of the B-25s. And on some nights, all remained silent and dark—no searchlights, no tracer fire, no flak bursts, no night-fighters, and no mystery rockets.

Nocturnal raids worked just as well for the JAAF, which often dispatched night intruders to the field at Liuchow. On September 23 Japanese bombers took out two B-25s and twelve thousand gallons of precious aviation fuel. Just four days later, the JAAF caught a P-51 on the ground and ignited another sixteen thousand gallons of avgas. On September 28 Japanese bombers damaged a B-25 and then did even better on September 29, when they set another eleven thousand gallons of fuel ablaze. On October 4 a series of well-placed fragmentation bombs wrecked a P-51 and left a B-25 tilted on a flat right tire and thoroughly sieved in the wings, fuselage, and tail assembly.[10]

During the raids flown over the airfields at Canton and Hong

Kong, more than one B-25 got slammed by the concussion of flak bursts that detonated close enough to light up the interior of the darkened aircraft. However terrifying the flak nonetheless proved to be highly inaccurate. During the twenty-five missions flown over the airfields, just three B-25s returned to base with shrapnel gouges and 7.7 mm machine-gun bullet holes. Not a single aircraft went down as a result of enemy action. However, for reasons unknown one B-25 from the 491st Bomb Squadron crashed in a rice paddy shortly after takeoff and exploded, killing all seven crew members, and one B-25 from the 11th Bomb Squadron ran out of gas on the return leg. The crew of the latter aircraft bailed out over friendly territory and reported for duty at Kweilin two weeks later.[11]

LIKE ALL THE units in the 14th Air Force, the 308th Bomb Group functioned as a jack-of-all-trades outfit capable of flying a wide variety of missions. Consummate multitaskers, the pilots and crewmen of the Kunming-based 308th chewed up Japanese supply lines to slow the momentum of the Japanese advance during Ichigō. They provided close air support, and on a few occasions the B-24s even got down on the deck and functioned as gunships. Flying low enough to graze the treetops, gunners spat out streams of tracer fire at IJA cavalry and armored units. In addition the hard-pressed unit also continued to fly nocturnal sea sweeps over the South China Sea. With their long-range capabilities, the B-24 LABs could still patrol far from shore even with the loss of forward airbases to the fury of Ichigō. They mined rivers and harbors, too. Whenever a full moon and favorable weather conditions converged, the 308th also ran night raids on various targets, including the same Canton airfields that the B-25s had been harassing with such dogged persistence.

During the summer of 1944, the 308th Bomb Group targeted Canton with two-dozen aircraft on the night of June 15, seventeen aircraft on the night of July 5, and eighteen aircraft on the night of July 8. Straight B-24Js without radar flew these missions, which necessitated visual bomb runs. For this reason each raid coincided with the full-moon conditions necessary for night bombing. Like the B-25s that had been harassing the Canton airfields, the Liberators carried a mix of one-hundred-pound bombs, including AN-M1 fragmentation clusters, AN-M30 GPS, and AN-M47 incendiaries. Overcast conditions and ground haze reduced bombing accuracy to a humbling 60 percent on the first mission, but during the second mission accuracy improved to a more respectable 80 percent. For the third mission, the overcast conditions and ground haze again interfered, causing a third of the strike force to hit alternative targets in the Canton area. Like a string of giant Chinese firecrackers, the one-hundred-pounders dropped during each raid banged their way across assorted godowns, oil depots, railroad yards, barracks, runways, and revetments. Each raid left flames, the agonized cries of wounded men, and a trail of craters four feet deep and nearly as wide. After the July 5 raid, some of the tail gunners reported that they could still see the glow of the conflagrations ignited by the incendiaries when their planes had flown one hundred miles back toward Kunming. Searchlights and flak menaced each raid, but only one "boxcar" went down during the three night raids on Canton. While returning from the run on July 8, one B-24 failed to make the field, and the entire crew had to bail out five miles short of Kunming. One of the gunners broke a leg, but everyone else returned to duty within twenty-four hours.[12]

On September 30 the 308th took advantage of the moonlight and dispatched twenty-nine aircraft to pummel Tien Ho airfield at Canton. Virtually every straight B-24 in the group went on the raid, including the B-24 piloted by Second Lieutenant Wind and his copilot, Second Lieutenant Haynes, who now had eleven missions recorded in his flight log. Even some of the precious B-24 LABS joined the mission to serve as pathfinder aircraft. While inbound to the target, the squadrons ran into a violent weather front. Faced with thick curtains of rain and a cauldron of thunderstorms boiling up to twenty thousand feet, the formation broke up, and each aircraft proceeded to the target individually. With the help of a good navigator, who charted a southerly course that allowed them to skirt the worst of the weather, Wind and Haynes popped out of the clouds above Tien Ho, which stood out brightly in the moonlight. Their aircraft stood out equally well to antiaircraft units on the ground, however, and searchlights started probing for their B-24 as flak rounds began flashing in the air around them. When the two lieutenants returned to Kunming, they discovered that only thirteen other aircraft had unloaded their payload of one-hundred-pound fragmentation and demolition bombs, and only half of these were over Tien Ho when they did so. Eight of their fellow pilots had turned back after yanking their salvo handles and jettisoning their bombs, while another seven pilots had opted to truck their bombs back to base—a risky practice made necessary by the general shortage of ordnance, which had to be flown over the Hump along with fuel, spare parts, and everything else the unit needed to stay in business. "Overall," Haynes would later write with laconic understatement, "the strike was not very successful."[13]

ON TOP OF the sea-sweep missions, the daylight interdiction of Japanese supply lines, and the nighttime bombing of the Canton airfields, the 308th returned to its project of mining harbors along the coast of occupied China and French Indochina in June 1944. By blocking harbor channels with airdropped mines, the 308th sought to deny the enemy the use of key ports like Hong Kong and Canton. Rendering these harbors unusable remained the primary goal, while sinking ships ranked as a secondary, albeit important, objective of the operation. Any vessel sunk in the relatively shallow channels where the mines would be dropped would block the passage to maritime traffic, though that same shallow water meant that sunken vessels could be raised, towed to dry dock, and repaired.

On moonlit nights between June and August, the 308th sent at least seven different mine-laying missions to block the Pearl River and the eastern and western channels into Victoria Harbor. On each mission the army provided the aircraft and aircrew, while the navy provided the one-thousand-pound magnetic and acoustic mines—airlifted over the Hump like everything else used by the 14th Air Force. A navy officer joined the army crew of each B-24 and fused the mine, advised the pilots on the where and when of dropping the mine, and charted its location once it splashed.

As each aircraft approached the target, the pilots shut off all navigation and formation lights and then throttled back to about 150 miles per hour to reduce the telltale glow of the engine exhaust. Each plane flew alone along a predetermined course from a preset checkpoint to assure accurate placement of the mines. Weaving in and out of islands and fogbanks in the luminous moonlight, the B-24 pilots looked for the cables strung between islands that they had been briefed to watch out for. Army intelligence believed that the Japanese had erected these cables to catch low-flying American planes, and while no B-24 ever ran into any of the rumored cables, at least one pilot claimed that he flew so low he could look up into the brightly lit portholes of Japanese ships.

Flying at the recommended drop altitude of two hundred to four hundred feet, the B-24s placed mines in the narrow eastern entrance to Victoria Harbor at Lei Yue Mun, between Lai Chi Kok and the western end of Hong Kong Island, in the Sulphur Channel between Green Island and Hong Kong Island, in the Rambler Channel between Tsing Yi and Tsuen Wan, and in the Ma Wan and Kap Shui Mun channels at the northern end of Lantau Island. In total the 308th dropped nearly 170 mines, each capable of sinking a large ship, and lost just one mine-laying B-24 in the process to causes unknown, but likely not a steel cable strung like a giant spider web across one of the channels.

Both the magnetic and the acoustic mines—the former triggered by the proximity of a metal hull and the latter by the noise of a passing ship—could be cleared by IJN minesweepers, but dropping a mix of the two types made sweeping much more difficult. In any case the IJN did not have an adequate number of minesweeping vessels stationed along the China coast, and by the beginning of September, the 14th Air Force believed that the channels into Victoria Harbor had been completely blocked. The 308th flew two more mine-laying missions at the end of September to refresh the cordon with a new set of mines to replace those that had exploded, drifted loose, sunk too deeply into the mud, or been disabled by the Japanese. As might be expected, Japanese vessels struck mines at a steady rate, including the IJNS *Saga*. The gunboat hit a mine in the Kap Shui Mun strait on September 26 and foundered in shallow water, thus putting out of action one of the few oceangoing escort vessels of the 2nd CEF.[14]

ON OCTOBER 5 Capt. Hajime Saito led the 1st Chutai of the 85th Sentai into battle over the suburbs of Canton with seventeen aircraft, proving that the extensive pounding of Tien Ho and White Cloud had failed to put the JAAF out of business. The pilots of the 85th Sentai had recently received nine brand-new Ki-84s, which represented the apex of Japanese aviation design. Just the day before Lt. Col. Yukiyoshi Wakamatsu, executive officer of the 85th Sentai, had flown his mint Ki-84 into combat for the first time and downed an American P-51. Two other pilots from the 85th had bagged two more Mustangs during the same encounter, so as Captain Saito flew over Canton that day he felt confident that the Ki-84 could hold its own against the best American aircraft.

At the start of Ichigō in April 1944, the 85th Sentai had possessed thirty-two operational Ki-44-IIs split between Canton and Hankow but not nearly enough experienced pilots to fly them. To rectify this problem, the unit added a fourth training *chutai* equipped with eight Ki-43-IIs for inexperienced replacement pilots who needed more training before flying the hard-to-handle Ki-44 Shōki. When the 85th Sentai received its first six Ki-84s in late September 1944, they went to the few remaining veteran pilots, including Lieutenant Colonel Wakamatsu and Captain Saito, who had taken over the command of the 1st Chutai after the death of the squadron commander in December 1943.

The Nakajima Ki-84 Hayate—variously translated as "Hurricane," "Gale," or some other form of violent storm—first went into service in April 1944. As a fighter the Ki-84 combined the range and maneuverability of the Ki-43 with the speed, climb rate, and heavy armament of the Ki-44. Equipped with a Ha-45 air-cooled

**1.** Col. Robert L. Scott stands in front of his P-40, which displays ten kill flags below the cockpit. Air Force Historical Research Agency, Iris no. 106440.

**2.** Col. Bruce K. Holloway sits in his P-40K with a canine companion. Air Force Historical Research Agency, Iris no. 106440.

**3.** Lt. Col. David "Tex" Hill stands by the nose of his shark-mouth P-40. Air Force Historical Research Agency, Iris no. 106440.

**4.** Eleven P-40s with drop tanks on the flight line at Kweilin. Air Force Historical Research Agency, Iris no. 106440.

**5.** Armorers clean and oil the .50-caliber wing guns of a P-40 while a mechanic stands atop a garbage can to work on the innards of the propeller assembly. Air Force Historical Research Agency, Iris no. 106440.

**6.** Nationalist Chinese soldier guarding American C-47 transport planes at Kweilin. Air Force Historical Research Agency, Iris no. 106440.

**7.** Chinese construction workers pulled giant rollers to pack down the gravel runway at Kweilin, where most repair work was done by hand. Air Force Historical Research Agency, Iris no. 106440.

**8.** B-25 Mitchell of the type flown by the 11th Bomb Squadron over Hong Kong in October 1942. Special Collections and University Archives, Grand Valley State University, Naval Recognition Training Slides.

**9.** A B-25 sits in a revetment at Kweilin with a stockpile of bombs in the foreground. Air Force Historical Research Agency, Iris no. 106440.

**10.** Airmen and ground crew pose with a B-25H armed with eight .50-caliber nose guns and a 75 mm cannon. Air Force Historical Research Agency, Iris no. 106440.

**11.** Recon photo taken by the 21st Photographic Reconnaissance Squadron on November 16, 1943, depicts the tip of the Kowloon Peninsula (*left*) and the HK and Whampoa dockyard at Hung Hom (*right*). Air Force Historical Research Agency, Iris no. 916428.

**12.** Flying on the deck, B-25s from the 11th Bomb Squadron caught a Japanese freighter in Victoria Harbor on November 16, 1943. Air Force Historical Research Agency, Iris no. 106440.

**13.** Capt. Richard D. Furbush with air evacuation nurse Lt. Eula M. Blackburn, likely aboard a C-47 leaving from Kweilin. Air Force Historical Research Agency, Iris no. 106440.

**14.** As the Japanese army approached, Chinese workers buried one-thousand-pound bombs in preparation to blow the runways at Kweilin in September 1944. Air Force Historical Research Agency, Iris no. 106440.

*FTC* *2900 GT*

*64th. Target*

*Before Bombing*

**15.** (*opposite top*) Bracketed by flak bursts, B-24s from the 90th Bomb Group hit the HK and Whampoa dockyard on April 2, 1945. Air Force Historical Research Agency, Iris no. 81021.

**16.** (*opposite bottom*) A Lockheed P-38 Lightning similar to the one piloted by Lt. Col. Gerald R. Johnson, who shot down a Japanese Ki-44 over Hong Kong on April 2, 1945. Special Collections and University Archives, Grand Valley State University, Naval Recognition Training Slides.

**17.** (*above*) B-24s from the 43rd Bomb Group sank a Fox Tare Charlie (FTC) anchored to the north of the Royal Navy dockyard on April 3, 1945. Air Force Historical Research Agency, Iris no. 79878.

**18.** A B-24 from the 43rd Bomb Group over Kowloon and Stonecutters Island, with the rectangular compound of the Sham Shui Po POW camp visible in the lower center of the photo. Air Force Historical Research Agency, Iris no. 79878.

**19.** (*opposite top*) A B-24 from the 43rd Bomb Group over the Canton airfields on May 9, 1945. Air Force Historical Research Agency, Iris no. 79879.

**20.** (*opposite bottom*) A fifty-five-gallon drum of napalm of the kind dropped by the 22nd and 43rd Bomb Groups on the Causeway Bay area of Hong Kong Island on June 12, 1945. Air Force Historical Research Agency, Iris no. 79879.

FIRST DAYLIGHT MISSION
OVER THE CHINA MAINLAND

**21.** Second Lt. Robert W. Jensen, the future pilot of *Bold Venture*, standing next to a B-25 during flight training at Columbia Army Air Base in South Carolina. Courtesy of Chris McWilliams.

**22.** The heavily armed B-25J nicknamed *Bold Venture* packed nine .50-caliber nose and cheek guns, plus two more in the top turret. Courtesy of Chris McWilliams.

radial engine rated at 1,875 horsepower, a Hayate in top form could hit 427 miles per hour, making it the fastest Japanese fighter of the war. Moreover, it could ascend to ten thousand feet in 2.6 minutes, which meant it could outclimb the P-51H and P-47N, though these two U.S. fighters had a slightly higher top speed in level flight. With a range of 1,800 miles when equipped with two 175-gallon drop tanks, the Ki-84 had about the same endurance as a P-51H, one of the longest-ranging fighters of the war. Earlier generations of Japanese fighters like the Ki-43 and A6M had lacked the rugged construction of American fighter aircraft. However, the Ki-84 featured a sturdy airframe, bulletproof windshield, self-sealing fuel tanks, and armor for the pilot. Armed with two Type-103 12.7 mm heavy machine guns in the cowling and two Type-5 20 mm cannons in the wings, the Ki-84 also carried a much heavier weapons package than the earlier Japanese fighters. In the hands of an experienced pilot, the Ki-84 could match anything the Americans flew, including the P-51 and the F6F Hellcat.[15]

Captain Saito flew a Ki-84 that day along with five other pilots. Eleven other pilots went aloft in Ki-44s, the workhorse of the 85th Sentai. Together the seventeen pilots attempted to intercept an American formation of twelve B-25s just after the Mitchell pilots had completed their bomb run on Samshui to the west of Canton. An escort of twelve P-51s and seven P-40s from the 118th Tactical Reconnaissance Squadron (TRS) and the 76th Fighter Squadron interceded, and in the ensuing battle the Americans shot down Captain Saito in his Ki-84. Sgt. Maj. Toshiji Shoji and Staff Sergeant Nishimori also went down while flying Ki-44s. None of the three pilots bailed out. The pilot of a fourth Ki-44 force landed due to battle damage but walked away from the wreck. When the 118th TRS returned to Liuchow, the American pilots debriefed and concluded they had downed three enemy fighters for certain, probably dispatched a fourth, and damaged two additional fighters. This tally represented a surprisingly precise estimate given the difficulty of making accurate observations during the disjointed, whirling, split-second dramas of air-to-air combat. Due to the visual similarities of the Ki-44 and ki-84, however, none of the American aviators seemed to know that they had gone up against seasoned JAAF pilots flying the ki-84, arguably the best all-around Japanese fighter of the war.

In their own debriefing, the fourteen surviving pilots of the 85th Sentai concluded that they had downed one or possibly two B-25s along with four or five P-51s. In fact two B-25s had sustained multiple hits in the cockpit area, injuring five crewmen, and three fighter pilots had returned to Liuchow with bullet-holed Mustangs, but only one American plane had been dispatched by the guns of the 85th Sentai. An unknown Japanese pilot managed to stitch the Mustang flown by 2nd Lt. Jack E. Gocke, who saw black-and-white smoke pouring from his engine as it began to vibrate in its final death throes. Gocke pulled into the overcast, jettisoned his canopy, and prepared to go over the side. His Mustang then popped back out of the clouds and promptly attracted the attention of a ki-44 pilot, who came at Gocke in a head-on dive. Gocke dropped back into his seat, lifted the nose of his Mustang, fired a long burst, and saw the ki-44—perhaps piloted by Shoji or Nishimori—trail smoke and fire as it continued diving past his aircraft. With his propeller barely spinning, Gocke crawled out on the wing just before his Mustang snapped into its final stall. Whipped clear from the wing, he smashed both legs against the rear stabilizer and tumbled ragdoll-style into the slipstream. Moments later Gocke's chute slapped open, and as he began drifting to earth with a broken femur, he watched the ki-44 dive into the ground and explode. He saw no other pilots hanging from a parachute, so he knew with certainty that he had just killed a Japanese pilot. Gocke evaded capture and walked out—or more accurately, was carried out—and returned to the 118th TRS on October 20.[16]

To maintain steady pressure on the 85th Sentai and other surviving air units in Canton, the 308th Bomb Group planned a daylight raid on White Cloud airfield. On October 15 Second Lieutenant Haynes took off from Kunming on his nineteenth mission as a B-24 pilot. While a few of the missions had involved nothing more than moving his plane from one airfield to another, the majority had been combat missions or equally perilous flights over the Hump.

Haynes had lost more than a few friends since arriving in China, and this trauma transformed every combat mission into an act of vengeance. Still, although he rarely discussed the matter with his fellow pilots, Haynes knew in his gut that with each mission his chance of surviving the war decreased.

Haynes welcomed anything that would improve the odds, such as the close escort of P-40s from the 76th Fighter Squadron and the 118th TRS that rendezvoused with his diamond-shaped formation of B-24s. He could occasionally catch sight of the Mustangs flying top cover, and while he couldn't count the number, he guessed that at least thirty P-51s had taken up station overhead. Inbound to Canton two boxcars aborted the mission—always a difficult call for the pilot and certainly a controversial action without hard proof of mechanical failure, such as a dead engine—and banked back toward Kunming. As the twenty-six-plane formation of B-24s approached White Cloud at midafternoon, the gunners aboard Haynes's aircraft started calling out sightings of Japanese fighters.

Two pilots from the 85th Sentai swooped down from six o'clock high and ambushed one of the elements in the top cover in a move taken from the playbook of American P-40 pilots. Both JAAF aviators shot up the Mustang flown by 2nd Lt. Jerome F. Eisenman of the 76th Fighter Squadron, who had evidently failed to check his six. Trailing coolant and white smoke, his aircraft headed straight down toward White Cloud in a seventy-degree dive.

As the aerial melee continued, the badly outnumbered pilots from the 85th Sentai abandoned any hope of reaching the bombers and focused on fending off the far more numerous P-51s. Second Lieutenant Haynes watched from his cockpit window as Sgt. Major Hiroji Shimoda and Sgt. Tatsuji Uebo went down with their planes. Heavy machine-gun rounds hammered the Ki-84 flown by Warrant Office Akiyoshi Nomura, who bailed out after his left wing tank ignited and began trailing a plume of flaming aviation fuel.

Flying at seventeen thousand feet and passing through scattered clouds and inaccurate flak bursts, Second Lieutenant Haynes felt his Liberator respond to the sudden release of weight as the bombs left the bomb bay. All twenty-six boxcars rained one-hundred-pound fragmentation bombs on the aircraft revetments at White Cloud. "Vengeance," Haynes thought and then focused on maintaining position as the formation executed its combat break and swung back on its return bearing to Kunming.

After a successful bailout from his burning Ki-84, Warrant Office Nomura had the good fortune to land among friendly Chinese who helped him return to his unit. Second Lieutenant Eisenman's squadron mates assumed he had augured in at the end of his seventy-degree dive, but Eisenman had actually managed to punch out and drift to earth. Hospitable locals took care of him just as they had taken care of Nomura, and the American pilot walked out, returning from the dead as well as for duty at the very end of October.[17]

ON THE CLEAR-SKIED afternoon of October 16, 1944, the air-raid siren blared at the Sham Shui Po camp in Kowloon. As usual the camp guards ordered the prisoners into the meager shelter offered by their barracks, but many of the men peered eagerly out windows and doors in the hopes of catching a glimpse of the Yankee flyboys. Graham Heywood thought it prudent to take cover under his iron-framed army cot.

"They're coming, boys; they're coming!" his fellow prisoners exclaimed not long after the air-raid siren had sounded.

"Can you see them?" Heywood asked from beneath his cot.

"Not yet," one of the prisoners said as he craned his neck out the window. "Yes, I can now . . . coming straight overhead. One, two, three . . . it's a big formation of bombers. I make it twenty-eight altogether, not counting those fighters in attendance. By Jove! This is the biggest raid we have had yet!"[18]

Those prisoners who dared to keep watching saw puffs of flak chase the high-flying B-24s, which glinted silver in the sunlight and stayed bunched in a tight formation despite the antiaircraft fire. Moments later a grand total of 294 bombs from the 308th Bomb Group whistled earthward toward the HK and Whampoa dockyard from seventeen thousand feet. Falling short, ten of the five-hundred-pounders burst among some garden plots on a hillside half a mile north of the dockyard. Another twenty-eight went into the water west of the docks. A cluster of twenty-two bombs fell into the civilian neighborhood adjacent to the docks, igniting the gasoline supplies stored in the British-built air-raid tunnels on Chatham Road, while ten bombs bracketed an armed passenger ship offshore from the Tai Koo dockyard. All the rest of the ordnance—about 76 percent of the bombs released—fell within the perimeter of the HK and Whampoa dockyard.

JAAF fighter pilots from the 85th Sentai harassed the formation throughout its bomb run and penetrated the screen of American P-51s, provoking sustained fire from the B-24 gunners. At least one JAAF pilot approached close enough for the gunners to see the red *hinomaru* on his wings. Still, the JAAF pilots failed to score any hits on the bombers and had to spend most of their time dodging P-51 pilots from the 76th Fighter Squadron and the 118th TRS.

As the floor of the barracks trembled with the reverberations of the American bombs, Heywood stayed under cover beneath his cot and mattress. He knew from past raids that plenty of rubbish would soon start falling on the camp—shards of flak shrapnel, spent machine-gun bullets, and stray automatic cannon rounds.

"Hullo, are you comfortable under there?" one of the younger prisoners asked Heywood as he dashed back and forth from window to door, trying to catch a glimpse of the bombers.

"Quite, thank you; tell me what's going on."

"Come and see for yourself. You won't get hit unless the bomb has your name on it!"

"Well, I'm taking no chances. It would be just too bad to be bumped off in an Allied air raid."

"Look at this!" another soldier shouted from the door as the unmistakable roar of aircraft engines filled the barracks. "My God, look at this! You can even see the stars on their wings!"[19]

Hedgehopping over the roofs of Kowloon at a mere seventy-five feet, seven B-25s from the 11th and 491st Bomb Squadrons swept over the Sham Shui Po camp in line abreast formation. A top cover of eight P-40s followed in train. The pilots could see dozens of ships spread out before them in the harbor, which despite initial and rather optimistic assessments by 14th Air Force intelligence staff had not been closed by the mines dropped by the 308th Bomb Group. Reconnaissance photos in early October had revealed a port clogged with more than forty merchant ships, a dozen patrol vessels, and innumerable small craft. Faced with this bonanza of maritime targets, General Vincent had ordered the 68th Composite Wing to go after Hong Kong even though the wing had been fully committed to slowing the Ichigō offensive.

Heywood heard the deafening clatter of machine guns as the B-25 pilots triggered their nose guns. In response the camp guards fired rifles at the bombers. Heavier antiaircraft fire crackled and boomed from the harbor. Shell casings ejected from the .50 calibers aboard the B-25s dinged and rattled on the barracks roof as the aircraft roared past at 250 miles per hour.

Though the B-25 pilots had planned to time their attack with the bombing of the HK and Whampoa dockyard in the hopes that this would distract Japanese flak defenses, they arrived a few minutes after the B-24s and faced fully alerted gun crews. As the B-25 pilots approached the harbor, they could see rapid sequences of red muzzle flashes on the decks of the many ships spread out before them at right angles. They spotted additional fire coming from gun positions on Stonecutters Island as well. Tracers arched toward them and flashed past to either side of the cockpit. White and black puffs from exploding shells danced just above the surface of the water. Short rounds foamed into the harbor in bursts of spray.

To suppress the incoming fire, the B-25 pilots and gunners strafed any ship where they saw muzzle flashes. The formation of seven aircraft included three H-models with a 75 mm pack howitzer in the nose—a weapon that usually served as a light artillery piece pulled behind a jeep or, when broken down, carried by a team of pack animals. A series of booms punctuated the chatter of the .50 calibers as the lone pilot aboard each B-25H fired howitzer shells into the hulls and the superstructure of various ships moored in the harbor. Unlike all the other models of the B-25, the H-version had just one pilot and no bombardier. In a well located behind and below the pilot, the navigator rapidly hand-loaded each cannon round in a role not all that different from an artilleryman. The pilot, meanwhile, had to fly the aircraft and fire the cannon.

As they winged into the cauldron of flak fire, the B-25s immediately started taking hits from machine guns and automatic antiaircraft cannon. One B-25 absorbed an explosive 25 mm round in the left engine nacelle, though the big Wright-Cyclone kept spinning, and then sponged up still more machine-gun rounds in the bomb bay. Another B-25 took a similar engine hit as well as a shell that punctured the retracted nose wheel and penetrated the flight deck, where it blew out the windows and shredded the pilot's parachute without harming the pilot, though the navigator received multiple lacerations to the head. Still more machine-gun rounds tore through the nose and tail. A well-aimed volley of machine-gun bullets shattered the Plexiglas of the tail turret in a third B-25, though the gunner escaped injury. A fourth B-25 caught an explosive round that blew off the escape hatch in the top of the cockpit, shattering most of the windows and wrecking much of the instrument panel. A red-hot spray of shrapnel ripped into the bombardier, radio-gunner, and pilot. Though no longer able to operate the 75 mm cannon, the flight crew kept the plane airborne despite the 250-mile-per-hour wind blasting through the cracked-open cockpit.

Acting on instinct, adrenaline, and muscle memory, the B-25 crews selected targets and released their five-hundred-pounders, spat streams of tracer fire, and banged out 75 mm cannon rounds. White geysers of water erupted throughout the harbor as forty-two bombs exploded in rapid succession. Some vessels began to burn, while others settled low in the water. Though the H-model B-25s fired eleven 75 mm cannon rounds, only one aircraft scored any hits. The well-trained crew fired seven rounds, which amounted to a rate of fire of roughly one howitzer shell every 6.5 seconds, and scored three hits on a freighter, plus one shell lobbed into a warehouse for good measure. Ships lucky enough to avoid a bomb or a howitzer shell still got raked by ten thousand rounds of .50-caliber machine-gun fire, which tore up deck planking, punched holes through the superstructure, blew out portholes, and tore apart the sailors manning the antiaircraft guns. Many ships likely took friendly fire hits from the crisscrossing streams of antiaircraft fire as well.

Chased by tracers hammered out by the surviving gun crews, the B-25 pilots executed a sharp break to the west, winged around Green Island, and disappeared behind the protective bulk of Hong Kong Island. Moments later the P-40s crossed the harbor without taking any flak hits and followed the B-25s. From start to finish, the entire gun run had taken a mere forty-five seconds.

A poststrike tally determined that four B-25s had been badly shot up, three B-24s had been pinged by flak, and two P-51s had taken superficial hits. Four B-25 crewmen had been injured, though none seriously. A P-51B flown by 1st Lt. Charles F. Porter had been shot down northwest of Macau. With the help of BAAG agents, Porter eventually walked out in the company of six crewmen who had bailed out of a B-24 LAB when a sea sweep went bad on October 26.

The Japanese, however, had fared far worse, though perhaps not as badly as American bomb-damage assessments suggested. No JAAF pilots had died that day over Hong Kong despite claims to the contrary by American pilots, and the initial tally of ships sunk or damaged almost certainly inflated the results of the raid. Damage assessment remained difficult because the B-25 crews had made just a single run over the harbor, and during that forty-five-second run each aircraft had bombed and strafed multiple vessels. Flying in a line abreast formation had ensured that no two aircraft bombed the same ship, but the turret and tail gunners had enjoyed interlocking fields of fire that likely meant some vessels got shot up by more than one B-25. The sheer number of ships also made damage assessment tricky. In the final analysis, the B-25s likely inflicted significant damage on seven vessels in the harbor and superficial strafing damage on several more, but failed to sink a single ship.

Flying in tight formation and benefiting from the skill of a highly experienced lead bombardier, the B-24s had pummeled workshops and warehouses at the HK and Whampoa dockyard. The bombs also destroyed the 1,990-ton *Bunzan Maru* in the dry dock and badly damaged a second 190-foot vessel hauled ashore for maintenance.[20] Several landing craft and other small vessels docked at the facility likely suffered damage as well. Though bracketed by an impressive pattern of geysers, the passenger vessel bombed near the Tai Koo dockyard received little or no damage. A single bomb dropped alongside the hulk beached at the tip of the Hung Hom Peninsula likely put still more holes in the side of this much-abused wreck.

At the Sham Shui Po camp, the all clear sounded at five, and Heywood crawled out from under his bunk. Though his barracks had not been hit, stray rounds and shrapnel had whizzed through the camp. Shells from automatic antiaircraft guns had blown through the roofs of several barracks and the camp hospital. An unexploded flak shell had crashed through the ceiling of the barracks for convalescing Canadian soldiers, gouged a hole in the floor, and failed to detonate. Sergeant Major Honda, a guard generally respected by the prisoners for his evenhanded treatment, went from barracks to barracks checking for wounded. This check determined that at least thirteen men had been struck by shrapnel, and that while some of their wounds necessitated a stretcher ride to the camp hospital, none of the men faced life-threatening injuries.

Camp life soon returned to its normal routine. Heywood had rice and bean stew for dinner along with a mug of straight tea and a smoke. Then he endured yet another roll call, planted some sweet-potato cuttings in his garden, took a cold shower, and lay down on his cot just before lights out at 9:30 p.m. Moments later he was fast asleep.[21]

THOUGH THE AMERICANS had maintained air superiority over southern China, the IJA pressed forward with the third phase of the Ichigō offensive and moved south from Hengyang along the railway line while additional forces pushed out of Canton toward Liuchow. Like a string of aviation dominoes, Paochang airfield fell in July and Lingling and Tanchuk in September, with Kweilin poised to topple next. General Vincent kept the 68th Composite Wing in Kweilin for as long as possible, but after the fall of Lingling he knew that he would have to order the evacuation of Kweilin and relocate to Liuchow to the south. Before abandoning each of the three airfields at Kweilin, the departing squadrons executed a scorched-earth policy that razed the entire airbase and destroyed stockpiles of precious aviation fuel, munitions, and other supplies hauled at great cost over the Hump. Demolition charges improvised from one-thousand-pound bombs ditched the runways and demolished crew hostels, maintenance facilities, fuel depots, and anything else of value to the enemy.

General Vincent and Lieutenant Colonel Hill collected their gear, which included six bottles of bourbon and a pillow slip. "My wife, Peggy, gave me that," Vincent told Hill, "and I'll be damned if I'll leave it for the Japanese."[22]

By the early morning hours of September 15, Vincent could hear Japanese gunfire from where he stood on the taxiway. "Blow the last runway," he told the small team of Americans who would complete the demolition job and then escape by road. "Make sure no American strays are left behind. Then get out in your truck and car."[23]

General Vincent and Lieutenant Colonel Hill then departed for Liuchow in Vincent's personal aircraft, a stripped-down B-25H named *Silver Slipper* that had the honor of being the last aircraft to leave the field. When the two veteran pilots circled Kweilin, they observed clouds of smoke and dust from the demolition of the sprawling airbase.

"Someday I'm going to write a book about this," Vincent said. "I'm going to call it 'Fire and Fall Back.'"[24]

The complex of airfields at Kweilin, which included the limestone cavern from which General Chennault had directed the first air raids on Hong Kong, soon fell to the IJA. Encircled by September 28, the city of Kweilin did not fall until November 11.

Though often moving at the pace of a marching soldier or cantering cavalry horse, the IJA continued to press south like a relentless juggernaut toward Liuchow, where General Vincent had relocated his headquarters. Vincent had to order his men to rig up yet more improvised one-thousand-pound demolition charges when the 68th Composite Wing abandoned the airfield at Liuchow in early November. The airbase at Nanning near the Indochina border also had to be abandoned at the end of November, though the city held out until December 24. Vincent had no choice but to resituate his headquarters and squadrons at airfields in western China. Meanwhile, IJA units thrusting north from Indochina linked up with the IJA units moving south. A land corridor from Saigon to Manchuria had been established, virtually the entire Chinese rail network had been captured, and almost all the airbases in southeastern China had been overrun.

In late 1944, however, two of the forward airfields in southeastern China still remained in Chinese hands: Suichuan and Kanchow. Both fields were situated in a large pocket of Chinese-held territory to the north of Hong Kong that had been cut off by the IJA advance. Though the fields now sat behind enemy lines, they seemed secure for the time being, and General Vincent planned to make full use of them. On November 12 a dozen P-51s, a lone P-40, and two C-47s carrying mechanics, tools, spare parts, and other necessary gear landed on the 7,200-foot runway at Suichuan. The 118th Tactical Reconnaissance Squadron had arrived.[25]

## 13

## The Death of Chan Lim-pak

The final moments of Chan Lim-pak can never be known for sure. He may have simply been shot by strafing American pilots, as the *Hongkong News* reported. According to legend, however, he tossed himself over the rails of the sinking ferry *Reinan Maru* and into the frigid waters north of Lantau. As the sea boiled with machine-gun bullets fired by American P-51s, Chan tried to rescue one of his three mistresses, who clung to him in her terror even as the bag full of gold strapped to her body weighed her down like a human anchor. Entangled in her embrace, unable to tread water, Chan felt the ocean slip over him as they sank to the bottom in a corkscrew of phosphorescent bubbles. The shredded bulk of the *Reinan Maru* soon followed, as did many more bodies, which slowly spiraled like feathers down to the muck of the seafloor.

Chan Lim-pak had long been a major player in the politics of Canton and Hong Kong. Arguably, he was the highest-profile public figure in Hong Kong to die in an American air raid. Born in 1884 into a wealthy family in Kwangtung Province, Chan acquired an English education at Queen's College in Hong Kong, one of the city's most prestigious educational institutions. By age twenty-four he had taken over the family silk business and went on to secure a position with the Hong Kong and Shanghai Banking Corporation (HSBC), one of the most powerful colonial enterprises in Hong Kong. As the comprador of the HSBC branch in Canton—that is, the man who facilitated business relations between the bank's British owners and the Cantonese business community—he moved in elite circles that included prominent local merchants and politicians as well as foreign bankers, business owners, and diplomats. During this time he met a young Japanese military attaché named Isogai Rensuke, who would later become the governor of occupied Hong Kong, and a Nationalist politician named Wang Jing Wei, who would later lead the Japanese puppet state in occupied China. During the Republican revolution, Chan commanded a powerful private militia that had been funded by both local and foreign Canton merchants to safeguard their businesses at a time when the country had fallen into turmoil. He hoped to take control of the city with this militia, in fact, but both Nationalist and Communist forces united to defeat his private army in 1924, and Chan fled to Hong Kong.

The British colony abounded in opportunities for ambitious, well-connected men like Chan Lim-pak. He shrugged off the loss of his position at HSBC and soon worked his way up to managing director of Nanyang Brothers Tobacco. By 1932 he had been appointed chairman of the board of the Tung Wah Group of Hospitals, which placed him at the apex of Cantonese elite society. However, Chan had to abandon this prestigious position two years later when the police arrested him for embezzling funds from Nanyang Brothers. He jumped bail and slipped out of Hong Kong but returned three years later when the charges against him were dropped.

The Sino-Japanese War broke out in 1937, and as might be expected, public opinion in Hong Kong strongly favored the Nationalist Chinese. Chan, however, continued to espouse his rather contrary anti-Nationalist and pro-Japanese positions, which did not endear him to the British. When the IJA invaded Hong Kong in December 1941, the colonial authorities happily tossed Chan in a jail cell for aiding and abetting the enemy. The Japanese military released Chan after the surrender of the British garrison, and in February 1942 he was reunited with Isogai Rensuke, his old acquaintance from Canton who had just been appointed governor-general of occupied Hong Kong. This development proved most fortuitous for Chan's political and financial ambitions.

An ardent supporter of the Japanese regime, Chan prospered during the early years of the occupation. He took a lead role in the

Chinese Representative Council, an organization of key Chinese figures formed by the Japanese to oversee the local population on behalf of the Japanese military administration. Chan also became managing director of Fook Hing Oil Refinery Company, one of the first manufacturing enterprises allowed to reopen by Governor-General Isogai's administration. The firm was granted a monopoly in the production and distribution of cooking oil—peanut oil until the stocks ran out, and then coconut, cottonseed, and rapeseed oils. Chan acquired considerable wealth as a result. However, Chan had a keen sense of which way the wind blew, and by 1944 he could sense that the prevailing currents had shifted in favor of the Americans and their Nationalist Chinese allies. When Tokyo abruptly recalled Governor-General Isogai from Hong Kong in December 1944 and installed Lt. Gen. Tanaka Hisakazu, the commander of the 23rd Army in Canton, as the new governor of Hong Kong, Chan knew that the time had come to jump ship. He converted his personal fortune into gold and decided to flee Hong Kong once again, this time to Macau, the neutral Portuguese colony some forty miles southwest of Hong Kong.[1]

The *Reinan Maru*—also known as the *Lingnan* or *Ling Nam*—served the Hong Kong–Macau line for the Inland River Steamship Company, which also ran steamers to Canton and other coastal destinations in southern China. By this stage of the war, the constant threat of air attacks and airdropped mines made any voyage in the Pearl River delta extremely perilous. These factors as well as the ever-increasing shortage of fuel, spare parts, and just about everything else had all worked to severely curtail service. The *Reinan Maru*, however, continued to make the run to Macau and may have owed its continuing survival to its relatively small size. By the end of 1944, however, American aircrews had begun to run out of larger targets. In such a target-lean environment, 125-foot river steamers had become fair game.

For the sixty-year-old Chan, the *Reinan Maru* offered an escape route to Macau, where he hoped to ride out the rest of the war in relative safety. Whether he had the permission of the Japanese authorities to depart, and if so how he obtained it, remains unclear. However, a man of his influence and wealth likely knew who needed to be paid to stamp the requisite travel documents and then look the other way. On the morning of Christmas Eve 1944, Chan boarded the *Reinan Maru* with three mistresses and, as the story goes, a quantity of gold. The ship cast off its lines and steamed for Macau under cloudless skies and visibility in the eight-to-ten-mile range.

While these clear skies made for good sailing weather, they made for equally good flying conditions for the Suichuan-based pilots of the 118th TRS under the command of Lt. Col. Edward O. McComas. Many of the unit's silver P-51s sported the squadron's distinctive black-lightning war paint, a color scheme based more on the supply of available paint cans than anything else. Originally, the pilots had hoped to call themselves the "Blue Lightning Squadron," but a lack of blue paint and a surplus of black changed the plan, and they became the "Black Lightning Squadron" instead.[2]

The pilots of the 118th had been trained in low-level flying and reconnaissance photography as well as standard fighter tactics. They had originally flown P-40Ns when they first arrived in Kweilin, but they soon transitioned to P-51 Mustangs specially equipped with fifty-pound cameras mounted in the fuselage and controlled from the cockpit. Unlike the unarmed F-4s and F-5s of the 9th Photographic Reconnaissance Squadron, which flew high and alone on long-range scouting missions, the P-51s of the 118th flew in packs and retained all their .50-caliber wing guns. They could also carry drop tanks, bombs, and rockets on hard points under each wing. The idea was that when the P-51 pilots of the 118th launched a fighter sweep and spotted a target, one pilot would take the lead and zoom in for low-level target photos just before the strike while the rest of the flight provided top cover. The lead aircraft would then rejoin the strike force, and the whole squadron would pile in, unloading five-hundred-pound bombs, rockets, and machine-gun fire on the train, ferry, truck convoy, or whatever luckless target of opportunity had caught their attention. Immediately after the strike, a P-51 would take another round of photos, giving the squadron before-and-after shots of the target that could be used for assessing damage and planning future raids. The unit often functioned as a straight-up fighter squadron, however, and dispensed with the aerial photography.[3]

From its new forward operating base at Suichuan, the Black Lightning Squadron flew counter-air missions against the dwindling number of Japanese air units still operating from the fields at Canton, Hong Kong, Hankow, and Shanghai. The 118th also launched a series of raids on the Japanese supply lines that primed Ichigō with rice, diesel, 7.7 mm ammunition, and everything else necessary to sustain an offensive involving a half-million men. Shipping on the Yangtze River and at Hong Kong ranked high on the target priority list for the 118th, which maintained a high sortie rate throughout December. The proximity of the Suichuan airfield to Hong Kong meant that the 118th could hit the city in the morning, refuel and rearm, and strike the city again in the afternoon.[4]

On the morning of December 8, eleven Mustang pilots led by Lieutenant Colonel McComas unloaded five-hundred-pound bombs on ships in Victoria Harbor and then shot up Kai Tak for good measure. To maintain the pressure on Hong Kong, two more pilots followed up with an afternoon raid later that day against the same targets. On the cold and bright winter day of December 19, the 118th sent a pair of planes to Hong Kong in the morning and then again in the afternoon. In both cases the pilots went after shipping and aircraft on the ground at Kai Tak.

Flying low-level gun and bomb runs over well-defended targets always remained a hazardous venture, and the 118th lost pilots and machines at a steady rate. On December 20 the unit lost its first aircraft over Hong Kong when 1st Lt. Carlton Covey took multiple hits from ground fire while strafing Kai Tak. Trailing a spray of coolant, he disappeared to the north of Hong Kong as he tried to make it back to Suichuan. On December 22 the 118th sent eight P-51 pilots on a fighter sweep over the Canton airfields, where flak hit the P-51C flown by 1st Lt. Blanton S. Keller. With a chemical vapor trail streaming from his punctured coolant system, Keller managed to nurse his Mustang back over the lines and bail out safely over friendly territory.

Between December 8 and December 22, the pilots of the 118th struck Hong Kong eight times and claimed that they had sunk seven ships in Victoria Harbor and damaged another six. However, postwar assessments only confirmed the sinking of the 5,320-ton *Hida Maru*, so the other six ships claimed as sunk likely sustained non-fatal damage.[5] The pilots also claimed to have destroyed twenty-one aircraft and damaged another five during the December missions to Hong Kong, but given the small numbers of JAAF aircraft still operational in the Pearl River delta, this number likely represented an inflated total resulting from the inevitable duplicate kill claims during dogfights and the strafing of wrecks and dummy aircraft.[6]

At 10:00 a.m. on December 24, ten P-51s led by Capt. John E. "Jason" Meyer of the 118th took off from Suichuan airfield and flew south at low altitude. The short flight to Hong Kong did not require drop tanks, which meant that each P-51C could carry a pair of five-hundred-pound demolition bombs under its wings fused for a four- to five-second delay. In addition the C model of the Mustang mounted two .50-caliber heavy machine guns in each wing. With Meyer in the lead, the heavily armed Mustangs crossed the Hong Kong border just ninety minutes after takeoff.[7]

The *Reinan Maru*, meanwhile, traced the coast of western Kowloon, passed by Stonecutters Island and Tsing Yi, and then entered either the Kap Shui Mun or Ma Wan channel—the two narrow passages running to either side of Ma Wan Island that had been seeded with American airdropped mines. Kap Shui Mun had been where the gunboat *Saga* of the 2nd CEF had struck a mine and sunk in late September. The captain of the *Reinan Maru* would have been acutely aware of the risks he faced in navigating through these same straits. However, the steamer passed through the channel without incident, and the threat of mines diminished as the ship entered the more open waters north of Lantau.

At 11:25 a.m. the incoming sweep of P-51s split into three echelons as it approached the ridgeline that sealed Kowloon off from the New Territories like a giant palisade. Captain Meyer had planned for a three-pronged attack involving simultaneous strikes on Victoria Harbor and Aberdeen. Meyer and three other pilots would sweep in from the northwest over Stonecutters Island and western Kowloon. First Lt. John F. Egan and three more pilots would come in from the northeast over Port Shelter and eastern Kowloon. The last two aircraft would swing around to the south side of Hong Kong Island and strike a radar station at Aberdeen. After completing their initial bomb runs, the three echelons would then rendezvous over the open waters south of Hong Kong Island, reform into a single flight, and return to the harbor to strafe targets of opportunity at Kai Tak.

The Mustang pilots of the 118th specialized in skip-bombing, which had proven to be a particularly effective form of ship-busting. In the early days of the war, American pilots had learned from trial and error that dropping a bomb on top of a ship might scramble the superstructure and set the vessel on fire, but the ship often remained afloat because the hull had not been breached. Larger merchant vessels and warships could take multiple bomb hits topside without going under and sometimes without even stopping. However, a single torpedo below the waterline would cause far greater damage and sometimes sink a ship in a matter of minutes. Since no aircraft flown by the 14th Air Force could be configured to carry torpedoes, P-40 pilots had turned to skip-bombing in the summer of 1943. By late 1944 P-51 pilots had perfected the tactic, which required a fifty-fifty mix of courage and skill. During a skip-bombing attack, a Mustang pilot would approach the target ship at a right angle, often at mast height. When he got within shooting range, the pilot would hose down the decks of the rapidly approaching ship with his .50 calibers in an attempt to kill the antiaircraft gun crews that would be trying their utmost to put a tracer round through his windscreen. A short distance out from the target, the pilot would release his pair of five-hundred-pound bombs, which would literally bounce or "skip" off the waves and into the side of the ship, which the resultant blast would tear open. In many cases a single five-hundred-pound bomb flung against the hull of a ship would be enough to send the vessel to the bottom.

Captain Meyer certainly hoped for just this kind of outcome when he swept into Victoria Harbor and spotted a medium-sized freighter near Stonecutters Island. As recounted in the flight intelligence report filed after the mission, Meyer bored on in and released both of his bombs, but they "skipped over," a term used to describe bombs that struck the water and literally bounced over the decks of a ship without hitting it. The antiaircraft gunners on Stonecutters banged away at Meyer but failed to hit him as he raced away from the watery geysers raised by his exploding five-hundred-pounders. Second Lt. Silven E. Kosa, who had stayed on Meyer's wing during his run on the first freighter, then made a pass on a second freighter anchored offshore from the Kowloon wharves. He skipped one of his five-hundred-pounders directly into the side of the four-hundred-foot ship, while the other bomb exploded close enough that it likely breached the hull. First Lt. Everson F. Pearsall and Flight Officer John E. Voznica attacked a pair of smaller freighters to the west of the Kowloon wharves, but their bombs either exploded short of the target or sailed over the deck to detonate on the far side of the vessel.

First Lieutenant Egan led the second flight of four aircraft as they flew in from the northeast and passed near Sai Kung. Egan skip bombed a 250-foot freighter in Port Shelter and then winged around to strafe the ship for good measure, leaving it engulfed in flames from the bow to amidships. The four pilots then continued over the eastern half of Victoria Harbor, where they spotted no targets, and then went after ships to the west of Stonecutters Island. Second Lt. Coleman N. York tried to hit a small freighter near the island, but his bombs overshot the target. First Lt. Richard K. Warrington spotted a 125-foot ferry west of Stonecutters, and with 1st Lt. Raymond A. Trudeau following, commenced his run on the ship. Warrington and Trudeau had no way of knowing that they were about to attack the *Reinan Maru*, which carried civilian passengers bound for a neutral port, and it is doubtful that this knowledge would have caused them to break off the attack. American pilots considered motorized vessels of any size in Hong Kong to be legitimate targets.

Warrington released his pair of five-hundred-pounders but failed to hit the *Reinan Maru*. Trudeau proved to be more adept at the art of skip-bombing and bowled both of his bombs directly into the side of the ferry. Given the relatively small size of the *Reinan Maru* and the blast power of two five-hundred-pound bombs, Chan Lim-pak and his three unlucky mistresses may well have died instantly. Or perhaps they survived the initial explosions and leapt into the water as the ship foundered in less than five minutes somewhere between Castle Peak and a trio of islets known as The Brothers. They may have then been diced to pieces as Warrington and Trudeau strafed the survivors bobbing in the waves. Or perhaps the legend was true, and ill-gotten gold pulled Chan Lim-pak and his mistress down to the ocean floor.

The last two P-51s flown by 2nd Lt. Paul A. Petris and 2nd Lt. Richard P. Chouinard, meanwhile, had broken off from 1st Lt. Egan's formation and continued on to the south side of Hong Kong Island to hit the suspected radar station on Ap Lei Chau, an island just off the Aberdeen waterfront. The pilots spotted an antenna array and what they believed to be the radar-control building on the southeast tip of the island. Petris managed a pair of near misses on the station, while both of the bombs dropped by Chouinard nosed into the dirt without exploding. The frustrated pilots then strafed the antenna and control building until their red-hot tracer bullets set them alight.

All ten P-51 pilots then formed back up into a single flight over the waters south of Aberdeen, swung around on a northern heading, passed back over Hong Kong Island, and strafed Kai Tak airfield. While the pilots failed to spot any aircraft on the ground, they did encounter two unlucky Japanese fighters—a Ki-43 and a Ki-44—that happened to be in the air when the Mustangs arrived. Voznica riddled the tail and cockpit of the Ki-44, whose pilot had apparently been caught on his initial landing approach. The plane flipped on its back and headed straight down, which caused Voznica to lose sight of the aircraft. Perhaps the pilot had successfully executed a desperate escape maneuver, but just as likely the plane had splashed into the harbor. Meyer shot the Ki-43 to pieces as it flew on the deck about five miles out from Kai Tak. He and two other pilots saw it slam into a hillside, which meant that Meyer could officially take credit for the shoot-down.

Meyer led the flight back to Suichuan, where all ten P-51s landed safely just before one o'clock in the afternoon. Ninety minutes later a second flight of five P-51s led by Lieutenant Colonel McComas took off for a follow-up strike on Hong Kong. The other pilots included 2nd Lt. Max Parnell, 1st Lt. Bryan L. Kethley, 2nd Lt. Frederick A. Lanphier, and 2nd Lt. Harold B. Tollett. The planes cruised south at low altitude under clear flying conditions until they reached the coast, then banked south to follow the shoreline into Hong Kong. Flying in trail formation with McComas in the lead, the five pilots swept into Victoria Harbor from the east at about 3:45 p.m.

McComas failed to spot any large vessels afloat in the harbor, but he did observe a partially submerged freighter of medium size to the west of the Kowloon wharves. This ship had perhaps been sunk earlier that day by Second Lieutenant Kosa. Flying just above the waves, McComas made an east to west run on a small freighter near the Kowloon wharves but missed with both of his five-hundred-pounders. Parnell took the next crack at the freighter, at which point the mission rapidly unraveled. Though the precise sequence of events could not be determined due to their pyrotechnic violence, it appeared that Parnell had slung his bombs directly into the side of the freighter, which caused them to explode on impact rather than after the usual four-to-five-second delay. The freighter erupted in a massive blast just as Parnell pulled up to clear the mast and stack. He felt the shock wave slam into his plane from behind, and a blinding combination of smoke and flame immediately swept into the cockpit. Kethley then flew directly into the shrapnel-filled ball of fire triggered by Parnell's bombs, lost his entire left wing, and spun down into the harbor not far from the freighter.

Unable to see through the smoke, Parnell hauled back on the stick and managed to climb to five hundred feet before jettisoning his canopy and attempting to bail out from the left side. The Mustang had gone into a right turn at high speed, however, and he found himself pinned to the seat as the slipstream tore off his goggles and helmet. He managed to get his boots on the seat and dove out the right-hand side headfirst. He broke his ankle when he struck the tail on the way out and went into the salt water seconds after his chute opened. After ditching his parachute harness, Parnell inflated one of the $CO_2$ cartridges in his Mae West and corked up to the surface north of Stonecutters Island. Bullets splashed into the water around him, and he heard the distant pop of small-arms fire as riflemen and machine gunners on Stonecutters and Kowloon began taking long-range potshots at him.

McComas had wheeled around over Hong Kong Island after pulling out of his bomb run and spotted a single Ki-43 stalking Tollett and Lanphier, who were focused on finishing off the freighter. Tollett released his bombs, which fell short, but Lanphier, the last pilot in the formation, appeared to score double hits on the stern of the ship. McComas, meanwhile, maneuvered behind the Ki-43 and opened fire at a distance of about seven hundred feet. The fighter's wing caught fire, and then the silver-colored aircraft flipped over and went straight down. McComas caught sight of a second Ki-43 in the distance, but its pilot chose to avoid contact with the three surviving P-51s.

McComas led his much-reduced flight back to Suichuan, where he reported the probable death of Kethley and the likely capture of Parnell. Tollett and Lanphier had both seen Parnell's parachute fluttering down into the harbor north of Stonecutters Island, so they felt reasonably sure that he had safely escaped from his aircraft before it went down.

In a series of stories spread out over several days, the *Hongkong News* reported that more than four hundred of the six hundred passengers aboard the *Reinan Maru* had died. However, the newspaper stated that a number of passengers had survived, including a woman identified, perhaps rather euphemistically, as Chan Lim-pak's wife. As eyewitness accounts published in the *Hongkong News* made clear, first-class passengers had a higher survival rate, as their berths in the upper decks had allowed them to more easily jump clear of the rapidly sinking ship, while second-class passengers had not been able to escape from the lower decks before the steamer went under. Those who did make it over the side had then been machine-gunned in the water. Chan Lim-pak himself was said to have died this way. Moreover, the American aircraft had strafed a rescue vessel that arrived after the sinking, killing an officer identified as Captain Yuasa and injuring eight Japanese and Chinese crewmen.[8]

American and Japanese pilots often strafed the crews of sunken ships or downed aircraft as they bobbed in the sea, so the *Hongkong News* may well have been giving a truthful account when it claimed that the "American butchers" had machine-gunned survivors as they struggled to stay afloat in the water. The 118th may not have been the culpable unit, however, since a flight of eight P-51s from the 74th Fighter Squadron had arrived over Hong Kong not long after the 118th sank the *Reinan Maru*. Flying on the deck, the 74th had proceeded to bomb and strafe six different vessels at various locations that included the general coordinates of where the ill-fated river steamer had gone under. Possibly the 74th had taken up where the 118th had left off and strafed the survivors still in the water as well as the rescue ships, killing Captain Yuasa. The pilots of the 74th had left Hong Kong before the arrival of the second strike flown by the 118th and returned to Kanchow, the other airfield in the pocket of friendly territory that held the Suichuan airbase. Regardless of the unit involved, there was no disputing that civilians aboard the *Reinan Maru* had been killed by the 14th Air Force. The *Hongkong News* capitalized on the incident by stating, "The Chinese, who had always been told of the high humanitarian principles of the Americans, were thus starkly made aware of the real nature of these barbarians."[9]

The *Hongkong News* also reported that the P-51s had bombed and set afire the SS *Chepbetpon*, a Soviet-owned freighter of 850 tons and one of several Russian ships in port for repair and refitting when the Japanese took Hong Kong in December 1941. By the end of 1943, these freighters had all been written off by their Russian owners as derelict, though the hulks remained intact enough to attract the attention of American pilots. All these ships qualified as neutral vessels, since Stalin had opted for neutrality in the war against Japan. Sensing another opportunity to portray the Americans in a dastardly light, the *Hongkong News* claimed that the "uncalled for and wanton attack on neutral ships has greatly aroused the indignation of neutrals and Chinese in Hong Kong."[10]

Despite the hyperbole the *Hongkong News* did present an accurate tally of American losses when it reported that antiaircraft fire had downed two P-51s, and that one American pilot had been captured. The assertion that only two ships had been sunk—the *Reinan Maru* and the Russian hulk—was likely true as well. The flight intelligence reports for the two missions flown that day by the 118th had rather optimistically claimed that one four-hundred-foot freighter had been heavily damaged and two smaller freighters and a ferry had likely been sunk. The pilots of the 74th Fighter Squadron, meanwhile, claimed two more sinkings plus four ships damaged. More sober postwar analyses of Japanese ship losses inflicted by the U.S. military did not list any sinkings of Japanese ships on this date, but neither the *Reinan Maru*—technically a Chinese ship—nor the Russian vessel would have appeared in these tallies. In all probability they were the only vessels to go down that day, though other ships had almost certainly been damaged.

The name of the captured American pilot, of course, was Max L. Parnell, who had survived both his bailout and the rather inaccurate small-arms fire that peppered the water around him as he bobbed in the harbor not far from the freighter that had exploded with such spectacular violence. Though burning the ship somehow remained afloat. At dusk Parnell saw a patrol boat coming his way with two crewmen stationed at the bow, Arisaka rifles at the ready. Figuring they could only get him killed, Parnell let his holstered .45 and survival knife sink to the harbor floor. The crew of the patrol boat hauled him out of the water, clubbed him senseless, and then blindfolded his eyes and tied his hands behind his back. Several beatings later and after losing consciousness a number of times, Parnell found himself on the cold stone floor of a cell in Stanley Prison.

That evening the guards stripped him of his clothes and hauled him up to the third-floor interrogation room in handcuffs, where he faced two naval officers sitting at a table. An interpreter and several guards also stood in the room. Speaking through the interpreter, the officers stated that Parnell had strafed women and children. Though the Japanese military had no shortage of accurate information on American air units in China, the officers asked a series of questions about Parnell's unit, squadron officers, and aircraft types. Parnell offered nothing more than his name, rank, and serial number. The officers then produced Parnell's Mae West and asked him how to inflate the life vest. Without giving the action any real thought, he pulled the release cord, which popped the remaining $CO_2$ cartridge with a loud retort that sent the vest jetting across the room like some kind of downed-aviator secret weapon. Officers and guards alike flung themselves to the floor, and Parnell found himself laughing with hysterical glee for a few incongruously mirthful seconds before the inevitable avalanche of fists, rifle butts, and army boots that followed the release of his errant life vest. In the days that followed, he would endure numerous beatings with whatever seemed to be handy—bamboo poles, rifles, wet ropes, boots—as well as a second interrogation by a pair of mild-mannered naval officers who never laid a hand on him and seemed concerned primarily about a brother held in an American internment camp.

On New Year's Day 1945, Parnell's captors loaded him aboard a freighter. This may have been an act of mercy by the two naval officers, who would have understood that if Parnell remained in Hong Kong he would almost certainly be executed. The freighter crew beat the odds and successfully ran the gauntlet of American submarines, skip-bombing aircraft, and airdropped mines. Parnell spent the entire voyage in handcuffs. Three weeks after leaving Hong Kong, he arrived at Ōfuna POW camp in Japan.[11]

# 14

## Convoy Hi-87

For the first two weeks of January 1945, the aircraft of the 118th TRS remained in their revetments at Suichuan, grounded by low-hanging clouds that made flying impossible. The weather cleared on January 15, however, which gave the 118th a clear run into the Pearl River delta. Sixteen P-51 pilots made a midmorning takeoff from Suichuan and flew at low altitude to Waichow, where the squadron split into two separate formations. The first group of eight Mustangs led by 2nd Lt. Melvin G. Scheer had been ordered to strafe the airfields at Canton, while the other group led by 1st Lt. Russell D. Williams had been tasked with skip-bombing ships in Victoria Harbor.

The game plan for the Hong Kong strike resembled the one used during the raids on December 24, when the 118th had sunk the *Reinan Maru*. First Lieutenant Williams divided his formation into two flights of four planes each, and as discussed during the mission briefing, his flight would approach Victoria Harbor from the northwest, while the second flight led by 1st Lt. Carl E. Colleps would approach from the northeast. Both flights would fly at minimum altitude and arrive over the harbor simultaneously so that each would benefit from taking the enemy by surprise. If all went according to plan, the eight Mustangs would be able to make their bomb runs, shoot-up Kai Tak, and hightail it back to Suichuan before the flak crews had a chance to pin them in their gunsights.

Williams waggled his wings as his flight approached the undulating ridgeline that hid Kowloon and the harbor from view. On this prearranged signal, all four Mustang pilots throttled up. With

Williams in the lead, the bomb-laden P-51Cs raced into Victoria Harbor from the northwest at ten minutes past noon. To their complete astonishment, the pilots saw ships ahead, and lots of them—tankers, destroyers, freighters, patrol craft. An entire fleet appeared to be arrayed before them on the gently corrugated waters of Victoria Harbor.

Williams and his fellow Mustang pilots had stumbled on a southbound tanker convoy codenamed Hi-87 by the Japanese. Convoy Hi-87 had left the port of Moji in southern Japan on the last day of 1944. The convoy included nine escort vessels and eight oil tankers laden with nothing but saltwater ballast. By this stage of the war Japan had become critically short of oil as well as tankers, and the convoy's mission represented a desperate attempt to import enough crude to keep the national war machine from sputtering to a complete halt. The convoy would slip south past the American submarines and aircraft to Japanese-held Singapore, went the plan, load up the tankers with crude oil, and run the gauntlet a second time on the return trip north. However, a U.S. Navy submarine torpedoed one of the tankers off Formosa, and American carrier–based aircraft claimed two more tankers when the convoy reached the port of Takao (Kaohsiung). The convoy soon left Formosa and resumed its journey south but then had to divert to Hong Kong to avoid U.S. Navy aircraft carriers operating in the South China Sea.

All sixteen ships of convoy Hi-87 had entered Victoria Harbor by the morning of January 13. A triangle of three tankers moored offshore from Kennedy Town on Hong Kong Island with a ring of nine escort vessels anchored around them in a protective circle. A fourth tanker tied up at the Kowloon wharves, and a fifth nestled against the quay at the Royal Navy dockyard with two escorts anchored just offshore.

The aircraft carriers belonged to Task Force 38 (TF 38), a powerful naval armada commanded by Admiral William F. "Bull" Halsey. Halsey's fleet had been rampaging through the South China Sea in search of Japanese warships that could threaten the American amphibious landings on Luzon in the Philippines. The mission went by the memorable codename of Operation Gratitude and involved nearly a hundred surface combatants, including six battleships and thirteen flattops that could launch more than eight hundred aircraft. Unable to find the IJN battleships and cruisers reported to be in the South China Sea, Halsey had ordered the air groups aboard his carriers to hit merchant convoys, airfields, port facilities, and anything else of military value from Indochina to Formosa. On the morning of January 15, more than fifty Grumman F6F-5 Hellcat pilots had run fighter sweeps over Hong Kong and Canton, where they had easily established local air superiority and cleared the way for the waves of dive bombers and torpedo planes scheduled to strike ships and port facilities later that day. However, the deteriorating weather conditions offshore had forced Halsey to curtail further carrier operations for the remainder of the day, which meant that First Lieutenant Williams and the pilots under his command never saw any evidence that naval aviators had been over Hong Kong.

Intelligence reports on the movements of convoy Hi-87 or the presence of TF 38 in the South China Sea had never reached the 118th at its isolated airbase behind enemy lines. Naval fleet movements ranked as top secret, and even General Chennault had likely been given only the sketchiest of details about the U.S. Navy carriers operating in the South China Sea. Due to the rules of need-to-know intelligence sharing, Lieutenant Colonel McComas of the 118th remained entirely out of the loop when it came to the actions of TF 38 or the whereabouts of convoy Hi-87. If McComas had known that five oceangoing tankers and eleven IJN escort vessels bristling with automatic antiaircraft cannon had anchored in Victoria Harbor in well-chosen defensive positions, he would likely have sent all sixteen of his P-51s to Hong Kong with a full bomb load. Instead, he divided his force and sent half his fighters on a guns-only strafing mission to Canton.

Fortunately for Williams and the other seven pilots sent to Hong Kong, McComas had ordered his men to go in on the deck. Flying just above the waves masked their approach and allowed them to buzz into the harbor undetected. Williams observed very little fire coming their way from the circle of warships anchored between

Kennedy Town and Stonecutters Island. Though he had no way of knowing this, the flak gunners aboard the destroyers and other escort vessels had been watching for more U.S. Navy carrier aircraft, which earlier that morning had come from different directions and at higher altitudes than the low-flying Mustangs.

Williams immediately skip bombed a freighter east of the Kowloon wharves and believed he scored a direct hit amidships at the waterline. His wingman, Lt. Col. John K. Hester—the A-3 officer of the 68th Composite Wing—made a run on a freighter near Stonecutters Island, but his bombs apparently failed to detonate as his fellow pilots did not observe any explosions. Hester also strafed the freighter and at least two other ships. Second Lt. Claude S. Jackson and his wingman, 2nd Lt. James B. Baker, went after the circle of ships moored off Kennedy Town. Jackson skip bombed a tanker, which he claimed to have hit in the bow, while Baker went after one of the escort vessels. He also believed he had landed at least one hit, since he saw the ship smoking.

After making their passes on the ships in the harbor, Williams and the other three pilots skimmed past Tsim Sha Tsui and Hung Hom. They then bored in on Kai Tak in the hopes of catching enemy aircraft on the runway or in the revetments spaced around the field. Williams saw no sign of First Lieutenant Colleps and the second flight, however, which should have joined up with his flight for the attack on Kai Tak after first unloading their bombs on the ships in the harbor. If he saw no sign of Colleps and the second flight, Williams detected no sign of Japanese aircraft either. In fact all four pilots failed to locate any Japanese planes in the air or on the ground. With no aircraft on the tarmac, Lieutenant Colonel Hester contented himself with perforating a truck instead.

By this point the gunners aboard the escort vessels as well as ashore had gone into action, and First Lieutenant Williams noted with more than a little concern that the naval gun crews could depress their barrels low enough to fire at aircraft flying on the deck. Tracers flashed past his windshield, and glancing up through his cockpit canopy, he saw strange purple-colored flak bursts erupting higher overhead.

As it turned out, First Lieutenant Colleps had missed his check-point when inbound to Hong Kong, and rather than lead his flight in from the northeast at the same time that Williams brought his flight in from the northwest, Colleps had been forced to trace the route flown by Williams instead. The first bomb run by Williams and the other three pilots in his flight had alerted the Japanese gun crews to the low-flying p-51s; moreover, their attention had been drawn to the path his flight had flown. Consequently, Colleps and the other three planes in his flight flew into a maelstrom of antiaircraft fire.

Despite his position as the lead plane, Colleps successfully executed his bomb run on a ship southeast of the Kowloon wharves without getting struck by antiaircraft fire. The second and third planes in his formation got shot to pieces, however, though they managed to drop their brace of five-hundred-pounders before being hit as they pulled out of their runs and banked around to the east. The p-51 flown by Maj. David H. Houck caught fire, clawed for altitude, and then did a wingover directly into the harbor. Meanwhile, 2nd Lt. Galen C. Theobold's Mustang trailed smoke as it flew eastward at mast height along the coast of Hong Kong Island like a clay pigeon for the gunners of Hi-87. The tail-end aircraft in the flight piloted by 2nd Lt. Harold B. Tollett—a repeat visitor to Hong Kong who had participated in the December 24 raids that sank the *Reinan Maru*—completed its bomb run against a small freighter. Like Colleps Tollett could not observe the results of his attack.

In the confusion and chaos of combat, Colleps and Tollett lost sight of the crippled p-51 flown by Theobold. This did not bode well, as none of the Mustang pilots still airborne observed any parachutes, though they did notice more of the multicolored flak bursts exploding harmlessly overhead. IJN gunners often used shells with colored smoke to improve fire control—a fact well known to the navy Hellcat pilots who had struck the harbor earlier that day but unknown to the army pilots of the 118th, who had never encountered IJN warships before and thus failed to grasp the significance of the colorful exploding ordnance.

When Williams landed at Suichuan, he learned that in addition to

Houck and Theobold, two other pilots from the squadron had gone down while strafing the airfields at Canton. No enemy fighters had challenged the Mustangs over White Cloud and Tien Ho, but the flak had been heavy and accurate. With four Mustangs lost, the raids on Hong Kong and Canton had been costly. Four pilots had gone missing, and at least one of them—Major Houck—was presumed dead. Fully a quarter of the attacking fighters had been shot down, which amounted to an unsustainable 25 percent loss rate. However, the squadron pilots had dropped sixteen five-hundred-pound bombs and claimed two freighters sunk and one escort vessel damaged. They had also fired eleven thousand rounds of .50-caliber ammunition at various ships as well as at a half-dozen enemy planes—or dummy aircraft built with bamboo and rice paper—on the ground at Canton. In addition there was Lieutenant Colonel Hester's truck, which he rather modestly claimed as "damaged" in the flight intelligence report.[1]

As it turned out, the two pilots shot down over Canton—1st Lt. Frank S. Palmer and 2nd Lt. Daniel J. Mitchell—avoided capture and returned to the squadron without injury. Theobold survived as well, albeit with injuries that left him unable to fly. He had nursed his smoking P-51 back to friendly territory before rolling back the canopy and tossing himself overboard. He broke his leg in the jump, but local guerrillas soon rescued him. Major Houck's fate remained unknown. However, Tollett had witnessed the plunge of his fighter into the harbor. He felt certain that Houck had died in the crash.[2]

By the early morning of January 16, the unruly weather in the South China Sea had settled down enough to permit the resumption of carrier operations. Starting at 8:30 a.m. waves of naval aircraft began pounding the dockyards as well as the tankers with everything from five-inch rockets to two-thousand-pound blockbusters. Lieutenant Colonel McComas of the 118th TRS ensured that the army got in on the action by sending in a quartet of Mustangs. Four aircraft may have been all that his depleted, overtaxed flight line could muster. Perhaps just as likely the colonel did not fully understand the size of the target. With five tankers and eleven escorts, convoy Hi-87 substantially outweighed and outgunned anything the 118th had ever encountered before in Hong Kong.

At approximately 10:30 a.m., the four P-51s led by 1st Lt. John F. Egan buzzed into Victoria Harbor to skip bomb the tankers. Second Lt. Coleman N. York flew on Egan's wing. A pair of P-51s flown by 2nd Lt. Richard P. Chouinard and 1st Lt. Robert G. Murray constituted the second element. Egan, Chouinard, and York were familiar with the target zone because they had taken part in the raids on Christmas Eve that had sunk the *Reinan Maru*. The short duration of the flight from the airbase at Suichuan to Hong Kong allowed for heavy loadings, which meant that Egan and his comrades arrived with a five-hundred-pound demolition bomb hanging from each wing—the same loading used during the raid that had sent Chan Lim-pak to his death.

Like everyone else in the 118th, First Lieutenant Egan and the other three pilots in his flight had no knowledge of the massive carrier assault under way against Hong Kong. By sheer coincidence they arrived during one of the intervals between carrier strikes to find the skies empty over the harbor. Flying on the deck, the four pilots proceeded to skip bomb the tankers and warships moored between Kennedy Town and Stonecutters Island. First Lieutenant Egan went after an escort vessel, but his bombs overshot, while Second Lieutenant York made a run on a merchant ship but could not observe the results. First Lieutenant Murray felt sure he had dispatched a destroyer escort with double hits at the waterline, while Second Lieutenant Chouinard believed he had hit a tanker. However, both pilots had quite possibly mistaken damage inflicted by navy pilots earlier that morning as proof they had scored hits of their own.

As they streaked across the harbor to make their escape, all four Mustang pilots suffered from the focused wrath of Japanese flak gunners firing from gun tubs aboard the escort vessels as well as positions on Stonecutters Island. During the carrier raids earlier that morning, the Japanese gunners had been forced to scatter their fire among dozens of American naval aircraft, but the 118th arrived with just four P-51s. As might be expected, the Mustang pilots quickly heard the bangs and rattles of enemy steel perforating the vulnerable undersides of their liquid-cooled aircraft. The Mustang piloted by First Lieutenant Murray absorbed multiple rounds but kept on flying, while the P-51B piloted by First Lieutenant Egan began trailing flame from its right wing root. Egan radioed his wingman that he had been hit, and then Second Lieutenant York lost sight of him over Hong Kong Island. On the return run back to Suichuan, Murray focused on keeping his Mustang airborne, while York and Chouinard strafed a Kowloon-Canton Railway locomotive somewhere in the New Territories.

As it turned out, First Lieutenant Egan made it only a few miles before he had to hit the silk north of Kowloon and spiral earthward beneath his parachute canopy. Looking down between his swinging feet, he saw a whirling mix of undulating ridgelines interspersed with the geometric lines of lowland rice paddies. Egan braced himself as the crazy-quilt topography of the New Territories rushed up at him, alternatively resembling a giant pillow or a massive fist, and hoped he would land gently among friendlies.

Back at Suichuan the S-2 officer compiled the missing air crew report (MACR) for First Lieutenant Egan, which among various other details included a litany of serial numbers for Egan's P-51B-7 Mustang, for the aircraft's V-1650-7 engine, for Egan's .45-caliber pistol, and, of course, for Egan himself. All these numbers could help identify the wreckage at a crash site and the body of a pilot killed in action, so they ranked among the most important blanks to fill when completing an MACR. Following a standardized template, the S-2 officer also filled out the mission report for the raid based on testimony from York, Murray, and Chouinard. Though the document offered a detailed account of the skip-bombing runs, antiaircraft fire, and loss of First Lieutenant Egan, the document made no mention of the U.S. Navy and indicated that the three pilots had failed to notice any signs that Hong Kong had been attacked earlier that morning. As far as the pilots and intelligence officers at Suichuan were concerned, the 118th TRS had been the only American squadron to put any aircraft over Hong Kong on the morning of January 16, 1945.[3]

# 15

## Devils Incarnate

The 118th Tactical Reconnaissance Squadron had flown a dozen sorties over Hong Kong on January 15 and 16 and lost three Mustangs. Over the same two-day period and unbeknown to the pilots of the 118th, the naval aviators of TF 38 had flown some 750 sorties over the Pearl River delta and subjected Hong Kong to the most intense air bombardment of the war. Pilots flying Grumman F6F Hellcats, Curtis SB2C Helldivers, and Grumman TBM Avengers had inflicted massive damage on the dockyards at Hong Kong and knocked convoy Hi-87 to pieces. Japanese flak had taken a heavy toll, however, and nineteen navy planes had gone down in the face of some of the most intense antiaircraft fire the pilots had ever encountered.[1] TF 38 withdrew on the evening of January 16 and exited the South China Sea four days later. After hammering targets in Formosa and the Nansei Shoto island chain at the extreme southern end of the Japanese home islands, TF 38 steamed eastward and Operation Gratitude drew to a close.

Accompanied by four escort vessels, the lone surviving tanker of convoy Hi-87—the *Sarawak Maru*—continued south for Singapore on January 17. The captain of the *Sarawak Maru* had been wise to flee Hong Kong because the very next day General Chennault ordered all four squadrons of the 308th Heavy Bomb Group to polish off the Tai Koo dockyard.

Second Lt. Elmer Haynes would be flying the raid as the check pilot for a green crew with a factory-fresh B-24 they had just flown all the way from the United States. As check pilot Haynes would train the new flight crew, measure their proficiency, acquaint them with routines and procedures specific to flying with the 308th over China, and provide a veteran presence in the cockpit during their first combat mission. When Haynes interrogated 2nd Lt. Edwin Baxter about the idiosyncrasies of his B-24, Baxter warned him that it guzzled gas at an abnormally high rate of sixty gallons an hour per engine. When Haynes ran some calculations, he realized that they would be lucky to make the 1,500-mile round-trip flight on their 2,750 gallons of aviation fuel.

After a 6:00 a.m. briefing, Haynes and Baxter took off from Chengkung field near Kunming and formed up with the 374th and 375th squadrons. The two units proceeded to Luliang airfield, where they joined the 373rd and 425th squadrons, and then the entire group maneuvered into a diamond formation and headed east toward the China coast. Haynes found that Baxter's B-24 handled like a truck with a flat tire, and that as Baxter had promised, its four engines consumed fuel at a rapid rate. Weather conditions deteriorated, and the group arrived behind schedule at the predetermined point for linking up with the fighter escort from the 74th Fighter Squadron and the 118th TRS. After circling in hopes of rendezvousing with the fighters, the bomber formation continued on toward Hong Kong without fighter cover. Hampered by the overcast, the Mustang pilots never did find the bombers. In the end they wormed beneath the ceiling and contented themselves with shooting up a train on the Kowloon-Canton Railway and other targets of opportunity.

When the twenty-eight planes from the 308th arrived over Hong Kong, the pilots found double-layered cloud cover, which forced Haynes and the rest of the group to run circuits over the target zone in pursuit of a break in the soup. A thoroughly disgusted Haynes observed the ragged state of the group formation, and his disgruntlement only increased when one squadron dropped its bombs prematurely into the water due to a malfunction in the bomb-release mechanism in the lead aircraft. After they had orbited for an hour, an opening in the clouds revealed White Cloud airfield, and the group leader gave the order to drop even though the field had not been on the secondary target list for the mission. Jostled by flak

Haynes and Baxter successfully released their load of five-hundred-pounders over White Cloud along with the rest of the group. Cloud cover rendered bomb-damage assessment impossible, though at least some of the bomb trains apparently rolled across the airfield.

To make matters worse, on the return haul back to Kunming, Haynes had to drop out of formation because keeping up with the group required him to burn more fuel than he could afford. Hampered by an inexperienced navigator, heavy clouds, and then total darkness, he had to draw on all the experience he had acquired during his forty-three missions to keep the plane on course. The fuel supply rapidly drew down, and they failed to locate the field at Kunming, however, which forced Haynes to prepare the crew for an emergency bailout. Just minutes before he planned to give the jump order, the radioman made contact with Kunming. Using the radio transmission as a beacon, Haynes and the crew adjusted their heading and soon spotted the rotating strobe light of the field. With less than two hundred gallons in the tanks, Haynes made a rough landing at what he assumed to be his home field of Chengkung. When Haynes deplaned, however, he learned that he had actually touched down at Luliang instead—a field seventy miles from Chengkung.

Still, Haynes counted himself lucky. One of the B-24s from his squadron had run out of gas, forcing the crew to bail out through the bomb bay. First Lt. Ernest G. Swart had held the plane level and ordered his crew to jump as the plane rapidly lost altitude. When the last crewmen had parachuted clear, Swart hurled himself out of the bomb bay at an altitude of just 250 feet, but his chute failed to fully deploy, and he plummeted to his death. All the other crewmen walked out, however, carrying .45 pistols, jungle kits, silk escape-and-evasion maps, and the heavy weight of knowing that Swart had traded his life for theirs.[2]

In addition to destroying the dockyards at Hong Kong, the 14th Air Force continued its efforts to deny the port itself to the Japanese by placing additional airdropped antiship mines in the channels leading into Victoria Harbor. Seven B-24s laden with four MK-26 mines apiece took off from Kunming late in the afternoon of January 20 and reached Hong Kong after nightfall. In an attempt to zipper up the channels into Victoria Harbor, the B-24s sowed the mines in the western approaches between Hong Kong Island and Kowloon as well as in the narrow passages at Kap Shui Mun and Ma Wan. Due in part to a mechanical failure that prevented one aircraft from releasing its mines, the radar-guided operation only partially sutured the eastern approach to the harbor at Lei Yue Mun. As soon as the crews had been debriefed in Kunming, the planning began for a follow-up mission to block the eastern passage.[3]

The next day thirty B-24s from Kunming flew to Hong Kong for another shot at the Tai Koo dockyard. Fully 10 percent—three aircraft—of the strike force had to abort, but that still put twenty-seven fully loaded Liberators over Hong Kong late in the afternoon. Thwarted once again by cloud cover, the formation failed to link up with its fighter escort and never sighted the Tai Koo dockyard. However, the lead bombardier found a hole in the clouds above the Royal Navy dockyard, and the entire formation dropped its load there instead. The resultant detonations inflicted yet more damage on the dockyard's already-scrambled workshops and godowns. Lucky bomb hits also inflicted the coup de grâce on the long-suffering IJNS *Saga*, which had been strafed on at least two different occasions before finally striking a mine at Kap Shui Mun in September 1944. Raised and refloated, the gunboat had been towed to the Royal Navy dockyard for extensive repairs, where the 14th Air Force did it in once and for all. In addition to the *Saga*, the raid also sank the salvage ship *Haruta Maru* and an assortment of small craft.[4]

Due to the cloud cover and the change in target, more than half of the B-24s missed the dockyard and trained their bombs down the length of Wan Chai to Morrison Hill instead. Though the British Military Hospital sat some distance above the city center on Bowen Road, the widely scattered bombs landed close enough to break windows and send bits of plaster raining down on convalescing POWs. Throughout the raid the POWs could hear the guards dutifully firing their rifles as ordered, though the American bombers remained so far out of range that the soldiers might as well have been throwing stones.[5]

As explosions erupted near the horse track in Happy Valley, punters and jockeys alike scrambled for cover just before the fourth race of the day. At the Chinese Methodist Church at the junction of Hennessy and Johnston Roads, a series of blasts shattered windows and swatted doors from their hinges. Dust and smoke engulfed the building, which had been bracketed by bombs on all sides.

"The cries for help by the wounded and dying in the streets were terribly heart-rending and almost indescribable," the Reverend Kwan Gan Yau told the *Hongkong News*. "The sights were also pitiful—men, women and children, some without hands or feet, and others horribly mutilated. So far as I know, three members of the congregation were killed while two are missing and believed dead."[6]

An editorial in the *Hongkong News* titled "Devils Incarnate" put the number of civilian dead at more than a thousand, with several thousand more who had been wounded. A report from the BAAG later estimated 1,500 Cantonese had been killed in Wan Chai, with additional civilian fatalities at the Royal Navy dockyard. A large number of Chinese tenement houses had been wrecked as well. Though the exact number of dead and wounded could not be determined, no other raid had inflicted so much harm on the city's civilian population.[7]

On the night of January 22, a pair of B-24s from the 308th seeded the Tathong channel with another eight MK-26 mines. This action denied the eastern channel to the Japanese, who lacked the minesweeping vessels needed to clear the passage into the harbor. The raid marked the final mission by the 308th Bomb Group over Hong Kong, a city that the unit had targeted repeatedly since July 1943. With the harbor channels mined, Kai Tak reduced to an aviation junkyard, and the dockyards thoroughly thrashed, General Chennault and his staff no longer categorized Hong Kong as a high-priority target. While a detachment of B-24 LABs continued to fly sea sweeps, most of the 308th redeployed to bases in Chengdu with orders to interdict the railroads that had been moving supplies for the IJA during the latest phase of Operation Ichigō.[8]

Despite the devastating military reversals suffered by the Japanese in the Pacific, the Ichigō offensive continued to roll forward into 1945. In the final phase of the offensive, IJA units cleared the Canton-to-Hengyang railway and gobbled up the remaining American airbases in southeastern China. As Japanese troops approached, the 118th TRS evacuated the field at Suichuan, which fell on January 22. Less than a week later, the IJA took the nearby airfields at Sincheng and Kanchow, at which point Operation Ichigō, at long last, finally began to run out of steam.

Despite conquering huge swaths of China, Operation Ichigō had been all for naught. While the American airbases in southeastern China had been taken as planned, the strategic equation had changed, and the USAAF no longer needed them for bombing Japan, severing the sea lanes in the South China Sea, and hitting key targets on the southern China coast like Hong Kong. Squadrons of B-29s launched from Chengdu, deep in the Chinese interior, had hit Japan as early as June 1944, and once the Mariana Islands chain had been captured, even more B-29s began flying raids against the Japanese home islands in late 1944. American aircraft operating from the reoccupied Philippines dominated the Japanese supply line that ran through the South China Sea and could also strike coastal targets in southern China. Technological developments had also rendered Ichigō irrelevant. Unlike the relatively short-ranged P-40s, which had once been the primary warhorse of the 14th Air Force, newly introduced long-range aircraft like the P-51 could take off from inland airbases, overfly the lost southeastern airfields, and continue on to hit targets along the China coast with fuel to spare.

Operation Ichigō had accomplished its objective of opening a land route to Indochina, but relentless air interdiction by the 14th Air Force prevented anything from moving along the roads, rails, and rivers of this lengthy supply route. An impressive chunk of Chinese real estate had been captured as well, but the IJA understood that this territorial windfall would be impossible to hold. Moreover, while the Nationalist army had suffered a massive and humiliating defeat to the tune of 750,000 casualties, Chiang Kai-shek's regime continued to totter along, propped up by American military might.

Though epic in their scope, the IJA victories during Operation Ichigō rang as hollow as the empty fuel tanks of its trucks and tanks.[9]

THE AMERICANS HAD been capturing airfields of their own in the Philippines, where the IJA had been routed and the JAAF completely eradicated. Hong Kong now fell within range of the 5th Air Force, which based its aircraft on the Philippine islands of Leyte, Luzon, and Mindoro. In February 1945 the first B-25s from the 5th Air Force appeared over the Pearl River delta in pursuit of a diminishing pool of available targets. Flying so low that they had to pull up to clear the masts and smokestacks of their targets, the pilots of the 345th Bomb Group—the self-proclaimed "Air Apaches"—bombed and strafed anything that floated and flew the flag of the Rising Sun. In their prop wash, they left only life rafts, oil slicks, and sheer terror. Highly skilled in the dangerous art of skip-bombing, the pilots of the 345th flew twin-engine B-25s configured for low-level attack runs. Gun packages varied from one field-modified aircraft to the next, but the most heavily armed B-25s mounted fifteen .50-caliber machine guns. Packing that many weapons aboard a Mitchell meant filling the nose compartment with five guns and then adding two .50 calibers in external cells on each side of the nose. That made nine forward-firing weapons, augmented by the flight engineer's top turret, which held two more .50s. Amidships the radio-gunner had two waist guns fired from open windows on each side of the fuselage, and in the rear of the aircraft the tail gunner manned twin .50s. Gun configurations differed from aircraft to aircraft, but every B-25 in the 345th Bomb Group packed a devastating weapons package that could bore holes through the side of a steel-hulled freighter and tear a wooden junk to pieces.

One of the unit's first forays to Hong Kong occurred on February 27, when B-25Js from the 499th and 500th Bomb Squadrons ran a shipping search along the south China coast. In the vicinity of Hong Kong, the flight crews from the 500th counted an estimated 225 junks, which they chose to attack due to the paucity of larger nautical targets. Capt. Herman F. "Rex" Reheis and the other pilots had been briefed on the rules of engagement, which stipulated that single junks should be considered civilian Chinese fishing boats and left alone. However, junks in groups of two or more as well as motorized small craft of any kind were to be considered military targets, albeit low-priority ones. Reheis and his fellow pilots proceeded to sink ten motorized junks and damage another eight with five-hundred-pound bombs. At least one bomb punched straight through the sail of a junk before exploding in the water. Collectively the six aircraft from the 500th expended 20,250 rounds of .50-caliber ammunition on the junks, whose crewmen managed to ping one of the B-25s with small-arms fire.[10]

On March 15 twelve B-25s from the 498th and 500th Bomb Squadrons of the 345th Bomb Group took off from San Marcelino airbase on Luzon. Many of the planes featured the distinctive group emblem of the Air Apaches—the profile of a Native American warrior in a full headdress—on their twin tail rudders. Additional artistic flourishes unique to each squadron decorated the gun-whiskered snouts of individual B-25s. The men of the 498th called themselves the Falcons, while the 500th Bomb Squadron was known as the Rough Raiders, and the names of famous racehorses adorned the noses of its aircraft.

Organized in a pair of six-plane flights, the war-painted gunships sped over the blue waters of the South China Sea as the Philippines faded away behind them like the remnants of a half-remembered dream. By midmorning the pilots and copilots could see the first faint lines of the China coast, and they passed the word to the gunners that they would soon be over the mainland. At Chelang Point, a promontory ninety miles northeast of Hong Kong, the first flight from the 498th Bomb Squadron turned north, its crew searching for coastal shipping vessels and the small warships that escorted them. The second flight from the 500th Bomb Squadron turned to the south, overflew Bias Bay, and swept over the mountainous islands, inlets, and peninsulas of Hong Kong.

Captain Reheis commanded the flight and took the lead position. He flew *Seabiscuit*, the same B-25J that he had piloted when bombing and strafing the junks on February 27. During that mission he had destroyed two junks and acquired a general sense of Hong Kong's complex coastal geography. He expected that this tactical knowledge would serve him well as he led his flight on another mission to Hong Kong. Second Lt. Robert W. Jensen followed the B-25 piloted by Reheis, with four more B-25s in trail behind. Jensen flew a B-25J with the nickname *Bold Venture* emblazoned on the nose. Like Reheis Jensen had maintained the squadron tradition of naming its aircraft after champion racehorses. Though the twenty-three-year-old pilot had not flown the mission against the junks, *Bold Venture* had gone on the raid with another flight crew in the cockpit.

Jensen's copilot, 2nd Lt. Orville L. Garrison, was flying his first combat mission with the Rough Raiders. An experienced B-24 pilot, Garrison had been transferred into the 500th as a replacement for men who had been reassigned to other units, or rotated home, or all too often, blown out of the sky. Three enlisted men rounded out the five-man crew. Sgt. Henry M. Worley held dual roles as the flight engineer and top-turret gunner. His power turret held two .50s, which could be fired forward to contribute to a strafing attack or swiveled to track an incoming enemy fighter. Sgt. Frank M. Tubb had the double-duty of operating the radio and manning the .50 calibers mounted in open windows on each side of the fuselage. The tail gunner, Sgt. Robert H. Waggy, knelt in the very rear of the plane behind two .50-caliber machine guns. On this particular mission, the B-25s had not been assigned any fighter cover, so Worley, Tubb, and Waggy remained vigilant, their .50s chambered up and ready to fire.

As Captain Reheis banked his aircraft toward the mouth of the Pearl River, he spotted a freighter anchored between the island of Lung Kwu Chau and the shoreline of the New Territories.[11] The ship had been heavily camouflaged to make it resemble a small wooded island, but Reheis saw through the disguise and identified the ship as a Sugar Baker Sugar—the Office of Naval Intelligence (ONI) codename for a 295-foot-long freighter that weighed in at 1,900 tons empty. Reheis came out of the west, overflew Lung Kwu Chau, and winged across the water toward the Sugar Baker at an altitude of just fifty feet.

His tail gunner could see Jensen's *Bold Venture* trailing just behind them off to one side. Surprised by the lack of return fire, Reheis released a single five-hundred-pound bomb, pulled up, and passed over the ship as he radioed the aircraft behind him to steer clear. Jensen may have failed to hear the warning, or he may have been tucked in so close to *Seabiscuit* that he never had time to react. Either way the bomb dropped by Reheis bounced off the surface of the water and slammed into the hull of the Sugar Baker, detonated, and triggered a massive secondary explosion just as *Bold Venture* flew overhead.

At the controls of *Bold Venture*, Second Lieutenant Jensen saw a brilliant flash and heard the brain-rattling boom of the explosion just beneath his aircraft. Shards of metal ripped into the belly of his B-25, and he felt the aircraft shudder and stall as the right engine died. Jensen feathered the propeller and clawed for altitude to give his crew a chance to bail out, but the crippled gunship failed to respond. He crossed over the coast, saw a ridgeline filling his windshield, and executed a desperate bank to the right in an attempt to clear the rocky spine. *Bold Venture* made it over the ridge only to slam into the crest of an even higher hillside a half mile inland, raising a small mushroom cloud of greasy black smoke near the village of Nam Long.

Captain Reheis circled back with the other four B-25s, searching for chutes or other signs of survivors, but he doubted there had been enough time to bail out and knew that the parachute packs would have failed to fully deploy at such a low altitude. As for surviving the crash, nobody had any illusions about walking away from a dive into a hillside speckled with house-sized boulders. Using K-20 and K-21 recon cameras, the crews of the B-25s took photos of the sinking Sugar Baker as well as the crash site of *Bold Venture*. They then banked to the south and threaded through the mountainous islands of Hong Kong, hoping to pounce on any ship luckless enough to be caught outside Hong Kong's well-defended harbor. As they droned to the south of Hong Kong Island, Reheis and the other flight crews spotted two motorized sampans near the rocky offshore island of Po Toi.

Perhaps the men aboard the sampans blinked when they first saw the black dots flying in the distance, hoping that by clearing their vision they could confirm those dots as seabirds or a trick of the eyes, hoping that the dots would prove to be anything but enemy warplanes. The men on the sampans would have known that when they headed out into the waters off Hong Kong they risked getting bombed and strafed, particularly on a day free of the fog and mist typical for that time of year in Hong Kong. When the roar of aircraft engines left no doubt that they would soon be under attack, the helmsmen pointed the bows of their wooden-hulled vessels toward Po Toi, which could provide concealment, cover, and dry land for a shipwrecked sailor to swim to. Some of the crewmen picked up their Arisaka rifles, pulled back the bolt, and slid a round into the breach. Perhaps the steel-on-steel click of the bolt comforted the crewmen and made them feel that they were something other than helpless prey as the enemy aircraft bore down on them.

Flying in trail on the deck, Captain Reheis and the other pilots could see men on the sampans firing rifles at them with hopeless defiance. This resistance ended quickly as each b-25 pilot put one of the sampans in his gunsight and fired thousands of .50-caliber slugs that raised white geysers in the water and splintered wood and bone. The turret, waist, and tail gunners poured out still more fire. Four five-hundred-pound bombs tossed the sampans out of the water and flayed them with shrapnel. The b-25s left the sampans shot to pieces and sinking, kept afloat by the natural buoyancy of their wooden timbers and little else. With spectacular overkill Reheis and his fellow pilots had fired 9,300 rounds of .50-caliber bullets, nearly all of them at the sampans. Satisfied that the sampans would soon slip beneath the waves and that they had killed all the sailors aboard, Captain Reheis and the rest of the flight photographed the smoking hulks with the recon cameras and then banked out over the South China Sea for the long run back to San Marcelino.[12]

THE TANKER *SARAWAK Maru*, which had escaped damage during the carrier raids on Hong Kong and continued south to Singapore,

never had the chance to load up with crude oil and make the perilous return voyage north to Japan. Just four days after *Bold Venture*
had disintegrated in a hilltop fireball, the *Sarawak Maru* struck an
airdropped mine near Singapore and foundered in shallow water.
Convoy Hi-87, one of the last to leave Japan, had now been completely destroyed. By the end of March, maritime traffic between
Japan and Southeast Asia had ceased altogether.[13]

Few oceangoing ships now called at Hong Kong, which had lost
its strategic relevance and become a military backwater. The air
campaign against Hong Kong continued unabated, however, and
in addition to the B-24 LABS of the 308th Bomb Group, the PB4Y
patrol bombers of the navy fleet air wings, the B-25 gunships of the
Air Apaches, and the P-51 Mustangs of the 23rd Fighter Group flew
missions in the crowded airspace above Hong Kong. On March 28
the 74th and 76th Fighter Squadrons staged a sweep through the
Pearl River delta. Fifteen Mustang pilots from the 76th went after
Tien Ho and White Cloud, where they machine-gunned vehicles
and parked aircraft, which may or may not have been derelict airframes or decoys constructed from bamboo and rice paper. Inaccurate and meager ground fire failed to hit any of the American
planes, and all the pilots from the 76th returned to base.

Led by squadron commander Maj. Philip G. Chapman—a seven-
kill ace and veteran pilot—nine P-51Cs from the 74th barreled into
Victoria Harbor in the early afternoon. They flew low and fast under
a ceiling that ranged from 600 to 1,500 feet, as it so often did in Hong
Kong in early spring. After assigning two Mustang pilots to fly top
cover, Major Chapman and the other six pilots bored in on Kai Tak
and shot up a pair of seaplanes—a big Kawanishi H6K5 four-engine
flying boat and a smaller single-engine Aichi E13A. Having drawn
very little ground fire, Chapman opted to circle back and zoom in
for another strafing run. However, the crews manning the antiaircraft guns near Kai Tak had been fully alerted and began pumping
out a heavy volume of automatic cannon fire. As Chapman made
his run on Kai Tak, an explosion rocked his aircraft, blowing five
feet off his left wing, and the intense flak brought down the Mus-

tangs flown by 2nd Lt. Stanley J. Chmielewski and 2nd Lt. Albert H. Sims. Both pilots failed to bail out. Major Chapman, meanwhile, had no interest in becoming a prisoner of the Japanese and decided to make a run for the nearest emergency landing strip. He made the 250-mile flight and found the field, but when he cut back his speed in preparation for landing, his Mustang stalled out due to the missing portion of the left wing. Chapman augered in and died in the resultant crash.[14]

On the same day, 1st Lt. Bob A. Howard of the 35th Photo Reconnaissance Squadron lost his bearings while returning from a solo recon mission over Bias Bay to the northeast of Hong Kong. When his twin-engine F-5E had just a few gallons left in the tanks, he pulled the emergency canopy release and cranked down the side window in preparation to go over the side. Slowing the plane to 110 miles per hour, Howard lowered full flaps and pushed the nose down into a thirty-degree dive. Then he simply rolled out of the left side of the cockpit, slid back along the wing, and sailed out between the tail booms. Moments later his parachute snapped open. Howard fluttered to earth to the west of Hong Kong and eventually walked out. Despite this happy ending to Howard's escape and evasion story, March 28 had been a bad day for the fighter pilots of the 14th Air Force, who had lost four aircraft and three pilots over Hong Kong, including a squadron commander.[15]

In the weeks to come, the silver P-51s of the 23rd Fighter Group would become increasingly rare birds over the Pearl River delta as the 14th Air Force shifted its focus to elsewhere in China. Meanwhile, the 5th Air Force was just getting warmed up on the other side of the South China Sea. In briefing rooms and intelligence huts, B-24 pilots, navigators, and bombardiers studied maps and recon photos of Victoria Harbor. Having sent a single medium bomb group—the Air Apaches—to Hong Kong as the opening act in February and March, the 5th Air Force now prepared for the main event in April, which would star not one, not two, not three, but *four* heavy bomb groups.

# 16

## Gangway Special

Twenty-four-year-old Lt. Col. Gerald R. Johnson stood on the wing of his P-38 and surveyed the field at Lingayen, one of the busiest American airbases in the reoccupied Philippines. He commanded the 49th Fighter Group, a unit equipped entirely with the Lockheed P-38 Lightning. However, numerous other squadrons shared the eight-thousand-foot runway on the shore of Lingayen Gulf, and Johnson could see B-25 medium bombers, C-47 transports, and even an occasional pint-sized L-5 spotter plane. Mostly, however, he saw fighter aircraft, and lots of them.[1]

As Johnson adjusted his flight gear, a continuous procession of aircraft touched down and lifted off from the runway of the beachfront airbase. The pierced-steel planking (PSP) of the runway wreaked havoc on landing gear and tires, Johnson knew, and the salt spray and sand caused all manner of mechanical problems, particularly when it came to the carburetors of his P-38s. His overstretched ground crews worked round the clock in the heat and humidity to keep the group's planes in the air. They had managed an aircraft operability rate of over 80 percent in February and March, which Johnson reckoned to be a near miracle, given the chronic shortage of spare parts and tools, not to mention mechanics and armorers. It was now April 2, and Johnson hoped his men could maintain the same rate of aircraft serviceability for the rest of the month.

In the prewar military a twenty-four-year-old lieutenant colonel would have seemed about as likely as a Japanese naval air strike on Pearl Harbor. However, the IJN had disemboweled the battlewagons of the Pacific Fleet in Hawaii, and in the bloody years that followed, men like Gerald R. Johnson who possessed the right combination of talent, dedication, courage, and survivor's luck had moved quickly up through the ranks due to the exigencies of war. Johnson flew P-40s during his flight training in 1941, P-39s on combat missions over the Aleutians in 1942, and P-38s, P-40s, and P-47s in the Southwest Pacific in 1943 and 1944. By the end of the summer in 1944, Johnson commanded the 9th Fighter Squadron of the 49th Fighter Group. By March 1945 he had attained the rank of lieutenant colonel and commanded the entire group, which had deployed all three of its squadrons to the Philippines. Johnson—known to family and friends as Jerry—had killed men multiple times and without mercy during his career as a combat pilot. As he climbed into his silver P-38 for his first mission to Hong Kong, he fully expected to kill still more men that day.

Johnson eased the twin throttle knobs forward until the contra-rotating twin propellers of his P-38 had spun up to a barely visible blur and he could see only the red-painted spinners. After the ground crew removed the wheel chocks, he released the brakes on the tricycle landing gear, taxied over the PSP to the end of the runway, spun his aircraft around, and began his takeoff roll. The Lightning rapidly accelerated and soared free of the airstrip. As he climbed, Johnson worked the knob of the lever that retracted the landing gear with his left hand while holding the yoke with his right. He heard the hydraulic whining of the wheels folding into the plane as his eyes swept across the dials of the instrument panel, which apprised him of the aircraft's flight performance with an artificial horizon, compass, rate of climb indicator, bank and turn indicator, airspeed indicator, and altimeter. Still more dials and gauges told him about the performance of the plane's twelve-cylinder Allison V-1710 engines—tachometer, manifold pressure, oil temperature and pressure, fuel pressure, and carburetor air temperature. Like the inline engines of the P-39s and P-40s that Johnson had flown in combat earlier in the war, the P-38 engines relied on liquid coolant, and a gauge on the right side of the panel told him the coolant temperature for each engine.

Crucially, given the long overwater flight to Hong Kong, two gauges indicated fuel levels for the internal fuel tanks. For the two drop tanks hanging from his wings, Johnson had to estimate fuel levels based on miles flown since the external tanks lacked fuel gauges. Johnson flew on his internal fuel tanks for the first fifteen minutes of flight and then switched over to the drop tank hanging from his left wing. As per standard procedure, he planned to feed fuel from this tank into both of his twin engines until it had nearly run dry. Then he would switch over to the right drop tank. If he encountered enemy aircraft over Hong Kong, he would jettison the tanks.

Johnson saw nothing out of the ordinary as he scanned the array of instruments in front of him, his feet and hands guiding the aircraft by instinct honed by years of combat flying. The butterfly yoke in his hands featured buttons on the grips that fired the plane's four .50-caliber machine guns and its single 20 mm cannon. Johnson could choose to fire the machine guns or the cannon, depending on the range and target. He could also trigger both simultaneously and had witnessed on numerous occasions what the resultant stream of shells would do to an enemy aircraft.

The administrative duties of commanding the 49th Fighter Group sometimes kept Johnson on the ground. However, he frequently led from the front, and on this particular day he would be flying the 9th Fighter Squadron into battle. Johnson positioned his Lighting at the front of Red Flight, which cruised at the vanguard of the 9th Squadron formation. His old friend Capt. James A. Watkins flew as his wingman, and collectively Johnson and Watkins constituted the lead two-plane element of Red Flight. The second two-plane element consisted of P-38s flown by 1st Lt. Rudolf A. Bellan and 2nd Lt. Walter J. Koby. Johnson, Watkins, Bellan, and Koby referred to their flight as "Bison Red Flight" since the squadron had been assigned the call sign "bison" for the first week of April. When Johnson craned his neck around to check his six, he could see the other three flights from the 9th Squadron stacked up just above and behind his own Red Flight. Each flight consisted of four P-38s divided into two elements of two aircraft, the smallest unit of the squadron. In total Johnson led sixteen aircraft, including his own. Attack as a squadron, Johnson had repeatedly drilled into the heads of his pilots, but fight with your element. Above all else never lose your element.

Johnson led Red Flight out over the South China Sea on a straight course to Hong Kong. The other three flights followed, with each group of four aircraft flying two thousand feet higher than the last. Johnson's orders from the 5th Bomber Command had been straightforward: The 9th Fighter Squadron would protect the 90th and 380th Heavy Bomb Groups during their strikes on Hong Kong. Johnson and his P-38 pilots would operate independently of the B-24s and fly to Hong Kong on a different flight path from Lingayen. In accordance with these orders, when Johnson and the rest of the 9th Fighter Squadron arrived over Hong Kong they would sweep the area to clear out any enemy fighters that might attempt to intercept the incoming B-24s. Meanwhile, two-dozen P-51Ds from the 3rd Air Commando Group (ACG) would provide close escort and take down any JAAF pilots who penetrated the screen of P-38s.[2]

Any JAAF pilot brave enough to risk an intercept would certainly not lack for targets, since the American air raid involved nearly fifty B-24s from two bomb groups. General Chennault's China-based 14th Air Force had long made do with a single heavy bomb group—the perennially gas-strapped and understrength 308th. However, the muscular 5th Air Force could field four heavy bomb groups from its newly recaptured bases in the Philippines, not to mention three light bomb groups and two medium bomb groups. The various bomb groups enjoyed the protection of six fighter groups, including Johnson's famed 49th, the deadliest USAAF fighter unit in the Pacific theater. Maj. Richard I. Bong, the highest-scoring American fighter ace of the war, had flown with the 49th. So too had Thomas B. McGuire, another top-scoring ace who had died while dueling with a Ki-43 piloted by Warrant Officer Akira Sugimoto in January 1945.[3] The airbase on Mindoro, one of the busiest in the 5th Air Force, had been named in McGuire's honor. Johnson himself had racked up over twenty kills, and Watkins had been credited with nine, which put them both in an elite league of American fighter pilots.

Several hours before Johnson had climbed into his P-38, the four squadrons of the 90th Bomb Group had launched two dozen B-24s from McGuire airstrip, which slashed across the dirt of Mindoro, an island that lay a considerable distance to the south of the airstrip at Lingayen. The mission marked the group's premiere strike on Hong Kong and its first daylight raid over the Chinese mainland. The four squadrons flew separately through intermittent rain and rendezvoused at eight thousand feet over Scarborough Shoal. The entire group then formed up and continued on a northwest heading toward Hong Kong. The 90th had been designated as the lead group and would hit its target first, followed shortly thereafter by the 380th Bomb Group, which had sent another twenty-four Liberators aloft from McGuire as soon as the ships from the 90th had cleared the field. The 380th formed up at its designated rendezvous point and trailed the 90th Bomb Group on a direct route to Hong Kong. Collectively the two groups packed considerable destructive power, with six one-thousand-pound bombs nestled in the bomb bay of each aircraft. In addition every boxcar carried 2,700 gallons of fuel, full loads of .50-caliber ammunition, and three hundred pounds of oxygen.[4]

The tail gunners caught distant glimpses of the reefs of Scarborough Shoal through the ragged overcast as the two bomb groups continued on a northwest heading toward Hong Kong. By the time the bomb groups came within visual range of the Chinese mainland north of Hong Kong, the overcast had dissipated considerably, which meant the bombardiers could make visual bomb runs and would not have to rely on the H2X system used for bombing at night or through cloud cover. However, runaway props, gas leaks, and other mechanical failures had caused six Liberators to abort the mission and return to base, though that still left forty-two heavy bombers inbound to Hong Kong. This display of 5th Air Force firepower substantially outgunned the 14th Air Force, which had never managed to put more than half that number of Liberators over Hong Kong.

As the B-24s banked to the south over the islands and inlets of the China coast, the navy PBM-3R Mariner that had shadowed the bomb groups took up station just offshore. The big flying boat had spooled up its engines earlier that day and lifted off from Lingayen Gulf. The twin-engine Mariner belonged to vh-4, a navy rescue squadron attached to Fleet Air Wing 10 of the 7th Fleet, which had been operating out of the gulf from the seaplane tender uss *Orca*. The pbm-3r flight crew would circle offshore with its own fighter escort during the strike and then trail the bombers during their return flight across the South China Sea. If a p-38, p-51, or b-24 had to ditch due to battle damage or fuel exhaustion, the Mariner— codenamed "Playmate"—would be vectored to the location of the crash, where it would land and retrieve the downed fighter jock or Liberator flight crew. For the navy pilots, the key question was not *if* a Mustang, Lightning, or Liberator would go into the drink during the raid. Rather, the key question was *how many* would splash down and *where*.[5]

Everyone flying the mission—the navy seaplane crew, Lieutenant Colonel Johnson and his Lightning jocks, the Mustang pilots from the 3rd acg, and the b-24 aircrews—expected the airspace over Hong Kong to be crisscrossed with tracers and spangled with flak bursts. During the prestrike intelligence briefing at McGuire, the bomber crews had been warned to expect significant antiaircraft fire from 120 mm heavy flak guns. Intelligence analysts estimated that nearly three dozen of these potent gun tubes ringed Victoria Harbor. Moreover, as the briefing made clear, these guns would be augmented by the antiaircraft weapons of any naval vessels that happened to be in port.[6]

The jaaf had evacuated its decimated air units from the Philippines back to Japan earlier in 1945, but the battered China-based squadrons still remained on station. The American pilots had learned during the prestrike briefing that photo-recon reports suggested the jaaf still possessed 158 serviceable fighters in the Hong Kong–Canton area, and that anywhere from 15 to 25 aircraft might attempt to intercept the b-24s. That this might represent a substantial over-estimate of what the jaaf could put in the air over the Pearl River delta was evidenced by the fact that the first Japanese fighter attack of the day consisted of just a single aircraft. Thirty miles out from Hong Kong, an intrepid enemy pilot made a head-on hit-and-run attack on the lead squadron of the 380th. The pilot failed to score any hits and disappeared before Johnson and his P-38s had a chance to catch him. By the spring of 1945, the badly outnumbered Japanese pilots in China had been forced to fall back on these kinds of guerrilla tactics, since any attempt to engage the Americans in sustained dogfighting almost always ended badly for the JAAF. Remarkably, however, Japanese fighter pilots had been consistently harassing American aircraft over Hong Kong despite the extended pounding of the Canton-area airfields and the near-total severing of the Japanese supply lines and resultant lack of fuel, spare parts, and replacement aircraft.

Undeterred by the lone enemy fighter, the B-24s continued to drone south over Tolo Harbor and across the Kowloon hills. The B-24 crews found perfect bombing weather over Victoria Harbor when they arrived at about one in the afternoon, with scattered clouds below six thousand feet and visibility out to twenty-five miles. The clear weather also favored the Japanese gun crews, who greeted the diamond-shaped formations of heavy bombers overhead with the forecasted volleys of flak shells fired from positions near Kai Tak airfield, the Royal Navy dockyard, and the Tai Koo dockyard. As had been presaged during the preflight intelligence briefing, naval escort vessels in the harbor added to the barrage. To foil radar-directed antiaircraft guns on these ships, crewmen aboard the B-24s dropped 250 units of chaff. The crews called these bundles of radar-reflecting aluminum strips "rope," and as they fluttered in the slipstream they created decoy radar signatures. If the rope worked as designed, Japanese radar operators would see fuzzy snow on their scopes instead of the precise blips of American aircraft.[7]

Harassed by inaccurate flak, the 90th Bomb Group commenced its run on the HK and Whampoa dockyard in Hung Hom. Flying at 15,200 to 16,200 feet in CAVU conditions, the four squadrons released 144 thousand-pound bombs, which blanketed the dockyard and triggered two particularly impressive secondary explosions. The resultant mile-high eruption of smoke and dust made bomb-damage assessment difficult, but the Liberator crews reported that three bombs had sledgehammered the 2,800-ton *Yokai Maru*. This pounding wrecked any repairs made to the ship after it had been repeatedly hit by carrier-based navy aircraft on January 16 and all but ensured that the vessel would never leave its position in dry dock number 2.[8]

The 380th Bomb Group found no significant shipping targets in the harbor and opted instead to hit the Tai Koo dockyard, the group's secondary target. The B-24 pilots overflew the runway at Kai Tak, which had been painted in rather ineffectual camouflage colors, and crossed the harbor at altitudes of 15,000 to 16,500 feet, depending on the squadron. The bomb-bay doors of each aircraft retracted, and one-thousand-pound bombs spilled out from the Liberators in trains of six, though the bombardiers in the 380th proved less adept than their comrades in the 90th and sent quite a few bombs whistling into the hills or the harbor. Those bombs that did impact within the perimeter of the dockyard tore up various buildings and may have damaged an already mangled 9,500-ton merchant vessel cradled helplessly in the main dry dock. Smoke spired upward to six thousand feet, further dirtying a sky already marred by the black pall over Hung Hom and the gray-black smudges left by bursting flak shells.

From his vantage point at fourteen thousand feet, Lieutenant Colonel Johnson had watched the B-24s hitting their targets on both sides of Victoria Harbor. No enemy fighters interfered with the bombers during their runs over Hung Hom and Tai Koo, but as the two bomb groups executed their target breaks, Johnson spotted a pair of Ki-44-IIs about ten miles northwest of the harbor. Flying at ten thousand feet, the Shōki pilots appeared to be lining up for head-on passes against the 380th Bomb Group. Johnson and the rest of Red Flight immediately dived on the Ki-44s, while the remaining three flights from the 9th Squadron flew top cover. The Japanese pilots fled in separate directions, which forced Red Flight to split into two separate elements—the first consisting of Johnson and Watkins, and the second consisting of Bellan and Koby.

Approaching from directly behind, Johnson closed on the left-hand Shōki. He waited until the wings of his target protruded beyond the diameter of his ring sight and then opened fire with all five gun tubes. He felt the hammering vibration of his guns as the nose of his aircraft erupted in flame. A barrage of shells exploded against the left wing root of the Shōki and gouged out large chunks of flap and other debris. Johnson made a second pass on the same aircraft and squeezed off a twenty-degree deflection shot that sent still more slugs into the engine and fuselage. The Ki-44-II spiraled into a dive and exploded in a dry riverbed in the New Territories.

Captain Watkins, meanwhile, flashed past Johnson in pursuit of the other Shōki. He fired a sustained burst as the Ki-44 pilot rolled his aircraft upside down at about three thousand feet, dived sharply, and reversed direction—a common maneuver known as split-essing. Watkins saw his shells ripping into the engine cowling and cockpit of the Shōki and guessed that he had incapacitated the pilot, since the aircraft failed to pull out of the split-ess and drilled into the ground about five miles away from the black smoke marking the crash site of the Shōki shot down by Johnson.

In addition First Lieutenant Bellan and Second Lieutenant Koby believed they had shot down a third aircraft that they identified as a Ki-43 Hayabusa. However, Blue Flight pilots flying top cover only confirmed two smoke plumes on the ground, suggesting that Bellan and Koby may have simply delivered the coup de grâce to one of the Ki-44s that had been mortally wounded by Johnson and Watkins. Still, Koby received credit for the Ki-43, and Johnson and Watkins each earned one more official kill as well. The three aircraft claimed over Hong Kong that day marked the final kills of the war for the 9th Fighter Squadron and brought the unit's official tally to 254 enemy aircraft destroyed.

Johnson had tangled with some of Japan's best pilots earlier in the war and held great respect for their flying skill as well as the maneuverability of their aircraft. They had killed more than a few of his squadron mates. However, he could tell that the Shōki pilots over Hong Kong lacked combat experience, for they had failed to capitalize on their principal advantage over the P-38—the ability of the Ki-43 and the Ki-44 to turn inside the twin-engine Lightnings. The pilots had also failed to take advantage of their camouflage paint, which might have allowed them to evade the Americans by flying on the deck and blending into the dark terrain of the New Territories. The engagement had certainly been a one-sided affair, as the four P-38s of Red Flight had expended an impressive 3,950 rounds of .50-caliber ammunition and 359 rounds of 20 mm cannon shells without facing a single round of return fire. In a dogfight that had proved to be just as lopsided, the Mustang pilots of the 3rd ACG claimed an additional three JAAF fighters, bringing the total for the day to six enemy aircraft.

As the pilots of the 9th Fighter Squadron and the 3rd ACG mixed it up with the JAAF, the B-24s crossed over Hong Kong Island and nosed back out over the South China Sea. Some of the Liberator pilots forming up for the long flight back to base caught a reassuring glimpse of the PBM-3R from VH-4. Protected by their own dedicated fighter escort, the navy pilots had circled offshore in anticipation of a rescue call, but no American aircraft had gone down during the raid. As Johnson led his fighters after the departing B-24s, the navy flight crew banked their big seaplane around for the return trip to Lingayen and the USS *Orca*.

After round-trip flights of ten to twelve hours, the Liberators began touching down in the Philippines. Most of the crews made it all the way home to Mindoro, but some of them had to drop out of formation and land at Lingayen or San Marcelino due to mechanical failures or empty fuel tanks. Inspection of the B-24s turned up a few flak holes but no significant damage. All the Mustang pilots from the air commando squadrons returned to their home base at Mangaldan. Combat damage amounted to a single bullet hole in the propeller spinner of one P-51D—the only hit scored by a Japanese fighter on an American aircraft that day.

Johnson and his P-38 pilots, meanwhile, banged down onto the PSP-lined runway at Lingayen. They had sore rear ends from sitting on their parachutes and life rafts for so long but were otherwise no worse for wear. Some of the Lightning pilots discovered that their empty drop tanks had damaged their wing flaps when they were jettisoned—a known risk for P-38s, which had to fly not much above stall speed to safely release empty tanks—but no pilots reported any battle damage. However, one pilot had lost fuel pressure in both engines as he approached the coast of Luzon. Both of his Allison engines had sputtered out just fifteen miles from the beaches of Luzon when they could no longer draw fuel from the tanks. The pilot traded altitude for distance, and by the time he glided over the beach, he had dropped from ten thousand to three thousand feet. He bailed out over the northern tip of Luzon, floated safely to earth, and landed in friendly hands. His unmanned P-38 eventually slammed into the jungle, and the crash site marked the end of the only American aircraft lost during the entire mission.[9]

To KEEP UP the pressure on Hong Kong, the 5th Air Force ordered its other two heavy bomb groups—the 22nd and the 43rd—to strike targets in Victoria Harbor the next day. The mission began just after first light on April 3 when the pathfinder B-24s lifted off from Clark Field on Luzon with Col. James T. Pettus Jr. in the lead aircraft. Call-signed as "Gangway Special," the pathfinder flight consisted of just three aircraft—one each from the 64th, 65th, and 403rd Bomb Squadrons of the 43rd Bomb Group, which Pettus commanded. The trio of aircraft overflew Luzon and then headed out to sea on a northwest heading to Hong Kong, at which point the pilot flying the B-24 from the 403rd Bomb Squadron signaled he would have to abort due to engine failure. Pettus continued on toward Hong Kong in the B-24 from the 64th Bomb Squadron with Capt. James Klein in the B-24 from the 65th tucked in close on his wing. Together they flew across the South China Sea.[10]

Like Lieutenant Colonel Johnson of the 49th Fighter Group, the twenty-six-year-old Pettus habitually positioned himself at the tip of the spear. He shared Johnson's philosophy that he should never ask his men to take risks that he would not take himself. Pettus had always been eager to fly and to fight, in fact, so leading a hazardous pathfinder mission suited his skills as well as his temperament. He had learned to pilot an airplane in his late teens and had planned to go to college and study aeronautical engineering, but he rather presciently understood that the United States would soon be at war and decided he needed to don a uniform instead. However, in pre-war days the U.S. Army Air Corps had no interest in pilots who had never been to college, so in 1940 he left his home state of Missouri and headed north to Canada instead. The Royal Canadian Air Force (RCAF) needed pilots with or without university degrees and gladly commissioned Pettus as a combat aviator. When the United States entered the war, the RCAF released him from service, and he returned home to join the USAAF in 1942. Pettus's career had a head start because he had already completed multiengine flight training with the Canadians and logged plenty of hours in the clouds. He never graced the cockpit of a pursuit plane and soon found himself behind the yoke of a four-engine B-24. By 1945 he had attained the rank of colonel, survived dozens of combat missions, and commanded an entire heavy bomb group.[11]

Pettus believed that the pathfinder aircraft would be essential to the success of the mission. During the previous day's raid, the 90th and 380th Bomb Groups had focused their destructive power on just two targets: the HK and Whampoa dockyard and the Tai Koo dockyard. The choreographing for this raid had been relatively uncomplicated, and there had been no need for pathfinder aircraft. However, Pettus planned to use his two bomb groups to strike a much larger number of targets, which would require careful command and control over Victoria Harbor. Pettus intended to arrive over the harbor forty-five minutes before the main strike force, identify the ships most worth sinking, and then use a simple target grid to assign those vessels to the seven incoming squadrons of the 22nd and 43rd Bomb Groups.

At Clark Field the intelligence officers had analyzed photographs of Victoria Harbor taken during the previous day's raid and identified the hulks and grounded vessels in the photos that did not rate a bomb run. After discounting the derelicts, the photo interpreters still cataloged thirty-nine merchant vessels and thirteen naval ships in the harbor. Not many of these ships topped one thousand tons, as very few sizable Japanese vessels remained afloat in the South China Sea, but these smaller ships still qualified as viable targets. When the intelligence officers had finished their analysis of the photographs, they superimposed a target grid over the black-and-white photos and distributed copies to every aircrew assigned to fly the mission. When the pathfinder aircraft reached Hong Kong, the spotters aboard the two B-24s would call out a specific grid coordinate to each of the inbound squadrons. Each bombardier would then know to hit the ship in the box of the grid assigned to his squadron. Since every aircraft flying the mission carried the same photographs and the same grids, communicating targeting information over VHF became a relatively simple matter. In theory this would prevent B-24s from bombing targets of little value, or hitting the wrong targets, or plastering targets already assigned to other aircraft. In anticipation of follow-up raids, the camera-equipped pathfinder aircraft would also take a fresh series of recon photos that could be used to fashion an updated target grid for air strikes the next day.

With Captain Klein still flying on his wing, Colonel Pettus reached Hong Kong just before noon and commenced his first run across the harbor, weaving as he did so to make his aircraft a more difficult target for the flak gunners far below. The spotters aboard Pettus's B-24 began calling out shipping targets for the inbound 22nd Bomb Group. The weather cooperated for the second day in a row, with CAVU conditions aside from some scraps of clouds hanging at three thousand feet. Sporadic and inaccurate flak began to rip through the air around the two B-24s, but the expected enemy fighters failed to materialize. However, Pettus noted with some concern that the squadron of P-38s assigned to cover the pathfinder flight had also failed to appear. The two Liberators would have to rely on their own .50 calibers for defense if any JAAF pilots decided to brave a gun run on the big American ships.

As the pathfinders completed their first run across the harbor, the 22nd Bomb Group arrived for its inaugural raid on Hong Kong with twenty-two boxcars, which proceeded to dispense thousand-pound bombs with scattershot accuracy despite the CAVU conditions. Explosions echoed across the water as bombs fell on Stonecutters Island, the Royal Navy dockyard, and merchant and naval ships at various points in the harbor. The system for calling out targets broke down in some cases, and a known hulk took several hits due to confusion in the communications between the spotters aboard the pathfinder aircraft and the various squadrons of the 22nd Bomb Group. Despite monitoring C channel on the VHF as ordered, some bomber crews never heard their targeting instructions. An increasingly rapid tempo of flak fire further confused matters, with black or white bursts detonating at altitudes ranging from four thousand feet all the way up to eighteen thousand feet. In response crewmen tossed out packets of rope, and while this seemed to degrade the accuracy of the antiaircraft guns, the chaff had no impact on the volume of fire. The persistent flak rattled the bombardiers and punched holes in seven aircraft, though these perforations caused no serious damage.

During Pettus's second run across the harbor, the spotters aboard his aircraft as well as aboard Klein's machine assigned targets to the second wave of Liberators from the 43rd Bomb Group. Some bombers hit targets assigned by the pathfinders, while others struck targets selected by the individual squadron bombardiers. Several Liberators from the 64th Bomb Squadron targeted a freighter northwest of the Royal Navy dockyard as well as a merchant ship moored offshore from Tsim Sha Tsui with a litter of lighters nuzzled alongside. Both vessels carried multiple antiaircraft guns, and flak that may have come from one of these ships ripped into the lead bomber and wounded the pilot. Undeterred by the flak, the B-24s executed conventional bomb runs from between eleven thousand and twelve thousand feet. Hitting ships in this manner had never been easy, but on the other hand, a single hit might be all that was required since a one-thousand-pound bomb packed enough destructive power to blow a small freighter to pieces. U.S. Navy dive-bombers routinely used one-thousand-pound bombs against the larger and more heavily armored warships of the IJN, so using a half-tonner against a small merchant ship amounted to spectacular overkill. Though they plunked plenty of bombs into the harbor, the bomber crews believed they had also scored multiple direct hits on both ships and caused fatal damage. Meanwhile, the 65th Bomb Squadron walked its bombs across the dry docks and slipways of the Cosmopolitan dockyard in Kowloon, while the 403rd unloaded on ships taking evasive action near Stonecutters Island. One stick of thousand-pounders trained across the decks of the escort vessel IJNS *Manju*, scoring three hits that left the ship dead in the water.

Individual B-24s that failed to receive instructions from the path-finder aircraft chose their own targets of opportunity on the Kowloon Peninsula. At least one B-24 struck Nathan Road near Whitfield Barracks, while several more tried to take out Holt's Wharf on the Tsim Sha Tsui waterfront. One of the harbor's most eye-catching targets, Holt's Wharf consisted of a distinctive T-shaped pier backed by a hulking, slab-sided godown that had been daubed in an ineffec-tual camouflage paint scheme. The bombs meant for Holt's Wharf whistled inland, just missing Signal Hill and slamming into a vacant lot beside the Peninsula Hotel. Though the blasts shattered the win-dows on the eastern face of the camouflaged building, the grand old hotel had been built to last and sustained no structural dam-age. The vacant lot on the corner of Nathan Road, meanwhile, now resembled the pitted face of the moon, and Salisbury Road sported a crater large enough to swallow a cargo truck.[12]

With a mix of giddy jubilation and unvarnished terror, Graham Heywood and the other Allied prisoners in the Sham Shui Po POW camp watched the B-24s line up for multiple runs on the nearby Cosmopolitan dockyard. Aircraft from all three squadrons of the 43rd Bomb Group trained their bombs across the entire facility, smashing a ship in the main dry dock and igniting a fuel storage tank. Several thousand-pounders from one Liberator fell short and leveled a theater and a row of shophouses on Lai Chi Kok Road, just five hundred feet beyond the perimeter fence of the Sham Shui Po camp. Shrapnel pummeled the camp with a hail of metal fragments, including a nine-pound chunk from the baseplate of an exploding bomb. A smaller piece of shrapnel punched through the knee of one of the prisoners, but this bloody wound represented the extent of the injuries suffered by the POWs. However, the civilians outside the camp fared far worse. Peering beyond the wire fencing that encircled the camp, the prisoners could see rescue teams picking through the rubble of Lai Chi Kok Road and pulling ragdoll-limp corpses from the bricks and splintered timbers. Meanwhile, an oily black smoke pyre rose eight thousand feet into the air over the Cosmopolitan dockyard.[13]

During his third and final run across the harbor, Colonel Pettus hoped to hit one of the largest ships himself. By this time the 22nd Bomb Group had executed its target break and swept back out to sea, while the squadrons of the 43rd had commenced their own bomb runs. This left the pathfinder flight alone in its corner of the sky, since none of the three P-38 squadrons assigned to the mission had arrived over the harbor. This presented the JAAF with a rare opportunity to gang up on outnumbered and unescorted American bombers. Quick to take advantage of their superiority in numbers, three JAAF pilots braved their own flak to go after the pathfinders. Flying in train with their guns hammering, they made a head-on run, closed to within thirty feet of the plane flown by Pettus, and zoomed under his left wing. Cannon and machine-gun fire ripped through the waist section of his plane and tore up the vertical stabilizers. One engine ground to a halt. Sergeant Gangler in the top turret took a round in his left leg just above the ankle, though he kept firing his twin .50 calibers as his blood poured onto the floor of the cockpit. Captain Klein, meanwhile, nearly fell into a stall when he yanked back on the yoke to avoid a line of tracers lancing past the nose of his aircraft. Pettus and Klein both got an up-close look at the green-painted enemy fighters, which sported distinctive red engine cowlings. They might have been older Ki-43s and Ki-44s or they might have been newer Ki-84s; Pettus could hardly say for sure, given their high closing speed and the fact that all three types of radial-engine aircraft looked pretty similar in the adrenal blur of air combat.

Cursing the missing escort of P-38s, Pettus feathered the propeller of his dead engine and aborted the bomb run. He knew he could still fly with three engines and a belly full of bombs, but he did not consider this a good idea, as his ship had become much harder to control and far less forgiving. Pettus made the prudent move and dumped the six thousand pounds of deadweight in his bomb bay—an action that raised some impressive saltwater geysers three hundred feet shy of the Cosmopolitan dockyard. Determined to stick with Pettus, Klein jettisoned his bomb load seconds later and kept his ship tucked in close to provide cover fire for his commander's badly shot-up airplane. Ignoring their own antiaircraft barrage, the JAAF fighter pilots made several more runs against both B-24s, but scored few additional hits. The flak shrapnel, however, caused still more damage to both Liberators and perhaps put a few holes in the JAAF fighters as well.

The JAAF fighters disappeared as Pettus and Klein banked out to sea for the long return flight to the Philippines. Pettus and his copilot monitored their three remaining Pratt and Whitneys, one of which had developed a serious oil leak. If the big radial seized up, they would be forced to limp across hundreds of miles of open ocean on just two engines. Pettus figured that they could still make it home on a pair of engines, but his margin for error would be thinner than the aluminum skin of his aircraft. On the floor of the cockpit behind the pilot and copilot seats, meanwhile, several crewmen worked to stabilize Sergeant Gangler, who had lost a great deal of blood to a wound so serious that Pettus thought it might require the amputation of the sergeant's lower leg.

With Captain Klein riding on his wing like a bodyguard, Colonel Pettus crossed the South China Sea, overflew the coast of Luzon with all three engines still spinning, and began descending toward Lingayen, the first available airfield. His emergency landing required considerable finesse, given the damage to his aircraft, but he put his boxcar down safely on the PSP. Sergeant Gangler went straight to the operating table, where surgeons performed a series of operations on his mangled ankle. The rest of the bomb group, meanwhile, passed by Lingayen and continued south over Luzon to Clark Field. Several of the squadrons reported that they had been intercepted by JAAF fighters over Hong Kong, but as it turned out only the pathfinder aircraft had taken any hits from the JAAF. The IJA and IJN antiaircraft gunners defending Victoria Harbor had not done much better. Though many Liberators returned to Luzon with flak holes punched in their wings and fuselage, all aircraft from both the 22nd and the 43rd Bomb Group made it home from the mission. Several crewmen had been injured by shrapnel, though none had been wounded as seriously as Sergeant Gangler. For the second day in a row, not a single American aircraft or airman had been lost over Hong Kong.

SWEAT-GLOSSED AND BUG-BIT, the ground crews at Clark Field labored through the tropical night in a race to have their B-24s operational by sunup. Each team of mechanics, ordnance men, and armorers checked their thin-skinned Liberator for flak damage and patched up any holes punched through the wings and fuselage. They pulled hoses from dusty tanker trucks and filled the wing tanks with 2,700 gallons of one-hundred-octane aviation fuel. Hands black with oil, they tuned the four R-1830 Pratt and Whitney engines, whose mechanical idiosyncrasies they had come to know intimately from hours of backbreaking, knuckle-skinning repairs. They replaced the empty oxygen canisters, they cleaned and oiled the .50s, they removed any spent brass, and they restocked the ammunition cans. When the bomb service trucks arrived, they wrestled eight one-thousand-pound GPs into the bomb bay. They even cleaned the cockpit windshield. By the time the tropical sun began to lighten the eastern sky on the morning of April 4, they had readied their battered boxcar for another day of combat.

Soon the ground crews heard jeeps rattling over the PSP as the rising sun shot its rays low across the field. The jeep drivers dropped the flight crews in front of their aircraft, where the ground crew helped the airmen crawl into the familiar confines of their B-24s. Belching smoke the four engines of each aircraft revved to life, and a trio of enlisted men pulled out the wheel chocks. By 7:45 a.m. Clark Field reverberated with the powerful thrum of over 160 Pratt and Whitneys as the B-24s of the 22nd and 43rd Bomb Groups began taxiing out to strip number one and rumbling aloft for another mission to Hong Kong. Their work completed, the ground crews tried to catch some sleep, but mostly they hung around the field, anxiously waiting for their planes to return from harm's way.[14]

That morning no pathfinder aircraft preceded the strike force, which flew under the leadership of Col. Leonard T. Nicholson, the commander of the 22nd Bomb Group. The recon photos taken by Colonel Pettus and Captain Klein the day before had offered a comprehensive inventory of targets—so comprehensive, in fact, that they had obviated the need for a pathfinder flight on the next raid. Targets could simply be assigned beforehand by Pettus and Nicholson. After analyzing the recon photos, the two colonels ordered the 43rd to hit the Royal Navy dockyard, the Tai Koo dockyard, and Holt's Wharf. Once the 43rd completed its bomb run, the 22nd would then hit oil tanks and shipping at Causeway Bay.

For the third day in a row, the air-raid sirens in Hong Kong began to wail at midday. Shortly thereafter the 43rd Bomb Group arrived with eighteen B-24s split among the 64th, 65th, and 403rd Bomb Squadrons. The pilots evaluated the weather conditions—scattered low clouds with ground haze—and quickly ascertained that they could make a standard visual bomb run. Meanwhile, the escorting P-38 pilots swept the Hong Kong area, and though they spotted a few enemy fighters in the distance, they soon determined that the JAAF had opted to avoid combat.

The 65th Bomb Squadron—the "Lucky Dicers"—approached Victoria Harbor from the northeast, overflew the knuckled ridges of the Kowloon hills, and passed over the camouflaged runway at Kai Tak. Crewmen dispensed rope every three seconds during the forty-five-second bomb run across the harbor to the Royal Navy dockyard. They picked up flak the whole way in and could see the guns firing from positions around Kai Tak. They also observed a Japanese escort vessel passing beneath them, its guns sparking and smoking. Still more guns fired from positions near the navy yard. Flying between twelve thousand and thirteen thousand feet, six B-24s unleashed nearly fifty one-thousand-pound bombs on the main dry dock in the Royal Navy dockyard, which held the seventeen-thousand-ton fleet tanker IJNS *Kamoi*. Though badly damaged during the raid by U.S. Navy carrier aircraft on January 16, the big oiler had remained afloat. Tugs had towed the *Kamoi* to the navy yard and shoved it into the flooded dry dock. Once the dry-dock gates had swung shut and the dockyard's massive pumps had emptied the dry dock of salt water, repair crews sheathed the ship in bamboo scaffolding and set to work repairing the damage inflicted by U.S. Navy dive bombers. Unlike the naval aviators of TF 38, the Lucky Dicers failed to score a single hit on the *Kamoi*. Instead, their bombs fell east of the dry dock on the other side of the boat basin and trained southward, romping through workshops and godowns all the way to Queen's Road. Black smoke rose to nine thousand feet, indicating that at least some of these buildings had been set ablaze.

An ad-hoc flight composed of wayward B-24s from all three squadrons of the 43rd hit the Tai Koo dockyard. Referred to in post-strike mission reports as the "bastard" or "mongrel" formation, this impromptu unit performed no better than the Lucky Dicers. All the bombs from the motley collection of aircraft fell five hundred feet south of the dockyard perimeter and trained inland, causing no damage whatsoever. Six more B-24s from the 64th Bomb Squadron had better luck. They unleashed forty half-tonners from 11,500 feet, thirty of which hit within the confines of the Tai Koo dockyard. At least two hit the bow of an already damaged 10,000-ton ship in the main dry dock—referred to in some poststrike documents as the *San Jose*—while several other bombs struck a smaller freighter tied to one of the wharves. The 403rd went after a 5,100-ton freighter at Holt's Wharf without success, though its bombs mangled the middle and western piers. As an added bonus, a small tug and a slew of lighters lashed to the wharf pilings got caught in this high-explosive rain and went under.

Collectively the four squadrons of the 22nd Bomb Group totaled twenty-four aircraft, and this armada released nearly two hundred thousand-pound bombs over Causeway Bay and North Point. The group also dropped a pair of belly doors for good measure when the bomb bay of one B-24 failed to open and all eight of its thousand-pounders crashed straight through the doors, which broke free and sailed off the aircraft. The bombs whistled earthward toward the typhoon shelter—a local term for a cove protected by a breakwater—as well as nearby oil tanks and refueling piers, which in prewar days had been the property of Asiatic Petroleum and the Vacuum Oil Company. Many bombs flew wide of the mark, however, hitting the North Point power station and leaving a scattershot trail of destruction through several districts of Hong Kong Island.

Bombs fell to the west of the Happy Valley racetrack, demolishing the Anglo-Chinese primary school on Gap Road.[15] Fortunately, the near-total collapse of the educational system under the Japanese occupation meant the building had been empty of students. Bombs also tore up the nearby Muslim cemetery and slammed into the Sikh temple on the corner of Kennedy Road and Stubbs Road, killing head priest Bab Sri Harbhajan Singh and at least two other Indians. With surgical precision a bomb erased the middle of the building but left the front facade and rearmost rooms intact. Body recovery and salvage work continued for days after the bombing as the Indian community combed through the rubble of the temple.[16]

Up to a half dozen bombs fell on the Leighton Road complex housing St. Paul's Hospital, which the locals almost universally referred to as the "French hospital." Operated by the nuns of the Order of St. Paul de Chartres, the complex also included a church, a convent, an orphanage, and a shelter for the homeless. Much of the complex occupied the grounds of the former Hong Kong Cotton Spinning, Weaving, and Dyeing Company. The cotton-spinning mill had been built by Jardine Matheson and Company, which later closed the facility and shipped its machinery to Shanghai. The sisters purchased the vacant mill buildings and remodeled them as a hospital, an orphanage, and a homeless shelter. Since the sisters had a long history of taking in orphans, impoverished children, and homeless elderly women, the Japanese administration had allowed the European nuns to remain at liberty in the city and to continue their charitable works during the occupation. The entire complex had been heavily shelled during the battle for Hong Kong in December 1941, but the bombs dropped by the 22nd Bomb Group caused much greater damage and numerous casualties.[17]

According to the *Hongkong News*, the bombing caused the death of over fifty children and eight Chinese nuns, none of them listed by name, and one European nun identified as Eulalie Chopier. Bishop Enrico Valtorta reported that while the hospital and church remained unscathed, the orphanage, the convent, and just about every other building within the perimeter of St. Paul's had been destroyed or damaged beyond repair. Valtorta had managed to avoid internment in the Stanley camp, and though he owed his freedom partially to his Vatican passport, his reputation for tirelessly serving the poor of any religion had done more to keep him outside the wire. In an interview with the newspaper, Valtorta carefully chose his words, balancing the need to stay in the good graces of the Japanese administration with his own unwillingness to choose sides or betray his own beliefs. "I don't know what to say. It is beyond my imagination to understand why they would bomb the French Hospital and Convent," the newspaper quoted him as saying. "The only war which I approve of is the war against ourselves—our greed, our lust, and our pride. This is the secret to peace in families, in clubs, in society and even among nations."[18]

The French hospital faced Leighton Road just one block west of the Causeway Bay typhoon shelter, which also received its share of one-thousand-pound bombs. Since many families lived aboard the wooden sampans and junks tied up in the shelter, bombing the boat basin caused the same civilian casualties as hitting a residential neighborhood on land. In a watery blast of collateral damage, the bombs splintered and capsized many of the small craft in the typhoon shelter. However, the venerable Tin Hau temple, which overlooked the typhoon shelter, escaped the fate of St. Paul's and the Sikh temple.

On the south side of Hong Kong Island in the Stanley camp, the Allied civilian internees heard the bombs falling for the third day in a row. All three raids had been big ones, they knew, but they could only guess about the targets. Curious for news they watched as a truck arrived that evening with a load of vegetables for the camp kitchen. Deliveries of the *Hongkong News* had become increasingly sporadic, but that warm April evening the truck brought three copies of the April 4 issue. Those internees who still deigned to read the *Hongkong News* scanned a brief front-page article on the raid that had occurred the previous day. The article reported that anti-aircraft fire had downed or damaged three American B-24s and that "some damage was caused to vessels on the Japanese side." Since shipping losses nearly always went unreported in the *Hongkong News*, the internees shrewdly concluded that the raid must have caused significant harm to merchant vessels in Victoria Harbor. This assessment turned out to be accurate, as poststrike analysis later confirmed that the vessels *Heikai Maru* and *Shozan Maru* had been destroyed during the raid coordinated by Colonel Pettus and his pathfinders. In addition more than fifty crewmen had died aboard the IJNS *Manju*, which had foundered off Stonecutters Island after taking multiple bomb hits. The Cosmopolitan dockyard had also sustained significant damage, and facilities on Stonecutters Island had received a thorough working over. For the men, women, and children behind the wire at Stanley, however, the bombing might as well have been taking place on another continent, and their immediate concern centered, as always, on food.[19]

Across the South China Sea at Clark Field, the concern of the ground crews centered on the safe return of their aircraft. The first Liberators arrived between four and five in the afternoon, and within a few hours all the planes that had departed for Hong Kong had been accounted for. A few had landed at Lingayen and other alternate fields, but none had gone missing, and even the expected flak damage proved to be lighter than usual. As the exhausted flight crews tried to get some sleep, the mechanics, ordnance men, and armorers began another long night of repairing, refueling, and rearming their B-24s. The scuttlebutt said that the 43rd would be heading for Hong Kong again in the morning in search of a big Japanese convoy.

THE 5TH AIR Force had enjoyed an atypical run of clear, sun-dappled skies over Hong Kong for the first four days of April. When Gangway Special arrived at midday on April 5, however, the pathfinder pilots discovered that a more seasonable overcast had descended over the city. Flying above the clouds, the pathfinder aircraft—one each from the 64th, 65th, and 403rd Bomb Squadrons of the 43rd Bomb Group—rendezvoused with a squadron of Luzon-based P-38s over the southern tip of Hong Kong Island.[20]

The Liberator and Lightning pilots then proceeded to fly south across the wide mouth of the Pearl River delta in search of what had become the rarest of big game: a Japanese convoy. According to U.S. Navy reports, the convoy had been recently sighted in the vicinity of Macau. As the trio of pathfinder aircraft made the forty-mile flight from Hong Kong to Macau, the cloud cover gradually dissipated, revealing the diminutive Portuguese colony far below. Crewmen scanned the inner harbor with binoculars and observed a number of sailing junks as well as two medium-sized ships nestled against the wharves—likely the tramp steamer SS *Masbate* of neutral Panamanian registry and the hulk ship *Tungwei*, which had been pressed into service as a home for wartime refugees—but saw no sign of a Japanese convoy.

Having come up empty, the disappointed pathfinder pilots banked back toward Hong Kong. As they retraced their flight path across the mouth of the Pearl River, the undercast quickly thickened to conceal the sea below. Periodic gaps opened up in the clouds, however, and the crew of the B-24 from the 64th thought they caught a glimpse of a six-ship convoy. Their radio calls failed to raise a response from the lead pathfinder aircraft, and since the weather appeared to be deteriorating, all three machines continued on to Hong Kong.

The pathfinders arrived over Hong Kong ten minutes before the main strike force and found the harbor blanketed in low-hanging clouds. As per standard procedure, the 43rd had been briefed to hit two sets of targets—one set if the group bombed visually in clear conditions and one set if the group bombed blindly through heavy cloud cover. The pathfinder crews quickly determined that the weather would force the 43rd to abandon its preassigned visual targets, which could not be seen through the undercast. Instead, the lead aircraft of each squadron would have to use its H2X radar to hit the squadron's preassigned blind-bombing targets, the HK and Whampoa dockyard and the Causeway Bay typhoon shelter.

The H2X air-to-ground radar system had been designed for high-altitude bombing through cloud cover—a form of weapons release known as bombing through the overcast, or BTO. When an H2X radar unit carried aboard a heavy bomber scanned the ground far below the aircraft, it created an image of cities and other prominent geographical features on a radarscope. This allowed the radar operator to see the target through cloud cover or darkness. By synching the H2X radarscope with the Norden bombsight, the H2X operator could work with his bombardier and, at least in theory, hit targets accurately without ever actually sighting them. Researchers at the Massachusetts Institute of Technology Radiation Laboratory first developed the AN/APS-15 radar, which went into service with the USAAF with the designation H2X. Initially, H2X radar arrays had been mounted in bulbous housings on the noses of B-17s, and because the ugly protuberances looked "Mickey Mouse" to the first airmen who saw them, the H2X soon became known as the "Mickey." The name stuck even after the H2X had been tucked into stream-lined radomes housed where the belly turrets would normally be on a B-17 or B-24.

Typically only the lead bomber in a formation carried an H2X and its associated Mickey operator, who coordinated the bomb drop with the lead bombardier. As an integrated weapons system, the H2X and the Norden worked in conjunction to compute the optimal moment for bomb release. To ensure the attainment of that optimal moment, the bombardier turned control of the plane over to the AFCE, which synched with the Norden during the final stages of the bomb run. When the lead bombardier dropped his bombs at the optimal release point, the bombardiers in the other non-H2X aircraft in the formation followed his cue.

The H2X system had been designed for the European theater, where inland targets hidden beneath cloud cover remained the norm. However, the 5th Air Force had found that the H2X worked particularly well against the coastal targets so often struck by its heavy bomber units in the Pacific theater. An H2X radar set could easily differentiate water from coastline, making accurate high-altitude bombing of socked-in shoreline targets possible. While misty April weather had scrubbed missions against Hong Kong earlier in the war, by 1945 spring cloud cover remained a nuisance rather than a barrier to the radar-equipped bomb groups of the 5th Air Force.

The main formation of the 43rd Bomb Group reached the southern edge of Hong Kong Island at around one in the afternoon. The 64th and 65th Bomb Squadrons overflew Hong Kong Island, crossed the harbor, and commenced radar-guided "Mickey runs" over Hung Hom. Flying at ten thousand feet, the 65th went in first as sporadic but accurate flak fire punched through the clouds. Figuring that the antiaircraft guns must be radar guided, the B-24 crewmen in the lead flight dropped bundles of aluminum rope and watched in relief as the chaff appeared to throw off the aim of the flak guns. H2X runs could be quite hazardous, after all, since an aircraft controlled by the AFCE autopilot flew straight and level in response to commands from the H2X, making it vulnerable to flak and fighters alike during its bomb run. The crewmen in the second flight watched in consternation as the flak fire simply shifted from the first flight to their own aircraft. Several boxcars picked up flak holes. Fortunately for the B-24s, however, the weather and the protective screen of P-38s ensured that no JAAF fighters chose to contest the skies over Hong Kong that day.

The lead aircraft of the 64th and 65th Bomb Squadrons carried an H2X unit, and when the bombardiers aboard these two aircraft released their bomb loads, the rest of the formation immediately released as well. Each of the twelve aircraft dropped eight one-thousand-pound bombs fused for instant detonation, and the bomb trains ran from the tip of the Hung Hom Peninsula south to north, pummeling the hulk beached at the very tip of the peninsula and striking the HK and Whampoa dockyard. Bombs also hit the Green Island Cement Company and the electrical plant for China Light and Power. More than a few thousand-pounders went into the sea as well.

Due to a malfunctioning H2X unit in the lead aircraft, the 403rd Bomb Squadron lost its ability to bomb accurately through the undercast. Like a blindfolded man throwing darts at a dartboard, the lead bombardier took his best guess and released his eight one-thousand-pounders. The first three aircraft put much of their payload into the harbor, though some bombs fell within the Causeway Bay typhoon shelter. The fourth aircraft strayed so far from the mark that its bombs detonated far inland, further terrifying the already petrified inhabitants of Causeway Bay, Wan Chai, and Happy Valley. A fifth aircraft operating independently managed to crater Kai Tak. A sixth never made it to Hong Kong at all, as it had aborted the mission when it suffered a substantial rip in one of its vertical stabilizers immediately after takeoff.

Handicapped by yet another inoperative H2X unit, the pathfinder crew from the 403rd dropped their eight one-thousand-pound bombs through the soup with unknown results. Though the H2X aboard the pathfinder B-24 from the 64th remained fully functional, the bombardier and the Mickey operator only managed to kill fish north of the Tai Koo docks when they dropped through the undercast. Only the pathfinder crew from the 65th could claim a bull's-eye, as they went after the *Kamoi* at the Royal Navy dockyard and walked their bombs across the stern of the already-damaged tanker.

All twenty-four aircraft assigned to the mission returned safely to Clark Field. Just five B-24 crews reported flak damage, and no airmen had sustained any injuries. For the 43rd the mission had been an unqualified success despite the many bombs that had splashed into the harbor. For starters the HK and Whampoa dockyard had been thoroughly worked over. Moreover, it turned out that despite the poor weather conditions and malfunctioning H2X equipment, the 43rd Bomb Group had managed to hit a number of ships. Postwar analysis determined that aside from mangling the high-and-dry *Kamoi*, the 43rd also damaged the escort vessels CD-1 and CD-52 as well as the subchasers CH-9 and CH-20.[21] Exactly how these four naval ships had been hit remained unclear—perhaps they had been caught at the HK and Whampoa dockyard by the 64th and 65th Bomb Squadrons, or maybe they had been unlucky enough to be straddled in the harbor by the bombs dropped blindly by the 403rd. Fog, scud, mist, and cloud no longer offered refuge for the ships of the IJN.

FOR A WEEK Hong Kong enjoyed a respite from the mass bombing raids of the 43rd Bomb Group. On April 13, however, a trio of pathfinder aircraft from the 65th Bomb Squadron appeared over the harbor just after lunch and began scouting targets. All the city's air-raid sirens remained silent, however. A recently instated policy reserved the sirens for large-scale raids, apparently because incursions by one or two American warplanes had become so common that the siren would have been wailing virtually around the clock. In any case the civilian population of Hong Kong had figured out that when several four-engine bombers circled over the city like a wheel of hungry vultures they could expect a major air raid within the hour. They didn't need the siren to tell them that they should seek whatever shelter they could find, which typically wasn't very much, since the Japanese regime refused to allow civilians into the extensive network of air-raid tunnels that ran beneath the city. Originally constructed by the British to protect the civilian population, the BAAG reported that the tunnels now housed stores of gasoline, ammunition, and other military supplies.[22]

In accordance with the new air-raid warning policy, the sirens went off when the main bomber formation arrived thirty minutes after the pathfinder aircraft. Using the grid system, Gangway Special assigned targets to fourteen B-24s from the 64th, 65th, and 403rd Bomb Squadrons. Grid coordinate G-6 went to the 64th, which

would hit the HK and Whampoa dockyard, where the pathfinders had spotted a bomb-worthy vessel of medium size. The 403rd
received orders to strike grid coordinate I-5, which held shipping
and the Tai Koo dockyard. The 65th had been broken into two
separate three-plane elements at the start of the mission, with the
first element consisting of the pathfinder aircraft. The pathfinders
instructed the second element from the 65th to go after the Texaco oil storage facility.[23]

When the five B-24s from the 64th arrived at sector G-6, which
put them out over open water east of the HK and Whampoa dockyard, they could not find the ship they had been assigned to bomb.
The squadron leader gave the signal to drop anyhow, and the rest
of the squadron obediently unloaded on cue. Nearly all the bombs
hurtled toward a cluster of tide-stained boulders sticking out of the
water four thousand feet east of the China Light and Power electrical plant. Explosions erupted around the rocks but rather miracu-
lously missed some junks moored nearby.

Despite the CAVU conditions, the six boxcars from the 403rd fared
no better when they made their run on grid I-6. With no merchant
shipping in sight, the 403rd unloaded on the Tai Koo dockyard. A
total of thirty-seven out of forty-eight bombs went into the water,
and even the one-thousand-pounders that hit land still fell outside
the dockyard fence. Aggressive flak fire, meanwhile, punched ten
holes in one of the squadron's Liberators.

The second element from the 65th dropped as ordered on the
Texaco oil storage area, which sat on the Rambler Channel between
Tsuen Wan and Tsing Yi. Only two of the three aircraft released their
bombs, and neither stick hit the tanks, though three large godowns
absorbed multiple blasts. Unable to release its load due to a bomb-
rack failure over the target, the third aircraft finally managed to jettison its bombs in the water near Kai Tak.

Flying at twelve thousand feet, the Gangway Special pilots sighted
a large tanker moored between Stonecutters Island and the coastline of Lai Chi Kok. The pathfinders identified the ship as a Sugar
Able Love—an ONI codename for a ten-thousand-ton tanker—

and concluded that the long-suffering *Kamoi* had been patched up after the raid on April 5, refloated in the flooded dry dock at the Royal Navy dockyard, and towed out to a mooring buoy. With clear skies, no Shōki or Hayabusa buzzing around, and only desultory flak, the pathfinders had little to distract them as they lined up on the tanker. They scored several direct hits, though given the rickety state of the *Kamoi*, even near misses would likely have buckled its hull plates. As the three Liberators banked back out to sea, the big ship listed hard to port beneath a halo of smoke. Shortly thereafter the *Kamoi* foundered once and for all as its surviving crewmen abandoned ship.[24]

All seventeen boxcars returned safely to Clark Field after a 1,200-mile round trip, though the flak-peppered Liberator from the 403rd blew a tire on landing. Shaken, the crew emerged unharmed from their pranged B-24. Two more aircraft had picked up flak holes over Hong Kong in the engine cowling and tail turret, but no crewmen had been hit. For the 43rd the run on Hong Kong had been another casualty-free mission, though the day had not been without loss. When the crews returned to Clark, they learned to their shock that President Roosevelt had died the day before at age sixty-three. His vice president, Harry S. Truman, had already been sworn in as the thirty-third president of the United States.

Confused targeting and inaccurate bombing had plagued the mission that day, leaving more than a few bomber crews feeling badly disgruntled. Indictments and recriminations, in fact, characterized many of the mission reports filed after the raid. In its narrative report written after the mission, the 65th exonerated its own pathfinder pilots of any blame for the seventy-six bombs that had gone into the drink. The 65th instead blamed its sister squadron for hitting the wrong target. The report stated, "Due to improper use of the grids, the 64th bombed some rocks in the water east of the assigned target. The 403rd had no trouble with the grid system, and the 65th second element bombed as ordered."[25] As this assessment of squadron performance made clear, the 65th believed that the boulder-bombing 64th had screwed up badly.

In its own mission reports, the frustrated 64th admitted that it had failed to hit anything worth mentioning, though it pinned the blame for this waste of ordnance on the pathfinders from the 65th Bomb Squadron. The reports filed by the 64th excoriated Gangway Special and claimed that the pathfinders had denied the 64th permission to bomb the Texaco oil tanks on the grounds that the 65th had already destroyed them. However, the 64th noted that its aircraft had radioed the pathfinders to report that the tanks had in fact survived the run by the 65th. The pathfinders failed to act on this information, and the 64th suggested that Gangway Special had issued poor targeting instructions, which explained why the unit had bombed a guano-stained rock pile. For its part the 403rd noted that the promised shipping in grid 1-5 had failed to materialize and as a result the squadron had bombed—albeit entirely without success—hulks at Tai Koo and previously damaged ships in the dry dock. Despite the accusations and finger-pointing, all the reports from the 43rd Bomb Group recognized that Hong Kong had been so thoroughly pounded during the month of April that one poorly executed mission hardly mattered, especially since it had come without loss of life or Liberator.

Over a two-week period, the 5th Air Force had visited Hong Kong five times, and despite the number of sorties involved it had lost only a single P-38. No pilots or air crewmen had been killed either. The flak had been a nuisance, and shrapnel had struck numerous box-cars, though in nearly every case the damage had been superficial and easily repaired. Several airmen had been wounded by the persistent flak as well. A gaggle of intrepid JAAF pilots had managed to shoot up Colonel Pettus's pathfinder aircraft and badly injure one of his gunners. All things considered, however, the cost of the raids for the 5th Air Force had been negligible in military terms.

In contrast Hong Kong had suffered heavily. The 22nd, 43rd, 90th, and 380th Bomb Groups had unloaded well over a thousand bombs on the city and harbor. The resultant explosions killed some Japanese, more than a few Cantonese civilians of all ages and both genders, a handful of Indians, and one European nun named Eulalie

Chopier. The bombs hit escort vessels in the harbor. They hit merchant ships in the dry docks. They hit tugs, lighters, sampans, and junks. They hit the *Kamoi* and then they hit it again. They sprinkled bombs across Kowloon and Hung Hom. They scrambled Holt's Wharf, cratered Salisbury Road, and shattered the windows of the Peninsula Hotel. They wrecked the orphanage, the convent, and the homeless shelter at St. Paul's. They set the oil tanks at North Point and Lai Chi Kok ablaze and smashed up both of the city's power plants for good measure. They hit shophouses and tenements in Wan Chai and Sham Shui Po. In Happy Valley they blasted the Sikh temple and the Gap Road primary school. They even disturbed the already dead in the Muslim graveyard. The bomb groups of the 5th Air Force, however, were not yet finished with Hong Kong. They would be back, and this time they would be back with one of America's newest and most terrifying weapons. It came in fifty-five-gallon drums with a single word stenciled on the side in block letters: *Napalm*.

## 17

## Playing with Fire

During the next four weeks, American aircraft from the 5th Air Force appeared over the Pearl River delta on a daily basis, though Canton received almost all the attention. Road, rail, and river traffic faced the continual risk of air interdiction from units like the 345th Bomb Group, which had lost *Bold Venture* over Hong Kong in March. On April 14, B-25 gunships from the 345th rampaged up the Pearl River, leaving a trail of bullet-riddled and bombed-out godowns, barges, railroad spurs, and lighthouses.[1]

Tien Ho, White Cloud, and various satellite airstrips bore the brunt of the air attacks, however. Most of the raids on the Canton airfields occurred during armed reconnaissance missions flown by a single night-flying B-24. These sorties usually fell to the 63rd Bomb Squadron—the "Sea Hawks"—of the 43rd Bomb Group. Unlike the other three squadrons in this unit, the 63rd flew Liberators configured for low-altitude radar-guided bombing, which allowed them to hunt ships in the darkness. Few Japanese vessels remained afloat on the South China Sea, however, so the nocturnal B-24 LABS of the 63rd usually had to hit their secondary target—the Canton airfields—instead. The 403rd Bomb Squadron occasionally flew these night intruder missions as well and bombed the Canton airbases using their H2X-equipped B-24s.

On May 9 news arrived in the Philippines that the war in Europe had ended with Germany's unconditional surrender. In the Pacific the war continued unabated, however, and all four heavy-bomb groups of the 5th Air Force carpeted Tien Ho and White Cloud airfields at midday with hundreds of fragmentation bombs and a confetti of propaganda leaflets. Though the fragmentation bombs barely scratched the runways, the bomb-damage assessment written up after the raid rather optimistically concluded that the overlapping sprays of red-hot shrapnel had shredded numerous Japanese aircraft in their revetments. Even this damage may have been overstated, however, since the carcasses of warplanes wrecked during previous raids cluttered the field along with dummy aircraft built of bamboo and rice paper.[2]

Though Canton had been struck repeatedly between April 14 and June 11, Hong Kong enjoyed a lull in the American air attacks. At about 10:45 on the hot, overcast morning of June 12, however, the ominous drone of aircraft engines announced the return of the 22nd and 43rd Bomb Groups. During the preflight briefing the pilots, bombardiers, and navigators had been told they would hit small craft in the Causeway Bay typhoon shelter. Colonel Pettus asked why the fishing junks in the typhoon shelter had been targeted. He argued that the families living on the junks would never leave them voluntarily, since the vessels served as their homes, savings, and livelihoods. He also said that bombing the typhoon shelter seemed to contradict the policy of not hitting junks, since the crews of these sailing vessels had often helped downed American aviators. The officers giving the briefing assured Pettus that the families aboard the fishing vessels would be warned beforehand and that, furthermore, the typhoon shelter qualified as a military target. Two high-speed wooden patrol boats had tied up among the fishing junks and would be primary targets. In addition, due to the lack of larger all-metal vessels, the Japanese had been increasingly relying on small wooden motor vessels to transport men and material along the China coast. Hitting the Causeway Bay typhoon shelter would help cut this last remaining Japanese seaborne supply line.[3]

All seven squadrons expected to use their H2X radar, but at the last minute the clouds parted and the bombardiers in some squadrons switched over from radar-guided Mickey runs to visually guided runs. Flying between 11,500 and 13,500 feet, all sixty-one bombers dropped on the Causeway Bay typhoon shelter. In total they released 448 drums of napalm, which amounted to 26,640 gallons of jellied gasoline. Each drum created a ring of flame fifty feet in diameter. Like liquid fire the napalm burned everything it touched—human flesh, canvas sails, and even the surface of the harbor. Water and junks alike erupted in flame, as did godowns and other buildings onshore. Even the breakwater ignited. As the bombers executed their combat break, the tail gunners could see angry towers of smoke rising nearly a mile high over Causeway Bay.

Along with the drums of napalm, the Liberators dropped more than sixty thousand propaganda leaflets, many of which likely burned up in the conflagration ignited by the napalm. Crewmen also dispensed generous quantities of rope, which failed to completely distract the Japanese gunners manning the flak guns. Razor-edged shrapnel pierced seven Liberators but failed to inflict significant harm. A lone enemy fighter approached a trailing B-24, but the tail gunner dissuaded the pilot from further attack with a fifty-round burst from his dual .50 calibers.

Despite the sporadic flak and the one fighter, the bomber crews feared the napalm drums more than the enemy. Unlike the usual cargo of one-thousand-pound demolition bombs, the crews considered the leaky drums to be highly unstable and likely to torch their aircraft at any moment. During the long flight across the South China Sea, the crews had carefully monitored the barrels cached in their bomb bays and inspected them for signs of leakage. This proved wise, as crews discovered a leaking drum on two different aircraft. In both cases the bombardiers jettisoned the drums without incident.

As it turned out, the primary objective of the raid had been to test the effectiveness of napalm on concentrations of small wooden vessels, which the 5th Air Force expected to target during the impending invasion of Japan. Documents from the 22nd Bomb Group described the raid as a "bombing experiment" but admitted that the results remained inconclusive at best. The photo interpreters back at Clark Field credited the 22nd and 43rd Bomb Groups with burning a small tugboat, a dozen lighters, and up to twenty fishing junks. However, the two Japanese patrol boats that had served as the ostensible justification for the raid had escaped harm and may not have actually been berthed in the shelter when its waters caught fire.

The *Hongkong News* edition for June 13 ran a story subtitled "Incendiary Bombs Used for First Time: Foe's Devilish Design." An accompanying editorial excoriated the "Anglo-American devils" for dropping drums of gasoline on civilian targets.[4] As the 43rd Bomb Group acknowledged in its own mission reports, at least three plane-loads of napalm drums had been dropped directly onto the streets of Wan Chai to the west of the typhoon shelter. Blazes immediately broke out among the closely packed tenement buildings, which remained highly vulnerable to fire. Two more planes had trained their napalm bombs across King's Road to the east of the shelter, igniting still more fires that burned largely unchecked since the city lacked a functioning fire brigade. According to BAAG reports, the city's pre-war fleet of American-made fire engines had been shipped to Japan in 1944.[5] Though a definitive casualty figure could not be compiled, the errant barrels of gelled petroleum may have killed or wounded at least 130 civilians and left more than 2,000 homeless. Most if not all would have been Cantonese. The Americans, meanwhile, flew all sixty-one of their Liberators back to Luzon for a casualty-free conclusion to what would prove to be the last heavy bombing raid ever flown by the 5th Air Force against targets in Hong Kong.

ONE OF THE final raids flown over the Pearl River delta by the medium bombers of the 5th Air Force occurred less than two weeks later. On the hot and cloudy morning of June 22, six B-25s from the 345th Medium Bomb Group—the Air Apaches—bypassed Hong Kong and flew up the Pearl River in search of targets. The bomber crews feathered some 250-pound para-frags into a suspected factory compound, shot up some river navigation buoys, and went gunning for a meager selection of powered junks and sampans. Whizzing along just above the surface of the river, one pilot ran his B-25 straight through the rigging of a junk while trying to dodge a second Mitchell making a gun run on the same unlucky vessel. Though the pilot had performed a unique feat of combat flying by dismasting a sailing vessel with an airplane, his crew reported that their B-25 had sustained significant damage to the fuselage. Later in the mission, a second B-25 absorbed a number of enemy machine-gun rounds, and as the Air Apaches winged back to the Philippines, a third B-25 ran out of gas and ditched just shy of the beach on Luzon. All five crewmen survived the surprisingly gentle water landing and waded to shore, where a welcoming committee of two hundred Filipinos and the local chief of police feted their arrival. A U.S. Army cargo truck picked them up the next day and dropped them at Lingayen. Despite the safe return of the missing crewmen, the 345th had been badly banged up, with two aircraft sidelined for repairs and another half-submerged in the surf.[6]

After the river sweep on June 22 by the Air Apaches, the 5th Air Force began to shift its attention to targets in Japan. From a strategic standpoint, Hong Kong and Canton had become irrelevant as the front lines of the war shifted northward. Isolated, starved of vital supplies, and stripped of air and naval assets, the Japanese garrisons in the Pearl River delta presented little threat to the Allies. Hong Kong and Canton no longer rated full-court presses by the 5th Air Force, so there would be no more napalm strikes on Hong Kong or sixty-plane carpet bombings of the Canton airfields. This reassessment of mission priorities reduced the presence of 5th Air Force aircraft over the Pearl River delta to reconnaissance overflights and small-scale harassment raids.

Most of the missions flown during the final week of June and the month of July involved lone aircraft from the 43rd Bomb Group. All these raids took place at night, which necessitated bombing with the H2X, and they usually targeted Canton. Despite the darkness the bombardiers might actually have been able to pull off a visual run on occasion, since haphazard enforcement of blackout restrictions by the Japanese meant that on some nights Hong Kong and Canton glowed with the incandescent brilliance of fully electrified peacetime cities. Standard operating procedure called for a P-61B Black Widow from the 418th Night Fighter Squadron to shadow each B-24 like a protective phantom. While the Liberator crew made a Mickey run on the Whampoa docks or industrial areas of Honam Island, the three-man crew of the P-61 orbited at a distance, ready to pounce on enemy night-fighters. Sleek, futuristic looking, and painted entirely in black, the twin-engine P-61 had been purpose-built for nocturnal dogfights. Highly maneuverable and capable of impressive acrobatics, it carried radar in its nose and had one of the heaviest weapons packages ever mounted on an American fighter aircraft—four 20 mm cannons and four .50-caliber heavy machine guns. As P-61 pilots had discovered to their delight, a quick burst from their eight gun tubes would knock down even the largest of enemy aircraft.

The 43rd Bomb Group sent a B-24 to make a Mickey run on Canton targets on eleven different nights during the latter half of June, and on every single mission the crew reported that they had been harassed by JAAF night-fighters.[7] Despite the extended pounding of the Canton airfields by both the 5th Air Force and the 14th Air Force, despite the thousands of fragmentation, incendiary, and high-explosive bombs strewn across the runways and revetments since 1942, despite the tens of thousands of .50-caliber rounds fired by strafing P-40s and P-51s, despite the total severing of supply lines by U.S. Navy submarines and the resultant lack of fuel, spare parts, and replacement aircraft, despite the devastating casualty rates for its pilots, despite all this, the JAAF in southern China could still put enough warplanes into the night sky over the Pearl River delta in the summer of 1945 to make missions real nail-biters for the B-24 crews flying nocturnal solo raids over Canton.

General Chennault's 14th Air Force had downsized its air operations over Hong Kong and Canton, which now offered few targets consequential enough to require an air strike. P-51 pilots from the 23rd Fighter Group still ran an occasional fighter sweep or recon mission over the Pearl River delta in the summer of 1945, and P-61 crews from the 426th Night Fighter Squadron, which had deployed to China in October 1944, flew some ground-attack sorties in the area as well. The war, however, had largely moved on, and the fortunes of General Chennault and the 14th Air Force declined with the winding down of the fighting in China and the shifting of priorities in Washington. Both President Truman and the high command of the U.S. military had grown increasingly disillusioned with Chiang Kai-shek's Nationalist regime, which they viewed as corrupt and militarily incompetent; moreover, American attention had shifted from China to geopolitical concerns in postwar Europe and the daunting task of invading Japan. Chennault had also acquired his share of enemies in the military and political establishment—General Bissell and General Stilwell chief among them—who wanted to terminate his command of the 14th Air Force. The recapture of Rangoon in May 1945 and the conclusion of major combat in Burma led to a reorganization of the U.S. Army Air Forces command structure on the Asiatic mainland. A new China-theater air command emerged from this reshuffling, but Chennault would not be the general to lead it. The Chungking-based headquarters would be commanded by Gen. George E. Stratemeyer instead, and the 10th Air Force, newly deployed to China from India and Burma, would be the dominant unit in this new command. For the time being, Chennault would retain control of the sidelined and subordinated 14th Air Force, but he understood that powerful forces would continue to work for his ouster. Beset by personal scandals, exhausted by eight years in China, and with few allies in the upper echelons of American power, Chennault resigned in early July 1945. A month later he boarded a c-47 at Kunming and flew out of China.

THE U.S. ARMY Air Forces had been bombing Hong Kong in earnest since July 1943, but the U.S. Navy would have the honor of carrying out the last American air strike on the battered port city. Naval patrol aircraft from Fleet Air Wing 17 of the 7th Fleet had continued to fly daylight missions over the Pearl River delta during the spring and summer of 1945, leading to frequent air-raid alerts in Hong Kong during the waking hours. On August 14 a Luzon-based PB4Y-2 Privateer—the naval version of the B-24—sank a small Japanese vessel offshore from the Stanley Peninsula. Just one day later, Japan declared its unconditional surrender.[8]

# 18

## *Bold Venture*

Second Lt. Elmer E. Haynes had flown his first combat mission over Hong Kong in August 1944 when he and 2nd Lt. Milton Wind had been pinned by searchlight beams after bombing the HK and Whampoa dockyard. Haynes had gone on to rack up more than fifty missions by April 1945, including four combat missions over Hong Kong and Canton and eight flights over the Hump. He had been shot up but never shot down, though he had scrubbed one of his battle-damaged B-24s in a crash landing at Chengkung airfield. In May 1945 Haynes received his stateside orders and rotated home to his wife as a newly promoted captain drawing $478 a month. His good friend Milt Wind made it home safely, too.[1]

Col. James T. Pettus ended the war with fifty-nine combat missions to his credit, including the dicey pathfinder run over Hong Kong on April 3, 1945. He still commanded the 43rd Bomb Group, which had left its base on Luzon and deployed to Ie Shima, a small island off the coast of Okinawa. From the bustling airbase on Ie Shima, the bomb group flew missions against the Japanese mainland, Korea, and northern China. Pettus had lost plenty of men during the war, and he was determined not to lose any more men after the news of the unconditional Japanese surrender reached Ie Shima. Understanding the risk posed by celebratory gunfire, the pragmatic and proactive Pettus confiscated every firearm in the entire bomb group. He then ordered that the impressive haul of .38-caliber revolvers, .45-caliber pistols, M-1 carbines, M-1 Garands, and assorted other small arms be secured in an impromptu armory room. Even war souvenir Nambu pistols and Arisaka rifles went into the lockup. For good measure Pettus then announced that any-one who fired a weapon could expect an immediate court-martial. More than a few men died from stray bullets and other pyrotechnic mayhem as thousands of American servicemen whooped it up on Ie Shima, but Pettus could proudly say that none of the dead men wore the shoulder patch of the 43rd Bomb Group.[2]

In the weeks that followed the surrender, American airmen from the 43rd Bomb Group and dozens of other units emerged from POW camps scattered across the now-defunct Japanese empire. Some had been imprisoned for years, such as Staff Sgt. James N. Young, who had bailed out of a crippled B-25 during the very first raid on Hong Kong in October 1942. He and his crewmates—1st Lt. Howard C. Allers, 2nd Lt. Murray L. Lewis, and Staff Sgt. Paul G. Webb—had been sent to the Kiangwan POW camp in the suburbs of Shanghai in December 1942. Their arrival caused an immediate sensation among the Allied prisoners, who had all been captured in the first weeks of the war and been cut off from any news since then. Young and his fellow crewmates brought word from the outside world to the inmates at Kiangwan, who included U.S. Marines from Wake Island and the north China garrison, merchant seamen from Brit-ish, Norwegian, and American ships, civilian construction work-ers from Wake Island, Chinese and Guamanian civilians who had worked in the mess and laundries for the marines, and a handful of U.S. Army and U.S. Navy men. The prisoners pressed Young for details on the progress of the war, but they also wanted up-to-date Major League Baseball scores and the lyrics for the latest hit songs back in the States. Fortunately for First Lieutenant Allers, who had been shot through the foot shortly after he had crash-landed his B-25 in a Kwangtung paddy field, the prison population at Kiang-wan included several navy doctors. Despite the limited medical facilities, the doctors managed to save Allers's foot and, given the risk of gangrene, most likely save his life as well. In spring 1945 the Japanese shipped Young, Allers, Lewis, Webb, and most of the men held at Kiangwan to northern Hokkaido to work as slave labor in the coal mines. Young survived this punishing work regimen, and so did Lewis, Webb, and Allers. In the autumn of 1945, they joined the exodus of demobilized American servicemen sailing eastward to the continental United States, where Young's beloved home state of Oregon awaited.[3]

Second Lt. Glenn A. McConnell and Staff Sgt. Tony M. Spadafora had been the only survivors of the ill-fated *Sweepy-Time Gal*, which had cartwheeled into the waters of Victoria Harbor in April 1944. By the first of May, both men had arrived at Ōfuna POW camp outside Yokohama, where they endured solitary confinement and torture-based interrogations that focused on the radar systems aboard B-24 LAB aircraft like *Sweepy-Time Gal*. Apparently satisfied that they had extracted whatever information of value the two airmen might possess, the camp administration transferred McConnell and Spada-fora to Shinjuku POW camp in Tokyo in January 1945. From inside the camp perimeter, they had front-row seats for the destruction of the city by their comrades in the USAAF. McConnell and Spadafora soon came to appreciate the camp's fortuitous location in the midst of a railroad yard. When the B-29s burned the city to the ground and incinerated its civilian population, the railroad tracks served as a firebreak that kept the camp from catching fire. When the war ended, McConnell and Spadafora boarded a C-54 for the first leg of the long journey home, transferred to a troopship in the Philippines, and reached the United States by early fall.[4]

Second Lt. Max L. Parnell of the 118th TRS had bailed out over Hong Kong on Christmas Eve 1944. He had been fished out of the harbor by the Japanese, and after a spell in Stanley Prison, had found himself handcuffed in a cage aboard a freighter bound for the Land of the Rising Sun. He arrived at Ōfuna in January 1945 at about the same time that McConnell and Spadafora transferred to Shinjuku. Parnell wore the same tattered shirt and pants for his entire eight and a half months at Ōfuna, most of which he spent in solitary confinement. He endured beatings far worse than the ones meted out to him in Stanley Prison and starvation-level rations that left him with beriberi. He never received medical attention, and during one particularly dark stretch his jailers forced him to go forty-four days without so much as washing his face. When liberation came, he possessed nothing more than the rags on his back, but in the days after the surrender a fellow prisoner found Parnell's watch, fountain pen, ring, and dog tags while rifling through the desk drawers of the departed Japanese camp commander. He returned these items to an astonished Parnell, who had never expected to see them again when they had been taken from him in Hong Kong. When Parnell had bailed out of his P-51 over Victoria Harbor, he had weighed a healthy 170 pounds. After two weeks aboard the navy hospital ship USS *Benevolence* in Tokyo Bay, he could manage 90 pounds. Despite his exhaustion on the second of September Parnell took great satisfaction in watching the surrender ceremony unfold aboard the battleship USS *Missouri*, which rode at anchor close to the hospital ship.[5]

ONCE THE POWS and civilian internees had been liberated, repatriated, and reunited with their families, American investigative teams fanned out across Asia in an attempt to determine the fate of thousands of missing army, navy, and marine airmen. Since the Pearl River delta had been a locus of American air activity from mid-1942 onward, the China Theater Search Detachment (CTSD) deployed a team designated as the Canton Sub-Detachment to Canton under the command of Capt. Franklin J. Wallace, an infantry officer. A substantial number of American servicemen had gone missing while flying missions over Hong Kong and Canton, including army pilots from the 14th Air Force and navy air crews from the flat tops of TF 38. Some of the missing aviators had turned up in prison camps at the end of the war, half-starved but alive. A substantial number remained unaccounted for, however, and the fact that many of these airmen had been shot down over the water made determining their fate all the more difficult. In January 1946 the British 3rd Commando Brigade in Hong Kong provided the Canton Sub-Detachment with a report of a crash site on land. According to the report, which immediately struck the sub-detachment investigators as quite promising, an American bomber had gone down in an isolated corner of the New Territories in March 1945. Cantonese farmers who lived in the rural community of Nam Long had buried the bodies of the five men killed in the crash and could guide American investigators to the location of the graves. Agencies of the Nationalist Chinese government, civilians in Hong Kong, and the American Office of Strategic Services (oss) all corroborated the report from the commandoes.

On the morning of February 5, 1946, an American investigation and recovery team from the Canton Sub-Detachment journeyed by boat from Kowloon to Nam Long, which could not be reached by road, and landed on a beach near the western edge of the village. The team knew that an identity bracelet engraved with the name "Robert Henry Waggy" had been recovered immediately after the crash by the villagers, who had then passed the bracelet along to Maj. Merrill S. Ady, an oss operative. Major Ady had forwarded the bracelet to the 14th Air Force. However, the team had little else to go on. They suspected that Robert Henry Waggy had been a crewman aboard a b-25, but they needed more information to determine exactly who he was and what plane he had been flying in.

After a series of interviews conducted on the beach, the team determined that the residents of Nam Long had found three badly burned bodies in the wreckage of an American bomber, which had been one of six aircraft that attacked a Japanese ship just offshore on March 15, 1945. A fourth airman had been thrown clear of the wreckage and died instantly. A fifth crewman had hurled himself out of the plummeting aircraft, but his parachute had failed to open. He had fallen from the sky, sustained severe injuries when he landed north of the crash site, and remained alive for just a few minutes before succumbing to his wounds. In the course of the interviews, a young boy from the village handed over an identification tag that bore the name "H. M. Worley" on one side and the serial number "18176644" on the other side. Careful questioning determined that the boy had found the tag in the vicinity of the crash site but not in the burned-out wreckage of the aircraft.

Though the men and women of Nam Long had understood with

absolute clarity that they would be risking reprisals from the Japanese, they had nonetheless proceeded to hack two graves out of the hard laterite soil and bury all five men as quickly as possible. They had placed the remains of the first four men in a single grave at the crash site, but the airman who had attempted the parachute jump went into a separate grave some distance from the wreck. The Nam Long villagers asserted that they had not removed any items from the bodies and that they had buried the men as they had found them. However, soldiers from the Japanese garrison had soon arrived in search of the downed American aviators. When the soldiers had determined that no Americans had survived the crash, they demanded that the men of Nam Long disinter the four airmen in the common grave. Once the bodies had been uncovered, the soldiers removed dog tags and other items from the corpses. Nobody in Nam Long revealed the grave holding the fifth crewman, which the Japanese never discovered.

Before boarding their boat for the journey back to Kowloon, the Japanese soldiers had ordered the villagers to leave the bodies of the American airmen unburied. However, after four days the leader of Nam Long had requested permission to rebury the corpses, which had attracted the attention of feral dogs. After the Japanese had granted permission, men from Nam Long had reburied the four sets of remains in the same single grave. They told the investigative team that the five bodies in the two separate graves had not been disturbed since.

Guided by the villagers, the investigation and recovery team hiked through rugged, boulder-strewn terrain to the top of a small hill that overlooked the sea. There the Americans determined that the plane had impacted just below the crest of the hill, shed a portion of the tail, bounced over the peak, and disintegrated in a massive explosion on the other side. Half of the tail gunner's compartment as well as pieces of the tail assembly remained on the front of the hill, while on the opposite side of the hill the rest of the plane had been reduced to ashes and gobs of molten aluminum. A debris field stretching for more than one hundred yards yielded shards of Plexiglas, safety-belt harness clips, snaps, grommets, rivets, bits of wire, .50-caliber bullets, and other unidentifiable bits of metal, but nothing with serial numbers or other identifying markings.

The recovery team exhumed four skulls and a jumble of other bones from the first grave, all of which they placed in a single coffin. When the team exhumed the fifth body from the second grave, the skeleton exhibited signs of massive trauma from the aborted parachute jump, including two broken shinbones. They laid the body in a second coffin and then hand-carried both caskets down to the beach. The team then shipped the five sets of remains—labeled x-184, x-185, x-186, x-187, and x-188—to CTSD headquarters in Canton.

CTSD personnel focused on determining the identity of the aircraft that had crashed at Nam Long, since once they knew the specific plane they would be able to obtain the crew roster. Evidence at the crash site, such as the .50-caliber rounds and remnants of the tail assembly, strongly suggested an American twin-engine bomber. This almost certainly meant a B-25, since other twin-engine American bombers like the B-26 Marauder had never been used over Hong Kong. Moreover, B-25s often flew with a five-man crew, which matched the number of bodies recovered from the crash scene.

CTSD investigators soon ascertained that only one B-25 had been lost over the Pearl River delta in March 1945; moreover, it had gone down on March 15, the crash date reported by Major Ady of the OSS, the British military, and the residents of Nam Long. Nicknamed *Bold Venture*, the B-25J had belonged to the 500th Bomb Squadron of the 345th Bomb Group, a unit of the 5th Air Force. The CTSD tried to track down a MACR for the plane, since standard procedure required squadrons to file such a report whenever an aircraft went down on a combat mission, but the MACR for *Bold Venture* had either never been filed or had been lost during the war years.[6] However, the CTSD located the mission report that had been written after the raid as well as the casualty report for *Bold Venture*. Both documents listed the name, rank, and serial number for each of the five crewmen who had been aboard the plane. CTSD investigators also discovered that the crews of the other B-25s assigned to the mission had taken aerial photographs that placed the crash at the location where the recovery team had found the charred remnants of the American plane. Both the mission report and the casualty report stated that all five men aboard the downed aircraft had been killed in the crash, and neither document mentioned the failed parachute attempt by one member of the crew. Upstaged by the detonation of the B-25 as it rammed into the hillside, this desperate act had gone unnoticed by the crews of the other five B-25s.

The CTSD determined that names on the crew roster matched names on the bracelet and the identification tag found at the crash site. However, the team still had to match the five names with the five bodies. This task proved more difficult, and even the identity of the relatively intact body of the man who had tried to bail out could not be determined. CTSD personnel concluded, however, that the man who had been ejected from the aircraft upon impact as well as the man who had attempted to bail out would have almost certainly occupied crew stations in the rear of the plane. Since investigators could not make a definitive identification of any of the five sets of remains, the CTSD recommended in April 1946 that the "killed in action" status of the five men be amended as "remains recovered, identified as a group, not individually."

From Canton the bodies traveled to the American Graves Registration Service (GRS) unit in Shanghai for identification and temporary burial. Using dental records the GRS unit identified Unknown X-184 as Sgt. Robert H. Waggy. This finding established the identity of the airman who had attempted to parachute from the plummeting B-25. However, GRS could not determine the identities of the other four bodies. Since the religious preferences of the five men remained unknown, a trio of Catholic, Protestant, and Jewish chaplains administered the burial rites during a service in the American military section of the Hungjao Road Cemetery on April 23, 1946. The GRS buried Sgt. Waggy in grave 346-A beside the unknown soldiers X-23 and X-6. The remains of the other four men were buried in grave 347-A between the graves of Unknown Soldier X-10 and

Capt. Samuel H. Dance of the 23rd Fighter Group. Collectively, the four bodies received the designation "Common Grave 115."

In 1947 the GRS unit at Shanghai disinterred the two caskets holding the five bodies and shipped them to the Central Identification Laboratory at Schofield Barracks in the Territory of Hawaii. At the laboratory the investigators relied on dental and medical records to identify Unknown X-185 as 2nd Lt. Robert W. Jensen in July 1948. No definitive identification could be made for Unknowns X-186, X-187, and X-188. After a period of temporary interment in Row Q, Casket 9 of U.S. Army Mausoleum number 2 at Schofield Barracks, in 1949 Second Lieutenant Jensen was buried at the request of his widow, Ruth M. Jensen, in the National Memorial Cemetery of the Pacific in Honolulu. Under the auspices of the Return of World War II Dead Program, the Office of the Quartermaster General sent a casket containing the remains of 2nd Lt. Orville L. Garrison, Sgt. Frank M. Tubb, and Sgt. Henry M. Worley back to the continental United States for final burial at Fort Smith National Cemetery in Arkansas. In 1949 the body of Sergeant Waggy came home aboard the army freighter USAT *Dalton Victory*, which docked in New York City. Sergeant Waggy's body and the remains of sixty-three other American servicemen who had died overseas were transferred to a mortuary train car and taken to Arlington National Cemetery, where a military honor guard buried Sergeant Waggy with his family in attendance.

As the bodies of the five men killed in the crash of *Bold Venture* had made their way from Hong Kong to their final resting places, reams of military paperwork typed out in triplicate had both preceded and trailed the caskets. This bureaucratic paper trail included "report of interment" forms filled out by the GRS and "laundry inventory" forms filled out by the Army Effects Bureau, an office tasked with returning the personal property of deceased service personnel to their next of kin. There were "intraoffice reference sheets" from the Office of the Quartermaster General as well as "correspondence action sheets" and "request for new letter of inquiry" forms. The various telegrams, letters, reports, and memos stated that the men had been KIPC (killed in plane crash) and included extensive maps of their teeth and extended narratives of their dental history. The thick files for each man revealed individual and very human details about the crew of *Bold Venture*: Tubb had been stationed in eight different states before deployment overseas and wore size 9D shoes; Jensen had 20-20 vision and webbing between the second and third toes of his foot; Worley was a Baptist and collected foreign coins as souvenirs; Waggy liked to read the New Testament and owned four cotton T-shirts; Garrison weighed in at a trim 131 pounds and had $31.80 in personal funds at the San Marcelino airbase when he died, and the money eventually reached his widow, Norma, in the form of a check from the Army Effects Bureau. The five men came from families rooted in West Virginia, Missouri, Connecticut, and Texas. Four of the five men left wives behind. When Jensen's widow, Ruth, gave birth to their son in May 1945, she named him Robert after her late husband. He grew up to become an air force pilot, just like his father.[7]

# ACKNOWLEDGMENTS

Various individuals and institutions in Hong Kong assisted me in my research for this book project. David Bellis, founder of the online Hong Kong history forum Gwulo: Old Hong Kong (www.gwulo.com), helped me track down obscure points of Hong Kong history and provided a venue for networking with experts on various aspects of Hong Kong's past. Over beers at the Foreign Correspondents Club, Craig Mitchell generously shared his expertise as well as his collection of U.S. Navy aircraft action reports and other primary documents. Craig saved me many hours of research work, and for this I am particularly grateful. Clement Cheung and the staff of the Hong Kong Heritage Project of China Light and Power facilitated my research of the archival documents in the Elizabeth Ride Collection. Elizabeth Ride herself shared additional documents above and beyond those she has already most generously donated to the HKHP archives. Richard Wesley, director of the Hong Kong Maritime Museum, provided access to research materials in the museum's Resource Center, particularly prewar charts of Victoria Harbor. Eric Huen shared his research on the Chinese American Composite Wing and filled in some of the gaps in my knowledge of the missions flown by this unit over Hong Kong.

In Alabama the staff of the Air Force Historical Research Agency assisted with my research in the air force archives at Maxwell Air Force Base. The mission reports and other wartime documents that I examined at the AFHRA are the bedrock on which this book has been constructed. Retired U.S. Air Force historian George Cully tracked down mission reports, wartime photographs, and other documents in the AFHRA archival collection. I know a thing or two about military aviation, but George knows far more, and he was unfailingly generous in sharing his encyclopedic knowledge about everything from HVAR rockets to Form 34s.

I owe a particular debt of gratitude to the many authors who have written about wartime Hong Kong and the American, Japanese, and Chinese squadrons that fought in the skies over China. Their articles, chapters, and books are listed in the bibliography. In writing this book, I have attempted to extend the conversation begun by these authors, and I hope that in doing so I have broadened our understanding of Hong Kong's experience during the Second World War.

Col. Chris J. McWilliams told me the story of his uncle 2nd Lt. Robert W. Jensen, pilot of the B-25J *Bold Venture*, for which this book is named. Chris Davis, whose grandfather Capt. Earl J. Davis flew with the 118th Tactical Reconnaissance Squadron, shared his extensive knowledge of the 118th as well as *Bold Venture*. Chris created and maintains websites devoted to the 118th TRS (www.118trs .com) and *Bold Venture* (www.boldventureb25.com) that will be of interest to readers of this book.

This book could not have been written without the research funding provided by Central Michigan University (CMU). A Creative and Scholarly Support Grant and a Faculty Research and Creative Endeavors Grant from CMU funded the archival research for this book project at the Air Force Historical Research Agency in Alabama. These grants also funded my research at the Hong Kong Heritage Project archives, the Hong Kong University Library, and other institutions and locations in Hong Kong. Micki Christiansen in the Department of English Language and Literature and Rick Middleton, Mary Montoye, Jamie Fockler, and Melinda Brackenberry in the Office of Research and Graduate Studies at CMU assisted with obtaining these research grants and helped me navigate the intricacies of funding, record-keeping, and reimbursement.

Libraries at various institutions played a key role in my research. In particular the CMU Library proved to be an invaluable research tool, and I am most fortunate to work for a university with such a fine library. Reference librarians Aparna Zambare and Susan Powers provided research tips and tracked down hard-to-obtain documents located at other institutions. The Hong Kong University Library granted me full access to its Special Collections, and the Special Collections and University Archives at Grand Valley State University provided digital copies of the U.S. Navy aircraft-recognition training slides that are included in the photographs for this book.

Anne Devlin of Max Gartenberg Literary Agency made it all happen. In short order she identified potential publishers and found a home for my manuscript at Potomac. I could not ask for better literary representation, and I could not ask for a better publisher either. I am grateful to Tom Swanson, my editor at the University of Nebraska Press, for seeing the potential of this book project and for taking a chance on an author who had never published a book-length work of military nonfiction before. Thanks are due as well to Sara Springsteen, the project editor for this book, and Barbara Wojhoski, who copyedited the final manuscript with precision and grace.

Most of all I am glad to thank my family—for everything, but particularly the slideshows that nurtured my interest in traveling overseas. On special occasions when I was a young boy, my father and mother would set up the slide projector and screen after dinner. My brother and sister and I would then watch slides of Greece, where my parents had lived in the mid-1960s while my father served as a lieutenant in the U.S. Air Force. I was born in a USAF airbase hospital in Libya—then a pro-American monarchy—and spent the first year of my life in Athens. Growing up in New England, I remember my father's collection of foreign coins, which he had picked up while traveling in the service, and how he always seemed to have an AHM model tank or box of 1/76th scale Airfix soldiers to give me. From my father, Edward "Curt" Bailey, I gained a fascination for all things military as well as for foreign travel. From my mother, Eleanor "Ellie" Bailey, I gained a facility with the written word, a passion for reading, and a love of history. In their own ways, both of my parents shaped who I am today—a writer and well-traveled academic—and made this book possible. I thank them for this. I also thank my maternal grandparents, Richard and Elva Stang, who intervened at a key moment in my education and made it financially possible for me to go to graduate school. I thank my wife, Jill Witt, and son, Kip, for their love, support, and good humor as I worked on this book project over a span of many years, sometimes while far from home in Alabama and Hong Kong. I say with the greatest of thanks that this book belongs not just to me but to my family as well.

# APPENDIX

**Units and Aircraft of the 1st American Volunteer Group (AVG), December 7, 1941–July 4, 1942**

  1st Fighter Squadron (Adam and Eves)
  2nd Fighter Squadron (Panda Bears)
  3rd Fighter Squadron (Hell's Angels)
  Aircraft: P-40B and P-40E[1]

**Units and Aircraft of the China Air Task Force (CATF) of the 10th Air Force, July 4, 1942–March 10, 1943**

23rd Fighter Group
  74th Fighter Squadron
  75th Fighter Squadron
  76th Fighter Squadron
  16th Fighter Squadron (attached from 51st Fighter Group)
  Aircraft: P-40B, E, and K; P-43A
11th Medium Bomb Squadron (attached from 341st Medium Bomb Group)
  Aircraft: B-25C
9th Photographic Reconnaissance Squadron
  Flight A
  Aircraft: F-4
Transport Flight
  Aircraft: C-47, C-53[2]

## Fighter Groups of the JAAF 3rd Hikoshidan (Air Division) Stationed in Canton during the American Air Raids of July–November 1942

24th Sentai (based in Canton July–September 1942)
> Commander: Maj. Takeshi Takahashi
> 1st Chutai
> 2nd Chutai
> 3rd Chutai
> Aircraft: Ki-43-1C

33rd Sentai (based in Canton September 1942–July 1943)
> Commander: Lt. Col. Kiyoshi Harada (to August 1942); Maj. Tsutomu Mizutani
> 1st Chutai
> 2nd Chutai
> 3rd Chutai
> Aircraft: Ki-43-1C

54th Sentai (based in Canton February–July 1942)
> Commander: Maj. Yasunari Shimada
> 1st Chutai
> 2nd Chutai
> 3rd Chutai
> Aircraft: Ki-27[3]

## Crew of B-25C number 055, 22nd Bomb Squadron, 341st Bomb Group, on October 25, 1942

> 1st Lt. Howard C. Allers (pilot)
> 2nd Lt. Nicholas Marich (copilot)
> 2nd Lt. Murry L. Lewis (navigator)
> 2nd Lt. Joseph W. Cunningham (bombardier)
> Staff Sgt. Paul G. Webb (flight engineer/top-turret gunner)
> Staff Sgt. James N. Young (radio operator/belly-turret gunner)[4]

## Units and Aircraft of the 14th Air Force, March 10, 1943

23rd Fighter Group
> 74th Fighter Squadron
> 75th Fighter Squadron

76th Fighter Squadron

16th Fighter Squadron (attached from 51st Fighter Group)

Aircraft: P-40B, E, and K; P-43A

11th Medium Bomb Squadron (detached from 341st Medium Bomb Group)

Aircraft: B-25C

308th Heavy Bomb Group

373rd Bomb Squadron

374th Bomb Squadron

375th Bomb Squadron

425th Bomb Squadron

Aircraft: B-24D

9th Photographic Reconnaissance Squadron

Flight A

Aircraft: F-4

Transport Flight

Aircraft: C-47, C-53[5]

---

**Fighter Groups of the JAAF 3rd Hikoshidan (Air Division) Stationed in Canton during the American Air Raids of July–September 1943**

25th Sentai (one or more *chutai* based in Canton September–October 1943)

Commander: Maj. Toshio Sakagawa to July 1944 (KIFA December 1944)

1st Chutai

2nd Chutai

3rd Chutai

Aircraft: Ki-43-II

33rd Sentai (one or more *chutai* based in Canton September 1942–July 1943 and September 1943)

Commander: Maj. Akira Watanabe (KIA August 1943); Maj. Isao Fukuchi (MIA November 1944)

1st Chutai

2nd Chutai

3rd Chutai

Aircraft: Ki-43-II

85th Sentai (one or more *chutai* based in Canton July 1943–December 1944)

    Commander: Maj. Goro Yamamoto

    1st Chutai

    2nd Chutai

    3rd Chutai

    Aircraft: Ki-44-II[6]

---

**Organization of the 14th Air Force, Summer 1944**

68th Composite Wing

    23rd Fighter Group

69th Composite Wing

    51st Fighter Group

    341st Medium Bomb Group

312th Fighter Wing

    33rd Fighter Group (April–September 1944 only)

    81st Fighter Group

    311th Fighter Group

Chinese American Composite Wing

    3rd Fighter Group

    5th Fighter Group

    1st Medium Bomb Group

308th Heavy Bomb Group[7]

---

**68th Composite Wing, 14th Air Force, Summer and Fall 1944**

    Commander: Brig. Gen. Clinton D. Vincent

    Headquarters: Kweilin

23rd Fighter Group

    74th Fighter Squadron

    75th Fighter Squadron

    76th Fighter Squadron

    Aircraft: P-40K, M, and N as well as P-51A, B, and C

118th Tactical Reconnaissance Squadron (attached to 23rd Fighter Group)

Aircraft: P-40N, P-51B and C, and L-5

5th Fighter Group (seconded from Chinese American Composite Wing)

    17th Fighter Squadron

    26th Fighter Squadron

    27th Fighter Squadron

    29th Fighter Squadron

    Aircraft: P-40N

341st Medium Bomb Group (detachments seconded from 69th Composite Wing)

    11th Bomb Squadron

    491st Bomb Squadron

    Aircraft: B-25D, H, and J

1st Medium Bomb Group (seconded from Chinese American Composite Wing)

    3rd Bomb Squadron

    4th Bomb Squadron

    Aircraft: B-25D and H

308th Heavy Bomb Group (detachments under operational control of 68th Composite Wing)

    373rd Bomb Squadron

    374th Bomb Squadron

    375th Bomb Squadron

    425th Bomb Squadron

    Aircraft: B-24D and J

21st Photographic Reconnaissance Squadron (detachments)

    Aircraft: F-4, F-5

322nd Troop Carrier Squadron

    Aircraft: C-47[8]

---

## Command Structure of the 5th Air Force in the Philippines, 1945

5th Air Force Headquarters

    Based on Leyte from November 1944, Mindoro from January 1945, and Luzon from April 1945

5th Fighter Command

85th Fighter Wing
86th Fighter Wing
Each wing commanded multiple fighter groups.
5th Bomber Command
308th Bomb Wing
309th Bomb Wing
310th Bomb Wing
Each wing commanded multiple bomb groups.
91st Reconnaissance Wing
54th Troop Carrier Wing
5th Air Service Command[9]

---

## Combat Air Groups of the 5th Air Force, April 1945

Light Bomb Groups
3rd Bomb Group
312th Bomb Group
417th Bomb Group
Aircraft: A-20
Medium Bomb Groups
38th Bomb Group
345th Bomb Group
Aircraft: B-25
Heavy Bomb Groups
22nd Bomb Group
43rd Bomb Group
90th Bomb Group
380th Bomb Group
Aircraft: B-24
Fighter Groups
8th Fighter Group
35th Fighter Group
49th Fighter Group
58th Fighter Group
348th Fighter Group

475th Fighter Group
Aircraft: P-38 (8th, 49th, 475th), P-47 (58th, 348th), P-51 (35th)
Independent Night Fighter Squadrons
418th Night Fighter Squadron
421st Night Fighter Squadron
547th Night Fighter Squadron
Aircraft: P-61
6th Photographic Reconnaissance Group
Aircraft: F-5 and F-7
71st Tactical Reconnaissance Group
Aircraft: B-25, P-38, P-51, L-5, and L-6
3rd Air Commando Group
Aircraft: P-51, C-47, and L-5
Transport Groups
2nd Combat Cargo Group
317th Troop Carrier Group
374th Troop Carrier Group
375th Troop Carrier Group
433rd Troop Carrier Group
Aircraft: C-46 and C-47[10]

---

## Heavy Bomb Groups of the 5th Air Force, April 1945

22nd Bomb Group (Heavy)
Commander: Col. Leonard T. Nicholson
Base: Clark Field, Luzon
2nd Bomb Squadron
19th Bomb Squadron
33rd Bomb Squadron
408th Bomb Squadron
Aircraft: B-24
43rd Bomb Group (Heavy)
Commander: Col. James T. Pettus Jr.
Base: Clark Field, Luzon
63rd Bomb Squadron

64th Bomb Squadron
65th Bomb Squadron
403rd Bomb Squadron
Aircraft: B-24
90th Bomb Group (Heavy)
Commander: Col. Ellis L. Brown
Base: San Jose, Mindoro
319th Bomb Squadron
320th Bomb Squadron
321st Bomb Squadron
400th Bomb Squadron
Aircraft: B-24
380th Bomb Group (Heavy)
Commander: Col. Forrest L. Brissey
Base: San Jose, Mindoro
528th Bomb Squadron
529th Bomb Squadron
530th Bomb Squadron
531st Bomb Squadron
Aircraft: B-24[11]

## 345th Medium Bomb Group (5th Air Force), February 1945

Commander: Col. Chester A. Coltharp
Base: San Marcelino, Luzon
Motto: Air Apaches
Squadrons
498th Bomb Squadron
499th Bomb Squadron
500th Bomb Squadron
501st Bomb Squadron
Aircraft: B-25[12]

## Crew of B-25J *Bold Venture* (Serial Number 43-36171), 500th Bomb Squadron, 345th Medium Bomb Group

2nd Lt. Robert W. Jensen (pilot)

2nd Lt. Orville L. Garrison (copilot)

Sgt. Henry M. Worley (flight engineer/gunner, likely in top turret)

Sgt. Frank M. Tubb (radio operator/gunner, likely at waist guns)

Sgt. Robert H. Waggy (gunner, likely at tail guns)

---

# NOTES

## 1. Eyes over Hong Kong

1. Wartime spellings for Chinese cities, airfields, and other geographic landmarks are used throughout this book. In many cases these wartime spellings differ substantially from contemporary usage, for example, "Kweilin" rather than the present-day "Guilin."

2. Chennault, *Way of a Fighter*, 120, 126; Ford, *Flying Tigers*, 94; Hotz et al., *With General Chennault*, 119–20; Molesworth, *23rd Fighter Group*, 43.

3. Flight intelligence report filed by Maj. Bruce K. Holloway, 23rd FG, September 22, 1942, AFHRA, Iris no. 78304.

## 2. Chennault

1. Hagiwara, "Japanese Air Campaign in China," 245.

2. Chennault's rank appears to have been an honorary one, as he had never risen above the rank of major in the U.S. military and did not accept a commission in the Chinese air force. Ford, *Flying Tigers*, 12.

3. Ford, *Flying Tigers*, 40; A. N. Young, *China and the Helping Hand*, 146.

4. Hotz et al., *With General Chennault*, 8.

5. Chennault, *Way of a Fighter*, 93.

6. Hotz et al., *With General Chennault*, 47–48.

7. Frillman and Peck, *China*, 107–34.

8. Ford, *Flying Tigers*, 285, 287; Frillman and Peck, *China*, 143.

9. Chennault, *Way of a Fighter*, 163–64.

10. Ford, *Flying Tigers*, 293–94; Frillman and Peck, *China*, 144–45.

11. American CNAC aircrews were granted military veteran status in 1993 in recognition of their contribution to the Allied war effort in the CBI Theater.

12. A. N. Young, *China and the Helping Hand*, 23, 245–52.

13. Xu, "Issue of U.S. Air Support," 466–67, 476; A. N. Young, *China and the Helping Hand*, 245–52.

14. Ford, *Flying Tigers*, 300.

15. Glines, *Chennault's Forgotten Warriors*, 7, 54.

16. Hata, Izawa, and Shores, *Japanese Army Fighter Aces*, 54–56; Ichimura, *Ki-43 "Oscar" Aces*, 35.

17. Scott, *God Is My Copilot*, 64–65.

18. Chennault, *Way of a Fighter*, 178.

19. Assistant Chief of Air Staff, *Fourteenth Air Force*, 59; Chennault, *Way of a Fighter*, 186.

20. Glines, *Chennault's Forgotten Warriors*, 299.

21. Molesworth, *Sharks over China*, 83–84, 86.

22. Chennault, *Way of a Fighter*, 196.

23. Mission report 4, 11th BS, 341st BG, July 4, 1942, AFHRA, Iris no. 268973.

24. Ford, *Flying Tigers*, 303–4.

25. Hotz et al., *With General Chennault*, 273–74; National Museum of the U.S. Air Force, "Over the Hump: The China National Aviation Corporation," April 29, 2015, http://www.nationalmuseum.af.mil/Visit/Museum-Exhibits/Fact-Sheets/Display/Article /196206/first-over-the-hump-the-china-national-aviation-corporation/.

26. Mission report 5, July 4, 1942; mission report 8, July 18, 1942; mission report 11, August 6, 1942; mission report 12, August 8, 1942, 11th BS, 341st BG, AFHRA, Iris no. 268973.

27. Taylor, *Air Interdiction in China*, 2.

28. Chennault, *Way of a Fighter*, 196.

29. Chennault, *Way of a Fighter*, 195–96.

30. Kwong, "Failure of Japanese Land-Sea Cooperation," 81.

31. Hata, Izawa, and Shores, *Japanese Army Fighter Aces*, 136–38.

32. The Japanese HO-103 12.7 mm heavy machine gun is sometimes inaccurately referred to as a 13 mm heavy machine gun.

33. Ichimura, *Ki-43 "Oscar" Aces*; Molesworth, *P-40 Warhawk vs Ki-43 Oscar*.

34. Edwin Ride, *British Army Aid Group*, 97; Lindsay Tasman Ride, "Report on the Activities of a M.I.9/19 Organization Operating in South China," 25, ERC HKHP, EMR-1-05.

35. Kwong, "Failure of Japanese Land-Sea Cooperation," 77, 87; Edwin Ride, *British Army Aid Group*, 92–93, 96–97; "Waichow Intelligence Summary No. 12," November 18, 1942, BAAG, ERC HKHP, EMR-1B-01.

36. "October 1942," BAAG, ERC HKHP, EMR-1A-07, tab 12, 13, 22, 24, and 27.

37. "Report No. 8: Period 28th July to 6th August, 1942," August 7, 1942, BAAG, ERC HKHP, EMR-1A-05, tab 7; Edwin Ride, *British Army Aid Group*, 93.

38. Bond and Anderson, *Flying Tiger's Diary*, 187; Ford, *Flying Tigers*, 313.

39. Scott, *God Is My Copilot*, 166.

40. Radio telegram from Gen. Claire Chennault to Song Meiling, October 24, 1942, AFHRA, Iris no. 268973.

### 3. Fried Eggs or Scrambled?

1. Molesworth, *Sharks over China*, 64.

2. Bergin, "Interview"; Ford, *Flying Tigers*, 45.

3. Chennault, *Way of a Fighter*, 196; Scott, *God Is My Copilot*, 165.

4. The description of Staff Sergeant Young's role in the first raid on Hong Kong is based on his memoir, "P.O.W: Mayday over China: The Diary of Jim Young," copy of manuscript in author's possession.

5. CATF documents describing the raid flown against Hong Kong on October 25, 1942, do not indicate how many aircraft and aircrews were from the 22nd BS, but they do indicate that First Lieutenant Allers, his crew, and his aircraft belonged to the 22nd BS. Memorandum to commanding officer, bomber unit, re: aircrews and aircraft participating in mission 33, October 25, 1942, 11th BS, 341st BG, AFHRA, Iris no. 43545; "Unit History Covering Period from June 26, 1917 to June 1, 1943," 11th BS, 341st BG, AFHRA, Iris no. 43526.

6. In 1940s Hong Kong, warehouses were almost universally referred to as "godowns." The term remains in common use today.

7. Molesworth, *Sharks over China*, 64.

8. Scott, *God Is My Copilot*, 108–9, 189.

9. Ford, *Flying Tigers*, 75; Lopez, *Into the Teeth of the Tiger*, 3; Molesworth, *Sharks over China*, 64; Scott, *God Is My Copilot*, 93, 170.

## 4. Tai-tai! Planes Are Coming!

1. United States Army Air Forces, Historical Office, *Army Air Forces*, 175; "Unit History covering Period from June 26, 1917 to June 1, 1943," 11th BS, 341st BG, AFHRA, Iris no. 43526.

2. Nelson, *First Heroes*, 7–8, 140.

3. United States Army Air Forces, Historical Office, *Army Air Forces*, 175.

4. Lopez, *Into the Teeth*, 3.

5. Radio telegram from Lt. Nolan Drone to Gen. Claire Chennault re: supplies of belly tanks, oil, and aviation fuel, November 15, 1942, AFHRA, Iris no. 268973.

6. Flight intelligence reports filed by Maj. John R. Alison and Maj. Bruce K. Holloway, 23rd FG, October 25, 1942, AFHRA, Iris no. 78304.

7. Chennault, *Way of a Fighter*, 195.

8. The account of the raid on Hong Kong flown by CATF aircraft on October 25, 1942, is based on the following sources: Chennault, *Way of a Fighter*, 195–99; mission report 33 filed by Lt. Col. Herbert Morgan, 11th BS, 341st BG, October 25, 1942, AFHRA, Iris no. 268973; mission reports filed by Col. Robert L. Scott, Maj. David L. Hill, Capt. John F. Hampshire, 1st Lt. Mortimer D. Marks, 1st Lt. Robert F. Mayer, 1st Lt. William E. Miller, October 25, 1942, and 2nd Lt. Morton Sher, November 9, 1942, 75th and 76th FS, 23rd FG, AFHRA, Iris no. 78304; Scott, *God Is My Copilot*, 164–74; "Unit History Covering Period from June 26, 1917 to June 1, 1943," 11th BS, 341st BG, AFHRA, Iris no. 43526.

9. Bond and Anderson, *Flying Tiger's Diary*, 38–39; Chennault, *Way of a Fighter*, 113; Molesworth, *Sharks over China*, 25–26; Scott, *God Is My Copilot*, 92, 103–4.

10. Flight intelligence report filed by 1st Lt. Martin W. Lubner, 76th FS, 23rd FG, November 24, 1942, AFHRA, Iris no. 78304; Hotz et al., *With General Chennault*, 148.

11. Bond and Anderson, *Flying Tiger's Diary*, 148; Ford, *Flying Tigers*, 255; Hotz et al., *With General Chennault*, 113.

12. Molesworth, *Sharks over China*, 27.

13. Scott, *God Is My Copilot*, 92, 105.

14. Hotz et al., *With General Chennault*, 131.

15. Lopez, *Into the Teeth*, 6.

16. Molesworth, *Sharks over China*, 209; Molesworth and Moseley, *Wing to Wing*, 167.

17. In 1940s Hong Kong, a *tai-tai* was a wealthy woman of European descent. An amah was a domestic servant who cared for her employer's children and performed other household chores.

18. Hahn, *China to Me*, 379–80.

19. No one source maps out where the bombs fell, the damage they did, and the casualties they caused. However, by triangulating a wide variety of sources the point of impact for the bombs dropped on October 25, 1942, can be estimated with reasonable confidence. In addition to USAAF documents cited above, of particular value is "Waichow Intelligence Summary No. 11," November 11, 1942, BAAG, ERC HKHP, EMR-1B-0, and the eyewitness account of Paul Astroshenko available at https://gwulo.com /node/27194/view-pages.

20. Barbara Anslow, wartime diary, October 25, 1942, https://gwulo.com/node/9710 /view-pages; Corbin, *Prisoners of the East*, 187–88.

21. In a memoir published in 1988, Scott gave an account of his role in the October 25, 1942, raid on Hong Kong that differed substantially from the account in his wartime memoir *God Is My Copilot* as well as the original mission report that he filed immediately after the raid. Scott claimed that he and Major Hill strafed the Peninsula Hotel in both of his memoirs but not in the mission report. In his own mission report, Major Hill made no reference to strafing the Peninsula Hotel. Scott, *Day I Owned the Sky*, 62–66, 154.

### 6. Night Raid on North Point

1. Ford, *Flying Tigers*, 103.

2. Chennault, *Way of a Fighter*, 183, 197; "Summary of Tactical Operations since 4 July 1942," 11th BS, 341st BG, January 1, 1943, AFHRA, Iris no. 268973; Zhang, "China's Quest for Foreign Military Aid," 290.

3. The account of the raid on Hong Kong flown by the 11th BS on the night of October 25–26, 1942, is based on the following sources: mission report 34 filed by Lt. Col. Herbert Morgan, 11th BS, 341st BG, October 26, 1942, AFHRA, Iris no. 268973; "Unit History covering Period from June 26, 1917 to June 1, 1943," 11th BS, 341st BG, AFHRA, Iris no. 43526.

4. Chennault, *Way of a Fighter*, 198; radio telegram from General Bissell to General Chennault, October 25, 1942, AFHRA, Iris no. 268973.

5. Radio telegram no. 773 A 179 from General Chennault to General Bissell, October 3, 1942, AFHRA, Iris no. 268973.

6. United States Army Air Forces, Historical Office, *Army Air Forces*, 178.

7. The account of the raid on Canton flown by the 11th BS on the night of October 25–26, 1942, is based on the following sources: mission report 35 filed by Lt. Col. Herbert Morgan, 11th BS, 341st BG, October 26, 1942, AFHRA, Iris no. 268973; "Unit History covering Period from June 26, 1917 to June 1, 1943," 11th BS, 341st BG, AFHRA, Iris no. 43526.

8. Flight intelligence report filed by Maj. Bruce K. Holloway, 23rd FG, October 26, 1942, AFHRA, Iris no. 78304.

9. Chennault, *Way of a Fighter*, 198–99.

### 7. Somewhere in Southern China

1. Young provides differing accounts of his questioning by the Kempeitai in his memoir and in his war crimes testimony given in August 1946. However, his account of being tortured is consistent in both documents.

### 8. Dud Bombs and Dead Fish

1. Scott, *God Is My Copilot*, 109.

2. Ford, *Flying Tigers*, 255, 295.

3. Combat pilots used the numbers of a clock for calling out the location of other aircraft. When a pilot sat in the cockpit, straight ahead beyond the nose of the aircraft was twelve o'clock, and straight behind the tail was six o'clock. The hours of two through five were on the right side of the plane, and the hours of seven through eleven were on the left side. For precision pilots specified high or low as well. For example, when pilots checked their sixes, they were looking behind them for enemy aircraft, particularly aircraft diving down on them from a higher altitude. If a pilot saw an enemy plane in that location, he might call out, "Bandits at six o'clock high!" His wingman would immediately know where the threat was.

4. Chief of Staff, War Department, *Basic Field Manual 30-38*, 4.

5. The account of the raid against Hong Kong by the 16th and 75th FS, 23rd FG, on October 28, 1942, is based on the following sources: consolidated flight intelligence report filed by Maj. Bruce K. Holloway and individual flight intelligence reports filed by Maj. John R. Alison, 1st Lt. Jack R. Best, 1st Lt. Dallas A. Clinger, Capt. Edmund R. Goss, 1st Lt. Chester D. Griffin, Capt. John F. Hampshire, Maj. Bruce K. Holloway, 2nd Lt. Walter E. Lacy, 1st Lt. John D. Lombard, 2nd Lt. R. A. Mitchell, 1st Lt. Robert H. Mooney, 1st Lt. Robert A. O'Neill, and Maj. H. M. Pike, AFHRA, Iris no. 78304; Molesworth, *Sharks over China*, 67–68.

6. Greenhous, *"C" Force to Hong Kong*, 130.

7. "Little Damage Done by Enemy Raids on H.K.," *Hongkong News*, October 27, 1942, 3, SC HKUL, MF 2521517, reel 3.

8. "Allies Give False Story regarding Raids on Hongkong," *Hongkong News*, October 28, 1942, 3, SC HKUL, MF 2521517, reel 3.

9. "Waichow Intelligence Summary No. 14," December 16, 1942, BAAG, ERC HKHP, EMR-1B-01.

10. Edwin Ride, *British Army Aid Group*, 207–8; "Waichow Intelligence Summary No. 12," November 18, 1942, BAAG, ERC HKHP, EMR-1B-01.

11. An alternative possibility is that the leaflets were a wartime tall tale. In their memoirs both General Chennault and Colonel Scott recount the story of the leaflets dispersed over Hong Kong by General Haynes, but there is no corresponding mention of a leaflet drop in mission reports or other CATF documents.

12. Edwin Ride, *British Army Aid Group*, 207–8.

13. Edwin Ride, *British Army Aid Group*, 207–8.

14. Hahn, *China to Me*, 380.

15. Banham, *We Shall Suffer There*, 68; Greenhous, *"C" Force to Hong Kong*, 130; Heywood, *It Won't Be Long Now*; Lindsay, *At the Going Down*, 95.

16. Hahn, *China to Me*, 380; Edwin Ride, *British Army Aid Group*, 208.

17. Kwong Chi Man, "The Failure of Japanese Land-Sea Cooperation," 78; summary of interview of M. Kavarana, J. P. Moslchandani, and K. T. Shinchand conducted by Capt. Wilfred J. Smith, CATF, AFHRA, Iris no. 81954; Edwin Ride, *British Army Aid Group*, 207.

18. Chennault, *Way of a Fighter*, 197; flight intelligence report filed by Col. Robert L. Scott, 23rd FG, October 25, 1942, AFHRA, Iris no. 78304; "Unit History covering Period from June 26, 1917 to June 1, 1943," 11th BS, 341st BG, 22, AFHRA, Iris no. 43526.

19. For a cogent analysis of how American P-40 pilots and their Japanese adversaries consistently overestimated the number of enemy planes they had destroyed, see Ford, *Flying Tigers*, 332–34.

20. Edwin Ride, *British Army Aid Group*, 207–8.

21. Hata, Izawa, and Shores, *Japanese Army Fighter Aces*, 62, 285; Ichimura, *Ki-43 "Oscar" Aces*, 63.

22. Flight intelligence report filed by 2nd Lt. Morton Sher, November 9, 1942, 76th FS, 23rd FG, AFHRA, Iris no. 78304.

23. Flight intelligence reports filed by 1st Lt. Mortimer D. Marks, 76th FS, 23rd FG, October 25, 1942, and 1st Lt. John D. Lombard, 16th FS, 23rd FG, October 28, 1942, AFHRA, Iris no. 78304.

24. See, for example, Carter and Mueller, *U.S. Army Air Forces*, 62; Chennault, *Way of a Fighter*, 197; United States Army Air Forces, Historical Office, *Army Air Forces in the War*, 179.

25. United States Army Air Forces, Historical Office, *Army Air Forces in the War*, 173; Ford, *Flying Tigers*, 337; "Unit History covering Period from June 26, 1917 to June 1, 1943," 11th BS, 341st BG, AFHRA, Iris no. 43526.

26. McClure, *Fire and Fall Back*, 56.

27. Molesworth, *Sharks over China*, 73.

28. Military History Section, Special Staff, General HQ, Far East Command, *Imperial Japanese Navy*, appendix B, 271; "Waichow Intelligence Summary No. 15," December 30, 1942, BAAG, ERC HKHP, EMR-1B-01.

29. "Abortive Bombing Raid by Enemy on Canton," *Hongkong News*, November 27, 1942, 1, SC HKUL, MF 2521517, reel 3.

30. The account of the air raids on Canton on November 23, 24, and 27 is based on the following documents: flight intelligence reports filed by Col. Robert L. Scott, Lt. Col. Clinton D. Vincent, Capt. E. R. Goss, Capt. C. B. Slocumb, 1st Lt. G. R. Barnes, 1st Lt. Jack R. Best, 1st Lt. J. R. Carney, 1st Lt. Patrick H. Daniels, 1st Lt. William W. Druwing, 1st Lt. Charles H. Dubois, 1st Lt. Martin W. Lubner, 1st Lt. R. H. Mooney, 1st Lt. H. K. Stuart, 1st Lt. Heath H. Wayne, 1st Lt. J. O. Wellborn, 2nd Lt. W. S. But-

ler, 2nd Lt. Aaron Liepe, 16th, 75th, and 76th FS, 23rd FG, November 23, 1942; flight intelligence reports filed by Lt. Col. Clinton D. Vincent, Maj. Bruce K. Holloway, Capt. E. R. Goss, Capt. George W. Hazlett, 1st Lt. D. D. Bryant, 1st Lt. L. H. Couch, 1st Lt. Charles H. Dubois, 1st Lt. Martin W. Lubner, 1st Lt. Robert A. O'Neill, 1st Lt. H. K. Stuart, 1st Lt. J. O. Wellborn, 2nd Lt. W. S. Butler, 2nd Lt. L. E. Hay, 2nd Lt. G. V. Pyles, 16th, 75th, and 76th FS, 23rd FG, November 24, 1942; flight intelligence reports filed by Col. Robert L. Scott, Lt. Col. Clinton D. Vincent, Maj. John R. Alison, Maj. Bruce K. Holloway, Capt. Burrall Barnum, Capt. E. R. Goss, Capt. John F. Hampshire, Capt. E. W. Richardson, 1st Lt. Jack R. Best, 1st Lt. H. M. Blackstone, 1st Lt. Edward H. Calvert, 1st Lt. Dallas A. Clinger, 1st Lt. William W. Druwing, 1st Lt. Charles H. Dubois, 1st Lt. John D. Lombard, 1st Lt. Martin W. Lubner, 1st Lt. Robert A. O'Neill, 1st Lt. Harold K. Stuart, 1st Lt. Charles Tucker, 1st Lt. Heath H. Wayne, 2nd Lt. George R. Barnes, 2nd Lt. R. L. Tempest, 16th, 75th, and 76th FS, 23rd FG, November 27, 1942, AFHRA, Iris no. 78304; 10th Air Force operational diary, October–November 1942, AFHRA, Iris no. 267305.

31. Chennault, *Way of a Fighter*, 199–200; Scott, *God Is My Copilot*, 188.

32. Hata, Izawa, and Shores, *Japanese Army Fighter Aces*, 294.

### 9. It Was a Honey

1. Hahn, *China to Me*, 412–13.

2. Assistant Chief of Air Staff, *Fourteenth Air Force*, 14–15, 160.

3. Assistant Chief of Air Staff, *Fourteenth Air Force*, 1–7; Xu, "Issue of U.S. Air Support," 471–72.

4. Assistant Chief of Air Staff, *Fourteenth Air Force*, 44–49.

5. Glines, *Chennault's Forgotten Warriors*, 50, 58; "Organizational History of 308th Bombardment Group," 6–8, AFHRA, Iris no. 81952; E. M. Young, *B-24 Liberator Units*, 46.

6. Assistant Chief of Air Staff, *Fourteenth Air Force*, 57–64; Drea and Van de Ven, "Overview of Major Military Campaigns," 43–44; Molesworth, *Sharks over China*, 116–18.

7. Assistant Chief of Air Staff, *Fourteenth Air Force*, 69–71; Ford, *Flying Tigers*, 343; McClure, *Fire and Fall Back*, 110; Samson, *Flying Tiger*, 195; Taylor, *Air Interdiction in China*, 2, 4.

8. Baime, *Arsenal of Democracy*, 134, 157, 162, 286.

9. Baime, *Arsenal of Democracy*, 90.

10. Feuer, *B-24 in China*, 119–20.

11. Assistant Chief of Air Staff, *Fourteenth Air Force*, 83–84; flight intelligence reports filed by Capt. E. W. Richardson on July 27, 1942, and Capt. Arthur W. Cruikshank on July 27 and 28, 1942, 74th FS, 23rd FG, AFHRA, Iris no. 78304; interrogation form for mission 82, 11th BS, 341st BG, July 27, 1943, AFHRA, Iris no. 43546; interrogation form for mission 83, 11th BS, 341st BG, July 28, 1943, AFHRA, Iris no. 43547.

12. Squadron history for 449th FS, July 1943–May 1944, AFHRA, Iris no. 60556.

13. Coates, *Whampoa*, 222, 226–27.

14. Cameron, *Illustrated History of Hong Kong*, 208; Chiu, *Port of Hong Kong*, 42; Courtauld and Holdsworth, *Hong Kong Story*, 40–41.

15. Banham, "Hong Kong Dockyard Defence Corps"; Melson, *White Ensign, Red Dragon*, 45–47.

16. Alternative translations of the Japanese name for the Royal Navy dockyard include the No. 2 Naval Working Department, the No. 2 Department of the IJN, the 2nd Construction Department, and the 2nd Naval Construction and Repair Department.

17. Kwong and Tsoi, *Eastern Fortress*, 151–53.

18. Assistant Chief of Air Staff, *Fourteenth Air Force*, 83–84; flight intelligence report filed by Col. Bruce K. Holloway, 23rd FG, July 29, 1943, AFHRA, Iris no. 78304; Hata, Izawa, and Shores, *Japanese Army Fighter Aces*, 136; mission 12, "Organizational History of 308th Bombardment Group," 26–27, AFHRA, Iris no. 81952; Molesworth, *Sharks over China*, 131; squadron history for 449th FS, July 1943–May 1944, AFHRA, Iris no. 60556.

19. Hahn, *China to Me*, 413; Hahn, *Hong Kong Holiday*, 158–59.

20. Hahn, *China to Me*, 413.

21. Bob Hackett, Sander Kingsepp, and Peter Cundall, "IJN Gunboat *Suma*: Tabular Record of Movement," 2015, www.combinedfleet.com/suma_t.htm; Military History Section, Special Staff, *Imperial Japanese Navy*, part 8, 190.

22. Assistant Chief of Air Staff, *Fourteenth Air Force*, 103; flight intelligence reports filed by 1st Lt. William B. Hawkins, 74th FS, 23rd FG, August 25, 1942, AFHRA, Iris no. 78304; interrogation form for missions 87 and 88, 11th BS, 341st BG, August 25, 1943, AFHRA, Iris no. 43547.

23. Ichimura, *Ki-43 "Oscar" Aces*, 63–66; missions 14 and 15, "Organizational History of 308th Bombardment Group," 29–36, AFHRA, Iris no. 81952.

24. Assistant Chief of Air Staff, *Fourteenth Air Force*, 104; flight intelligence report filed by 1st Lt. William B. Hawkins, 74th FS, 23rd FG, August 26, 1943, AFHRA, Iris no. 78304; mission 16, "Organizational History of 308th Bombardment Group," 36–37, AFHRA, Iris no. 81952; group mission report 16, 308th BG, August 26, 1943, AFHRA, Iris no. 81962; squadron history for 449th FS, July 1943–May 1944, AFHRA, Iris no. 60556.

25. Cressman, *Official Chronology of the U.S. Navy*, 380; draft of unit citation for 74th FS, February 14, 1944, AFHRA, Iris no. 78297; flight intelligence reports filed by 1st Lt. William B. Hawkins, 74th FS, 23rd FG, August 30 and 31, 1943, AFHRA, Iris no. 78304.

26. Hahn, *Hong Kong Holiday*, 116.

27. Interrogation form for mission 99, 11th BS, 341st BG, September 2, 1943, AFHRA, Iris no. 43547.

28. Assistant Chief of Air Staff, *Fourteenth Air Force*, 118–19; Banham, *We Shall Suffer There*, 134–35; Ebbage, *Hard Way*, 219–20; flight intelligence reports filed by 1st Lt. William B. Hawkins, 74th FS, 23rd FG, September 2, 1943, AFHRA, Iris no. 78304; Lindsay, *At the Going Down*, 96.

29. "Bus Services Temporarily Suspended," *Hongkong News*, September 5, 1943, 3; "Kowloon to Have More Rickshaws," *Hongkong News*, September 7, 1943, 3; "More Horse Carriages for K'Loon Residents," *Hongkong News*, September 8, 1943, 3, SC HKUL, MF 2521518, reel 4.

30. Assistant Chief of Air Staff, *Fourteenth Air Force*, 122; flight intelligence report filed by Capt. William B. Hawkins, 74th FS, 23rd FG, September 9, 1943, AFHRA, Iris

no. 78304; Hata, Izawa, and Shores, *Japanese Army Fighter Aces*, 297; Ichimura, *Ki-43 "Oscar" Aces*, 66; interrogation form for mission 101 and supplement to mission report 101, 11th BS, 341st BG, September 9, 1943, AFHRA, Iris no. 43546.

31. Also spelled "Nakazono."

32. Assistant Chief of Air Staff, *Fourteenth Air Force*, 122–23; Hata, Izawa, and Shores, *Japanese Army Fighter Aces*, 64–65; Millman, *Ki-44 Tojo Aces*, 23; Molesworth, *Sharks over China*, 147–48; squadron history for 449th FS, July 1943–May 1944, AFHRA, Iris no. 60556; United States Army Forces in the Far East Headquarters and 8th U.S. Army, *Air Operations in the China Area*, 134–37.

33. Assistant Chief of Air Staff, *Fourteenth Air Force*, 124; Raymond Eric Jones, wartime diary, September 12, 1943, transcript in author's collection; Military History Section, Special Staff, *Imperial Japanese Navy*, part 8, 192; squadron history for 449th FS, July 1943–May 1944, AFHRA, Iris no. 60556.

34. Emerson, *Hong Kong Internment*, 64–71; Hahn, *Hong Kong Holiday*, 275–79.

### 10. Colbert's Walk Out

1. Assistant Chief of Air Staff, *Fourteenth Air Force*, appendix 6; Molesworth, *23rd Fighter Group*, 72–73.

2. Bergin, "Interview."

3. The account of the mission flown over Hong Kong on December 1, 1943, is based on the following documents: flight intelligence reports filed by 2nd Lt. Luther C. Kissick, 74th FS, and 2nd Lt. E. E. Paine, 76th FS, 23rd FG, December 1, 1943, AFHRA, Iris no. 78304; flight intelligence report filed by Capt. Archie H. McGray, 1st BG, CACW, December 1, 1943, AFHRA, reel 1118-130035-1BG; historical record, 1st BG, CACW, 19, AFHRA, reel 1118-130035-1BG; interrogation forms for missions 183 and 184, 11th BS, 341st BG, December 1, 1943, AFHRA, Iris no. 43547.

4. Interrogation report for mission 172, 11th BS, 341st BG, November 26, 1943, AFHRA, Iris no. 43547; Kwong, "Failure of Japanese Land-Sea Cooperation," 79; Military History Section, Special Staff, *Imperial Japanese Navy*, part 8, 194.

5. Hata, Izawa, and Shores, *Japanese Army Fighter Aces*, 298; group mission reports 29, 32, and 33, 308th BG, November 3 and 16, 1943, AFHRA, Iris no. 81962; missions 29, 32, and 33, "Organizational History of 308th Bombardment Group," 47–50, AFHRA, Iris no. 81952.

6. Sources differ on when the radar unit atop Tai Mo Shan went into operation as well as its effective range. See "World War 2 Japanese Radar Station on Tai Mo Shan," Gwulo: Old Hong Kong, January 25, 2016, https://gwulo.com/node/30456; "Japanese Radar Station on Tai Mo Shan," Industrial History of Hong Kong Group, November 14, 2014, http://industrialhistoryhk.org/japanese-radar-station-tai-shan/; Kwong, "Failure of Japanese Land-Sea Cooperation," 77–78; Lai, Ching, and Tan, "Survey Findings," 87–88; Millman, *Ki-44 Tojo Aces*, 24.

7. Millman, *Ki-44 Tojo Aces*, 17.

8. Hata, Izawa, and Shores, *Japanese Army Fighter Aces*, 63–64; Millman, *Ki-44 Tojo Aces*, 9–14.

9. Molesworth, *Sharks over China*, 167.

10. Millman, *Ki-44 Tojo Aces*, 91–92.

11. Bergin, "Interview."

12. Molesworth, *Sharks over China*, 168.

13. Military History Section, Special Staff, *Imperial Japanese Navy*, appendix B, 276; Joint Army-Navy Assessment Committee, *Japanese Naval and Merchant Shipping Losses*, 48.

14. The narrative of First Lieutenant Colbert's "walk out" is based primarily on the following documents: "Appendix A: Escape of Lieut. Colbert USAAF," "Kweilin Weekly Intelligence Summary No. 30," BAAG, ERC HKHP, EMR-1B-03; MACR for 1st Lt. Robert T. Colbert (aircraft serial no. 43-5277), 76th FS, 23rd FG, February 19, 1945, NARA/Fold3, https://www.fold3.com; narrative of Lieutenant Colbert's "walk out" prepared by Lt. E. E. Paine and Maj. Richard V. Taylor, December 27, 1943, 23rd FG, AFHRA, Iris no. 78304.

15. Colbert's English-speaking benefactor is not identified by name in any of the sources describing Colbert's walk out. He is referred to here by the common Cantonese surname of Leung for the sake of readability and narrative coherence.

16. *Pointee Talkie*, 26, ERC HKHP. As indicated by the signature and handwritten note on the back cover, the *Pointee Talkie* in the Elizabeth Ride Collection at the Hong Kong Heritage Project belonged to Capt. G. H. Reynolds, who served in the BAAG in the Yomping-Canton area, December 1944–October 1945.

17. *Pointee Talkie*, 46, ERC HKHP.

18. The names of the officers in the special operations unit have been spelled as they originally appeared in the narrative of Colbert's walk out prepared by the S-2 officers of the 76th FS and 23rd FG.

19. Edwin Ride, *British Army Aid Group*, photo section.

20. Flight intelligence reports filed by 2nd Lt. Luther C. Kissick, 74th FS, 23rd FG, December 23, 1943; flight intelligence reports filed by 2nd Lt. E. E. Paine, 76th FS, 23rd FG, December 24, 1943, AFHRA, Iris no. 78304; group mission reports 40 and 41, 308th BG, August 26, 1943, AFHRA, Iris no. 81962; missions 40 and 41, "Organizational History of 308th Bombardment Group," 58–60, AFHRA, Iris no. 81952; Molesworth and Moseley, *Wing to Wing*, 26.

21. Molesworth, *Sharks over China*, 167–68, 177–78.

22. Narrative of Lieutenant Colbert's "walk out" prepared by Lt. E. E. Paine and Maj. Richard V. Taylor, December 27, 1943, 23rd FG, AFHRA, Iris no. 78304.

## 11. *Sweepy-Time Gal*

1. Emerson, *Hong Kong Internment*, 55.

2. Corbin, *Prisoners of the East*, 207–8; Emerson, *Hong Kong Internment*, 52; Endacott and Birch, *Hong Kong Eclipse*, 215; Gittins, *Stanley*, 119–20, 126.

3. *Hongkong News*, April 20, 1944, 2, SC HKUL, MF 2521519, reel 5.

4. Raymond Eric Jones, wartime diary, April 21, 1944, transcript in author's collection.

5. Section 1, "Kweilin Weekly Intelligence Summary No. 49," May 19, 1944, BAAG, ERC HKHP, EMR-1B-04.

6. Molesworth, *Sharks over China*, 181–82.

7. Group mission report 53, 308th BG, January 25, 1944, AFHRA, Iris no. 81967; Joint Army-Navy Assessment Committee, *Japanese Naval and Merchant Shipping Losses*, 50; mission 53, "Organizational History of 308th Bombardment Group," 69, AFHRA, Iris no. 81952; Military History Section, Special Staff, *Imperial Japanese Navy*, part 8, 196.

8. Appendix 1: 74th FS missions flown during the month of January 1944, 74th FS, 23rd FG, AFHRA, Iris no. 78296; flight intelligence report compiled by Col. T. Alan Bennett, 3rd FG, CACW, January 23, 1945; flight intelligence report compiled by 1st Lt. Luther C. Kissick, 74th FS, 23rd FG, January 23, 1944, AFHRA, Iris no. 78304; interrogation form for mission 230, 11th BS, 341st BG, January 23, 1944, AFHRA, Iris no. 43548; mission 45, "Organizational History of 308th Bombardment Group," 65, AFHRA, Iris no. 81952; Molesworth and Moseley, *Wing to Wing*, 40; group mission report 45, 308th BG, January 11, 1944, AFHRA, Iris no. 81963.

9. Flight intelligence report compiled by Col. T. Alan Bennet, 3rd FG, CACW, February 11, 1945; flight intelligence report and supplementary report compiled by 1st Lt. Luther C. Kissick, 74th FS, 23rd FG, February 11, 1945; "Four Enemy Raiders Shot Down," *Hongkong News*, February 13, 1944, 3, SC HKUL, MF 2521519, reel 5; interrogation form for mission 239, 11th BS, 341st BG, February 11, 1944, AFHRA, Iris no. 43549; Molesworth, *Sharks over China*, 190–91; Molesworth and Moseley, *Wing to Wing*, 40–41.

10. Group mission report 72, 308th BG, March 10, 1944, AFHRA, Iris no. 81963; Raymond Eric Jones, wartime diary, March 10, 1944, transcript in author's collection; mission 72, "Organizational History of 308th Bombardment Group," 82–83, AFHRA, Iris no. 81952.

11. Frisbee, "Valor."

12. Glines, *Chennault's Forgotten Warriors*, 213–14; group mission report 75, 308th BG, March 10, 1944, AFHRA, Iris no. 81963; mission 75, "Organizational History of 308th Bombardment Group," 83–84, AFHRA, Iris no. 81952.

13. The account of the final mission of *Sweepy-Time Gal* and the fate of McConnell and Spadafora is derived from the following sources: Glines, *Chennault's Forgotten Warriors*, 212–23; MACR for crew of B-24DR (aircraft serial no. 42-40622), 373rd BS, 308th BG, May 1, 1945; mission 93, "Organizational History of 308th Bombardment Group," 93, AFHRA, Iris no. 81952.

14. Horsnell, "Note on the Japanese Gun Emplacement."

15. Burton, *Fortnight of Infamy*, 220; Ichimura, *Ki-43 "Oscar" Aces*, 31; McManus, *Deadly Sky*, 277–78; Scott, *God Is My Copilot*, 189.

16. Sakaida, *Aces of the Rising Sun*, 110, 141–44.

17. Endacott and Birch, *Hong Kong Eclipse*, 163.

18. "Kweilin Weekly Intelligence Summary No. 56," July 7, 1944, BAAG, ERC HKHP, EMR-1B-04.

## 12. Gulls, Pigeons, and Jays

1. Glines, *Chennault's Forgotten Warriors*, 129–34; Taylor, *Air Interdiction in China*, 7–10; E. M. Young, *B-24 Liberator Units*, 75–78.

2. Mission 193, 198, 205, 216, 230, 264, and 266, "Organizational History of 308th Bombardment Group," AFHRA, Iris no. 81952.

3. Feuer, *B-24 in China*, 28–29; group mission report 216, 308th BG, August 25, 1944, AFHRA, Iris no. 81964; mission 216, "Organizational History of 308th Bombardment Group," AFHRA, Iris no. 81952.

4. Military History Section, Special Staff, *Imperial Japanese Navy*, part 8, 201.

5. Hara, "Ichigo Offensive," 392; Tohmatsu, "Strategic Correlation," 435.

6. Mitter, *Forgotten Ally*, 333.

7. Hara, "Ichigo Offensive," 392–402.

8. Taylor, *Air Interdiction in China*, 7.

9. Hagiwara, "Japanese Air Campaign in China," 251; Tohmatsu, "Strategic Correlation," 435.

10. McClure, *Fire and Fall Back*, 202–4.

11. Operational intelligence reports D-27, D-31, D-34, D-37, D-40, D-41, D-42, D-43, D-44, D-45, D-75, D-82, D-85, D-87, D-88, D-90, D-91, D-92, D-94, D-95, D-104, 491st BS, 341st BG, July 4–October 31, 1944, AFHRA, Iris no. 47494; operational intelligence report 375, 11th BS, 341st BG, July 28, 1944, AFHRA, Iris no. 43550; operational intelligence reports 510, 519, 520, 521, 523, 526, 528, 530, 531, 545, 11th BS, 341st BG, September 25–October 31, 1944, AFHRA, Iris no. 43552; operational intelligence report 379, July 29, 1944, operational intelligence report 389, August 1, 1944, and supplementary operational intelligence report 379, August 11, 1945, 11th BS, 341st BG, AFHRA, Iris no. 43546.

12. Group mission report 147, June 15, 1944, 308th BG, AFHRA, Iris no. 81963; group mission reports 169 and 174, July 5 and 8, 1944, AFHRA, Iris no. 81964; mission 147, 169, and 174, "Organizational History of 308th Bombardment Group," AFHRA, Iris no. 81952.

13. Feuer, *B-24 in China*, 51; group mission report 265, September 30, 1944, AFHRA, Iris no. 81965; mission 265, "Organizational History of 308th Bombardment Group," AFHRA, Iris no. 81952.

14. Glines, *Chennault's Forgotten Warriors*, 96–97, 116–17; group mission reports 135, 164, 197, 222, 226, 250, and 251, 308th BG, June 6–September 22, 1944, AFHRA, Iris no. 81963, 81964, and 81965; Raymond Eric Jones, wartime diary, October 30, 1944, transcript in author's collection; Kwong, "Failure of Japanese Land-Sea Cooperation," 80; missions 135, 164, 165, 197, 222, 226, 250, and 251, "Organizational History of 308th Bombardment Group," AFHRA, Iris no. 81952; Military History Section, Special Staff, *Imperial Japanese Navy*, part 8, 208; Taylor, *Air Interdiction in China*, 10–11.

15. Aeronautical Staff of Aero Publishers, *Nakajima Ki-84*; Sakaida, *Japanese Army Air Force Aces*, 69.

16. The account of the dogfight over Canton on October 5, 1944, is based on the following sources: flight intelligence report 516, October 5, 1944, and supplement to flight intelligence report 516, 118th TRS, 23rd FG, October 22, 1944, AFHRA/118th TRS; Hata, Izawa, and Shores, *Japanese Army Fighter Aces*, 70, 168–70, 268–69, 305; Millman, *Ki-44 Tojo Aces*, 43; Molesworth, *Sharks over China*, 235–36; operational intelligence report D-93, 491st BS, 341st BG, October 5, 1944, AFHRA, Iris no. 47494.

17. Second Lt. Eisenman was killed in action on April 15, 1944. The account of the raid on White Horse airfield on October 15, 1944, is based on the following sources: Feuer, *B-24 in China*, 53; flight intelligence report 569, 76th FS, 23rd FG, October 15, 1944, AFHRA, Iris no. 57338; flight intelligence reports 556 and 556A, 118th TRS, 23rd FG, October 15, 1944, AFHRA/118th TRS; Hata, Izawa, and Shores, *Japanese Army Fighter Aces*, 67, 306; MACR no. 9611 for 2nd Lt. Jerome F. Eisenman (aircraft serial no. 43-7089), 76th FS, 23rd FG, October 16, 1944, NARA/Fold3, https://www.fold3.com; Millman, *Ki-44 Tojo Aces*, 44–45; mission 276, "Organizational History of 308th Bombardment Group," AFHRA, Iris no. 81952.

18. Heywood, *It Won't Be Long Now*, 127.

19. Heywood, *It Won't Be Long Now*, 128.

20. Some sources spell *Bunzan Maru* as *Buzan Maru*.

21. The account of the raid on October 16, 1944, and the estimate of ships sunk and damaged during this attack are based on the following sources: Corrigan and Corrigan, *Hong Kong Diary Revisited*, 280–82; Cressman, *Official Chronology of the U.S. Navy*, 556; flight intelligence report 559, 118th TRS, 23rd FG, October 16, 1944, AFHRA/118th TRS; Glines, *Chennault's Forgotten Warriors*, 158, 264; group mission report 278, 308th BG, October 16, 1944, AFHRA, Iris no. 81965; Heywood, *It Won't Be Long Now*, 126–30; Joint Army-Navy Assessment Committee, *Japanese Naval and Merchant Shipping Losses*; Kweilin weekly intelligence summaries Nos. 72–74, 76, ERC HKHP, EMR-1B-04 and EMR-1B-05; MACR no. 9721 for 1st Lt. Charles F. Porter (aircraft serial no. 43-7109), 26th FS, 51st FG, October 17, 1944, NARA/Fold3, https://www.fold3.com; mission 278, "Organizational History of 308th Bombardment Group," AFHRA, Iris no. 81952; Molesworth, *Sharks over China*, 235; operational intelligence report 354, 11th BS, 341st BG, October 16, 1944, AFHRA, Iris no. 43552; operational intelligence report D-96, 491st BS, 341st BG, October 16, 1944, AFHRA, Iris no. 47494; Military History Section, Special Staff, *Imperial Japanese Navy*; reports on ship movements and bomb damage, 18th Photo Intelligence Detachment, October 16, 17, 19, and 23, 1944, AFHRA, Iris no. 268762.

22. McClure, *Fire and Fall Back*, 186.

23. McClure, *Fire and Fall Back*, 187.

24. The account of the demolition of Kweilin airbase and the departure of General Vincent and Lieutenant Colonel Hill is based on the following sources: history of the 68th Composite Wing, December 22, 1943–January 31, 1944, AFHRA, Iris no. 106440; McClure, *Fire and Fall Back*, 14, 185–87, 194, 201; Molesworth, *Sharks over China*, 225.

25. Flight intelligence report 719, 118th TRS, 23rd FG, November 12, 1944, AFHRA/118th TRS.

### 13. The Death of Chan Lim-pak

1. Holdsworth and Munn, *Dictionary of Hong Kong Biography*, 71–72; Lethbridge, "Hong Kong under Japanese Occupation," 110; Snow, *Fall of Hong Kong*, 219.

2. Squadron history for 118th TRS, 23rd FG, September 15–November 7, 1944, AFHRA/118th TRS.

3. Molesworth, *Sharks over China*, 210–11.

4. Squadron history for 118th TRS, 23rd FG, November 12, 1944–January 22, 1945, AFHRA/118th TRS.

5. Joint Army-Navy Assessment Committee, *Japanese Naval and Merchant Shipping Losses*, 78; Military History Section, Special Staff, *Imperial Japanese Navy*, part 8, 218.

6. Flight intelligence reports 749 and 750 for December 8, 760 and 761 for December 19, 762 for December 20, 764 and 765 for December 21, 766 and 767 for December 22, 1944, 118th TRS, 23rd FG, AFHRA/118th TRS; MACR no. 10739 for 1st Lt. Carlton Covey (aircraft serial no. 45-25186), 118th TRS, 23rd FG, December 20, 1944, and MACR no. 10955 for 1st Lt. Blanton S. Keller (aircraft serial no. 43-24950), 118th TRS, 23rd FG, December 22, 1944, NARA/Fold3, https://www.fold3.com.

7. The account of the raids on Hong Kong flown by the 118th TRS on December 24, 1944, is based on the following sources: flight intelligence reports 769 and 771, 118th TRS, 23rd FG, December 24, 1944, AFHRA/118th TRS; MACR no. 16260 for 1st Lt. Bryan L. Kethley Jr. (aircraft serial no. not indicated), 118th TRS, 23rd FG, date of document not indicated, and MACR no. 10967 for 2nd Lt. Max L. Parnell (aircraft serial no. 43-24984), 118th TRS, 23rd FG, December 26, 1944, NARA/Fold3, https://www.fold3.com; unnumbered flight intelligence report, 74th FS, 23rd FG, December 24, 1944, AFHRA, Iris no. 57261.

8. The account of the sinking of the *Reinan Maru* is based in part on the following documents: "Soviet Ship Sunk by U.S. Airmen: Chan Lim-Pak Believed Killed" and "2 P-51s Bagged over Hong Kong," December 26, 1944; "Graphic Account of Inhuman Attack on *Reinan Maru*: Rescuers Strafed; Captain Yuasa, Crew Mowed Down" and "Passengers Mowed Down like Sheep," December 27, 1944; "Lady Passenger of *Reinan Maru* Saved by Junk," December 28, 1944; all from *Hongkong News*, SC HKUL, MF 2521520, reel 6.

9. "Soviet Ship Sunk by U.S. Airmen: Chan Lim-Pak Believed Killed," December 26, 1944, *Hongkong News*, SC HKUL, MF 2521520, reel 6.

10. "Soviet Ship Sunk by U.S. Airmen: Chan Lim-Pak Believed Killed," December 26, 1944, *Hongkong News*, SC HKUL, MF 2521520, reel 6.

11. Max L. Parnell and Wayne G. Johnson, "The Hell of Ōfuna as a 'Guest' of the Japanese in WWII," April 22, 2015, 118th TRS.

### 14. Convoy Hi-87

1. Flight intelligence report 14, January 15, 1944, 118th TRS, 23rd FG, AFHRA/118th TRS; squadron history for 118th TRS, 23rd FG, November 12, 1944–January 22, 1945, AFHRA/118th TRS.

2. MACR no. 11636 for 1st Lt. Frank S. Palmer (aircraft serial no. 44-11120) and MACR no. 11637 for 2nd Lt. Daniel J. Mitchell (aircraft serial no. 45-6751), 118th TRS, 23rd FG, January 17, 1945; MACR no. 11633 for 2nd Lt. Galen C. Theobold (aircraft serial no. 43-24972) and MACR no. 11635 for Maj. David L. Houck (aircraft serial no. 44-11105), 118th TRS, 23rd FG, January 18, 1945; all documents NARA/Fold3, https://www.fold3.com.

3. The account of the raid on Hong Kong by the 118th TRS on January 16, 1945, is based on the following documents: MACR no. 11634, January 18, 1945, and supplemental

MACR no. 11634, January 29, 1945, for 1st Lt. John F. Egan (aircraft serial no. 43-7056), 118th TRS, 23rd FG, NARA/Fold3, https://www.fold3.com; flight intelligence report 16, 118th TRS, 23rd FG, January 16, 1945, AFHRA/118th TRS.

## 15. Devils Incarnate

1. TF 38 aircraft losses, action report filed by commander TF 38, October 30, 1944–January 26, 1945, NARA/Fold3, https://www.fold3.com.

2. The account of the raid on Hong Kong by the 308th BG on January 18, 1945, is based on the following documents: Feuer, *B-24 in China*, 140–44; flight intelligence report 19 filed by Capt. Robert C. Burke, 118th TRS, 23rd FG, January 20, 1945, AFHRA/118th TRS; group mission report 498 and supplementary group mission report 498, 308th BG, January 18, 1945, AFHRA, Iris no. 81967; MACR for crew of B-24J (aircraft serial no. 44-41118), January 18, 1945, and supplemental MACR, January 29, 1945, 375th BS, 308th BG, NARA/Fold3, https://www.fold3.com; mission 498, "Organizational History of 308th Bombardment Group," AFHRA, Iris no. 81952.

3. Group mission 503, 308th BG, January 20, 1945, AFHRA, Iris no. 81967; mission 503, "Organizational History of 308th Bombardment Group," AFHRA, Iris no. 81952.

4. Military History Section, Special Staff, *Imperial Japanese Navy*, appendix A, 253, and appendix B, 261; group mission report 505, 308th BG, January 21, 1945, AFHRA, Iris no. 81967; Kwong, "Failure of Japanese Land-Sea Cooperation," 80; mission 505, "Organizational History of 308th Bombardment Group," AFHRA, Iris no. 81952.

5. "Air Raid Victims Relief Fund Drive Launched by Local Businessman," *Hongkong News*, January 25, 1945, SC HKUL, MF 2521521, reel 6; Bowie, "Captive Surgeon in Hong Kong," 244.

6. "Chinese Pastor Strongly Condemns U.S. Airmen's Savage Bombing of Wanchai on Sunday: Thousands Killed, Wounded," *Hongkong News*, January 23, 1945, SC HKUL, MF 2521521, reel 6.

7. "Devils Incarnate," *Hongkong News*, January 23, 1945, SC HKUL, MF 2521521, reel 6; "Kweilin Weekly Intelligence Summary No. 87," BAAG, ERC HKHP.

8. Group mission 507, 308th BG, January 22, 1945, AFHRA, Iris no. 81967; mission 507, "Organizational History of 308th Bombardment Group," AFHRA, Iris no. 81952.

9. Hara, "Ichigo Offensive," 392–402.

10. Narrative reports for mission FFO 58-D-22 and mission FFO 58-D-23, 500th BS, 345th BG, February 27, 1945, AFHRA, Iris no. 258863.

11. Referred to as Tungku Island in the mission report filed after the raid.

12. Narrative report for mission FFO 74-D-17, 500th BS, 345th BG, March 15, 1945, AFHRA/345th BG; author's phone interview with Col. Chris J. McWilliams, January 16, 2018.

13. Military History Section, Special Staff, *Imperial Japanese Navy*, appendix B, 271; United States Strategic Bombing Survey, *War against Japanese Transportation*, 105.

14. Flight intelligence report filed by Capt. Luther C. Kissick, 74th FS, 23rd FG, March 28, 1945, AFHRA, Iris no. 57261; MACR for Maj. Philip G. Chapman (aircraft serial no. 44-11055); MACR for 2nd Lt. Stanley J. Chmielewski (aircraft serial no. 43-24977); MACR

for 2nd Lt. Albert H. Sims (aircraft serial no. 44-11110); all 74th FS, 23rd FG, April 3, 1945, NARA/Fold3, https://www.fold3.com; Molesworth, *Sharks over China*, 260–62; unnumbered flight intelligence report, 76th FS, 23rd FG, March 28, 1945, AFHRA, Iris no. 57339.

15. MACR for 1st Lt. Bob A. Howard Jr. (aircraft serial no. 44-24972), 35th PRS, March 29, 1945; individual report of downed aircraft, plane no. 826, 35th PRS, March 30, 1945; casualty questionnaire, Capt. Bob H. Howard, 35th PRS; all documents NARA/Fold3, https://www.fold3.com.

## 16. Gangway Special

1. The account of the mission flown by the 9th FS over Hong Kong on April 2, 1945, is based on the following sources: Brischetto, *Twelve to One*; Bruning, *Jungle Ace*; unit narrative combat report filed by 2nd Lt. Kenneth B. Clark and individual combat reports filed by Lt. Col. Gerald R. Johnson, Capt. James A. Watkins, 2nd Lt. Walter J. Koby, 1st Lt. Rudolf A. Bellan, and 1st Lt. Noah C. Williams, April 3, 1945, all 9th FS, 49th FG, AFHRA, Iris no. 258874.

2. The account of the mission flown by the 3rd ACG over Hong Kong on April 2, 1945, is based on the following sources: final mission report, unit narrative combat report, and individual combat reports filed by 1st Lt. Glenn E. Lairmore and 2nd Lt. Barrett D. Wagner, all for mission 92-C-1-F, 3rd FSC, 3rd ACG, April 2, 1945, AFHRA, Iris no. 61666; history of the 3rd FSC, 3rd ACG, April 1945, and weekly status and operations report, April 1–10, 1945, 3rd FSC, 3rd ACG, AFHRA, Iris no. 61662; weekly status and operations report, April 1–10, 1945, 4th FSC, 3rd ACG, AFHRA, Iris no. 61683.

3. Records suggest that Sugimoto later died of wounds sustained during this dogfight. Hata, Izawa, and Shores, *Japanese Army Fighter Aces*, 312.

4. The account of the mission flown by the 5th Air Force over Hong Kong on April 2, 1945, is based on the following sources: final mission reports and narrative mission reports for mission 92-E-1 filed by 319th, 320th, 321st, and 400th Bomb Squadrons of 90th BG, April 2, 1945; field order 46 for mission 92-E-2 and intelligence annex to field order 46, 380th BG, April 1, 1945; mission board for mission 92-E-2, 380th BG, April 2, 1945; mission reports for 528th, 529th, 530th, and 531st Bomb Squadrons of 380th BG, April 2, 1945; reports on operation 92-E-2 filed by 528th, 529th, 530th, and 531st Bomb Squadrons of 380th BG, April 3, 1945; all documents AFHRA, Iris nos. 258874 and 258875.

5. War diary for April 1945, VH-4, FAW 10, U.S. Pacific Fleet, NARA/Fold3, https://www.fold3.com.

6. Intelligence annex, field order 46, mission 92-E-2, 380th BG, April 1, 1945, AFHRA, Iris no. 86281.

7. While the 5th Air Force referred to chaff as "rope," in the European theater the 8th Air Force referred to it as "carpet." The British, who originally invented chaff, called it "window." The Japanese referred to chaff as *giman-shi*, which is usually translated as "deceiving paper." Tillman, *Clash of the Carriers*, 154; Yenne, *Big Week*, 111.

8. Cressman, *Official Chronology of the U.S. Navy*, 654; Military History Section, Special Staff, *Imperial Japanese Navy*, part 8, 228.

9. Lt. Col. Johnson survived the war, but his B-25 disappeared without a trace over Japan during a typhoon in October 1945. Bruning, *Jungle Ace*, 240–42.

10. The account of the mission flown by the 5th Air Force over Hong Kong on April 3, 1945, is based on the following sources: Cherkauer, "Col. James T. Pettus' Manuscript," 85; final mission reports and narrative mission reports for missions 93-A-1, A-2, A-6, and A-7 filed by 64th, 65th, and 403rd Bomb Squadrons of 43rd BG and 2nd, 19th, 33rd, and 408th Bomb Squadrons of 22nd BG, April 3, 1945; all documents AFHRA, Iris nos. 258874, 258875, 44268, 78234, 79878.

11. Schmidt, "Interview of James T. Pettus, Jr.," 2.

12. The Sheraton Hotel now occupies this once-vacant lot on the corner of Nathan Road and Salisbury Road.

13. Corrigan and Corrigan, *Hong Kong Diary Revisited*, 326; Fisher, *I Will Remember*, 194.

14. The account of the mission flown by the 5th Air Force over Hong Kong on April 4, 1945, is based on the following sources: final mission reports and narrative mission reports for missions 94-A-2 and A-3 filed by 64th, 65th, and 403rd Bomb Squadrons of 43rd BG and 2nd, 19th, 33rd, and 408th Bomb Squadrons of 22nd BG, April 4, 1945; all documents AFHRA, Iris nos. 44268, 78234, 79878, 258875, 258877.

15. Gap Road no longer exists and was replaced postwar by the easternmost portion of Queen's Road East.

16. "Thanks to Helpers at Sikh Temple," *Hongkong News*, April 9, 1945; "U.S. Vandals' Puerile Try at 'War of Nerves,'" *Hongkong News*, April 6, 1945; both documents SC HKUL, MF 2521521, reel 7.

17. Wordie, *Streets: Exploring Hong Kong Island*, 143, 170–71.

18. "Blind Bombing," *Hongkong News*, April 5, 1945; "Bishop Deplores Wanton Bombing of Convent," *Hongkong News*, April 8, 1945; both documents SC HKUL, MF 2521521, reel 7.

19. Bob Hackett, Sander Kingsepp, and Peter Cundall, "IJN Escort *Manju*: Tabular Record of Movement," 2016, www.combinedfleet.com/Manju_t.htm; Raymond Eric Jones, wartime diary, April 4, 1945, transcript in author's collection; Military History Section, Special Staff, *Imperial Japanese Navy*, appendix A, 251, and appendix B, 261, 274.

20. The account of the mission flown by the 43rd BG over Hong Kong on April 5, 1945, is based on the following sources: final mission reports and narrative mission reports for missions 95-A-1, A-3, and A-5 filed by 64th, 65th, and 403rd Bomb Squadrons of 43rd BG; all documents AFHRA, Iris nos. 44268, 79878, 258874, 258875.

21. Sources agree that *Kamoi*, CD-1, CD-52, CH-9, and CH-20 were damaged by American aircraft in Hong Kong on April 5, 1945. However, the coordinates provided by *The Imperial Japanese Navy in World War II* place the four escort vessels near Hong Kong but not actually in Victoria Harbor. It is possible that other American aircraft not from the 43rd Bomb Group attacked these ships offshore on April 5, 1945. See Military History Section, Special Staff, *Imperial Japanese Navy*, appendix B; Cressman, *Official Chronology of the U.S. Navy*, 656; Bob Hackett, Sander Kingsepp, Allan Alsleben, and Peter Cundall, "IJN Seaplane Tender/Oiler *Kamoi*: Tabular Record of Movement," 2017, http://www.combinedfleet.com/Kamoi_t.htm.

22. "Kweilin Intelligence Summary No. 74," November 10, 1944, BAAG, ERC HKHP, EMR-1B-05; "Siren Only for Big or Night Air Raids," *Hongkong News*, March 31, 1945, SC HKUL, MF 2521521, reel 7; Snow, *Fall of Hong Kong*, 225–26.

23. The account of the mission flown by the 43rd BG over Hong Kong on April 13, 1945, is based on the following sources: final mission reports and narrative mission reports for mission 103-A-4 filed by 64th, 65th, and 403rd Bomb Squadrons of 43rd BG; all documents AFHRA, Iris nos. 44268, 79878, 258878, 258879.

24. Hackett et al., "IJN Seaplane Tender/Oiler *Kamoi*."

25. Narrative mission report for mission 103-A-4 filed by Capt. Baird J. Simpson, 65th BS, 43rd BG, AFHRA, Iris no. 258879.

### 17. Playing with Fire

1. Narrative report on mission FFO 104-D-19 filed by 1st Lt. Isaac E. Baker, 501st BS, 345th BG, April 16, 1945, AFHRA/345th BG.

2. The account of the mission flown by the 5th Air Force over Canton on May 9, 1945, is based on the following sources: final mission reports, narrative mission reports, and unit histories for missions 129-A-4, A-5, E-1, and E-2 filed by the following units: 2nd, 19th, 33rd, and 408th Bomb Squadrons of 22nd BG; 64th, 65th, and 403rd Bomb Squadrons of 43rd BG; 319th, 320th, 321st, and 400th Bomb Squadrons of 90th BG; 528th, 529th, 530th, and 531st Bomb Squadrons of 380th BG; all documents AFHRA, Iris no. 258887.

3. The account of the mission flown by the 5th Air Force over Hong Kong on June 12, 1945, is based on the following sources: Cherkauer, "Col. James T. Pettus' Manuscript," 118–19; final mission reports, narrative mission reports, and unit histories for missions 163-A-1 and A-2 filed by the following units: 2nd, 19th, 33rd, and 408th Bomb Squadrons of 22nd BG; 64th, 65th, and 403rd Bomb Squadrons of 43rd BG; all documents AFHRA, Iris nos. 44270, 78234, 79879, 79880, 258896.

4. "Three Enemy Raiders Bagged over Hongkong Yesterday: Incendiary Bombs Used for First Time; Foe's Devilish Design" and "Winged Devils," *Hongkong News*, June 13, 1945; "Practical Measures to Help Victims of Enemy Air Raid," *Hongkong News*, June 15, 1945; all documents SC HKUL, MF 2521521, reel 7.

5. "Kweilin Weekly Intelligence Summary No. 68," September 29, 1944, BAAG, ERC HKHP, EMR-1B-04.

6. Narrative mission report FFO-173-A-4 filed by 1st Lt. Isaac E. Baker and enclosure to narrative mission report FFO-173-A-4 filed by 2nd Lt. Donald J. Britton, 501st BS, 345th BG, June 24, 1945, AFHRA/345th BG.

7. Group history, 43rd BG, June 1945, AFHRA, Iris no. 79880.

8. Aircraft action report 396, VPB-104, FAW 17, August 14, 1945, NARA/Fold3, https://www.fold3.com.

### 18. *Bold Venture*

1. Feuer, *B-24 in China*.

2. Cherkauer, "Col. James T. Pettus' Manuscript," 144; Schmidt, "Interview of James T. Pettus, Jr.," 2.

3. Adjutant General's Office, War Department, records of World War II prisoners of war, December 7, 1941–November 19, 1946, record group 389, Electronic and Spe-

cial Media Records Services Division, NARA; James N. Young, "P.O.W.: Mayday over China; The Diary of Jim Young," ed. Andrew Priddy, unpublished manuscript, copy in author's collection.

4. Adjutant General's Office, War Department, records of World War II prisoners of war, December 7, 1941–November 19, 1946, record group 389, Electronic and Special Media Records Services Division, NARA; Glines, *Chennault's Forgotten Warriors*, 218–23.

5. Adjutant General's Office, War Department, records of World War II prisoners of war, December 7, 1941–November 19, 1946, record group 389, Electronic and Special Media Records Services Division, NARA; Max L. Parnell and Wayne G. Johnson, "The Hell of Ōfuna as a 'Guest' of the Japanese in WWII," April 22, 2015, 118th TRS.

6. For reasons that remain unclear, a casualty report for the crew of *Bold Venture* was included with MACR no. 15447 for a B-25J (aircraft serial no. 44-30258) from the 501st BS of the 345th BG that was lost offshore from Japan on July 31, 1945.

7. The narrative describing the recovery of the remains of the crew of the B-25J *Bold Venture* is based on the following documents: casualty report, 500th BS, 345th BG, March 16, 1945; individual deceased personnel files for 2nd Lt. Orville L. Garrison, 2nd Lt. Robert W. Jensen, Sgt. Frank M. Tubb, Sgt. Robert H. Waggy, and Sgt. Henry M. Worley; "Investigation and Recovery of Remains" and "Remarks on Investigation and Recovery," CTSD case 207, Headquarters, Canton Sub-Detachment, China Theater Search Detachment, February 18, 1946; narrative report for mission FFO 74-D-17, 500th BS, 345th BG, March 15, 1945.

## Appendix

1. Ford, *Flying Tigers.*

2. United States Army Air Forces, Historical Office, *Army Air Forces in the War,* 172; Assistant Chief of Air Staff, *Fourteenth Air Force,* 9–10.

3. Hata, Izawa, and Shores, *Japanese Army Fighter Aces,* 124–26, 136–38, 148–50.

4. Memorandum to commanding officer, bomber unit, re: aircrew and aircraft participating in mission 33, October 25, 1942, 11th BS, 341st BG, AFHRA, Iris no. 43545.

5. Assistant Chief of Air Staff, *Fourteenth Air Force,* 20, 22–23, 125.

6. Hata, Izawa, and Shores, *Japanese Army Fighter Aces,* 128–30, 136–38, 168–70.

7. Maurer, *Air Force Combat Units,* 404–5, 420–21.

8. Maurer, *Air Force Combat Units,* 404–5; Maurer, *Combat Squadrons,* 111–12, 396–97; McClure, *Fire and Fall Back,* 156; Samson, *Flying Tiger,* 231.

9. Maurer, *Air Force Combat Units,* 460–61; United States Strategic Bombing Survey, *Fifth Air Force,* 12.

10. Maurer, *Air Force Combat Units*; Thompson, *P-61 Black Widow Units,* 77–85; United States Strategic Bombing Survey, *Fifth Air Force,* section 2, figure 7.

11. Maurer, *Air Force Combat Units*; United States Strategic Bombing Survey, *Fifth Air Force,* section 2, figure 7.

12. Maurer, *Air Force Combat Units,* 223–24.

# BIBLIOGRAPHY

## Archival Sources

118th TRS. Historical documents collection. 118th Tactical Reconnaissance Squadron website. http://www.118trs.com.

345th BG. Historical documents collection. 345th Bomb Group website. http://www.345thbombgroup.org.

AFHRA. Archives of the Air Force Historical Research Agency, Maxwell Air Force Base, Montgomery AL.

ERC HKHP. Elizabeth Ride Collection. Hong Kong Heritage Project Archives, Hong Kong.

NARA. National Archives and Records Administration, College Park MD.

SC HKUL. Special Collections. Hong Kong University Library, Hong Kong.

## Published Sources

Aeronautical Staff of Aero Publishers. *Nakajima KI-84*. Fallbrook CA: Aero, 1965.

Alderson, Gordon L. D. *History of Royal Air Force Kai Tak*. Hong Kong: Royal Air Force Kai Tak, 1972.

Assistant Chief of Air Staff, Intelligence, Historical Division, U.S. Army Air Forces. *The Fourteenth Air Force to 1 October 1943 (AAFRH-9)*. N.p.: Army Air Force Historical Office, Headquarters, Army Air Forces, 1945.

Baime, Albert J. *The Arsenal of Democracy: FDR, Detroit, and an Epic Quest to Arm an America at War*. New York: Houghton Mifflin Harcourt, 2014.

Banham, Tony. "The Hong Kong Dockyard Defence Corps, 1939–41." *Journal of the Royal Asiatic Society Hong Kong Branch* 50 (2010): 317–42.

———. *Not the Slightest Chance: The Defence of Hong Kong, 1941*. Hong Kong: Hong Kong University Press, 2003.

———. *The Sinking of the* Lisbon Maru: *Britain's Forgotten Wartime Tragedy*. Hong Kong: Hong Kong University Press, 2010.

———. *We Shall Suffer There: Hong Kong's Defenders Imprisoned, 1942–45*. Hong Kong: Hong Kong University Press, 2009.

Bartsch, William H. *Doomed at the Start: American Pursuit Pilots in the Philippines, 1941–1942*. College Station: Texas A&M University Press, 1992.

Bergin, Bob. "Interview: Panda Bear Leader 'Tex' Hill." *Aviation History* 13, no. 2 (November 2002): 42–49.

Bond, Charles R., and Terry Anderson. *A Flying Tiger's Diary*. College Station: Texas A&M University Press, 1984.

Bowie, Donald C. "Captive Surgeon in Hong Kong: The Story of the British Military Hospital, Hong Kong 1942–1945." *Journal of the Royal Asiatic Society Hong Kong Branch* 15 (1975): 150–290.

Boyd, John, and Gary Garth. *Tenko! Rangoon Jail: The Amazing Story of Sgt. John Boyd's Survival as a POW in a Notorious Japanese Prison Camp*. Paducah KY: Turner, 1996.

Brereton, Lewis H. *The Brereton Diaries: The War in the Air in the Pacific, Middle East and Europe, 3 October 1941–8 May 1945*. New York: William Morrow, 1946.

Brischetto, Roy R. *Twelve to One: Fighter Combat Tactics in the SWPA*. N.p.: 5th Fighter Command, 1945.

Bruning, John R. *Jungle Ace: Col. Gerald R. Johnson, the USAAF's Top Fighter Leader of the Pacific War*. Washington DC: Brassey's, 2003.

Burton, John. *Fortnight of Infamy: The Collapse of Allied Airpower West of Pearl Harbor*. Annapolis MD: Naval Institute Press, 2006.

Cameron, Nigel. *An Illustrated History of Hong Kong*. Hong Kong: Hong Kong University Press, 1991.

Carter, Kit C., and Robert Mueller. *U.S. Army Air Forces in World War II: Combat Chronology, 1941–1945*. Washington DC: Center for Air Force History, 1991.

Chan Sui-jeung. *East River Column: Hong Kong Guerrillas in the Second World War and After*. Hong Kong: Hong Kong University Press, 2009.

Chennault, Claire Lee. *Way of a Fighter: The Memoirs of Claire Lee Chennault*. New York: G. P. Putnam's Sons, 1949.

Cherkauer, James. "Col. James T. Pettus' Manuscript." January 3, 2018. https://www.kensmen.com/ColJamesPettusManuscript.pdf.

Chief of Staff, War Department. *Basic Field Manual 30-38, Military Intelligence: Identification of Japanese Aircraft*. Washington DC: Government Printing Office, 1942.

Chiu, T. N. *The Port of Hong Kong: A Survey of Its Development*. Hong Kong: Hong Kong University Press, 1973.

Coates, Austin. *Whampoa: Ships on the Shore*. Hong Kong: South China Morning Press, 1980.

Corbin, Allana. *Prisoners of the East*. Sydney: Macmillan, 2002.

Cornelius, Wanda, and Thayne Short. *Ding Hao: America's Air War in China, 1937–1945*. Gretna LA: Pelican, 1980.

Corrigan, Leonard B., and Gladys Corrigan. *A Hong Kong Diary Revisited*. Baltimore ON: Frei Press, 2008.

Courtauld, Carol, and May Holdsworth. *The Hong Kong Story*. Hong Kong: Oxford University Press, 1997.

Cressman, Robert J. *The Official Chronology of the U.S. Navy in World War II*. Washington DC: Contemporary History Branch, Naval Historical Center, 1999.

Division of Naval Intelligence. *Standard Classes of Japanese Merchant Ships, Supplement 3 (ONI-208-J Revised)*. Washington DC: Office of Naval Intelligence, U.S. Navy, 1945.

Drea, Edward J., and Hans van de Ven. "An Overview of Major Military Campaigns during the Sino-Japanese War." In *The Battle for China: Essays on the Military History of the Sino-Japanese War of 1937–1945*, edited by Mark Peattie, Edward J. Drea, and Hans van den Ven, 27–47. Stanford CA: Stanford University Press, 2011.

Ebbage, Victor Stanley. *The Hard Way: Surviving Sham Shui Po Camp 1941–45*. Stroud, UK: Spellmount, 2011.

Emerson, Geoffrey Charles. *Hong Kong Internment, 1942–1945: Life in the Japanese Civilian Camp at Stanley*. Hong Kong: Hong Kong University Press, 2008.

Endacott, George Beer, and Alan Birch. *Hong Kong Eclipse*. Hong Kong: Oxford University Press, 1978.

Esposito, Vincent J., ed. *The West Point Atlas of War: World War II; The Pacific*. New York: Tess Press, 1959.

Feuer, A. B. *The B-24 in China: General Chennault's Secret Weapon in World War II*. Mechanicsburg PA: Stackpole Books, 2006.

Fisher, Les. *I Will Remember: Recollections and Reflections on Hong Kong 1941 to 1945—Internment and Freedom*. Totton, Hampshire, UK: Hobbs the Printers, 1996.

Ford, Daniel. *Flying Tigers: Claire Chennault and His American Volunteers, 1941–1942*. New York: HarperCollins/Smithsonian, 2007.

Frillmann, Paul, and Graham Peck. *China: The Remembered Life*. Boston: Houghton Mifflin, 1968.

Frisbee, John L. "Valor: Four-Engine Fighter Pilot." *Air Force Magazine: Online Journal of the Air Force Association*, June 1995. www.airforcemag.com/MagazineArchive /Pages/1995/June%201995/0695valor.aspx.

Gittins, Jean. *Stanley: Behind Barbed Wire*. Hong Kong: Hong Kong University Press, 1982.

Glines, Carroll V. *Chennault's Forgotten Warriors: The Saga of the 308th Bomb Group in China*. Atglen PA: Schiffer, 1995.

Greenhous, Brereton. *"C" Force to Hong Kong: A Canadian Catastrophe*. Toronto: Dundurn Press, 1997.

Hagiwara Mitsuru. "The Japanese Air Campaigns in China, 1937–1945." In *The Battle for China: Essays on the Military History of the Sino-Japanese War of 1937–1945*, edited by Mark Peattie, Edward J. Drea, and Hans van den Ven, 237–55. Stanford CA: Stanford University Press, 2011.

Hahn, Emily. *China to Me: A Partial Autobiography*. New York: Doubleday, 1944.

———. *Hong Kong Holiday*. New York: Doubleday, 1946.

Hara Takeshi. "The Ichigo Offensive." In *The Battle for China: Essays on the Military History of the Sino-Japanese War of 1937–1945*, edited by Mark Peattie, Edward J. Drea, and Hans van den Ven, 392–402. Stanford CA: Stanford University Press, 2011.

Harland, Kathleen. *The Royal Navy in Hong Kong since 1841*. Cornwall, UK: Maritime Books.

Hata, Ikuhiko, Yasuho Izawa, and Christopher Shores. *Japanese Army Fighter Aces, 1931–45*. Mechanicsburg PA: Stackpole Books, 2012.

Heywood, Graham. *It Won't Be Long Now: The Diary of a Hong Kong Prisoner of War*. Edited by Geoffrey Charles Emerson. Hong Kong: Blacksmith Books, 2015.

Holdsworth, May, and Christopher Munn, eds. *Dictionary of Hong Kong Biography*. Hong Kong: Hong Kong University Press, 2012.

Horsnell, Robert. "A Note on the Japanese Gun Emplacement at Tathong Point, Tung Lung Chau." *Journal of the Royal Asiatic Society Hong Kong Branch* 42 (2002): 399–404.

Hotz, Robert B., George L. Paxton, Robert H. Neale, and Parker S. Dupouy. *With General Chennault: The Story of the Flying Tigers*. New York: Coward-McCann, 1943.

Ichimura, Hiroshi. *Ki-43 "Oscar" Aces of World War 2*. Oxford: Osprey, 2009.

Jentschura, Hansgeorg, Dieter Jung, and Peter Mickel. *Warships of the Imperial Japanese Navy, 1869–1945*. Translated by Antony Preston and J. D. Brown. London: Arms and Armour, 1977.

Joint Army-Navy Assessment Committee. *Japanese Naval and Merchant Shipping Losses during World War II by All Causes (NAVEXOS P-468)*. Washington DC: Navy Department, 1947.

Kwong Chi Man. "The Failure of Japanese Land-Sea Cooperation during the Second World War: Hong Kong and the South China Coast as an Example, 1942–1945." *Journal of Military History* 79 (January 2015): 69–91.

Kwong Chi Man and Tsoi Yiu Lun. *Eastern Fortress: A Military History of Hong Kong, 1840–1970*. Hong Kong: Hong Kong University Press, 2014.

Lai, Lawrence W. C., Ken S. T. Ching, and Y. K. Tan. "Survey Findings on Japanese World War II Military Installations in Hong Kong." *Surveying & Built Environment* 21, no. 2 (December 2011): 78–94.

Lawson, Ted W., and Robert Considine. *Thirty Seconds over Tokyo*. New York: Fall River Press, 2007.

Lethbridge, Henry J. "Hong Kong under Japanese Occupation: Changes in Social Structure." In *Hong Kong: A Society in Transition*, edited by Ian C. Jarvie and Joseph Agassi, 77–127. New York: Frederick A. Praeger, 1969.

Lindsay, Oliver. *At the Going Down of the Sun: Hong Kong and South-East Asia, 1941–45*. London: Sphere Books, 1982.

———. *The Battle for Hong Kong, 1941–1945: Hostage to Fortune*. Montreal: McGill-Queen's University Press, 2005.

Lopez, Donald S. *Into the Teeth of the Tiger*. Washington DC: Smithsonian Institution Press, 1997.

Macri, Franco David. *Clash of Empires in South China: The Allied Nations' Proxy War with Japan, 1935–1941*. Lawrence: University Press of Kansas, 2012.

Maurer, Maurer. *Air Force Combat Units of World War II*. Washington DC: Office of Air Force History, 1983.

———. *Combat Squadrons of the Air Force, World War II*. Washington DC: Albert F. Simpson Historical Research Center and Office of Air Force History, 1982.

McClure, Glenn E. *Fire and Fall Back: Casey Vincent's Story of Three Years in the China-Burma-India Theatre, including the Fighting Withdrawal of the Flying Tigers from Eastern China*. San Antonio TX: Barnes Press, 1975.

McManus, John C. *Deadly Sky: The American Combat Airman in World War II*. New York: NAL Caliber, 2016.

Melson, P. J. *White Ensign, Red Dragon: The History of the Royal Navy in Hong Kong 1841–1997*. Hong Kong: Edinburgh Financial, 1997.

Military History Section, Special Staff, General HQ, Far East Command. *The Imperial Japanese Navy in World War II: A Graphic Presentation of the Japanese Naval Organization and List of Combatant and Non-Combatant Vessels Lost or Damaged in the War*. Japanese Operational Monograph Series 116. N.p., 1952.

Millman, Nicholas. *Ki-44 Tojo Aces of World War 2*. Oxford: Osprey, 2011.

Mitter, Rana. *Forgotten Ally: China's World War II, 1937–1945*. New York: Houghton Mifflin Harcourt, 2013.

Molesworth, Carl. *23rd Fighter Group: Chennault's Sharks*. Oxford: Osprey, 2009.

———. *P-40 Warhawk vs Ki-43 Oscar: China 1944–45*. Oxford: Osprey, 2008.

———. *Sharks over China: The 23rd Fighter Group in World War II*. Edison NJ: Castle Books, 2001.

Molesworth, Carl, and Steve Moseley, *Wing to Wing: Air Combat in China, 1943–45*. New York: Orion Books, 1990.

Morison, Samuel Eliot. *History of United States Naval Operations in World War II*. Vol. 13, *The Liberation of the Philippines: Luzon, Mindanao, the Visayas, 1944–1945*. Boston: Little, Brown, 1959.

Nelson, Craig. *The First Heroes: The Extraordinary Story of the Doolittle Raid—America's First World War II Victory*. New York: Penguin, 2002.

Office of the Assistant Chief of Air Staff, Intelligence. *Air Objective Folder No. 83.4: Canton Area, China*. Washington DC, 1943.

Research and Analysis Section of Combat Intelligence. *Canton-Hong Kong Black Book*. N.p.: Headquarters United States Forces, China Theater, 1945.

Ride, Edwin. *British Army Aid Group: Hong Kong Resistance, 1942–1945*. Hong Kong: Oxford University Press, 1981.

Ride, Elizabeth, ed. *Advance Headquarters, Waichow Field Operations Group*. BAAG Series 4. N.p., 2004.

Sakaida, Henry. *Aces of the Rising Sun, 1937–1945*. London: Osprey, 2002.

———. *Imperial Japanese Navy Aces, 1937–1945*. London: Osprey, 1998.

———. *Japanese Army Air Force Aces, 1937–1945*. London: Osprey, 1997.

Samson, Jack. *The Flying Tiger: The True Story of General Claire Chennault and the U.S. 14th Air Force in China*. Guilford CT: Lyons Press, 2005.

Schmidt, G. Lewis. "Interview of James T. Pettus, Jr." Association for Diplomatic Studies and Training, Foreign Affairs Oral History Project, May 30, 1990. https://www.adst.org/OH%20TOCs/Pettus,%20James.toc.pdf.

Scott, Robert L. *The Day I Owned the Sky*. New York: Bantam, 1988.

———. *God Is My Co-Pilot*. New York: Ballantine, 1971.

Snow, Philip. *The Fall of Hong Kong: Britain, China, and the Japanese Occupation*. New Haven CT: Yale University Press, 2003.

Taylor, Joe G. *Air Interdiction in China in World War II (AU-132-55-RSI)*. USAF Historical Studies 132. Maxwell Air Force Base AL: USAF Historical Division, Research Studies Institute, Air University, 1956.

Thompson, Warren. *P-61 Black Widow Units of World War 2*. Oxford: Osprey, 1998.

Tillman, Barrett. *Clash of the Carriers: The True Story of the Marianas Turkey Shoot of World War II*. New York: NAL Caliber, 2005.

Tohmatsu Haruo. "The Strategic Correlation between the Sino-Japanese and Pacific Wars." In *The Battle for China: Essays on the Military History of the Sino-Japanese War of 1937–1945*, edited by Mark Peattie, Edward J. Drea, and Hans van den Ven, 423–45. Stanford CA: Stanford University Press, 2011.

United States Army Air Forces, Historical Office. *Army Air Forces in the War against Japan, 1941–1942*. Army Air Forces Historical Studies 34. Washington DC: Headquarters Army Air Forces, 1945.

United States Army Forces in the Far East Headquarters and 8th U.S. Army. *Air Operations in the China Area, July 1937–August 1945*. Japanese Monograph 76. Office of the Chief of Military History, Department of the Army, 1956.

———. *Army Operations in China, December 1941–December 1943*. Japanese Monograph 71. Office of the Chief of Military History, Department of the Army, 1956.

———. *Army Operations in the China Area, January 1944–August 1945*. Japanese Monograph 72. Office of the Chief of Military History, Department of the Army, 1956.

United States Pacific Command, CINCPAC-CINCPOA. *United States Pacific Fleet and Pacific Ocean Areas: Air Target Maps and Photos; China Coast, Ningpo to Canton (A.T.F. No. 152A-44)*. N.p., 1944.

United States Strategic Bombing Survey. *The Fifth Air Force in the War against Japan*. Washington DC: Military Analysis Division, 1947.

———. *The War against Japanese Transportation, 1941–1945*. Washington DC: Transportation Division, 1947.

Wong Suk-har. "Disused Air Raid Precaution Tunnels: Uncovering the Underground History of World War II, Civil Defense Tunnels in Hong Kong." MA thesis, University of Hong Kong, 2010.

Wordie, Jason. *Streets: Exploring Hong Kong Island*. Hong Kong: Hong Kong University Press.

———. *Streets: Exploring Kowloon*. Hong Kong: Hong Kong University Press, 2007.

Xu Guangqiu. "The Issue of U.S. Air Support for China during the Second World War, 1942–45." *Journal of Contemporary History* 36, no. 3 (July 2001): 459–84.

Yenne, Bill. *Big Week: Six Days That Changed the Course of World War II*. New York: Berkley, 2012.

———. *When Tigers Ruled the Sky: The Flying Tigers; American Outlaw Pilots over China in World War II*. New York: Berkley Caliber, 2016.

Young, Arthur N. *China and the Helping Hand, 1937–1945*. Cambridge MA: Harvard University Press, 1963.

Young, Edward M. *B-24 Liberator Units of the CBI*. Oxford: Osprey, 2011.

Zhang Baijia. "China's Quest for Foreign Military Aid." In *The Battle for China: Essays on the Military History of the Sino-Japanese War of 1937–1945*, edited by Mark Peattie, Edward J. Drea, and Hans van den Ven, 283–307. Stanford CA: Stanford University Press, 2011.

# INDEX

Eglin Field, 112–13
Eisenman, Jerome F., 173, 174, 293n17

Ford Motor Company, 94
Fort Bayard, 92
Fort Smith National Cemetery, 264
"French hospital." *See* St. Paul's Hospital
French Indochina, 11, 92, 97, 139, 168
friendly fire, 20, 82, 159
Frillman, Paul, 7
Furbush, Richard D., 140

Gangler, Sergeant, 232, 233–34
Gap Road, 237, 297n15
Garrison, Orville L., 212, 264–65, 279
*Genchi Maru*, 114
General Motors, 6
Gocke, Jack E., 172
Graves Registration Service (GRS), 263–64
Green Island Cement Company, 243
GRS. *See* Graves Registration Service (GRS)
Gun Club Hill, 43

H2X air-to-ground radar system, 221, 241–44, 249, 250, 253
Hahn, Emily, 41, 77, 79, 89–90, 97, 102–3, 106, 110–11, 113
Haiphong, 97
Haiphong Road, 43
Hajime Saito, 170–71
Halsey, William F. "Bull," 197–98
Hampshire, John F., 30, 37, 44, 45, 70, 71, 73, 74–75, 77
Hankow, 11, 93, 104–5, 108, 162–63
Hankow Road, 43
Happy Valley, 77, 208, 237, 243, 248
*Haruta Maru*, 207
Haynes, Caleb V., 9, 10, 23–24, 27, 37, 42, 43, 44, 77, 285n11
Haynes, Elmer E., 160–61, 167–68, 172–74, 204–6, 256
Health Department (Hong Kong), 79
*Heikai Maru*, 239
Hengyang, 11, 93, 133, 162, 163, 179, 209
Hennessy Road, 208
*Hermes*, HMS, 100
Hester, John K., 199, 201
Heywood, Graham, 78, 107, 174, 175, 176, 179, 231

*Hida Maru*, 187
Hill, David L. "Tex," 13, 23, 30, 37, 43–44, 48, 57, 98, 112–13, 114–16, 120–21, 138, 141–42, 180, 284n21
Hiroji Shimoda, 173
HO-103 heavy machine gun, 17, 39, 117, 282n32
Holloway, Bruce K., 1–3, 21, 30, 36, 61–62, 70, 71, 72–73, 75, 98, 99, 102, 104, 113
Holt's Wharf, 231, 235, 236, 240
Honam Island, 254
Honda, Sergeant Major, 179
Hong Kong, 14, 16, 154; civilian casualties in, 75, 76, 77, 103, 192–93, 208, 232, 237–38, 247–48, 252; civilian morale in, 78–79; fuel shortages in, 107–8; geography of, 15–16, 18; loss of strategic relevance of, 208, 215, 253; port facilities in, 16, 99–101, 106–7; weather in, 18, 19, 106, 242
Hong Kong and Shanghai Bank, 137
Hong Kong and Shanghai Banking Corporation, 182
Hong Kong and Whampoa Dock Company, 99
Hong Kong and Whampoa dockyard, 16, 99, 101, 104, 105, 115, 121, 144, 160, 174–75, 179, 223–24, 243–44, 245
Hong Kong Island, 15
*Hongkong News*, 75–76, 77, 136–38, 143, 153, 154, 182, 192–94, 208, 238, 239, 252
Houck, David H., 200–201
Howard, Bob A., 216
Hump, 9–10, 59, 90, 91–92, 98–99, 145, 168, 180
Hung Hom, 16, 99, 179, 223–24, 242–43, 248
Hungjao Road Cemetery, 263

Ichigō sakusen (Operation Number One), 162–63, 166, 170, 176, 179–80, 180–81, 186, 208–10
Ie Shima, 256–57
IJA. *See* Imperial Japanese Army (IJA)
IJN. *See* Imperial Japanese Navy (IJN)
Imperial Japanese Army (IJA), 4, 5, 6, 7, 93–94, 108, 127–28, 130–31, 143–44, 162–63, 179–81, 183, 208–10
Imperial Japanese Navy (IJN), 5, 83, 101, 146, 153, 154–55, 169, 198, 200; 2nd China Expeditionary Fleet, 83, 101, 110, 161, 170, 187
Indians, 14, 79–80, 86, 237, 247

McConnell, Glenn A., 145–55, 258

McGuire, Thomas B., 220

McGuire airfield, 220–21

*Menado Maru*, 140–41, 145

Meyer, John E., 187–88, 189, 191

Miller, William E., 30, 37

mines (airdropped antiship), 114, 141, 168–70, 176, 184, 187, 206–7, 208

Mingaladon airbase, 7

missing air crew report (MACR), 203, 262

*Missouri*, USS, 259

Mitchell, Daniel J., 201

Monroe, Rose, 94

Mooney, Robert H., 74

Morgan, Harold "Butch," 24, 25, 27, 36, 37, 41–42, 43, 58, 60–61, 67, 68, 75, 78

Moritaka Nakasono, 108–9

Morrison Hill, 207

*Moth*, HMS, 83, 101. See also *Suma*, IJNS

Murray, Robert G., 202–3

Myitkyina, 9

Nam Long village, 213, 260–62

Namyung airbase, 71, 72, 75, 106

Nanking Street, 43

Nanning airbase, 181

napalm, 248, 250–52

Nathan Road, 231

Nationalist army, 4, 8, 93, 123, 162, 163, 209

National Memorial Cemetery of the Pacific, 264

New Territories, 15, 19, 203, 212, 225, 260

Nicholson, Leonard T., 235, 277

Nishimori, Staff Sergeant, 171–72

Nomonhan Incident, 17, 105, 151

Norden bombsight, 36, 41–42, 157, 241

North American (aviation manufacturer), 32, 94

North Point, 58–59, 237, 248

North Point power station, 59, 61, 75, 76, 77, 79, 237

Number 2 Repair Facility, 101, 103

*Oceanic*, RMS, 100

O'Connell, Philip B., 73, 74–75, 81

Office of Strategic Services (OSS), 260, 262

Ōfuna POW camp, 155, 195, 258

Operation Gratitude, 198, 204

Opium War, 15

*Orca*, USS, 222, 226

OSS. See Office of Strategic Services (OSS)

Palmer, Frank S., 201

Pan American World Airways, 8

Paochang airfield, 179

Parnell, Max L., 191–92, 194–95, 258–59

pathfinder aircraft, 167, 227–34, 235, 239, 240–41, 243, 244–47, 256

Pearl River, 12, 16, 58, 83, 109, 114, 168, 184, 240, 249, 252–53

Pearsall, Everson F., 189

Peninsula Hotel, 43, 231, 248, 284n21

Petris, Paul A., 190

Pettus, James T., 227–30, 232–33, 235, 239, 247, 250, 256–57, 277

*Pointee Talkie*, 124, 125, 126

Porter, Charles F., 178

Port Shelter, 189

Quarry Bay, 16

Quarry Point, 100

Queen's Road, 236

radar, 223, 242, 258; in American aircraft, 148, 156–59, 207, 241–42, 250, 254; Japanese, 116, 143, 144, 190, 289n6

RAF. See Royal Air Force (RAF)

Rambler Channel, 169, 245

Rangoon, 5–7, 255

Red Cross, 89, 110

Reheis, Herman F. "Rex," 210–14

*Reinan Maru*, 182, 184–85, 187, 189–90, 192–94, 196, 200, 202

repatriation, 89, 110–11, 259

Reynolds, G. H., 290n16

Ride, Lindsay T., 18, 20, 78

Ritter, First Lieutenant, 140–41

Rockwell, Ivan A., 110

Roosevelt, Franklin D., 5, 92, 246

rope, 223, 230, 235, 242, 251, 296n7. See also chaff

Rosie the Riveter, 94

Rough Raiders. See United States Army Air Forces (USAAF), 500th Bomb Squadron (Medium)

Royal Air Force (RAF), 5, 6, 19

Royal Army, 133; 3rd Commando Brigade, 259–60

Royal Canadian Air Force, 228